ALONE WITH YOUR HORSE

Drawings by
Anna Livia Holland
and Mary Jean Vasiloff

ALONE
WITH
YOUR
HORSE

Mary Jean Vasiloff

HARPER & ROW, PUBLISHERS
New York, Hagerstown,
San Francisco, London

FIRST EDITION

Library of Congress Cataloging in Publication Data

Vasiloff, Mary Jean.
  Alone with your horse.

  Includes index.
  1. Horses. I. Title.
SF285.V37 1977   633.1   76–5532
ISBN 0–06–014499–8

78 79 80 81 82 10 9 8 7 6 5 4 3 2 1

To Alex

Contents

A section of illustrations follows page 242

Acknowledgments

I wish to express my appreciation to several people for their generous help with this book: Frank Palka, D.V.M., who updated and corrected Chapter 13, "Your Horse's Doctor"; Justin Garziano, farrier, who did some corrective trimming of Chapter 14, "Your Horse's Farrier"; Judi Zielinski, who coordinated, and typed and retyped for endless hours; Bill Kilmer, who has contributed greatly to the chapters on understanding the horse's mind and behavior; Sandy Hough, who did still more retyping; and my niece, Anna Holland, and my mother, Rook McCulloch, who asked important questions and corrected mistakes as only members of a family can.

Introduction

This is a personal book. It is based on more than forty years of living with, caring for, and learning about horses. Instead of telling you how to buy the "ideal" horse, ride in the "correct" seat, and give the horse "proper care," I have endeavored to encourage you to seek the horse that will suit you personally—your character, your ability, your body shape, and your life style. I have detailed the horse's needs and offered suggestions on a number of ways to make him comfortable, happy, and useful to you.

This book is intended to enrich your life with a real understanding of the horse and to get you deeply involved in a sympathetic and responsive relationship with him. It stresses why horses are different from other animals and from people, offering insight into the workings of the horse's mind and body to help make you a more effective and knowledgeable horse person.

No relationship between living things is all milk and honey. There are days when nothing goes right; there are illnesses and distress, mistakes and even disasters. But with information and understanding, the bad moments can be held to a minimum and the triumphs rendered more glorious. This book requires a little from its readers. It asks you to do some soul searching, and expects you to make an effort to learn more than the bare essentials of horse ownership.

I have not attempted to tell you all about horses. Nobody could do that in a single book, because no one person has all the information on all aspects of the horse world. Hopefully it will whet your appetite for more knowledge, and also give you an inkling of how many different and fascinating horse sports there are in this country alone.

More than anything, I hope this book will free its readers from the notion that they must buy the kind of horse "everyone else" is buying. Each horse is as unique as each person. In this computerized world, where everything is so readily reduced to impersonal categories, the horseman has the best opportunity to do something totally personal—to select the right horse for himself and get to be good friends.

Finally, you will notice that I start by asking a lot of basic questions. These are the questions that must be answered before you buy a horse and launch yourself into a totally new world.

ALONE WITH YOUR HORSE

CHAPTER 1

Why Do You Want a Horse?

DAY IS BREAKING and the mist floats on the lake. High on the ridge of a hill a figure appears—the horse with his flying mane, silken and flowing in the breeze, his prancing gait so graceful and alive; the rider erect and still. They stop and gaze into the valley, then vanish from view in a floating gallop.

Have you dreamed of being that mysterious rider? If not, you probably have never really wanted a horse. Most of us who want a horse want it to fulfill a private image we have of ourselves. We want a live, soaring steed, and the power and excitement that only a horse can give his rider. Many want the feeling of mastery of this huge and spirited animal, and some desire the companionship and responsibility that come with ownership. This book is dedicated to you, the horseman,* and to helping you find that perfect friend, servant, and companion.

This book is also dedicated to the horse, for I mean to explain in detail all the things you will need to know that will make him happy, comfortable, healthy, and able to do your bidding. I am not writing for the person who wants a horse solely as a status symbol or an investment. This is a personal book, designed for the horse lover who

*Please note, dear reader, that the vast majority of horsemen I know are women and girls, and far and away the majority of horses I have owned are mares. The English language has not kept up with the times and I have therefore been left with only the masculine word "he" for both horse and horseperson throughout the text.

1

is planning to own and care for a horse himself.

Horses serve as a great stabilizer through the rough and uncertain years of adolescence. Horses help adults to release tensions after long and often grueling hours at work. They bring together families in a common endeavor and offer each member a chance to participate in the group. Owners of horses have the added bonus of an increased awareness of the fragile beauty of our natural surroundings.

A more recent role for horses has been as a form of therapy for accident victims, emotionally disturbed persons, and those with polio, cerebral palsy, and other diseases. A nurse in Colorado has used ponies and horses in her work with wounded soldiers, many of whom are multiple amputees. She brings a tiny pony stallion to the patient's hospital bed, and from this modest contact has worked until some patients have gone on to ride cutting horses on ranches and in open competition against professionals. They saddle and bridle their own mounts, climb aboard unaided from wheel chairs, and compete in cutting and reining competitions.

What About *You?*

There may be no doubt in your mind that you want a horse, but your reasons for wanting it should be examined as closely as your preparedness for ownership. Do you meet the requirements for being a horse owner? Loving and wanting a horse are really not enough. Once you have spent all your savings on buying a horse, how do you plan to pay for his care and keep? Have you the facilities, or is there a suitable stable nearby? If all this is under control, how about you yourself as an owner, rider, or driver? Do you know enough to use and care for the animal properly? A horse is a living animal, dependent upon you for his health and well-being. A horse is also an investment which must be protected by care and knowledge.

Let me start here with some finances. In 1945, a ton of hay cost from $15 to $25; a bag (100 lbs.) of grain was $1, and the farrier charged $4 to shoe a horse. Times have changed. Thirty years later, hay is as much as $300 a ton, grain is up eight to ten times what it was, and there is little reason to expect any reduction in price. Horses eat between 3 and 5 tons of hay each year, and anywhere from 2 to 20 or more quarts of grain a day. They need bedding, which is as expensive as hay. Farriers get $20 or more for a set of shoes—and I haven't even mentioned the veterinarian. Horses need their feet done at intervals of from four to eight weeks, and it would be a fair estimate with current prices to say that you must put away $75 per year per horse for the veterinarian bills. Some years you will have only routine worming and immunizations to pay for, but then there are other years when nothing seems to go right. One case of colic can run as high as $60, but not calling the vet can cost the life of the horse. Colic is often the result of ignorance or carelessness, and it is a beginner's greatest hazard. If you've been running a total in your head, you now know that a horse will cost at least $300 a year for maintenance, if you do all your own work and have the place to keep him before you start. Supplying a barn and pastures will add to the investment.

Your responsibility does not end with cleaning the stall and paying the bills. Your horse depends on you for his mental as well as physical well-being. Solitary confinement is no joy for a horse—a herd animal which is energetic and gregarious. If someone put you in a box and took you out to play for fifteen minutes a day and then locked you up again, it would make no difference if the box were lined with satin and fur and the meals served under glass. You would be miserable. Yet ignorant though well-meaning people treat horses this way.

Even if you board the horse at someone else's stable, you are still responsible for making sure he receives the care you are paying for. You must have enough knowledge about a horse's condition to recognize a change in his health or his attitude. Since the horse does not belong to the stable hands, they may not care if he is getting the water, daily exercise, grooming, and attention he needs. People tend to put a great deal of emphasis on clean stalls and fat on their horses; but there are other things that are far more important to the horse's well-being.

The care of a horse actually involves a big investment in time and energy, sustained over his entire life. He must be fed a *minimum* of twice a day and should be fed more often. He needs nearly 30 gallons of cool, fresh water a day. He needs clean, appropriate food, which has been inspected for mold and extraneous materials. He needs some sort of shelter from driving winds and rain or ice, and from heat and flies in summer. Ideally, this will be a shelter he is free to use or not, as he chooses. He needs a pasture, not just a small exercise paddock, where he can run long enough to stimulate his circulation, his mind, and his appetite. He should be groomed and spoken to and given company, if not by another horse, then by you; and he needs this same routine on the days when you are not feeling well and when you have other things you would rather do. He will have to be walked when he does get colic, and treated for the worms and minor wounds and other problems to which a horse is subject. He will require a vet checkup at least once a year to make sure he is protected against contagious diseases and that his teeth and feet are receiving proper care.

If you cannot feed and haul water at least twice a day, clean the stall, and be there when he needs you, then you do not have the right kind of life to be a horse owner. It is not too hard to find someone to drop in and water your potted plants when you go off to Florida for a month, but it may be very hard to find a responsible horse-sitter.

Now, all this may seem foolish. Of course, if you buy an animal, you plan to take care of it. But from the figures on horses that starve to death annually, and from the numbers of horses that the Humane Society and the ASPCA remove from stables and have to destroy, not everyone who buys a horse does know or understand these responsibilities. Lots of children want horses and are sure they will take care of them—until they are faced with the chores every day. Then somehow Mom, who never wanted the thing in the first place, ends up having to shovel out the stalls and dish out the hay and grain. After a while, the horse goes on the market at a loss and the whole family is down on horses from then on.

This is not the fault of the horse.

But what of those people who keep their horses well and then mishandle them once they are on their backs? The horse can be fit and happy, yet if you have bad hands, a shifting leg grip, or poor balance, you will make his mouth and his back sore. Take the trouble to find out whether or not you are a good enough rider by going to a riding teacher for advice and criticism. Make sure the teacher is versed in the style of riding you prefer. You do not want a teacher to pick on your style, but rather to determine how good or bad your hands are and how stable your center of gravity is. If you are still a beginner, that is nothing to be ashamed of; but thinking that you are a better rider than you are, is. Consider taking a few lessons, especially if you are getting a horse that is trained in a different style from the way you were taught.

What if the things I have said here have given you pause? What if you are *not* really ready to own a horse? If you are under eighteen, you are in luck. There are camps, Future Farmers of America, 4-H clubs, Pony Clubs, and even summer jobs for young people on farms where they can learn and improve their skills. For adults, it is a little harder but not impossible. If there is a horse breeder near you, that may be the best place to start. Ask him to recommend riding instructors, horse trainers, and stables in the area. Some breeders will take on a few people and help them along, either as friends or as potential customers. You may be able to "borrow" a horse in the herd, come and care for him, and so learn to handle horses under supervision. You may be able to lease a horse from a breeder or a stable, perhaps with an option to buy it. If you can keep the animal at the owner's stable, pay for his keep, and do the caring while you learn for a year, you will have a pretty good idea of whether you are really interested in actual ownership. Some stables can take on a few people as assistants, grooms, and stable hands in exchange for lessons. Do not expect to get paid for your labor; novice help is more of a liability than an asset to most horse owners. It takes as much time—and more thought—to watch a beginner and be sure he doesn't hurt an animal or himself as it takes a competent horseman to do his chores alone. Insurance is also a problem, so the owner may decline your offer if he is not covered for outsiders.

There are some stables which are run on a leasing basis; that is, every horse in the stable belongs to the stable, but each is leased to one or more people for their exclusive use. The riders each have a time schedule for using the horse. There is a monthly charge for the leasing, and if you get tired of it, you can cancel. In such a stable horses are not rented out on an hourly basis, so the quality and condition of the animals can be well maintained.

Another alternative to buying a horse might be to find a horse owner who will let you share the care of a horse in exchange for part-time use. Some farms will lease a mare for the purpose of raising a foal. You don't take the mare home; you pay a fee and her board, and the foal she has is yours. Meanwhile, you get a chance to handle horses and learn how to school your foal when it arrives. If you are a good rider, you may have a chance of being hired to show other people's horses; if you are a willing stable hand but as yet not as good a rider as you would like to be, you might apply to a professional stable to work as a student assistant.

While none of these things is quite like owning a horse of your own, they do add to your skill and knowledge, and if you get paid, make a tangible contribution toward a good horse of your own.

There are some valid reasons for *not* buying a horse of your own. Your financial circumstances, or a life that includes vacations away from home for long periods, are contrary indications. Some member of the family might be allergic to horse dander, in which case it would be unfair to subject him or her to asthma or painful skin problems for your pleasure. Sometimes careful planning can overcome the difficulties, but in certain cases the demands placed on the potential horse owner and the family are too great to justify ownership.

If none of the obstacles I have mentioned deters you, and you still feel you are willing to stick to it both good and bad days, and able both physically and financially, then you are ready to get involved in the exciting experience of finding the right horse for you. You will discover that every horse is a personality unto himself and the search can be as much fun as ownership itself. A new world will be opened up to you, and you will meet people who love horses and believe in what they are doing with them. The horse world is the smell of stables and leather, good company, and a warm nuzzle from a special and personal friend, your horse. The best moments will always be when you are alone with him.

CHAPTER 2

Where Will He Live?

A STABLE IS MORE than a place for the horse to live. You yourself will also spend a great deal of time there, and will appreciate comfort, convenience, and attractiveness far more than you may realize. Careful thought before the project is started can save you much in terms of money, injuries, and changes later on.

Barn or Stable Requirements

A barn must provide a safe and comfortable stall, which should have minimum dimensions of 8 by 8 feet, ideal dimensions of 12 by 12 feet, and be as near square as possible. It must have adequate storage for hay, grain, bedding, as well as tack and stall-cleaning equipment. You have to be able to remove manure piles, bring in new supplies, and have water available at all times. Electricity is not an essential but will certainly make life pleasanter and safer if you must stay with a sick horse late at night, or if your schedule dictates that you will do winter chores after dark. Your barn should also be accessible in severe storms, and its location in relation to pastures and exercising areas should be given careful thought. Run-off from barns, and mud and rain run-off into the barn from a nearby hillside, must be considered. Barns should not be higher than houses, they should be located where they will not foul wells or interfere with septic systems. Zoning regulations will also restrict the location of a barn in many communities.

The sun is high overhead in the summer and slants low on the southern horizon in the winter. In order to make a barn comfortable in all seasons, you should take this into consideration: the open side or long face of the barn should face south or southeast. Then the winter sun can warm the barn most effectively. Wind usually blows from northwest to southeast, so this should be considered in ventilating the barn. Drainage is essential; the subsoil should be properly investigated, and it may be necessary to install drains and trenches.

Once you have established the ideal location, you can begin to consider construction. The barn must be strong enough to hold a horse in his bad moments in life. Horses thrash about when they are hurt, frightened, or angry. They smash things. Barns that are built of flimsy materials sometimes become traps for a leg or head. If a horse feels trapped, he struggles even more violently, so plan to make everything stronger than you think necessary, and also to make things as easily replaceable and removable as you can. Stall walls are best constructed of 2-inch-thick oak planking—horses don't chew on oak as they do on other wood. It is better to put the planks up in slots or channels than to fix them with nails or screws. The stall doors should be a minimum of 4 feet wide. They can slide, swing, or even be made as a takedown barway for some horses. Personal preference and available space will dictate which is best. Floors should be warm, easily cleanable, and not slippery. Dirt (preferably clay) floors are the best for horses. Wood is the next choice, but it should be very thick and not nailed down but force-fitted into place with the floorboards at least 2 inches thick (nails work up as the horse walks about the stall). Cement floors, the third option, are the least satisfactory, being dangerous, cold, and requiring a great deal more bedding than either wood or dirt floors. Bedding is very expensive in most places. Some alternatives are thick rubber matting, carpet, or Homosote—a thick building board which is remarkable for its endurance, warmth, and resistance to deterioration. This makes excellent temporary flooring in a situation where a cement floor must be covered—for a converted garage, for instance. Horses stabled on cement floors are prone to foot and leg problems and subject to slipping accidents. Also, cement does not drain and therefore holds the moisture in the bedding, making it essential to change it more frequently.

Hallways should be a minimum of 6 feet wide. Less space can cause a horse to bruise his hip constantly as he turns to enter the stall; this also means that you will be crowded as you lead the horse beside you. Remember that anything hung along the walls is a hazard. Hall floors should again be of wood or dirt, not cement. The horse who comes into a barn in winter often has ice packed into his feet and he can take an awful skid on a slick floor. Even rain can make a cement floor unsafe for horses. Finally, if for some reason you must have cement in the barn, make certain that it has deep ridges running across every 2 inches or so. Some barns have asphalt floors and hallways; apparently these are just as treacherous as cement. We use rubber runners on the cement floors in our old barn.

The crosstie area, where you will tie your horse in order to groom or work on him, should be thought out with care. There has to be enough room on each side of the horse for you to stand, bend down, and step back at arm's length. You will want good light, and during the summer you will appreciate good air circulation in that area. The floor should be flat, for when the farrier works on the horse he will need to judge the level and position of the feet, which is usually done by standing the horse in crossties and looking at him from several

A horse standing in crossties. Note that the ties are secured to the wall well above the horse's withers. There is ample room to work around the horse.

angles, as well as by watching him move. The crossties should be located near the tack room. Grooming supplies should be kept in the crosstie area, you may also want to locate your medicine cabinet there. A crosstie area is best if it is at least 8 feet wide. Ours is almost 12 feet and very comfortable. The crossties themselves should be constructed of two big rings fastened securely to the wall well above your head. From these two stout ropes, fitted with large, easy to open snaps, are hung. The ropes should almost meet at your chest level.

The tack room should be one you can lock. Tack is expensive and there is a great deal of tack theft. Plan on room for more tack than you expect to own, it accumulates fast and you will find that as your interest and knowledge in horses grows your supply of equipment will increase, too. The stable-cleaning equipment should be stored in a separate place from the regular tack, not leaned against a wall where you can trip over a pitchfork in the dark. If you clean stalls into a wheelbarrow or a basket, that will take up at least 3 square feet of floor space. (If you store the wheelbarrow out of doors, it will deteriorate rapidly.)

When you are planning a barn, try to think of all the things you will want to store and use there, and then also consider if one horse is going to be your limit or whether you might take on a boarder for company and to help share costs. An extra stall might cost more to build in, but it can pay for itself in the extra storage space if you buy hay or bedding in larger quantities. In our area, people buy loads of hay or bedding on a cooperative basis, so that the load is bought at a discount. They all help to unload and store the supplies, and such sharing greatly reduces the individual labor and expense.

The stableboy may well be a girl, and perhaps a small one at that. It may be that Mother is pressed into service to do chores when the kids go off. A barn should be designed for easy handling of hay, grain, water, and stall-cleaning chores, with only limited strength required. Hay stored at ground level is far more convenient than overhead storage. Climbing a ladder is fine for the teen-agers in the family but may not be much fun for the less horse-minded members who are conscripted from time to time, and in any case, ladders can be dangerous. Overhead storage has other disadvantages, too. Barns for horses should be airy and have lots of circulation. Horses create humidity and suffer in what we might consider snug, cozy stables. They should *not* be kept warm in the winter, and are far healthier if they are allowed to go out of doors every day and to stay cool at night. During the summer, fresh air is of prime importance. Hay stored over the stalls cuts down on the ventilation in the stable, and also lowers the headroom. Eight feet is the minimum headroom for a small horse, tall horses should have far more.

Write out all your needs in an organized fashion and draw up plans from the information you have gathered on your visits to farms. An indoor ring is nice but few single-horse owners can justify such an expense. While storing a ton of hay at a time might save you money, there is little need to store several tons unless you plan to retail hay during the rough winter months to local people who don't have storage room. You don't want to overbuild, but neither do you want to shortchange yourself in space simply because you miscalculated. You should always build with the thought that you might want to add on in the future, and keep the plan flexible. Lumber companies and agricultural extension services will supply you with detailed plans for constructing stables if you do not want to use an actual building company.

Converting an Existing Building

Sometimes a building is available already that only needs some conversion to make it into an adequate stable. If it is located far enough from the house so that flies will not be a problem and the septic and well systems are not involved, that's fine. Most garages are too close to the main house to act as a stable. They usually have cement floors and not enough ventilation, in which case it may be better to use such a building for storage and to build a separate stable nearby, or perhaps a shed off the back or side of the garage for the stalls themselves. This usually ends up proving less costly than trying to break out cement flooring or make the drainage work.

In case you plan on owning more than one horse, or even having a breeding farm someday, let me tell you about the barn we have evolved. First, because I am physically very limited in the amount of wheelbarrowing I can manage, I installed a mechanical barn cleaner. Second, because I like to have fresh air and light, and want my horses to be healthy, our stalls are all faced with industrial-weight chainlink fencing, with grilles between the stalls from 4 feet up. Third, because watering horses is the slowest, least interesting, and most essential of all horse chores, we now have automatic water fountains in each stall. We buy our grain in bulk, 7 tons a month, which saves about $1 per 100 lbs. This is stored in ratproof bins.

Our old barn was a converted cow barn, which in turn had been converted from an old camp bunkhouse. It is not comfortable, practical, or really suitable for horses in the winter. It has cement floors, cramped stalls, and stone walls along one side as the barn is built into a bank. It is cold and damp and forbidding in the winter. Our second barn is what used to be our house, and before that was the milkhouse for the old cattle barn. It, too, has cement floors, with one cement wall running the entire length, and is built into the hillside. We have learned much from the conversion of these two buildings. The milkhouse now has nice big stalls, with windows open along the entire east side, open eaves, and open ends for ventilation, and a whole west wall with doors which we can open all summer (we tore down the ceiling, which gave us much more air circulation). We secured posts and walls into place with a gun that shoots studs into concrete. This makes construction far stronger and stalls far easier than when you have to jam posts into position between floor and rafter to hold up stall walls.

In the new barn, we took all these things into consideration. The construction is what is known as a *pole barn*. The entire building is held up by poles set on concrete pads which are three feet underground. The floor is just dirt—the way it was when we started to build. Every once in a while we add a load of sand to level out the stalls, which get dug down in the stall-cleaning process. The outside wall of the building is ⅝-inch Plyscore, stained brown. The roof, unfortunately, is of aluminum. It is insulated with Styrofoam to prevent condensation from dripping down on the horses. Had I realized that a standard wood and asphalt shingle roof would have cost the same, I would certainly have preferred that. It would have been quieter, warmer in the winter, less inclined to leak, and would not have caused the glare problem we get from this metal roof. We have huge sliding doors at each end of the barn so we can drive a horse trailer, bulldozer, or sand truck right in. There are Dutch doors on three front broodmare stalls, two sliding exit doors on the sides, and a sliding door to the grain room. We have just added an extension along the side of the barn for a sawdust bin and carriage shed, and to cover the side door to the pasture so that I can open it when there is snow on the ground. The snow comes off the roof in such a pile that it used to take me forty-five minutes to open the door on winter mornings.

The way my barn is laid out, it houses twenty horses comfortably in stalls 10 by 12 feet, with a 50-by-50-foot arena in the center where my weanlings live and play. I do not believe in locking up horses in stalls when they are young, so I do not start stalling my horses until they are yearlings. This system works out very well for us. The stalls line the outside of the barn, but along the outer wall of each is an uncovered cement gutter through which the barn cleaner runs. The cleaner is a continuous chain with scraper paddles, which is pulled by a motor mounted on the outside at the end of a track. The chain travels slowly along in the gutter, and as I toss the litter out of the stall into the gutter, it is conveyed outside to a pit. It can be set up to go directly into a manure spreader or into a methane generator digester. (The next project on the farm is to make our own power using horse manure.) The horses can step into the track if they want to. Most of them decide that it is not too interesting and so they stay out. Once in a while a nervous horse used to back into it, but would quickly step out again. We put up "butt bars" to prevent this and to keep the foals from falling in when they got to romping about their mothers—2-by-8-inch planks, dropped into slots, which run across the back of the stall above the near edge of the gutter. This is one single board which runs horizontally about 20 inches off the floor. That is all that is needed. For very nervous horses it might be necessary to cover the track with wood and make trapdoors to put the litter in, but I really think any horse would soon learn to stay out of it. There are no windows in my horses' stalls, so they are not inclined to stand in the very back of the stall anyway.

The kind of stable you want to build will clearly depend to some extent on the kind of horse you buy. If you plan to own a show American Saddle Horse or Tennessee Walker, or a park-type Morgan or Arabian, you are going to have to keep the horse confined and exercise him daily. If you choose a hunter, which you clip and blanket, you will want to keep that horse confined. If you decide on a trail or pleasure horse that has a normal foot and a light type of shoe, he can probably go out in a pasture for exercise without getting hurt. For the pleasure horse, a *free stall system* is ideal. This is also the very best way to house a broodmare or any growing horse. The system can be a real money and labor saver, for in many cases a horse will live out of doors most of the time and the stall will not need to be cleaned or bedded at all. Free stall simply means the horse has a shed, shelter, or stall that opens into a pasture and the door is never closed. He can come and go as he likes. Given the choice, most horses will stay out of doors in all but the worst blizzards and hot, bug-ridden days. If your horse is a free-stabled horse, you will only have to build storage space, tack room, crosstie area, and a shed roof. If you have sufficient pasture and he can live on pelletted complete feed, you need not figure on hay or bedding storage. In that case, you have already saved yourself hundreds of dollars.

Larger Stables

For those readers who are going to get into the horse business on a larger scale and plan to run a breeding farm, or a boarding, training, or livery stable, the whole concept of construction takes on a different view. You can convert an old chicken coop or cow barn, as we have, but if you really want to be a commercial success in this day and age, you must take advantage of every saving technique available. In the case of raising young horses, any breed will benefit by being shed-raised in large pastures. The young horses will look scruffy and shaggy and they may not sell as easily as fat, slick, hot-house-raised show horses, but they will be healthier, more valuable horses at maturity, and the buying public is beginning to be aware that "hothcuse" foals are very likely to be crippled by their fifth year of life. There will be a gradual trend among buyers to be impressed less by pushed and fattened foals, and more by these free-moving, healthy, normally grown youngsters. Veterinarians, farriers, and some intelligent breeders are already writing more and more articles urging people to abandon the fat show horse and huge racing infants for a sounder future for horses. So this brings us to practical methods of housing young and growing horses. Ideally, a shed which is carefully located on a pasture of sufficient size to support and exercise a group of young horses will prove the best arrangement. One of the most highly respected show stables raised all their young horses this way. The broodmares were also kept in compatible groups in sheds. Certain select horses were taken up into the show barn, fitted, and worked to be shown. The results were impressive, and this farm's horses have become the best-known name in their breed. Other farms have followed suit with good results. Any breed of horse can learn to live out of doors without clipping, blanketing, and pampering. I have seen Arabians, Thoroughbreds, and Saddlebreds all raised successfully this way, right here in New England. The horses develop the necessary winter coat and resistance to the cold, and their skin thickens enough to be comfortable. The incidence of respiratory diseases drops impressively in these stables by comparison to stall-raised horses. The one important thing to keep in mind with shed raising is that pastures have to be rotated and rested. It is a temptation to put horses in every shed and on every pasture at the same time. Parasite control must be carefully handled. You will still have to have some stalls to house a sick or injured horse, a horse being fitted up for work or show, and so on. You will need tractors and equipment for handling the hay and feeds that must be transported out to the sheds. You may have to protect your animals from hunters, which can be a major problem in parts of the country where deer are poached for profit or hunting is not properly regulated.

In the case of riding, livery, and training stables, you will almost certainly want an indoor ring or arena of some sort for year-round activity. Such buildings can vary from plastic geodesic domes to the common commercially constructed truss-roofed pole barns. If you plan to drive indoors and do harness training, an arena of 80 by 160 feet is adequate. Many stables have a wide working alleyway, and the horses are worked up and down the alley in hand and under saddle. Some barns are built with a group or cluster of stalls in the center, with a working track going around the stalls. And some, like ours, have the stalls around the perimeter and a working area in the center. Arena floors should be dirt, and should be surfaced with tanbark, shavings, or some other substance that can be wet down to keep dust from filling the air while working.

Those stables where several owners have horses together will have to provide places for privately owned equipment—in lockers or some other secure fashion so that people cannot "borrow" each other's things. Any stable, large or small, should consider the possibility that a horse might have to be completely isolated from other horses because of disease. A horse I sold this year just died because another horse with a "slight runny nose" was brought into the same barn and the disease she was carrying proved to be overwhelming to the horse already there. Last year I spent several hundred dollars trying to clear up a "bug" brought into our stable by a yearling colt who was to stay for a few days. He did not show signs of anything on the day he arrived, but by the next day his nose was running, and inside of a week nearly twenty-eight horses here were sick. Some farms have small isolation stables located at a reasonable distance from the main barn, where two horses can be housed and cared for as a complete unit. This makes good sense, particularly for a farm with young horses, who have not developed immunities to many diseases.

Your Own Needs

Before you put down any money for a stable or a horse, visit all the stables in your area with notebook in hand. Most stables are built the way they are for a reason. The owner either thought out the first plan or converted and rearranged his barn to suit specific circumstances. Try to understand your own needs and ways of doing things before you actually invest in the lumber and labor needed for construction.

If you plan to drive your horse, you will need a shed for vehicle storage where carts, wagons, and sleighs can be suspended when not in use. Poles and shafts take up quite a bit of room. Measure a few vehicles before you make the assumption that they can squeeze into the garage with the family car. If you plan to truck about to shows, rallies, and so on, you will need tack trunks to hold equipment. They, too, have to be stored somewhere between trips. A pencil and a pad of paper are the best money-savers in the world, providing you put them to use in listing all the things you will have to accommodate.

Obviously, you must have a stall to house the horse. This can have a drinking fountain or water bucket, a feed tub or bucket, and per-haps a hay manger. It should have a secure door, be light and airy, and easy to clean, with a nonslippery floor. Airy does not mean drafty —the walls should be solid up to 4 feet to protect the horse's chest from drafts. Hay can be stored by the bale or by stacks of bales, and these vary somewhat in actual measurement, but it is safe to assume you could store a full ton of hay in a 10-by-10 foot stall. Shavings and other forms of bedding come in bales and bags of about the same dimensions as the hay bales, that is, about 20 inches wide and 36 inches long. Measure the size of the bales you plan to purchase. Find out what the price break is for your area on quantity buying. There may be no savings in buying more than a daily or weekly supply for one horse; if so, the consideration will be what is most convenient for you. Would you prefer to drive down to the feed store once a week and buy a bag of grain and a few bales of hay, or have the grain company deliver a month's supply at a time?

Water is the one thing your horse absolutely cannot live without. He must have clean, fresh water in *adequate* supply. It is hard to carry enough water to a horse. It makes much more sense to invest in a water supply that is handy and will not freeze up in the winter. A hose from the house is not practical. You can buy fountains which are heated or fountains which are self-draining. It is not too expensive to dig a trench below frostline and lay a plastic pipe to the stable. Then you can install a hydrant (again, the self-draining kind) or put in drinking fountains. We are very satisfied with the plastic drinking fountains advertised nationally and guaranteed. The company has lived up to its guarantee—the ones our horses have broken were replaced without a murmur. They do freeze up on very cold nights, but they have not split and cracked, as the old metal cow fountains used to do. If you have a problem with freezing pipes and hoses, a heat lamp hung over the hose will help. Don't put it too close, though; I burned one hose in half that way. Electrical heat tapes, which are strips of wire imbedded in plastic which are wound around the pipes, are not safe to use on plastic pipe and hose, but work well on metal pipes. However, they have to be wrapped and the fiberglass and kraft paper wrap is tempting for a horse to chew. You must not use this system where a horse can reach it. We used unwrapped heat tapes on the metal pipes in our old barn and the horses ate all the little terminal connections on the ends!

Hazards

Fires are the major hazard in barns. Bedding and hay are very flammable. People do smoke in barns in spite of all warnings. When you have to get horses out of burning barns, a gate that is hard to open, a door that doesn't open all the way, or halters that are hung in inaccessible places can mean the difference between disaster and rescue. Install a light that you can get to right at the barn entrance. Install another light out of doors to flood a fair-sized area, if you can. Have a hose connected to the hydrant in case a fire starts. Have the fire station phone number posted next to your phone.

Besides the slippery floors (already mentioned), there are a few other hazards we have learned about to our sorrow. Buckets should be hung on a solid ring or screw eye by a double-ended snap. Never hang a bucket on an open hook, as horses can tear their eyelids off on these. Unprotected electrical wiring should be an obvious danger, but not everyone is aware how much chewing a horse can do. Plastic which can get chewed on is also potentially fatal. Obviously, glass bottles, wire, and nails are all dangerous. We decant things from glass to plastic containers if the chemical reactions won't be a problem. Remember that anything sold in a dark brown glass bottle must be protected from light, so it cannot just be put into a clear plastic bottle and then left on a shelf. If you want to keep a large supply of absorbent cotton in the barn, take it out of its box and store it in a food storage bag (the self-locking kind that doesn't require a twist tie is most convenient). Paints, kerosene, and other flammable substances should never be stored in a stable. Fly-killing strips cause respiratory problems to horses—don't hang them in your barn.

Lastly, don't plan on stabling a horse with either a tractor or a car. Exhaust fumes are deadly and people will warm up a car inside in the winter. Even if an animal doesn't die from inhaling such fumes, its brain cells can be destroyed in a matter of moments.

Your barn should be safe, convenient, and comfortable for both you and the horse. It need not be expensive or elegant to meet these requirements. But just as you differ from your neighbor, so your needs in a barn will differ. Gather all the ideas you can while you are looking for your horse.

CHAPTER 3

Where Will He Play?

YOUR BARN WILL BE the major expense and consideration before you bring your horse home. But unless you can ride, drive, or work that horse every day for an hour or so, he will also need some form of pasture. The easiest way to provide this is to make a paddock so that at the very least he can be turned out while you pick up his stall. If you have no room, the other alternative is to lead him for two or three hours every day.

He Needs Adequate Space

How many acres does a horse require? That depends on what those acres are supposed to provide. A horse can get exercise in a "run" of about 100 by 100 feet. Anything less than that will likely just make him pace the fence, although two horses together will take more exercise in a paddock than one alone. If he can gallop full out, he will freshen the air in his lungs and stimulate his circulation. If he just paces back and forth along one line or stands dejectedly in a tiny enclosure, he will fret, lose weight, and wear down his shoes. Even a 100-foot-square paddock is still no more than a place to move. It does not offer the things a real pasture should provide, and is no substitute for actual riding and driving, in terms of keeping the horse fit.

For some horses, however, a paddock is adequate because of the life they lead. Show horses are kept out of the sun because their coats fade, dry out, and become dull. Gaited or park horses with long feet and weighted shoes cannot be turned out in any area large enough to frolic, for they will tear off their shoes and a good portion of the hoof as well. They also hit themselves and inflict injuries when they try to play with those heavy feet. For most horses a pasture that affords some real grass, shade, water, and enough room to open up to a full gallop is great for muscle and spirit. Most people feed their horses enough so that they do not need pasture for survival; but grass is the natural food for horses and far superior to all the dried and concentrated feeds we can offer. In the case of breeding stock, grass is almost an essential for milk production in the lactating mare and helps in breeding. It is far easier to get mares in foal and to keep a stallion virile and potent if they have adequate grass daily.

The number of acres per horse depends upon the amount of food those acres offer. If the pasture is lush, fertilized, adequately clipped to keep down weeds, seeded with a real pasture mixture, and rotated • so that at no time does the grass grow rank or get eaten down too far, then 1 acre per horse is adequate. With trees, overgrazing, lack of liming and fertilizing, and zero rotation, the ratio doubles or triples.

If you are a beginner with a new home and 2 acres of uncleared woods, you have enough room to keep one or two riding horses as long as you also maintain their grain and hay rations year round. In pasture they will have places to roll, to rub on trees and play, and to supplement their regular diet. But this would never supply an adequate diet in itself. Woods alone, with no relief from deer flies, no clearing for any grass, and without rotation to kill off the worm population, will do little to maintain either a horse's condition or his spirit.

Is it essential to clear and bulldoze those 2 acres? No—and it is not recommended. The best procedure is to clear a path around the circumference of the proposed pasture first. Make it wide enough and clear enough to give yourself room to work, or to get a tractor through if possible. Then invest your money in the best fencing material you can afford.

Fencing

Fences are to keep horses in, not to hold people up. However, people like to climb and sit on fences, so this must be taken into consideration when a fence is being put up. One way to preserve the fence from the rump-rubbing, mane-scratching, over-the-top-grazing horse, and the visiting horse watchers alike, is a hot (and I mean hot) electric fence. I highly recommend the electric fence in combination with a regular pasture fence as the safest and most effective type of enclosure. Since most of us live near enough to a road to have to worry about auto accidents, it is well to consider a fence as a major investment in your horse's routine expenses. If your horse gets into a road and is struck by a car, you are financially responsible for all damages to the car and its occupants.

Fences constructed of wood posts and rails or boards are traditional on a horse farm. They afford safety to the horse, since the animal cannot get his feet twisted in wooden rails. However, wood fences require careful construction, starting with good materials. All fences require constant upkeep. There are a few rules to follow in making a fence that will help to keep the whole thing standing up longer. Here are a few suggestions:

Make all post holes 8 feet apart on center. Set posts 3 feet deep. Treating your posts with creosote or penta will literally add years to their life. Note: both penta and creosote are very poisonous substances. Use only on parts that will be underground.

Put rails or boards on the inside of the fence, so that the horse leans against the rails and cannot push them off the post.

Pre-drill all nail holes to avoid splitting. Space the boards no more than 2 feet apart, and make the fence high enough to discourage the horse from grazing over the top. Three boards will prevent grazing through the fence and so ruining the mane.

When a fence divides two pastures, plank or board both sides of the fence, or top it with electric fence.

Where the fence is likely to have to hold people, make a flat-topped caprail with a slight pitch to let water drain off.

If the fence is of cedar rails, the horse will rub his winter hair off on the knobs and stubble; it is better to cut the stubble flat to the surface of the rail.

A 4-foot-high fence is fine for most pleasure horses. Hunters and jumpers will do better with a 6- or 7-foot fence, but when erecting such a high fence, be sure to set the posts in deeper than 3 feet.

Some states require double fence and specify height and materials where stallions are kept; check your local regulations.

Woven stock wire fence is satisfactory for horses, providing it is kept tight enough. Once it starts sagging, the horses will get their feet into it. Top-railing a woven wire fence works very well. For this, you put up wood posts, wire fence, and a wooden rail at the top, and staple the top strand of the wire to the rail. This is good for a pasture where you keep foals, because sometimes they dive through a wide-spaced rail fence and frantic mares can do a lot of harm to themselves as well as the fence while their foals race about the perimeter of the pasture. If you put a woven wire fence between two pastures where horses are likely to visit or fight or play, then I strongly urge electric fence over this. If they strike, as horses do in conversation, they will tangle. Once a horse is trapped in a fence, other horses will sometimes attack him, and they can turn and kick a hind foot into the wire, too.

Combination fences of stone walls and rails or wire can work out

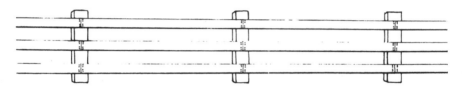

Post and three rail boards, 2 × 6, 10 inches apart.

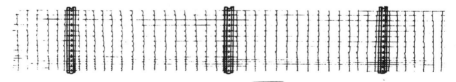

Rustic cedar rail.

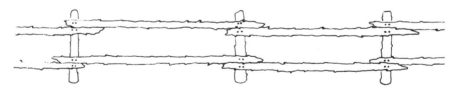

Stock wire fence on metal fence posts.

well and look very handsome. The old-time snake fences are beautiful and sturdy but require a large number of rails to gain enough height for horses.

Split-rail fences, threaded into drilled posts, are probably the strongest fences possible. The labor required to erect them, however, is impressive.

Barbed wire has no place on a horse farm, since horses apparently don't see single strand fences well and easily become entangled in them. When they do get tangled, they often panic and tear or cut their legs on barbed wire. Leg injuries are hard to heal, and the horse, like man, is subject to tetanus. It is far cheaper to avoid barbed wire entirely than to repair an animal when it is cut. We once bought a mare whose neck had been cut nearly in half as a foal when dogs chased her into a barbed-wire fence. It is not possible to keep dogs out of your pasture, so when dogs do get the horses running you can

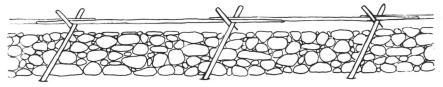

Stock wire fence, top rail and braced. Wooden gate hung on pintles and secured with a chain.

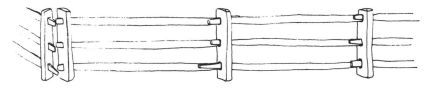

Post and rail with rails threaded through drilled posts.

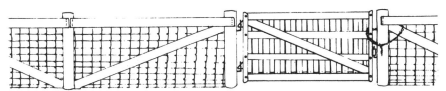

Stone wall with crossbuck and rail.

only pray the fences will hold and the horses not injure themselves. Where trespassers are a real problem and dogs are fierce, a cyclone fence is the surest protection for very valuable animals and for small enclosures. You have to be a millionaire to put up much of the stuff, but do consider, if you really have a bad situation in your area, making a small paddock if you have to be away from home frequently.

Plain, smooth wire and rope fences are essentially useless for the average horse. If you must string a fence in the woods from tree to tree or over extremely rugged grades, smooth wire in several strands will hold horses, providing it is tight enough.

Sheep-hurdle fences are great for temporary pastures or for rotating and separating pastures. These are a series of separate panels fastened to posts, usually metal stakes driven into the ground. The whole setup is removable for plowing and seeding in the fields, or to take with you when you move. The gates can be set up as temporary stalls, or used to divide a larger area for worm control or confinement of a sick animal. Such panels are not cheap, but they offer many advantages. Gate kits are available, consisting of metal ends that can be made up into gates for pastures or into sets of panels. If you are just starting out, a set of such gates would be practical; they can be employed to hold horses until permanent pastures can be made. When the pastures are complete, these panels can be used as the pasture gates.

Snow fences and single-strand electric fences are not much good for horses. If you have limited funds, make a three-strand electric fence and then tie white ribbon (or markers of some sort which you are certain the horse can see) every few feet along the fence. You will probably need to electrify only one strand of the wire, but put up all three, or better four, and make them tight.

Pasture

If your image of a horse farm is white-painted fences and rolling green hills and meadows, there is nothing but time and money to prevent you from turning your entire acreage into such a showplace. It is best to do it all at least a year before you plan on bringing the horses home. Be sure the fences are painted three times with non-leaded and non-mercury paint. Do leave at least one large tree in each paddock for shade as well as aesthetic reasons. Most of all, be sure those acres are broken up into enough paddocks for frequent rotation, or the fields will soon turn brown and dusty from overgrazing, and the fences will be chewed.

A second point is essential in pasture management. Fences protect your new seedlings and recovering pastures. Maintain strong fences and clip the grass along the fence lines to discourage the horses from leaning over the fences. The grass may be greener on the other side of the fence, but the fences rapidly break down and your nice divisions will once again be one big pasture. One pasture will not support as many horses as well or as safely as two or three totaling the same area.

Two of the most important services you can perform for your pasture are *mowing* and *dragging*. Horses do not like tall grass. They like short, new shoots and will eat the same shoots in the same spots constantly, ignoring the older woody stems of "rank" pasture. Mowing will discourage weeds and promote the tender grass. Also, horses tend not to eat where their own feces have dropped. This is fine, for it lessens the chance of reinfection by parasites, but it also makes rank growth of grass that is wasted. Dragging with a chain drag will break up the clumps of manure. The worm larvae are then exposed to the killing rays of the sun and to birds who eat them. Dragging also spreads the fertilizing and moisture-conserving properties of the manure over a wider space. Many big farms which raise both horses and cattle let the cattle graze the pasture first, then they rake it and drag it, and finally they pasture the horses. If the practice is carefully controlled so that the cows do not eat the grass too short and the horses are moved often enough to have parasite-free pasture, this is an extremely profitable way to utilize all the grass you can grow.

Fields of tall grass and brush are lovely to see, but they create an ideal breeding ground and habitat for mosquitoes and deer flies. They also create a terrible fire hazard when the grass dries in the fall. If you plan to cut hay, that's fine, but don't allow open meadows to grow untended anywhere near your house or horse pastures. If you can't pasture them, at least keep them mowed.

This brings up the question of pasture *rotation*. If you have one or two horses and one lovely big pasture, divide it. If one section grows up too fast, mow it, and feed the cut grass in the stalls while it is fresh. (Do not feed cut grass to horses if it has started to heat or "cure." It becomes highly toxic.) Worm the horses the last week on a pasture. Move them to the next pasture and drag the first with a drag.

Chain drags are expensive, but a brush drag is easy to make, and a cooperative horse can help with his own pasture maintenance by towing it about from one place to another from his saddle or harness. To make a brush drag, cut several small cedar trees or some young black birch saplings about 10 feet high. Nail the butts to a 2-by-4 about 4 feet long. Drill holes in each end and the center of the 2-by-4, and attach a trio of chains or ropes to these holes. Then attach these ropes to traces or a single rope, by which the drag is pulled. The horses can pull this from the horn of a Western saddle, with a regular breast collar, or just with ropes from the two holes on the end (it should not be heavy).

In our New England soil, it is not recommended that pasture be plowed and reseeded unless it is completely grown up to bush and bull brier. If there is any native grass at all, we try to fertilize for it and encourage its natural spread. Weedkillers are not safe in horse pastures, and it is best to cut or uproot such pests as burdock, briers, and deadly nightshade. I attended an extension-service lecture recently at which a woman asked how to get rid of burdock and poison ivy in her pasture. The agent recommended 2-4-D, 2-4-5-T, and other herbicides to be spread on the pasture. The weeds they were trying to dispel were not poisonous to horses, but the herbicides most assuredly were!

Fertilize in the spring or fall to encourage the grasses you desire, and cut weeds or mow entirely the section that the horses have just finished. Take a soil test before you fertilize. Horses do not really like much clover, and enough of it will grow naturally to balance their ration without additional fertilization for it. New England soil tends to be acid, so liming is generally indicated; our practice is to lime every three years and fertilize once a year. However, conditions will vary from year to year and from one field to another even on the same farm. Your state department of agriculture, college of agriculture, or field representative of cooperative farm exchanges can help in doing your testing. Their recommendations are based on the samples you send, so be sure you follow the instructions carefully.

The type of seeding mixture you use in a pasture will also depend on the drainage and the area of the pasture. Tender grasses, like blue grasses, are the horses' favorite; but in areas where horses stand for long periods of time, under trees and near gates, it will die off. For heavy traffic areas, fescue, red top, timothy, and vetch will tend to last longer. The University of Connecticut recommendations are as follows: for poorly drained soil horse pasture—10 lbs. Kentucky Blue Grass, 6 lbs. Reed canary grass, and 1 lb. ladino clover; in well-drained soil—10 lbs. Kentucky Blue Grass, 5 lbs. timothy or orchard grass, 1 lb. ladino clover.

The 4-H Extension Service publishes helpful reports on pasture care. Check with your own state for such aids.

The native grasses will survive and flourish with the least encouragement, and new grasses can be introduced by raking these into the established sod. Disk harrowing or spring tooth harrowing is preferable to deep plowing where the topsoil is light or the rainfall scant. Seed can be compacted and rolled in with a cultipacker or lawn roller. Your rainfall will determine to a great extent the results you get in seeding a pasture, and for this reason it is recommended that seeding be done early in spring or in fall. Be sure the weeds are mowed before they seed or they will defeat your grass. There are mixtures of grass seed called *conservation mix,* which will survive in poor soil, shade, and other places where lawn grass can't make it, but remember to check on the acidity of your soil.

Buy only as much seed as you need, for if allowed to lie around for too long, it can lose its germinating ability. Each time an area gets cleared, either by the demise of a tree or by the horses grubbing out brush, rush in with grass seed and sprinkle it liberally about. Ideally, grass should be sown in the spring and fall, but this spot system of reseeding often works effectively regardless of the time of year. You can also reseed by spreading hay chaff and seed in those bare spots. Put a fairly thick layer on, as the wind will blow some away. Water for a few days after seeding.

If your land is hilly, steep, and rocky, with a thin layer of topsoil, ferns, and woodland flowers, it will have to be watched for erosion. As horses walk, their hoofs do cut into the roots of plants. There are some ground-holding plants which are safe for horses and very useful for restoring land that has steep banks or has been bulldozed or burned over. Crown vetch, alfalfa, and other legumes are good for soil, as they put nitrogen into the earth; because of their extensive root system they are particularly valuable on slopes, where they help to hold soil. Sedums and other low-growing plants will help hold soil until more grass can be established, but again, consult your agricultural agent or a qualified landscaper before venturing on any major reclamation—even a little of that work can be expensive and frustrating unless it is done properly.

You can pasture horses in orchards and among trees, but you should be aware that they will kill a good number of them if they start to chew wood, unless the trees are protected. Gradually, horses will girdle and kill off most of the small trees in their pasture and sometimes an old giant as well. The trees you wish to preserve should be painted frequently with Carbolineum, or wrap ¼-inch mesh hardware cloth around them from the ground to about 7 feet high. When you cut down a tree, pull the stump or drill it down, fill with a stumpkiller, and burn it. If it can be grubbed out and the earth flattened, plant some grass seed in that spot to prevent the growth of bull brier and poison ivy.

At certain times of the year (and in certain years), horses chew more. During early spring, when the sap is starting to flow and the horses are shedding, they will chew wood even in their stalls. At that point, put them on the brushiest piece of land that you want cleared, protecting the trees you wish to preserve. It will save your barn from the ravages of their wood-chewing urges and you also will get a good head start on the bull brier, poison ivy, burs, and small weeds they like. Browsing on brush is very good for horses, so let the horses browse to reduce the undergrowth. At the time you switch them to the alternate pasture, go into the used pasture and grub out the roots of all the bull brier you can get. Do the same with all the small wild cherry trees they have stripped down. Spread seed or hay chaff on the bare spots immediately.

If you cut any tree branches, cut them flush and smooth and do not leave sharp stubble. Be sure not to cut any brush at or near ground level, as it leaves sharp stumps that remain alive and send up new and more vigorous growth. Since it is alive, the stubble can puncture a horse's foot. No matter how careful you are, you cannot get stubble from brush all the way down to the ground where it does not pose a threat to the animal. So save your efforts and leave it alone. The horses will kill it in time by walking about on it.

If you want a flat paddock, cut the trees and bulldoze, but remember that you must seed, fertilize, and mow that new area before the horses are ever allowed in it. If you clear, plow, and seed, and then put the horses into the new grass, they will destroy it. It has to have one full growing season in order to establish a root system that will resist the weight and cut of the hoofs and the pulling of the horses as they eat. So if you make a new paddock or cleared pasture, don't plan on using it the following year. Make the pasture in the fall, mow it once in the spring, and by the next fall, after the dry season is behind, it will likely survive pasturing.

Do *not* plant multiflora roses (living fences) or raspberries on your land. They will spread everywhere and choke out pastures. Birds spread the seeds of cherry, bull brier, poison ivy, multiflora, raspberries, deadly nightshade, and bittersweet. To eliminate these weeds, you must clear them out before fruit has formed. Pull up the entire plant if possible.

People often worry about poisonous plants in their pastures and want to know what is the best procedure for getting them out. For the most part, if you feed horses and cattle an adequate diet of appetizing food and do not leave them in a pasture until it is overgrazed, they will not normally eat enough noxious weeds to harm themselves. They can chew on bark, browse, and forage perfectly safely with no ill effects. If, however, you pasture them exclusively on clover or alfalfa, which are fine in very carefully controlled quantities, you can kill your horses. Clover is a pet peeve of mine. Horses don't really like it; given a choice, they'll eat many wildflowers in preference. Alfalfa, when wet or slightly frost-bitten, is poisonous to horses—though more so to white horses (as well as to donkeys, ponies, and mules) than to the darker-colored equines.

A few plants are no problem as long as they are green and growing and left alone. Most notable of these is the wild cherry, which horses eat with relish and impunity when it is part of a healthy live tree; but let the wind break a branch or a woodsman chop a limb, and the wilting leaves become a deadly source of cyanide, a very potent and painful poison. It smells like bitter almonds or peach pits. Check all the wild cherry trees in the pasture after a heavy storm or windy day for broken branches. Do not cut cherry trees when their leaves are on the branches. If you wish to eradicate cherry trees from the pasture, pull them out by the roots and drag them away while they are dormant. Our horses are gradually clearing out pastures of cherry. During the winter, they girdle the trees by chewing the bark off. The trees die slowly all the way down through the roots, and we

can then cut them with no danger of wilted leaves. Horses eat poison
ivy with very little adverse effect, but human beings can contract the
rash from contact with horses. Deadly nightshade does not attract
horses; I have loads of it gracing our fence lines, but I have yet to see
a horse eat enough to give him even a twinge. Ferns, if ingested in
quantity, can kill, but again, they are not very attractive to horses if
good pasture is available. I know of one mare who nearly died of
cedar bark, which is not poisonous; she was on a diet to reduce a hay
belly and so she gorged herself on bark, which swelled up and
bloated her stomach.

We harbor many highly toxic plants in our flower gardens; lark-
spur, lupine, lily of the valley, yew, and rhododendron are just a few.
Christmas roses and azaleas are other lovely but potentially dangerous plants. At times it is the molds which grow on plants that are the
source of trouble. Mushrooms are an example of a mold that can be
lethal.

Below is a list of poisonous plants. You can consult your botany
books for their scientific names and families and geographical locations:

> bracken (fern)
> wild cherry
> horsetail
> locoweed
> oleander
> raywort or groundsel
> hairless goldenrod
> St.-John's-wort (toxic to animals with very large areas of white skin)
> tarweed
> jimson weed
> skunk cabbage

The cynogenic plants (wild cherry is the major one and our real
consideration here) form a large group of poisonous plants. Sorghum,
a common plant in the hayfields and pastures, is one of them; Sudan
grass, Johnson grass, elax, and arrow grass are a few more. When
grown under normal conditions, the sorghums are considered very
good feed; but when the normal growth has been interrupted by
drought, frost, trampling, or other causes, hydrocyanic acid may
develop to a point where the plants become toxic.

Saponin is the toxic chemical in nightshade, sprouted potatoes, and bittersweet. All these are common in Eastern areas and more poisonous to human beings than to horses. The seeds of the rubberweed, a Western plant, sometimes get mixed into wheat and hence into our grains, so that it carries this same saponin into our barns and homes. Rhododendrons, azaleas, and laurels owe their toxicity to resinoids, as do water hemlock, which is extremely poisonous, and poisonous milkweed.

There is a great deal more to the management of grasses as pasture and forage than can be put into this general description. But if you plan to pasture animals in old hayfields and have questions about what is growing there and its safety, do have a biologist come down from the agricultural department and go over the fields with you.

Most of the deadly plants are *not* native to any one part of the country and it is unlikely that you would have to cope with them in large quantities, but some things do come into our barns and pastures in the form of chaff and seeds mixed with grain and hay. We have jimson weed and nightshade that came in with hay from out of state, and I have seen other exotics in pastures for the same reason. If you have questions about your hay, take a bale to your state university and ask them to go over it and tell you what they find. Sometimes the biology or botany teacher at your local high school can be of help. Try shaking the seeds and chaff out of the hay you get and planting them in flats. Find out what grows. Do the same with the grain you buy. You can pick out the obvious oats, corn, and wheat, but see what else is there. My oats contained large quantities of soybeans one year. This was because the mill where the grain was bagged doesn't clean the hoppers thoroughly all the time. There is no problem when the weed seeds are nontoxic, but who is to know when a batch of contaminated grain is brought in?

Why not get a good botany book from the library, one with detailed illustrations? Walk over the fields and along the streams where your horses eat, and see what they like and what they avoid. Then identify every plant you see in order to get a broader picture of their appetite and nutrition. They like variety. Dandelions are a favorite and chives interest them, while mustard is not their favorite seasoning. They love burdock when it is tiny and find thistle flowers irresistible. Don't overlook the bushes and trees they browse on, and taste some of the leaves and plants they like to eat.

CHAPTER 4

Where Will He Work?

HORSES CAN BE WORKED in a number of different kinds of areas, so you have several choices in design to consider. As always in making any permanent structure, you must first decide what the primary function will be. You may wish to do quite a bit on ground work, longeing to retrain a horse's spoiled mouth, or longlining a youngster. For this you will want a limited enclosure at first, probably not much more than 40 feet in diameter. This size is handy for working a horse on leads also, if he tends to go disunited or to gallop on instead of taking an easy rocking gait. A limited-size ring will not do for regular work; it is far too confining. Standard-size show rings are fine for driving, or working several horses, for riding lessons and jumping courses. But for a one-horse owner who just wishes to do some ring work or for dressage, they are probably larger than is really practical. Harness work really should be done on a track, hunting on an open course, and trail training on a trail. Not everyone has the acreage or the finances, or for that matter the desire, to own all these things. Each requires special terrain and surfacing.

The Training Area

The training area, which is the smallest, should be located where the horse will not be distracted by other horses, traffic, or activity. Ideally, it should not be very far from the stable, because training work should be done frequently and for very short periods. It takes time to groom, tack up, and get a young horse into the ring to work, and to cool him afterward. A long walk, or a hazardous one past vehicles or distractions, will mean that you will tend to work the horse less frequently, and for too long a period. If you have only one or two horses, consider making the training ring the start of one end of a regular riding ring; both take the same kind of ground surface and you will save on lumber. Make the fence out of panels, so that when you are ready for the final fence on the larger ring they can be removed and set into place. If you wish to train a harness horse, you will want a track. A quarter of a mile should be the minimum track. Of course, a long dirt road, driveway, or a good bridle path will do.

PERMANENT OBSTACLES

Since hunt and trail courses should be over rough and natural terrain and unfenced, it makes little sense to write out specifications; but if you have to school for these classes in the ring, then there are things you can plan into your ring as you set it up. First, plan on a muddy or wet spot. Somewhere off in one sector of the ring, most practically the lowest spot but preferably *not* on the rail, dig out some of the surface and line it with clay in a thick layer; this becomes as natural a water obstacle as you can provide. Set up a jump for hunters on the high side so that the horse can approach from either direction, and use the water obstacle as a regular spread jump and a routine part of the training program. For the trail horse, if the mudhole is a wide ditch, put a bridge over part of it and be sure the horse will go over the bridge or through the mud as you direct. A large barrel left open to catch the rain will help make it easier to refill the mudhole when there has not been enough rain. A few drops of oil or insecticide will prevent it from being a mosquito incubator. Make it a practice to carry the water from the barrel to the waterhole on horseback, so that your horse will learn to allow you to dip the water out, carry a sloppy pail, and dump it, without his shying. Even hunters should go through a certain amount of this sort of training.

Build a mound in another sector of your ring for both hunter and trail horse, and be sure the horse learns to approach and negotiate it in a straight line. A large fallen tree, preferably one with stubs of branches still on it, should be another regular part of the scenery. You can dream up as many other "natural" obstacles as you see fit. Oil barrels are a must. We sometimes hang the long streamer-type filling-station flags along our fence as high up as we can get them. Windmill figures, those that are used as weather vanes in gardens, are also startling to a horse at first sight and they are cheap and easily set up somewhere near the rail. Even for a three-or five-gaited horse, fine-harness, or equitation mount, it is a good idea to get your horse accustomed to some of the things that will make any horse shy, jump, or refuse to pay attention to the exhibitor. Before you go to a show with a youngster, practice with loudspeakers and recordings or radios. They should be planned for as part of your ring facilities—it is wise to have an outdoor electric outlet somewhere near the ring. I would keep most of the equipment off the track, particularly if you plan to do harness work, because it will be a nuisance to move things about too often.

SURFACING

Surfacing comes before fencing. I have mentioned the permanent obstacles in the first place, because the mound and the waterhole should be planned when the surfacing is undertaken. If you have a choice of places in which to lay out the ring, try to pick a high place where there will be drainage, so that your ring is usable summer and winter and all through the thaws as well. If it holds water it will also hold ice, and your use will be restricted. Mud is fine for a single section, but when you are schooling a horse to trot on boldly or to canter with a free shoulder, he will tend to resist or fret if the corners are all slimy with mud and he has to struggle for his balance. If the ring must be on a low area, then have a bulldozer push all the topsoil and much of the subsoil back (in two different piles) and lay a layer of coarse or sized gravel. Then spread the soil back and reseed. If there are some reasonably large trees in the ring area, but not right on the track, leave them there, and don't let the dozer get too close to their root systems.

Mixed peat moss and shavings makes a remarkably dust-free and smooth riding surface. Tanbark is, of course, the ideal surface, but it is fairly expensive for a single private ring. If you have a nearby polo club, show stable, or some such place that uses it, you might be able to get a part load at a reasonable rate when they order it to resurface their track. We have used wood chips by the ton; the power company is happy to come and dump them when they clear the lines each spring. We pick out the wire, and the logs and bottles, then rake it all down. It takes a while for it to settle, and you do have to watch a bit for sharp chunks of wood that could bruise a horse's foot; but it makes a good surface which is not slippery and is certainly as cheap as anything you can get. During the winter if the track does ice up, just clean your stalls into the wheelbarrow and dump it on the track. It will give you much more time to use the track and will nourish the grass. In the spring it will not be difficult to rake over and smooth down again.

A plain sand or gravel surface is very bad for a track. Gravel with small stones can cause stone bruises or send a horse sprawling. Sand is fine for Arabian horses, because it is their natural habitat. But in other horses, sand will work up into the hoof and cause sand cracks. If it is too deep it may well cause the horse to twist his fetlock or strain his tendons. A horse with high action and with any unnatural length to the hoof is especially subject to problems on sand. It is better to have the topsoil and mud to work on than either sand or gravel. If you can't afford to put a proper surface on your ring, don't touch it with a dozer at all. Rake it as smooth as you can and cover it with soiled shavings as you clean your stalls. Grass tracks are lovely, but they are very difficult to maintain, and tend to end up as pure dust.

RING FENCING

Once you have worked out the layout, obstacles, and surface, you are ready to think about a fence. There is really only one good ring fence and that is made of boards. Snow fence, wire, cedar rails, and rope are all asking for trouble and injuries. Smooth rails are lovely but very expensive and hard to keep in place when people sit on them. Flat 2-by-6 oak-board fences are more practical. The best and by far the simplest to construct, repair, and replace are sections of hurdles, or panels. This does not require the digging of holes. If a section is broken, it can be removed and replaced easily. The size of the ring can be changed, or the ring divided into pastures for temporary use, by shifting and adding panels. They can be made of common rough lumber, stained rather than painted for preservation. They will look and hold up well, certainly as well as or better than the conventional white board fence with set posts. There are a number of ways of constructing board fences so that the rails or boards can be easily removed and replaced. Whatever you work out, consider that for harness work you want the smooth surface, not posts, on the inside of the fence, and that you want one board all the way around at axle height so that there is no likelihood of hanging a wheel on a post or through a fence.

MOVABLE OBSTACLES

Now that you have the layout, permanent obstacles, and ring fence, it is time to consider the movable obstacles. You may not want to keep jumps and other trail obstacles set up all year, especially in the winter. Rails for cavallettis and the supports will be set up and removed. Think about a place to store these items; they will certainly deteriorate if left under a blanket of snow all winter long. If you construct a small shed at ring's edge, it can be handy not only for work but also for getting the horse used to judges' stands. If such a shed is so arranged and the ring does not directly join a pasture, you may find this a good isolation stall in the case of a sick horse that must be removed from others in an emergency.

It is remarkable what can be incorporated into each new project if you devote sufficient thought to the problems involved.

RING SPECIFICATIONS (SIZES)
Standard show ring (Conn. Horse Assoc.): minimum, 100 by 175 feet, rounded corners

1st and 2nd level dressage (AHSA): 66 by 132 feet, square corners

3rd and 4th level dressage (AHSA): 66 by 198 feet, square corners

Longe or longline ring: maximum for convenience, 40-foot diameter, square or rounded corners

Track for schooling in harness (horse size): minimum, quarter-mile oval with rounded corners

ADDITIONAL SPECIFICATIONS
Cavalletti at a walk or trot: 10 inches high, maximum 4 to 5 feet apart

Cavalletti at a canter: 18 to 20 feet at first, 9 to 10 feet after experience

Trail obstacle: 18 to 24 inches high

Hunter practice jumps: 2 feet 6 inches to 3 feet maximum

Open hunters: up to 4 feet 6 inches

CHAPTER 5

What Will He Need?

WHEN YOU VISUALIZE riding or driving a horse, a certain amount of equipment automatically comes to mind. Saddle and bridle, or harness and cart, are perhaps the first. But there is a greater variety of tack available than any one catalog or horse shop can list in one place. Each bit of tack or tool was designed to fill a specific need, and more experimental designs and new products are coming on the market all the time.

The basics are a halter, lead rope, saddle, bridle, harness, and cart, as well as grooming and stall-cleaning tools. You can limit yourself to these essentials and keep your expenses minimal, or you can get carried away and clutter your life, your car and living room, attic and hayloft with trunks of gear at a cost of thousands of dollars. Every horse magazine carries advertisements for saddle shops that offer catalogs. Invest in a few of these and study the drawings and information. When you look at horses to purchase, ask about the tack you see and why the owner uses one bit rather than another on any given horse. Before long you will have formed some idea of what equipment will be useful to you and what will just take up room and effort in maintenance.

Halters

The halter is the one piece of equipment with which most people are familiar; horses of every age and breed wear halters. Since many horses live in halters day in and day out, they can be a real source of discomfort if they are not fitted properly and are not clean and safe.

Properly fitted leather halter.

The first piece of equipment a horse wears is his baby halter, and the impression this makes on him will color his future reactions to both people and training. If the halter is light and soft, properly fitted, and handled by gentle, experienced hands, it will train the foal to respond willingly and without fear. He will accept other tack in its natural order. A stiff, ill-fitting foal halter can distress the baby; moreover, if the person who handles him by the halter is rough or ignorant, the halter becomes a trap and the foal's instinct is to free his head from this danger.

In our barn, halters are signals to the horses that something is going on. Grooming or classes, field days, walks on the trails, and visits from the veterinarian or farrier are all preceded by putting on a halter. The rest of the time the horses are led with just a rope tossed over the neck.

Halters vary as much in kind and materials as they do in use. The British call a fine show or stable halter a *head collar.* There are *track* halters, made of doubled and stitched rawhide, which are fine-looking and very strong. *Grooming* halters are made of leather, with the crown and noseband sewn to rings as on a normal halter, but the throat latch is completely removable for access to the chin and jaws. *Turnout* halters must be able to survive the elements, and must fit properly so as not to fall off during grazing. Again, they are made of leather, so that if a horse becomes snagged on a tree or fence he can get loose and not hang or break his neck. A new turnout halter with a safety system of special buckles has been announced and will soon be on the market. *Colt* or *show lead* halters resemble fine show bridles, and are often made of rounded leather, sometimes mounted in silver or gold. The best hardware is brass, solid nickel, or cadmium, and the cheapest is japanned (black enameled).

A show halter.

Halters are made in a variety of materials other than leather. Some very strong and handsome halters are made of nylon webbing, which is excellent. They are smooth and won't shrink, stretch, or twist. Some are made with slip-fitting buckles so that they are adjustable for proper fit. The cotton-web halters are not nearly so attractive or satisfactory; they shrink when wet and rot. Rope halters are made of cotton, polypropylene, or polyethylene rope. The rope halters are all of the same pattern, and the hardware is relatively difficult to adjust. They should *never* be left on a horse out in pasture. Those made of cotton rope get tighter and tighter as they shrink, and plastic won't break if the horse gets tangled. Because of their shape they hang down and forward at the chin; if they are loose enough for comfort, they are also loose enough for a horse to get his hind foot caught when he scratches his face. If you have ever tried to undo a horse in this predicament you will appreciate my urging that you never take the risk. These halters are fine for tying a horse who pulls back a lot, providing they are adjusted so that they won't pull off the nose. But they cannot compare with the leather or nylon web halters for leading control. It is also more difficult to use them with a chain lead shank over the nose. Two halters should be avoided: one is the rope halter that has a chain in place of the lower chin piece; the other has a strap that passes below the chin, through the lead ring. Ordinary halters have either a flat strap attached to both side rings, or an adjustable buckle and strap; these dangerous halters have the strap going through one ring, with another ring on the strap where the

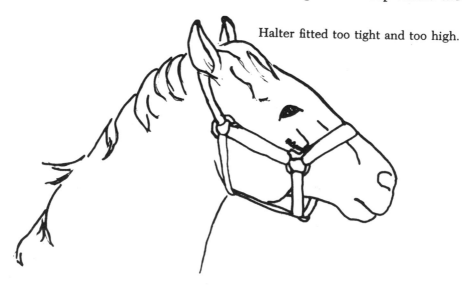

Halter fitted too tight and too high.

lead snaps in place. Both of these dangerous styles of halter tighten when you pull on them, often panicking a horse and causing a really rebellious fight.

No matter which halter is used, I would stress the importance of proper adjustment. The reason is obvious—if the halter doesn't fit, it can cause sores or fall off. In fitting a halter, there is one simple rule: the noseband should be halfway between the corner of the mouth and the end of the cheekbone. When you adjust the noseband, check it for fit by giving the horse a wisp of hay. As he chews, the halter should not quite come into contact with the bars of his jaw. It should not restrict the opening of his mouth when he yawns; on the other hand, it should not be loose enough to get his foot into. If the halter falls back on the neck, it will irritate the horse and can scare a young foal; it also allows the noseband to ride up on the face. Halters often wear holes in the horse's face, at the bottom of the cheekbone, at the jaw, and right behind the ears. These are the result of carelessness. It is the handler's responsibility to see to it that the halter is removed and checked for fit and cleanliness periodically. The most dangerous sore a horse can get is poll evil, or fistula of the poll. This is an abscess that can damage the brain and kill the horse, and it can be caused by halter pressure. Perspiration, mud, and hair can make the inside of a halter very rough and irritating, and metal edges can be sharp. Plastic and nylon halters benefit by a good washing—they can go right into the washing machine.

In order to prevent raveling, nylon fabric and poly rope are often finished on the edges by melting the fabric, which causes sharp ridges or points inside the halter. Always check a halter for this before you buy it. Sometimes careful sandpapering will soften the edge somewhat, but do not go so far as to release the fabric edges. If you have a growing horse, buy a series of halters in different sizes and switch to the new one as soon as the earlier one has been let out as far as it will go. If the halters are leather, oil them and store them in freezer-type plastic food bags and they will stay soft and ready for use. It is a temptation to go on using an outgrown halter if there is no new one handy, but the resulting injury to the delicate face bones over the sinuses is permanent and disfiguring. Tubes made of imitation sheepskin can be purchased to help prevent halter sores.

Tying the Horse

If you tie up your horse to groom him, crossties of strong rope are best. There are two theories about tying a horse. My neighbor, who is a trainer, ties his horses in light chain crossties with double-ended snaps on the halter. He feels that it is best if they can break loose if they are frightened rather than setting up hard, struggling, and possibly throwing themselves. My feeling is that once they are tied, they should stay there, even if they dump themselves once or twice until they learn to stand. I have to work alone and can't manage a horse who breaks and flies back when tied. We are both right, as is often the case when people differ in their opinions. You have to decide for yourself how you feel.

My crossties are of ¾-inch rope with panic snaps spliced in. I use the "unbreakable halters," which do in fact break once in a while. Never tie a horse with a leather strap of any sort. They are expensive and the horses do snap them, even by just turning to chase a fly off their backs.

Leading the Horse

Leads come in as many varieties as halters. Here, too, there are two schools of thought and you must decide which you prefer. I often lead my horses, even my stallion, just by a handful of mane and rarely have any problems. Some horses need a halter for control, and some must have both a halter and a rope because they will swing their heads and lift their leader off the ground if they turn suddenly. I never use a lead shank with a chain unless I have a horse who is a problem to handle. I feel they are unnecessary and cumbersome, and if they get dragged under the horse's feet and stepped on, they break. Also, a chain over the horse's nose or under his chin inflicts pain. That is why it is there, for "control." I don't keep horses who have to be hurt or punished to behave. A personal mount for the average person should be manageable in a simple halter with a simple lead. Even a spirited horse should be well-behaved enough to lead without such a device, otherwise he is not properly trained to lead! Chains are advisable for horses that rear.

Leather shanks are made for leading horses. And there are matching leads of nylon and poly rope to complement your stable halter.

There are ordinary hemp or sisal ropes, which do not belong in any stable because they cause rope burns and rot if they get wet. There are white cotton leads, which I usually find a foot too short. We make our own leads out of nylon or Dacron rope from the marine hardware store. It is soft and pliable, and comes in white, which I dye in my stable colors, or in a nice soft shade of gold. I buy the biggest snaps available with a trigger or thumb snap. These ropes last ten years or more if the snaps hold out. They are nice to handle, easy to untie. You have to get used to tying them because they require a little more length than a cotton rope. But for daily use there are no better ropes; the ones on the market all have very flimsy snaps. Choose the thickness that suits your hand. Marine ropes are strong enough to hold a horse when he tries to turn the whole world upside down.

You should have one long rope of soft-surfaced nylon with a big bull snap on it. This all-purpose rope can be used to tie a horse, load one into a trailer, or tow your car out of the snow. Make it at least 25 feet long, at least ½ inch thick, and back-spliced a good 8 inches.

SNAPS

Several kinds of snaps are available, the newest being the *panic* snaps. These are designed for tying horses in crossties and trailers and they are one of the best safety devices available. They are not as convenient for lead ropes because it takes both hands to attach them until you have become very comfortable with them. I carried one in my pocket and practiced with it for a few months so that I now can hook them one-handed in a hurry. They consist of a ring for the rope, a sliding collar, and a hinged loop which flips over the halter ring and then folds down into the collar. To release them, you simply slide the collar toward you and the rope. They are spring-loaded. The joy is that when a horse is setting back and pulling on a rope, or has his feet over the front of the trailer breast board, or is upside down and suspended by his halter, the average person hasn't the strength to pull the horse forward to unhook a regular snap. In such situations, the quick-release or panic snap is fast, safe, and simple.

The most common snaps are *trigger* snaps, which can be swiveled or dead, and the *thumb* snap or *bag* snap, which is the kind found on the halter throat latches. When they are new, you hurt your finger trying to press them in, and by the time they are flexible they are

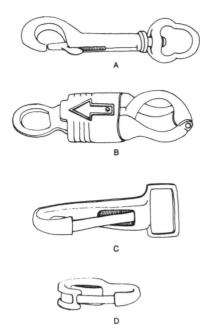

Assorted snaps that you will use at some time or another. *A*, the trigger swivel snap most commonly found on leads; *B*, panic or quick-release snap used in tying horses; *C*, bag snap, the type found on cheap leads and on halter throatlatches; *D*, bit snap, used in early training to hold a bit from the tie rings of a halter.

broken. Most snaps are made out of cheap, flawed metal. For this reason, I get the largest and best-made ones I can find; the initial cost and effort of finding them pays for itself in the first emergency.

Bridles

Bridles are designed to carry a bit in a horse's mouth, or a hackamore, which connects the horse's mouth and nose to the rider's hands via the reins. The rest of the bridle then acts as a support. The simplest form of bridle is the *Western split ear*. This is a strap which runs from the bit, over the horse's poll, and back down to the bit on the other side. It has a slot cut on one side for one ear to slip through, and this holds the bridle in place. The overhead strap on a bridle is called the *crownpiece*. The straps that run from the crownpiece to the bit are the *cheek pieces*. And the strap that runs behind the jaw from one side of the crown to the other (or as an independent loop around the throat) is called the *throat latch* (or throat lash). This serves to prevent the bridle from falling forward if the horse lowers his head. It should be loose enough so that if the horse's chin is pushed in against the windpipe, the throat latch will not restrict his breathing. If it is set just against the back of the jaw and swinging free, it will serve its purpose without irritating the horse. Many people take the throat latch up too tight because they think it looks neater that way. The usual bridle has a *browband*—a strap that goes across the front of the forehead and prevents the bridle from slipping back on the horse's neck. The browband must be long enough to allow the bridle to set behind the ears, not tight against the back of the ears. Many horses carry "sour ears" because of a tight browband that pinches them constantly.

After the bridle is in place, always run your hand under the browband on the forehead. There should be room enough to do this easily. Morgans, who have very wide heads, suffer frequently from tight browbands because saddlemakers design their equipment to fit Saddlebreds, which have much narrower heads. To be sure of fit here, remove the browband, place the bridle on the horse where it belongs, and measure from the back of the crownpiece across the forehead to the back of the crown on the other side. (The tape measure will be narrower and more flexible than the leather bridle front of the browband, so allow for that difference.) The wider the browband,

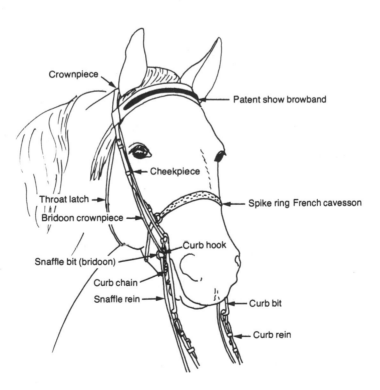

the more allowance you have to make, for the horse's head is tapered, and the lower edge of the browband may fall where the head is wider than where you have measured. You will notice that in the catalogs no mention is made of the length of browbands offered, but when you go to a tack shop you will find quite a variation.

There are at least a dozen different kinds of bridles, each of which is designed for a certain type of horse or style of riding. What you buy will depend on your horse and his training, or the use you wish to put him to. Starting with the simplest, there is the Western split ear, already mentioned, and the English variety or *snaffle* bridle, which is a single crownpiece with browband and noseband slid on and a single pair of reins. Next is the snaffle bridle with the separate *cavesson*, which is a noseband with its own crownpiece. The primary purpose of the cavesson is to attach to a standing martingale so as to prevent the horse from tossing his head. Many people use the cavesson primarily to keep the horse's mouth closed. Their theory is that if the horse can open his mouth, he can escape the action of the bit. The cavesson is often buckled so tightly that you cannot get one finger jammed in between it and the horse's jawbones under it. It should fit the same place as the halter: exactly halfway between cheekbone and mouth. Cavessons are part of the required tack at horse shows. The crownpiece of the cavesson slips through the browband under the crown of the bridle.

The *pelham* bridle is like the snaffle bridle in all details except that when you change from the snaffle bit to the pelham bit you add a second pair of reins: the wide, "snaffle" rein is on the top and should have a buckle at the hand part in the center; the narrower, "curb" rein is on the bottom and can be either buckled or sewn closed. The snaffle rein is buckled because it is the one that goes through the rings of a running martingale, if one is used. A *full* bridle or *Weymouth* bridle calls for the addition of another bit, called a *bridoon* (a fine snaffle bit) in the horse's mouth, and the change from the pelham to the Weymouth or curb bit. Yet another strap of leather is slid under that browband. This is the crownpiece of the bridoon bit. It must slide under the crown of the bridle but *in front of* the cavesson crownpiece. Both must lie flat, side by side. They are narrower than the bridle crown and will not be seen if properly in place. They should be slid in flat, not twisted. Many people put the full or double bridles together without the cavesson and put the cavesson on the horse separately first. If it is tight, it won't slip back or off the face. In a *driving* bridle, the cavesson is always put on separately and first.

Hunting and *jumping* bridles are made of heavy, wide leather. *Hacking* bridles are considerably lighter, and *show* bridles for gaited, pleasure, and park horses are of the lightest possible leather. *Dressage* bridles are sometimes of round leather. *Western* bridles vary from light straps, doubled and buck-stitched latigo, to wide, heavily ornamented or carved saddle-skirting leather. When you hack in the woods or compete in a trail ride, the choice of style is your own; but when you show, you must conform to the correct, required tack. Most modern English bridles are buckled at the cheeks, but attach to the bits by hook-in-stud closures. These are smooth on the outside and the attachments are made on the side facing the horse. Western bridles are held together in a number of ways. If, after you have taken a bridle apart to put in the bits or to clean it, you are confused, remember that the browband faces the front of the horse and the throat latch faces the rear. The rough surface of the leather faces the horse.

Bits

The choice of a bit is determined by the horse and his mouth. Young horses and untrained horses have tender, uneducated mouths and must be schooled to accept the bit and to understand its communication. A bit tells the horse several things. It indicates desired direction and speed, and it raises or otherwise alters the position of the horse's head. The head is raised by the action of the snaffle bit in the corners of the mouth. When the rein on the snaffle ring is pulled, it lifts the bit into the corner of the mouth and pulls the head back and upward, forcing the nose out in front. When the rein on the curb is pulled, it exerts leverage against the bars of the mouth and against the chin, pulling the nose down and tucking the horse's chin in toward his chest. In some cases, two bits are used in the mouth in both riding and driving. Each bit indicates to the horse where he is to hold his neck and head.

The *snaffle* bit is the simplest design of all. The bridle and a single rein attach to the bit at the edge of the mouth. A snaffle can have any one of several mouthpieces, which will be described further on. A

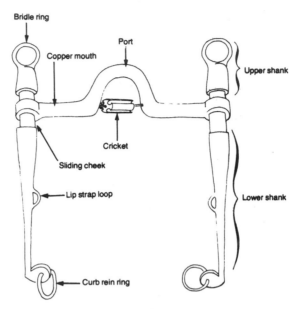

Bridle ring

Port

Copper mouth

Upper shank

Cricket

Sliding cheek

Lip strap loop

Lower shank

Curb rein ring

Anatomy of a bit. In this case, a loose-cheeked port-mouthed curb bit with a copper bar and a cricket.

curb bit has only one rein, but it is attached below the mouth at the end of a shank, and the bridle is also attached to a shank, which extends above the mouth. The curb bit is always used with a curb chain or strap under the chin groove. The *pelham* bit is like a combined snaffle and curb, having two reins, one at the corner of the mouth and one below, on a shank. The *Kimberwick* bit has a top and mouth like a pelham but without the lower shank. Hence it has some leverage but only one rein. Like the curb and the pelham, it is used with a curb chain.

In various sports certain bits are specified, traditional, or prohibited. It is customary to use curb bits with Western saddles, but it is not mandatory except in shows where so specified.

It is the mark of a good horseman to get the best performance from the mildest bits and a minimal signal. A severe bit or yanking and hauling are the mark of a failure on the rider's part and a spoiled mouth on the part of the horse.

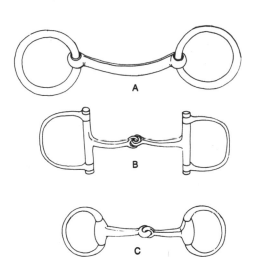

Snaffle type bits. *A*, flat ring, mullen mouth; *B*, Dee race bit, jointed mouth; *C*, egg butt, hunting snaffle; *D*, wire ring bradoon.

Pelham bits. *Top*, Mullen mouth Tom Thumb; *Center*, Kimberwicke or Spanish jumping bit; *Bottom*, Western pelham.

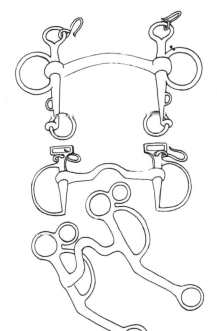

MILDNESS AND SEVERITY

The leverage of a bit is exactly like that of a seesaw. The further you get from the fulcrum (mouth), the more leverage there will be. This holds just as true for the upper shank of the bit, which goes from the mouth to the bridle, where the curb chain is attached, as it does for the lower shank, where the curb rein attaches. In the illustrations you will see many shapes and designs of curb and pelham shanks. The swept-back ones are used on Walking horses, Five-Gaited Saddlers, and on the Western grazing bits. The slim, plain upright shanks are correct in showing three-gaited park and pleasure horses and for hunters. The very short-shanked bits—curb or pelham—are known as *Tom Thumb*. The *Tom Bass* bit (which people often confuse with Tom Thumb) is a style of curb bit that has a swell where the mouth joins the shank in the corners of the mouth. The *shank,* sometimes called the *cheek* of the bit, can be in line with the mouth; or in the case of some Western bits, the mouth of the bit part is clearly laid back against the tongue. Cheeks of Western bits can be simple or ornate, inlaid with real silver, gold, and gemstones. Except for their additional weight, the ornamentation and weight have nothing to do with severity.

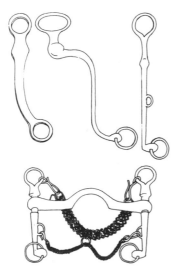

Curb bits. The style of the bit is determined by the shape of the shank, the severity by the heft of the mouth and the length and leverage of both the upper and lower shank. *Top* (l. to r.), Western grazing bit, walking horse bit, show or fine curb. *Bottom,* Tom Thumb complete with lip chain and curb chains.

The severity of the mouth is determined by the *heft* or thickness of the mouthpiece and by its shape. The thicker the heft, the milder the bit. If you try to carry a heavy package by a string, it will cut into your hand. But if you put on one of those round wooden handles, the carrying becomes much less painful. Heft doesn't have to mean weight in a bit mouth, either. Some mouths are made of rubber over a flexible chain. Some are of hard rubber or vulcanite, and some metal mouths are hollow. There are leather-covered bits available and it is a common practice to wrap bits with latex to make them milder. There is a growing acceptance now of copper mouth bits. These are sometimes called sweet mouth bits, and are said to help calm and steady a mare while she is in heat. I have not heard of anyone who has used them for this purpose, but a number of trainers say that copper bits are great for certain horses who seem resentful of a bit. They appear to tolerate the copper better.

In shape, the mouth of any bit—whether curb, pelham, or snaffle —can be mild or severe. The *bar,* either straight or mullen style (which has a gentle curve), is the mildest of all forms, for it lies quietly in the mouth and does not pinch or pry. Some horses learn to lift such a bit off the bars of the mouth with their tongue. Some dislike the even pressure, and for these horses a port is more comfortable. The *port* is just an arched spot in the center of the mouth. It allows the tongue to fold up into the port, and the bit then has greater contact with the bars of the horse's mouth. Ports are sometimes fitted with *crickets*—little wheels that the horse can turn with his tongue. The port is not made to press against the roof of the horse's mouth, as many people suppose. It prevents the horse from pulling his tongue back and over the bit, which is very painful. *Spade* bits are a form of port mouth bit that are designed for delicate hands and in particular for the extremely precise riders of the Southwest; such bits have no place in the hands of an average horseman. The spade bit is made with a spring and a sharp blade, which points back and into the horse's mouth. A hard pull on the reins can sever the tongue. Many horses seem to like and respond well to *Dr. Bristol* bits. These have a jointed mouth, with a flat plate between the two sides. The plate lies on the tongue, while the sides of the mouth pull back on the bars of the mouth. The least gentle of all common mouth shapes is the *jointed* or *broken* mouth, often called the *snaffle* mouth. These have a nutcracker effect on the mouth and are probably the most misused and misunderstood of all bits. From the simple broken or jointed mouth, we progress downward into the torture chamber of bicycle chains, mule mouth, twisted wire, double-jointed (two mouthpieces, each with a joint slightly offside from one another), knife edge or triangle, and some that are actually barbed. Many riders think that they must use a harsh bit in order to control the horse. Many others have been led to believe that a horse who goes on a snaffle bit has a good mouth. Try some of the bits in a tack shop on your own hand. Lay the bit across your palm. Put the chain, if it is a leverage-type bit, across the back of your hand and then pull on the rein rings. This experiment will give you a far better understanding of what the horse feels.

There is a distinct back or front to a bit and many novices make the mistake of putting their bits in backward. The mouth of the bit must curve forward or arch over the tongue. In the case of bits with rings for reins, it is usually easy enough to see that the rein faces the back of the bridle. But in bar bits and snaffles, that is not always so evident. The Dr. Bristol, for instance, is a relatively mild type one way and very harsh if put in in reverse. Some people deliberately use it thus, but such a mistake could make a horse very rebellious if the rider was not aware of what he was doing.

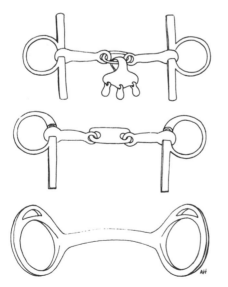

Specialized bits. *Top,* full cheek key bit used for "mouthing" or early schooling; *Center,* Dr. Bristol bit (half cheek, driving style); *Bottom,* mullen mouth bar bit with bridle attachment slots.

The bit you select must be suitable for the horse's type and degree of training, and it must also fit his mouth properly. Bits come as narrow as 4 inches and as wide as 6 inches. Narrow bits are for young horses and Arabians with the very fine mouth; wide bits are for draft horses and those with coarse muzzles. The height of the horse is not an accurate way of finding out his mouth size. A 15-hand horse might take a much wider bit than a 17-hand one. Head shape is not related to the length of leg. Too wide a bit will irritate the animal, for it will slide about and get lopsided. Too narrow a bit will pinch like narrow shoes. The horse will be uncomfortable and unable to perform with an ill-fitting bit. You may have to take a couple of bits home for trial or borrow some to see what is best for your horse. The corner of the bit mouth should be at the corner of the horse's mouth or be just a little wider. Properly adjusted, the snaffle bit wrinkles the corners of the mouth with one or two creases. The expression is that "He should smile but never grimace."

The curb or pelham bit fits lower and should not crease the corners of the mouth at all. It should lie on the bars of the mouth (that space between the teeth) and should never touch the back of the front teeth or the front of the back teeth. Many people err in making a bit too loose, thinking that it will be more comfortable. It won't. The lower the curb bit hangs in the mouth, the greater its leverage against the jaw. When the bit is fitted with a curb chain or strap, the chain must lie flat in the chin groove, not up on the jaw or down on the fleshy part of the chin. When two bits are used—as in driving with a bit and an overcheck bit, and in Weymouth and full bridles—the snaffle bit hangs in front of the bit (driving or curb). If both are properly in place, there should be a little space between them at the corners of the mouth.

Whenever you have any problem with a horse's mouth, assume that the horse is uncomfortable and start by blaming yourself, your hands, or your adjustment of bit. Then, when you have checked to be sure that you have done nothing wrong, look for a bruise, or a broken or emerging tooth, and especially for "wolf teeth," or a possible cut on the tongue. Have the veterinarian check for rough edges and have the teeth floated (see p.230). If the horse still rebels, you may have to wrap the bit with latex, change to a different style of bit, or go back a few lessons and do some reeducation. Getting a more severe bit is simply ignoring your responsibilities to the horse and giving up in defeat.

Curb hooks come in different sizes and styles. The most common is a simple loop, which hooks onto the bit end and is then squeezed closed with a hook below on which you hang the chain. In most pairs there is a right and left hook, so that when they are on the bit the hooks open away from the horse's mouth. Some horsemen give them a careful twist to make certain they do. The chain hooks should *not* be squeezed shut. The chain must be unhooked when the bridle is taken off the horse. The length of the hook will vary, as will the thickness or heft of the wire. There is a circular pattern hook which is miserable to fasten but can be a real lifesaver. Some horses get the hook caught in the corner of the mouth, which can be painful and damaging, and some horses get the bridoon caught in the hook, which changes the whole pull of the bit in the mouth. Circular hooks are the answer for these animals.

Hackamores

Hackamores look like variations of the cavesson or noseband, but hang freely on the nose below the cheek (though never so low that they cut off the horse's wind). Horses who have hackamores that are too low will fret, snort, and toss their heads. Adjusted too high, the hackamores are ineffective. The gentlest form of hackamore is the *jumping* hackamore. Next comes the *bosal,* then the *donal,* and the *mouthless pelham* or *mechanical* hackamore. The most severe (and far from gentle it is!) is the Easy Stop. The jumping hackamore is really just a loop of round leather with rings for the reins at the back on the sides. The bosal is usually a braided or heavy affair, with a large knot for attaching reins at the back. It is obvious that if the reins attach at the sides, you can guide the horse by pulling either rein; but when they both are attached at the bottom of the chin, the horse must learn to neck rein. Both work on the simple principle of pressure and signals to the sensitive nerves on the nose only. The donal hackamore has another feature: a loop over the nose, with two branches on the sides which are rigid metal pressing against the sides of the bars of the jaw. There are sensitive nerves along this bone. The donal works then on both the nose and the sides of the jaw. The mouthless pelham and the mechanical hackamore bit both have a curb strap or chain under the chin, and work on the principle of squeezing the nose and putting pressure on the chin simultaneously. They are a very effective means of control, and few horses need any more than this to respond and behave.

The Easy Stop hackamore belongs in torture museums—along with the double-twisted wire snaffle bits, and some of the hideous new creations sported in my latest catalogs, offering complete control for the barrel racer. Vicious bits are not a mark of a bad horse —they are the clear and unmistakable badge of a lousy horseman! The joy of the hackamore is that it does not cause pain and fear in the horse. It gives a young horse the necessary restraint, while at the same time causing no hardening or deadening of the mouth. Often hackamores are used with a snaffle bit in training. The horse learns to carry the bit and respond to it with minimal force. If force or pressure is needed to reinforce the education of the bit, it is applied on the hackamore. Once the horse has accepted the signals of the bit and understands them, the hackamore is removed and the horse continues his education with a light, sweetly responsive mouth. I also use the hackamore for the sake of the trained horses who are teaching beginning riders. The average beginner thinks of the reins as a means of holding himself on the saddle and forcing the horse to stop. Until such riders gain balance and understanding, they can be brutally hard on a horse's mouth. If the horse is properly trained, it is a shame to sour and injure him. So for us, the hackamore gives the rider enough control to make him feel safe while he practices balance and refinement of communication. That way my horses know that a hackamore means slow, quiet work with a jerky rider, and a bit means some other form of work.

Cavessons

The use of the cavesson or noseband to keep the mouth shut was mentioned earlier. There are several styles, ranging from the *simple* cavesson, with a show or harness bridle which buckles just 2 inches below the cheekbone where the halter fits, to those that hang below the bit (*dropped* noseband), clamping the mouth shut, or *figure-eight* nosebands, which cross over the nose and buckle below the bits. There is also an *anti-pulling* cavesson, made like a standard cavesson over the nose, but with crossed chains under the chin that hook to the curb hooks on the bit. These are effective devices for spoiled horses—if you see a horse wearing any of these it is a pretty good clue that either they have a problem or their rider has. Once you need these devices, you have lost communication and are involved with problems of control.

A cavesson I like very much is called the *Kineton* noseband. This fits over the nose and has two half-circles, which slide behind the rings of a snaffle bit. In use, it presses gently on the nose while you apply pressure on the reins, and releases immediately as you let up again. It is like having a hand on the horse's nose. There is no leverage of any kind. It does not interfere with the action of the snaffle bit, either. I have used this on horses who needed just a bit more signal than a simple bar snaffle yet were bothered by the curb chain or leverage of a Kimberwick.

Martingales

As stated earlier, the noseband and cavesson were originally designed to attach to a *standing martingale,* in the case of Western horses called a *tiedown.* This device prevents the horse from throwing his head up or carrying his nose poked way out in "star-gazing" fashion. Tiedowns and martingales are prohibited in most saddle classes in the show ring. A properly schooled horse should never have to wear them, but they are a necessity for badly schooled horses and a safety factor for certain kinds of jumpers. The tiedown or standing martingale does not act on the mouth, but it does limit the use of the horse's neck. It is a simple strap, buckled in a loop around the girth, running up between the horse's front legs, and looping around the cavesson under the chin. It is supported by a neck strap and sometimes held in place with a rubber ring called a *stop,* which prevents it from dangling down under the horse's chest and entangling his feet. All it does is limit the distance the horse can move his head up or forward.

The *running martingale* has two rings, through which the reins pass. These are sewn to a forked strap, which then attaches to a single strap to the girth. The running martingale places a constant downward pressure on the reins. The weight of the rings and straps alone holds the bit down in the mouth to a slight degree, but as the rider pulls on the rein there is an increased downward pull on the bit. In training young horses, often a rider will use two reins on a snaffle bit, one to the hand in a direct line and the other rein through the running martingale rings. This prevents the horse from rearing and pointing his head too high in the air.

Another system of control is the *draw rein*. Like the running martingale, this puts a different direction of pull on the snaffle rein. The draw rein is used for training. It consists of a long rein, running from the billets of the saddle or the girth buckle on each side of the horse, through the snaffle ring, to the hand. When the rider tugs on this rein, the horse's head is pulled toward his chest. There is no constant pressure; only as much pressure as the rider exerts is transmitted to the horse.

There are also anti-grazing *side checks* for horses and ponies who like to stop and eat. These run from the saddle dees through side check rings on a crownpiece and down to the bit. They do nothing while the horse's head is in the right position; but if he tries to throw his head down to buck or to eat grass, it lifts the bit into the top corner of the mouth and prevents the action.

Some Other Devices

We use other devices to alter the pressure and to correct problems in horses' mouths. When a young horse is cutting teeth, it is often hard for him to cope with a bit and learn new things, because he is in pain or fear of pain. Here the hackamore is the first choice for comfort, but not always applicable because the horse may be in training for the show ring and must wear a bit. *Wrapping* the bit helps prevent some soreness. Shoelaces or leather straps running over the nose from one side of the bit to the other will lift the bit, relieve painful pressure, and also sometimes prevent the horse from getting his tongue over the bit. We use *bit converters* for this purpose. They are designed to be used to make a pelham bit into a single rein bridle—by running from the snaffle ring to the curb ring and the rein attached to the strap. I have never used them for their original purpose, but have dozens of other uses for these handy straps.

Reins

Hunters and jumpers are ridden with quite a variety of reins, ranging from simple *flat leather* to *covered* reins with rubber hand parts, *plaited* reins, *laced* reins, and *woven-web* reins with hand-grip stops all along them. They are usually wide to afford the rider a good grip and enable him to really pull. *Western* reins and those on other English bridles are designed for much lighter signals and contact; the lighter the rein, the less it interferes with your communication with the horse. Just the weight of the rein alone is enough to speak to a sensitive, thoroughly schooled horse. Many good horses are so responsive that they can be ridden with knitting yarn for reins. We had a Morgan gelding who was just such a horse, and the lessons his riders had with the yarn reins were a joy to watch. Riders who depend upon their reins for security are at first terrified and then, when the realization sinks in, simply thrilled to be able to turn, stop, and guide the horse by just a squeeze of the fingers on that flimsy yarn. I wish every rider could take his first riding lessons on such a beautifully schooled animal, for it would eliminate much of the cruelty caused by ignorance we see in riders' hands. Reins should be soft in the hand and never rough. They should be comfortable. A small child should never be given great wide reins, for they will make his hands hard. The reins should lie lightly in the rider's hands—never with the fingers closed over them. When a full bridle or a pelham bridle is used, the reins run between the fingers. If you ever have a chance to see a really great Spanish cowboy riding, you will see that the reins are held so lightly and handled with such tact that the signals are as undetectable as those given to a finely trained dressage horse by a truly accomplished rider.

Saddles

Saddles may be the first thing you think of when you visualize tack; but in fact you can ride without one, you know. The saddle, cart, and harness are the most expensive tack you will buy. Style, of course, comes first. Western styles vary as much as English saddles.

WESTERN SADDLES

Western saddles are made for parade, roping, cutting, and general ranch work. *Roping* saddles must be rugged and can be lightweight or heavy, but made with the horn securely attached to the tree and the cinch rings or dees securely on, too, or else the saddle will tear apart in daily use. *Pleasure* or *trail* saddles can be of much lighter, less strong construction, and are therefore a lot less costly. The height of the cantle, the swell of the forks and padding, tooling or a rough-out surface, are all a matter of preference. My own choice is a *Monte Foreman balanced ride* saddle, because I was trained as an English rider and this kind of saddle lets me sit upright with my legs down along the horse's sides in what, to me, is the most natural and comfortable position. Most Western saddles slope upward in the front of the seat, making the rider sit way back and even forcing a slouch that I find unbearable. The saddle strings which dangle down the sides of the horse actually hold the saddle together. They are left long for repairs and are made of tough latigo, as a rule. They are handy for tying gear onto the saddle, too.

Even though most Western saddles are lined with sheepskin, they should still be used with a blanket or pad. This ensures the saddle a longer life and also protects the horse's back. It is not easy to clean the underside of a Western saddle properly if the sheepswool gets worn and grimy with sweat. Also, where the latigo tie strings pass under the saddle, they can make terrible sores on the horse's back. Before buying a Western saddle, try out a few and see which will best suit you. They can have a wide or narrow twist—the part of the saddle in front of your crotch, which can make you miserable if the fit is wrong. The slope of the seat, width of the forks and swells, all make a difference to the rider, as does the placement of the cinch rigging.

Western saddles come rigged several different ways. Mine is a single rig, with the girth well forward and flat in the saddle, so that there is no bulging knot in front of my leg. *Centerfire rigs* have their cinch under the stirrup leather and if tied they present quite a bulge under the leg. For this reason, they are often buckled rather than tied. *Three-quarter rigs* are similar, but the position of the girth differs, and a *full double-rigged* saddle has two cinches. Many Easterners, not understanding why the saddles are set up as they are, don't cinch their horses correctly. The front cinch is designed to hold the saddle in place; it needs to be only tight enough to keep the saddle from rotating about the horse's abdomen as you mount. The back cinch should be fairly snug, to prevent the saddle from rising up off the horse's back. Easterners keep their back cinches loose, and if they are not firmly anchored to the front one, they can sometimes ride back like a flank strap or bucking band and send the horse into a frantic flurry of leaps and bucks. We don't rope too many cattle in these parts and so the need to prevent the saddle from upending doesn't bother us much, but it sure does give our Western observers a laugh.

ENGLISH SADDLES

English saddles are also made for work and play. We rarely attach anything more than a rain slicker to an Eastern-style saddle, but hunting, polo, and competitive trail riding put quite a strain on them and certainly training saddles should always be rugged. Let us look at the *forward seat* saddles first. These are used for hunting and jumping and sometimes for competitive and endurance riding too, but they are not pleasure saddles for everyday hacking. They force the rider to sit over the horse's forehand, and weigh down the shoulders. Since the horse's front legs already carry most of his own weight, it makes little sense to burden him still more with the entire weight of the rider as well. He cannot use either his shoulders or his head and neck freely if they are carrying an extra burden of weight. There are varying degrees of forward seats. Some have skirts, which swell forward with knee rolls to help hold the rider's legs in place. The back tilts up in the air, pushing the rider to the front of the saddle. The point is to keep the rider as still as possible in one place on the horse's back so as to help the horse in jumping.

Anatomy of an English saddle. The one shown is a full-cut back flat show saddle commonly called a Lane Fox style.

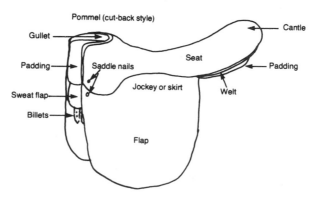

DRESSAGE

Dressage riders sit up straight and balanced, as good saddle seat riders should. In dressage, the rider sits with his legs down low against the horse's sides, with his hands also held very low and still. The saddle must offer sensitivity, for contact and communication come as much from the legs and seat of the rider as from the hands. The slightest tensing of the muscles of the rider's body cues the horse for changes of gait or attitude. The rider sits deep in the saddle, and since he must have no unintentional motion, the saddle is often of a sueded or rough surface to prevent slipping about.

POLO, HUNT, OR HACKING

Saddles made for hunting and hacking fall between the dressage and forward seat styles. The old *Whippy*-pattern saddle was by far the most popular riding saddle for the pleasure rider. These are getting harder to find all the time, because people fancy themselves as one special style of rider or another and the old-fashioned hacking style has no prestige. For the average rider who may not be fully decided what he will do eventually, a Whippy style of saddle is still the best choice. He can hunt or jump, practice dressage movements, and show in pleasure classes on the flat with any breed of horse. The old-style *polo* or *hacking* saddle does not force you to take one position and stay there. It has a deep enough seat for security, but the seat is not tilted to position you. It has panels or skirts, which are not too heavy or thick but still afford protection of the rider's leg from the horse on all but the most extreme stirrup adjustments.

SADDLE SEAT

The *flat* show saddles in Blue Ribbon, Lane Fox, or Equitation styles are made for the show ring. My own favorite saddle is so flat that I have to put my arms around my stallion's neck to stay on it going up mountains. It is not designed for everyday pleasure riding, but I like it. The flaps on a show saddle are made wide to protect the clothing of the rider from the horse's sweat. The seat is flat and smooth, so that by slight changes you can position yourself at just the right spot to enhance the horse's action in the front or to the rear. Show horses must have a very free shoulder to perform and some cannot stand a rider too far back on their loins. The flat show saddle is designed for these differences in the horse's anatomy and his preference. Riders who train young show horses can take on some pretty strange positions as they adjust themselves to suit the animal. When a horse is young, you must keep your weight farther forward because his back has not the strength or muscle to support the weight of the rider, particularly when he is made to hold his head way up and his chin tucked in toward his chest.

Saddle horse riders sometimes assume the "turtle" position, with their neck and head shoved way forward, their spines rounded, shoulders hunched, and legs just barely reaching the stirrups with the tips of their toes. They don't win beauty contests and they sure look ridiculous, but they somehow manage to get the horse to perform at the peak of his ability. The hands of the saddle seat rider should be held higher than those of the dressage and hunt riders, and sometimes they get up almost directly behind the horse's ears. As long as the touch is light, responsive, and gentle, and the communication is intact, the rest of the picture is of little importance. If the horse is open-mouthed, sour-eared, and lugging on the bit, the rider is wrong, no matter how much action the horse displays.

CHOICE OF SADDLE

There is no one right style of riding, and no single kind of saddle, bridle, or tack that is universally best. Everyone has his preferences. I am utterly miserable in a backward-sloping Western or a forward-pitching jumping saddle. I learned to ride bareback, which gave me complete freedom to place myself where the horse and I did best together. Don't be persuaded to ride in a saddle that is uncomfortable for you because someone else thinks it is "correct." Every style has variations. If you want to jump but don't want to be anchored to one position, try a variety of seats until one strikes you as most comfortable. People are all built differently. The stirrup bars, which support the stirrups, are set forward in some saddles and farther back in others. Their relation to the deepest part of the seat will affect your comfort as a rider, depending on your build. This ratio, together with the actual overall length of the saddle, will make a difference to your comfort and security. There is also a vast difference in the amount and thickness of padding in saddles, which affects both your comfort and your contact with the horse.

The saddle must fit the horse as well. Too narrow a saddle on a horse will pinch him and make awful saddle sores. Too wide a saddle will slip on his back, also creating sores. Again, a saddle that is too wide is preferable to one that is too narrow, because you can add saddle pads and tighten the girth but there is no way to relieve the pressure from too narrow a tree. Breeds vary; Morgans, Arabians, and the old-style Quarter Horses have a broader back as a rule than Saddlebreds and Thoroughbreds, who are usually both narrower in the shoulders and higher in the withers. But individuals vary within breeds, and you have to fit the saddle to the individual horse, not the breed's standard of perfection. The width of the tree is seen from the front of the saddle. Air should be able to pass between the saddle and the horse's spine through the gullet.

Saddles have either *straight* or *cutback* heads. It is a popular misconception that a cutback saddle is the best thing for a high-withered horse. A cutback saddle allows the saddle to sit lower on the horse's back, and if the front edge of the saddle rubs or even touches the back of the withers, the horse will develop a wither sore and perhaps a fistula. A cutback can pinch badly. A straight-headed saddle rides up over the withers, and if the saddle is properly padded it should be high enough to clear the withers entirely. You should be able to slide your hand into the front of the saddle on the horse's back. If not, you have to watch out for sore backs.

There are saddles that are close to being just a pad. These are treeless, made of felt or another material, and come complete with girth and stirrups. They are great fun if you can keep them on the horse, but are not acceptable in show rings or on many competitive trail rides either. They have a definite place for children, who like to take their horses swimming, and for young horses or those with problem backs. They cost little and surely will serve many people for hacking about in the woods. But if you can have only one kind, you'd do best to stick to a standard variety. Never pass up a chance to try a new style of saddle and see what it is like. *Sidesaddles* are the greatest thing for jumping once you get the knack, and can be ideal for handicapped riders with particular hip or spine problems.

Breastplates are a device for keeping the saddle from slipping back. These are commonly put on jumpers, hunters, and horses that climb hills a lot. They are used decoratively for parade outfits. *Breast collars* serve in towing a vehicle with a harness. If your horse has the reverse type of saddle slippage—that is, if the saddle slides forward —you can have it fitted with a *crupper*, which is a useful piece of equipment for children on fat-backed ponies.

Saddle pads vary in style to fit the saddles they shield. Some have forward flaps and some are straight-cut. Some curve down in the natural shape of a horse's back; others are straight, and some are seamed down the center. Most English-style pads have little straps or tapes, which fit around the front of the saddle and slip onto the billet. These prevent the pad from slipping backward out from under the saddle. They should always be put on the billet to which the girth is buckled, and should be snug around the front of the saddle. Saddle pads can be made of a variety of materials, including quilted cotton, felt, woven blanket, imitation and real sheepskin, or foam. You have to decide which you and the horse prefer. There is an advantage in being able to throw everything into the laundry once in a while! You may think that high price is a guarantee of satisfaction, but sometimes replacing a cheap pad frequently is better than trying to get your money's worth out of an expensive one. It depends entirely on your own style of riding. Most American riders use a pad, except in the show ring, under their show or flat saddles. The English use pads less often.

Girths (Cinches)

The saddle does not sit on the horse's back by itself. It is held in place by a girth. (Cowboys call them *cinches*, but the purpose is identical.) The proper girth for a flat English show saddle is a *white web* girth, either a "humane" tubular linen one with self-adjusting straps and pimpled rubber lining, or a simple flat white web girth with two buckles at each end. These are the only acceptable girths for a show saddle in gaited and park classes. Hunters are shown with *leather* girths and only occasionally with *string* girths. These vary in pattern from straight-folded baghide girths to shaped Balding, anti-chafe, and elastic-ended girths. The Fitzwilliams girth is a web girth, with another separate web girth over it, giving three buckles on each side of the saddle. My preference for pleasure riding is a mohair string girth. I have had many horses develop saddle sores from leather and web girths, but never from a mohair one. They are easy to wash in the laundry, do not get stiff or rub grit, and they allow air to circulate under them. Leather girths must be soaped frequently and must *always* be put on with the folded edge forward. Many people put them on backward and the stiff edge makes a sore.

The web girths are often like a row of saw teeth along the horse's elbows. If a horse is very fat, the girth will ride forward and rub. After you have gone through deep mud or sand, or if your horse flips his feet, the girth may well trap grit under it. Check for this from time to time. Western cinches are made of cotton and of mohair string. Again, the mohair is preferable. It is stronger and more enduring, and will not stiffen as easily as the cotton. There are nylon string girths and cinches, too; they are fine and very strong. We have a set of them for our drill team in bright blue, and they are easy to wash and come out looking brand-new again. Girths come in different lengths, from pony size to ones of 52 inches that fit our pregnant mares. If the billets are too short on the saddle (or are broken), there is a girth extender you can buckle in place to attach the girth to. This is sometimes referred to as a replacement billet.

Driving Harness

There are several basic styles of harness for different purposes. The *heavy work* or *draft* harness, made with a thick collar and hames, is used when a horse has to pull anything fairly heavy, for he leans

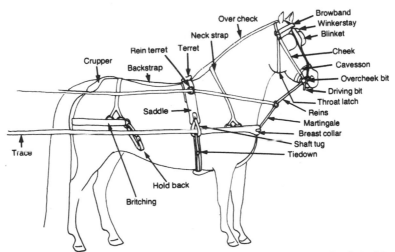

Parts of a harness. This is a buggy style single-horse harness with a britching.

forward and pushes the load with his hind legs through his spine and with the front legs. *Carriage* harness is sometimes used with collar and hames also. These are finer, prettier, and sometimes fancied up with patent leather. The light *buggy* harness is made of good rugged strapping for general driving; it is serviceable and stout. *Training* harnesses are usually of the same weight, and are useful for general driving, not show or draft work. These lighter harnesses are breast collar harnesses; that is, the horse pulls from his chest by means of straps or bands called *traces* running back along his sides to the cart. *Racing, fine* harness, and *roadster* harnesses are all breast collar harnesses in the same general style. They can be very fine and fancy, made of narrow leather or patent leather; and now even whole harnesses are made of nylon or plastic, which resembles patent leather, throughout. The fittings—which include the buckles, rein turrets, and rings—are made of brass, German and nickel silver, stainless steel, base metal, and japanned metal. Quality varies. Most of the new harness bridles that are made cheaply are stapled together. The staples can back out and cause awful sores so they bear watching. Harnesses must be strong. They must fit the horse and be kept in good order, or you will wind up in an accident. Carts, carriages, and buggies are expensive, and a cheap harness or one badly patched can spell disaster to horse, driver, passengers, and the vehicle as well.

DRIVING BRIDLES

Three different kinds of bridles are used for driving. The standard is an *overcheck* bridle with two bits—one the driving bit, to which the reins attach; the other the check bit, which sits above the main bit and lifts the horse's head by a strap running up his face over his neck and back to the saddle. In the show ring, the blinkers of a standard *overcheck bridle* are square. The *combination* bridle used for horses shown in a class both in harness and under saddle has round blinkers and side checks. Side checks are those that have a strap running from the rings of the check bit up through rings on the sides of the bridle near the browband and thence back to the saddle. There is growing acceptance in pleasure driving of using side checks with square blinker bridles and snaffle bits. Sometimes a horse is driven in an *open* (blinkerless) bridle. This is not acceptable in the show ring, however.

Harnesses come in black or russet, the latter being considered correct for informal, daytime, and natural-finished wood vehicles.

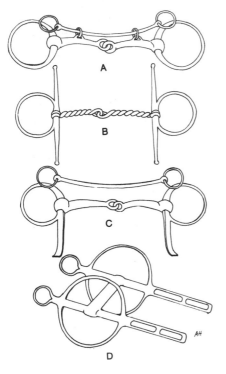

Driving bits. *A*, perfection or Norton bit; *B*, twisted mouth, full cheek; *C*, mullen mouth overcheck (wire ring) and half cheek driving bit with jointed mouth; *D*, Liverpool.

THE VEHICLE

You will need something to hitch your horse to in order to enjoy driving. The choice is between carts, buggies, or carriages, and working equipment such as plows, stone boats, or harrows and hay rakes.

Two-wheeled vehicles include road carts, sulkies and chariots, meadowbrooks and Governess carts, etc. Buggies, wagons, and carriages have four wheels, and include buckboards and the elegant landaus and broughams. Most horses are started in a two-wheeled breaking cart or jog cart. These are available in several weights and materials and are frequently homemade. There is little mystery in their manufacture, but the balance, weight distribution, and strength must be right or you're headed for an accident. Many horses are started in harness in a travois—two long poles dragging behind the horse. Others are started in a sleigh, on the theory that it is harder for a horse to run away in snow! The important thing in harness work is to make sure that the equipment you use is strong and comfortable, and that you go slowly enough in introducing each new piece so that the horse is never panicked. A runaway under saddle is never so disastrous as a horse attached to a rattling, clattering cart or buggy that keeps chasing him.

Grooming Tools

Before and after every ride, you must groom your horse. This takes equipment. First you loosen up the dirt with a plastic or rubber *curry comb*. This is essential. *Brushes* come in an assortment of kinds and uses. The stiff, long-bristled ones with a narrow back are called dandy brushes. Some are made small and very narrow for a child's hand, and some are very soft for smoothing off the hair after the rough grooming is done. Fiber or mud brushes are excellent for rough work. The fiber absorbs a certain amount of water and helps in drying a horse's coat and getting caked mud off the feet and legs. The flat, leather-backed brush with soft bristles is called a body brush or finishing brush. This is used to give the coat a smooth glow. Our practice is to keep the finishing brush absolutely clean and not allow it to be used for taking dirt off the horse at all. There is also an excellent rubber grooming mit on the market which doubles as curry comb and brush.

The Shed'n Blade—a flexible metal band with leather handles on each end, a saw-toothed edge on one side and a smooth one on the other—is fine for getting loose hair off the horse and as a sweat scraper, too. Hoof picks are simple loops with a bar and hook, although there are variations. One style folds flat, which is great for carrying on a trail ride.

You may want to get much fancier, too. There are electric vacuum cleaners for horses, several kinds of clippers, and blunt-ended scissors. If you pull the mane to braid it, you'll want a mane-pulling comb. Shaping the Quarter Horse tail requires a comb, too. I have an electric grooming head made for cattle that fits on my Sunbeam Clipmaster. The horses love it. It speeds up grooming with a deep massage from its spinning brushes that I cannot duplicate; and it gets them used to the noise of the clippers so that clipping is not a chore when the time comes.

You need a supply of disposable cotton or Handiwipes for the eyes and the dock, and towels can never be too plentiful in a stable.

You should have a special box for carrying and storing grooming tools; this avoids getting the equipment dirty or losing it. There are many suitable boxes and baskets, as well as a commercial grooming tray. Actually, every horse should have his own private set of grooming tools in order to prevent the spread of communicable diseases.

Blankets and Sheets

Blankets are a necessity for sick horses. They are a convenience for show horses and horses that are to be used hard during the winter. The all-wool "rugs" are thick and absorbent, and since they are not covered with a tightly woven outer shell, water can evaporate off the horse without his catching a chill. However, they are easily torn and hard to repair, and their soft surface picks up dirt more easily than the canvas-backed kind. It is customary to use the "rugs" under a sheet on a horse that needs the warmth for recovery from fatigue or injury, but not for everyday purposes. Most often the blankets you find are covered with a material called duck, which is light canvas, and they may be lined with jute fiber or with wool. Some, called turnout blankets, have straps and surcingles set up so that the horse can lie down and roll and the blanket will not shift or get around under his belly. There are new "ski jacket"–style blankets, quilted and fiber-filled like parkas, and waterproof so-called storm blankets, with a tail flap that protects the horse's rear end as well as his back.

Blankets are usually open in front and have grommeted holes for a strap, or a strap-and-buckle arrangement to close across the horse's chest. Some blankets close over the chest in a single piece, the whole thing being slid over the horse's head. Gather the blanket up like a donut and put it on the neck, then pull it out flat and arrange it. If your horse tends to be a little claustrophobic or head-shy, better buy the strap-and-buckle or grommeted kind of blanket. The closed front obviously gives the horse more protection from drafts and chills across the chest. It has to fit snugly enough so it will not shift position, but should not be so tight as to cause sores. You should have two blankets, in fact, so that if one gets wet it can have time to air and dry. Also, blankets should be hung in the sun and aired frequently; horses who remain blanketed during the year often suffer from lice, fleas, and mange. Be sure that you remove the blanket, shake, air, and brush it daily to prevent this. Our horses don't wear a blanket unless they are chilled or sick. They grow heavy winter coats and stay out, but then they are not ridden hard all winter or prepared for early shows in spring.

There is no breed of horse that *must* be blanketed. I hear Thoroughbred people saying that their horses can't stand being left uncovered, but that depends on the conditioning of the individual horse and is not a breed characteristic. Many horses are clipped of their winter hair and then kept blanketed, so that they do not stay wet after work with their heavy coats and can cool out faster. But you cannot leave an unblanketed and clipped horse standing still in the cold or he will chill.

Sheets are lightweight blankets, made of unlined duck or canvas, which serves to keep the horse clean and his hair lying smooth. They cut down a bit on drafts and are a good protection when trailering a horse if it starts to rain. You can get waterproof sheets for rain protection. Ordinary stable sheets are often thrown on a horse who is still a little sweated up after a workout, but they are not meant for that purpose.

Coolers and *anti-sweat* sheets are used for cooling out a hot horse. Most people think a horse is walked to make him cool off faster; in fact, you walk the horse to *prevent* him from cooling off too fast. You blanket the horse to prevent the sweat from evaporating at too fast a rate and thereby reducing the horse's temperature too quickly. The slower his temperature is returned to normal, the safer he is from founder, chills, and muscle stiffness. Horses are particularly susceptible to chilling. Coolers are usually made of wool; they are long blankets, which go all the way from the head to well over the tail and hang way down along the sides, letting air enter under the blanket and warm up before it hits the horse's body. This warm air becomes laden with moisture, which is absorbed and then evaporates off the surface of the blanket. The anti-sweat sheet is an open "fisherman's net" weave which acts as an insulator. Used with a light sheet, it does cool a horse very evenly; it is completely washable.

Scrim sheets are light mesh sheets designed to protect the horse from flies. They can be made like fitted sheets and blankets, or like walking covers or coolers to go from head to tail.

In an emergency, a bed blanket, several large safety pins, a tablecloth, and some strips of rug binding tape will make a fine double-layered blanket for a sick or chilled horse. Give some thought to what types of blanket you will really need or use. If you plan to use one only when the horse is sick, get one he won't destroy if he lies down in it in his stall for weeks. If you want one to throw on him when you go to a show and while trailering, get one that will maintain its good looks through launderings. Some of them shred and fade and look awful in short order.

Horses tear blankets with their teeth. To prevent this, the horse is fitted with a *bib*—a flap of wide, heavy leather suspended from his halter. This does not interfere with his eating, but prevents him from tucking his chin down and catching the end of the blanket in his teeth. It does *not* prevent him from reaching around to the side and ripping off the surcingles, however. If the horse does this and he must be blanketed, he may have to wear a *neck cradle,* which is a row of slats or aluminum bars encircling his neck and making it difficult for him to bend it in any direction. I have never felt that I needed to blanket a horse so badly that I wanted to truss him up in one of these contraptions, but if a horse is injured such measures do sometimes become necessary. These bibs and cradles prevent a horse from removing bandages from injuries, too. You may never need such a device, but it is good to be aware of its existence.

Some horses grow a layer of fat around their throats which makes flexion difficult and is unsightly. If your horse has this problem, there are a number of hood, jowl, and neck *sweat wraps* to reduce the fat around either the throat latch itself or the entire neck area. The newest ones are of neoprene and held with Velcro, whereas the older styles are made of felt, sheepswool, or rubber and buckled about the horse's neck. There are *shoulder sweats* also. There are even heated ones which plug into a wall outlet like an electric blanket.

Hoods, which match the shipping blankets, exist for protection against wind and rain. Fly scrim ear nets to keep flies out of the ears are also available. There is a hood with blinkers for use in early saddle training and ground work to help keep the horse's mind and his eyes on his business. The blinker hoods work wonders for some horses with wide peripheral vision, who tend to shy violently. These special items are not found in the general tack trunk, but knowledge of their existence can be a godsend for special problems.

Boots and Bandages

Every stable should have at least one complete set of leg wraps or bandages. If you get the kind that you wind around the legs and tie, you must have a supply of cotton wool or quilted pads to protect the horse from the cording effect of the bandages. You must also have someone show you carefully exactly how tight and in what direction to wrap, as too loose a bandage will slide down and tangle the horse's feet and too tight a bandage will cut off the circulation. Cording can result in a bowed tendon. I prefer the thick, padded, oblong bandages closed with Velcro, which do not need much skill to apply. Bandages for hind legs are taller than those for front legs, and should fit over the top of the coronet to protect it from cuts while the horse is being shipped—for they tend to step on their own feet if they lose their balance. We bandage horses when they have a chill, because they lose a great deal of heat from their feet and legs. Sometimes, if a horse must work in deep mud, he is bandaged to help support his tendons and prevent strains; bandages are needed that can be wrapped and adjusted for pressure and support. I don't suggest that you stock up on too many kinds of bandages, because if the horse has pulled or strained anything, the veterinarian will supply the first bandages he needs and tell you what to get.

Shipping boots of leather, or of foam, sheepswool, acrylic, or other shock-absorbing materials, are really the only essential sort of boot or bandage most people need regularly. At that, you will need them only if you plan to haul your horse about. If the horse trucks well and loads without a fuss, you may never use anything on his legs.

There are boots for specific problems, such as speedy-cut boots for splay-footed horses, which rap their cannons as they trot; overreach boots for horses that catch the front feet with the hind; bell boots for protecting the front foot from the hind foot (again in an overstride); quarter boots for action, to lift and increase the reach of the foot; run-out boots, ones for sliding stops, polo boots and shin guards, hock boots, and elbow boots.

The shoe-boil boot prevents a horse from lying down with his heel directly under his elbow and creating an abcess. It looks like a large leather donut, and it buckles around the pastern. Boots to prevent injury from a poor way of going are a temporary measure until the farrier can correct the problem. Bell boots do help a young horse while he is learning to carry weight and handle his growing legs. Once he has a good balance, maturity, and muscular control, he should no longer need the protection of bell boots. There are federal laws about boots in horse shows now. There has been quite a bit of abuse of certain horses for show purposes, known as "soreing," which is partially caused by and/or covered up by boots.

There are boots for therapy. Soaking swabs are thick felt boots that you wet down and buckle on the horse's pastern to keep the hoof wet or medicated. Rubber soaking boots fit like a fisherman's waders, with suspenders over the horse's shoulder to soak a leg up over the knees. Whirlpool boots pump water actively around the legs to reduce heat and swelling; these are useful for horses that are worked extremely hard or for large stables where there are so many horses that the task of soaking and massaging would be too time-consuming to be practicable. You can make soaking boots, poultice boots, and the like with burlap bags and a little imagination.

A new product called Easy Boots are shoes which fit over the whole foot, instead of being nailed to the bottom of the hoof. Since cold metal shoes draw heat out of horses' feet in winter, these boots should make a horse far more comfortable. Also, horses with brittle feet that can't hold nails and horses with tender-soled feet can all be shod with these boots and then allowed to go barefoot while not being worked. The initial cost is high, but may be well worth it for a problem. I have never had occasion to try them, but people have recommended them for many uses, although some have complained of damage to the horse's heels.

Restraining Devices

Hobbles are a form of footwear. Cowboys still use them, and if you show in Western classes with closed reins instead of open ones you are required to carry hobbles. They limit how far the horse can move one foot in front of the other, so that an animal can graze around a campsite, for instance, without wandering too far. Smart horses learn to rise up and jump forward with both front feet and can travel for miles at night in this fashion.

Breeding hobbles buckle around the hind feet; instead of tying one foot to the other, they attach both hind feet to the neck, limiting how high and how far back a mare can kick. The rope runs from the hobbles under her belly to a collar, and generally has a quick-release system of some sort.

Restraining a horse so that he can be worked on or treated is usually best accomplished with a *humane twitch*. This twitch looks like a giant nutcracker; it slips over the horse's upper lip and is held in a clamplike grip. (It is called the "AAA Humane One Man Twitch.") The Wilform twitch is another variety, designed for someone working alone; but this one is square, and has a screw which presses a bar down on the nose. The old-fashioned rope or chain twister is still around. This is more likely to come off the nose and can damage the horse's lips and teeth, to say nothing of the damage it does to the head of the person who lets it go when the horse yanks back! This is good only in the hands of experienced, tall, strong people. You must learn to handle a twitch sooner or later if you plan to help the veterinarian or farrier with your horse and the animal tries to resist. It hurts the horse temporarily, to be sure, but the pain goes away. There are some horses who resent a twitch and fight harder if one is used. We usually start without one, and if the horse squirms too much put one on. One last word: sometimes a twitch is applied to the ear or the horse is simply "eared down" by twisting his ear with your hand. Ear cartilage can be broken that way and I have had several horses made head-shy by such treatment. Be cautious about earing a horse. I do it if I must, but I never yank down on the ear, only squeeze and turn it.

Miscellaneous

There are assorted odds and ends you will gather, too. Leather punches, saddle soap, a leather-conditioner such as Lexol, will all be a regular part of your tack box. (Do not use neat's foot oil on tack because it rots stitches.) Whips, crops, spurs, training equipment, specialty items, measuring standards to see how tall your horse is, measuring tapes to see how heavy he is (a great help in figuring doses of medicine), all add up. Many of the items listed here are available at local horse and cattle auctions, through farm cooperatives, at hardware stores, and of course at tack and horse supply stores and grain companies. Most horse magazines list saddle shops that put out catalogs and it is wise to write for them, for there are many items not available through other sources. Catalogs help in comparison shopping for price, but remember that quality varies within given price ranges.

The things you should *not* buy yourself are horse-shoeing tools and medicine. Let competent professionals handle the feet and health supplies for your horse. When you know enough to do your own vetting and blacksmithing, you will know what to buy. If you feel you must have things on hand to treat wounds, buy a jar of Vaseline, a bottle of peroxide, and a role of sterile cotton. Put up a huge sign in your barn reading: "NEVER PUT WATER ON AN OPEN WOUND!" Use a saline solution (1 cup salt added to 1 quart water) instead.

The essentials will make your life workable. The additional items may make it more fun or more convenient, but too much equipment can cause confusion. Select your tack with care, favoring enduring and maintenance-free materials whenever possible. The time is past when people sat for hours polishing brass and soaping leather, but uncared-for tack is a hazard. There is no point in owning equipment you do not know how to use. It is fun to have all your own equipment in the same color or marked with colored tape, and to have things in boxes painted to match, which also makes it easier to identify your equipment on rides and at shows. Make a list of the things that you buy, with the date and amount paid, and where you purchased them. Some tack needs to be replaced yearly, and it is an expensive proposi-

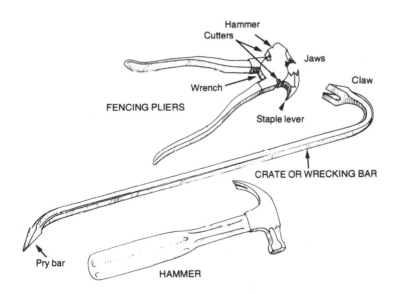

Emergency tools that should be kept in every stable. *Top,* fencing pliers to remove nails, staples, cut wire, hammer and squeeze; *Center,* crate or wrecking bar to pry boards loose and to remove nails; *Bottom,* hammer.

tion. Many people spend more on equipment than they do on their horse. Keeping a record facilitates replacement and helps you to keep control of the actual outlay. A visit to a tack room or shop is always fun, but it is also a grave temptation to splurge. Try to arrange it so that you spend most of your time with the horse instead of housekeeping for a lot of equipment.

Finally, every stable should have one set of emergency tools to free up a horse if he becomes entangled or cast in his stall and to repair stalls and fences. This includes a hammer, fencing pliers, and a wrecking bar. They should always be readily available and returned to their proper place after use. You simply don't have time to go looking for tools when a horse is in trouble.

CHAPTER 6

Where Will You Look

for Your Horse?

THERE ARE HORSES FOR SALE in virtually every county of every state of the Union. I know of people who have just driven down a road, spotted a horse they liked, stopped in at the house, and made their purchase. I have known others who have searched for months or even years with careful study in bloodlines, endless letter and phone contacts, and never found a horse that satisfied their needs. I have traveled thousands of miles in search of certain qualities I want in a horse and am still searching.

The single most important factor in buying the right horse is the person from whom you make the purchase. The fact is that every horse that is on the market is for sale for some reason. And the reason may be one that would make that horse wrong for you. Hence, the reputation and honesty of the seller is all-important, whether you spend $50 or $50,000 on a horse. Good horses, suitable for the novice who wants a safe and gentle companion, are sometimes available for a small amount of money and the guarantee of a good home. Better horses can command higher prices. Many people think that if they pay a high price, they are getting a better horse; this is not necessarily the case.

Auctions

The worst place to buy a horse is at an auction, for if the horse turns out to be a total loss, you have no recourse. When you buy at auction, you bid on the horse with all his faults; and when you have made the highest bid and the horse is "knocked down" to you, he is yours, even if he drops dead on the spot. Besides the fact that you might make a very poor purchase by buying at auction, you also miss out on a very important aspect of horse buying, which is the contact you make with the seller. If you visit a farm, see where the horses live, and observe the methods of handling by the present owners, you will know much more about your horse when you get him home. Most horse owners care about their animals and many care greatly about their customers and their reputations. The backyard pet owner, as well as the owners of the large horse-breeding farms, becomes attached to animals with their own personalities and feelings, and we all sleep better if we know we have sent those horses into good hands.

Even after investigating the reputation of the owner, you should still get advice on the actual horse you plan to purchase from a qualified veterinarian. This protects both you *and* the seller. The seller might not realize that a horse has a potential unsoundness which a veterinarian should recognize. Sometimes even a vet will fail to notice a weakness because it is only evident after a horse has had a real workout; but in general, once you have narrowed down the likeliest of prospects, it will pay you to hire a vet to check the animals for you.

The Registry

If you know that you want a registered horse, your best bet may be to start with the registry and ask them for a list of breeders in your area. If you have a well-run stable nearby with capable management, they can guide you to owners and breeders of repute. Even people who own a different breed can usually help you to contact someone with the breed you prefer. Every major breed has at least one magazine which carries advertisements; in addition, there are several national and regional magazines with ads of horses for sale. Your nearest tack shop, grain company, or stable should be able to start you out with contacts in the horse world of your choice.

The Price

The price you plan to pay for a horse will also establish the distance you are willing to travel. People who spend a great deal for horses travel miles to see them in person, acquire written purchase agreements and written guarantees, vet certification, and then cover the horses with insurance. When you are limited in what you can spend and must consider the cost of transportation as a part of the cost of purchase, you will be more likely to search in a limited area.

It costs far less to raise a horse where hay is raised than where it must be shipped in. It is literally one-tenth as expensive to raise a horse in the grain belt of the Midwest as in the Northeast, given that all the other expenses are the same. Feed is the major factor in the cost of horses, although not the only one. So it is that you can often find horses of comparable quality for far less money in the areas where feeds are available at less cost. You will also find that horses cost less in financially depressed areas of the country.

For this reason, many hundreds of horses are "picked up" by dealers in the middle states and shipped by the carload to the two coasts. These horses can be sold at prices far below the cost of the coast-raised native stock. These dealers tend, then, to depress the prices that the Eastern and Far Western breeders can get for their animals. Sometimes they flood the market, driving breeders out of business. In certain cases, these horses are kept well, schooled, and fitted, and have all the necessary veterinary work done on them to make them suitable for the market. But far too many are just picked up, thrown into pens with meager feed, their shipping papers filled out in blank by a negligent vet who is in on the deal, and then sold to unwary buyers.

Be Prepared

Impulse buying is something we all do. Even horse breeders who put much thought and study into their purchases end up buying on impulse quite often. There is a good reason for this. You are looking for an animal that appeals to you. If you fear you will fall in love with the wrong horse and don't trust your instincts, then make up a check list of particulars that the horse *must* meet, and take a firm-minded friend with you who can act as an observer and stabilizer.

You will need a notebook of the names and locations of prospective farms in the area; take the time to map out the most practical path from one to the next. In your notebook write down the name of the farm, the manager or owner, and the phone number, so you can call or write ahead to be sure there will be someone home to show the animals to you. It is common courtesy to make an appointment to see horses, for the owner will certainly want to spend some time with a serious customer to ascertain whether he is right for the horse and vice versa. Also, the horse you want to see may be out in the north forty, covered with mud and quite happy to stay there. You will save time and get a much better reception if you make and keep an appointment.

A word here to teen-agers who cannot drive themselves on horse-hunting jaunts. If you expect the family to cooperate on horse-hunting trips, especially where there are small brothers and sisters to take along, there are a few things you can do to make it all a fun outing instead of an ordeal. Search out some interesting sights on the way —caverns, forts, transportation museums, or whatever else might interest members of the family—and write away for necessary information. Pack a picnic lunch basket and include some surprises to keep younger children busy on the long car ride. If you suspect your mother might enjoy looking at horses with you, but not with a bored, fussing youngster in tow, see if you can exchange baby-sit for a neighbor or friend or even hire one of your school friends to give your mother a real day off with you. A promise of future rides in exchange for baby-sitting while you are looking for your horse might be considered a fair bargain. In any case, use your head! Contribute as much as you can to facilitate the traveling that is a necessary part of buying a horse.

Making Use of Photos

Find, borrow, or buy a simple camera for your horse-hunting trips. Use black-and-white film. Make the following two vital rules: that you will not buy a horse on the first visit, but will take all the information on a horse that interests you, including some careful photographs; and that you will have a veterinarian examine any horse you select. In all fairness to a seller, if you ask him for photographs, be certain to return them within a week, unless he tells you to keep them.

Photographs are expensive and we all get hundreds of requests for them. It is impossible to keep a current supply of pictures on hand unless you have many duplicates printed. I do my own darkroom work and still am constantly out of pictures to send because it is so time-consuming to set up and run a darkroom.

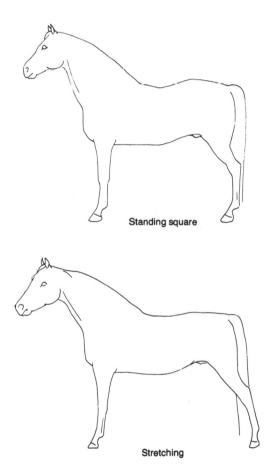

Standing square

Stretching

Two drawings of the same horse, standing in the normal, relaxed and square position and posed or stretched out. Note the effect of stretching on the apparent length of neck, refinement in the throat, level and length of hip and croup, and the fact that it is impossible to judge the angle or set of the hock. When the horse stands square it is evident that his hocks are set on behind his body, indicating that he will drag his hocks.

If you take your own pictures, stand at exactly the side of the horse about 15 feet away and with the horse standing square, not "posed." Be sure you take in the whole horse and that he is standing on level ground. Take two or three pictures, and try to get him with his ears up, looking at something. Then stand behind him and shoot a picture of his legs. Do the same from the front. Do this with every horse you consider and with some that take your fancy even if they are not for sale, or some that look weird to you but you can't quite figure out why.

Judge the horses against a good picture of a horse who is supposed to be correct for the breed. Make sure to find one that is not posed or taken from a concealing angle, and compare each horse, one against the other. Mark each picture with the horse's name so you don't get mixed up. In your own home you can examine the actual shape of the horse, measure his shoulder line, length of back and neck, and see if his legs are straight or crooked. It is hard to see these things while the horse is before you. If you see something in the picture you missed in person, note that in your special book and examine it with care when you return to see the horse. I find that no horse looks the same to me ever again once I have photographed him and studied the pictures. Some I like better, most I find fault with; but since I realize that no horse is perfect, I can make a better judgment armed with the pictures. Once the horse is stopped in motion and committed to print in a photo, some aspects of his conformation fairly jump out at you.

Registration Papers

If the horse is registered, ask to see the papers and copy down the names and *numbers* of the horses, but do not expect to be able to take the papers with you. They stay with the horse at all times. Note that the current owner is the person who has the horse for sale. In some cases, papers have not been properly transferred from one owner to the next. When the buyer tries to get the papers transferred into his name, he finds he must research back through several owners, pay a transfer fee for each, get all their signatures, and only then, if there is no broken link in the chain, does he have a registered horse. If he fails to get one owner, he is out of luck. For a pedigree to mean anything, both the sire and the dam must be shown and their parents also listed. If the horse has one registered parent and the other is an unknown, you have a half-breed; the papers serve only to indicate the age of the horse and who bred him or owned him, little more.

Horses are of two kinds: purebred, registered stock, and unregistered stock. Most people who work with one kind do not have much contact with people who work with the other. We live in two different worlds, with entirely different philosophies about animals. While some mongrel enthusiasts are contemptuous of anyone who "bothers about all those fancy papers and stuff," most purebred enthusiasts wouldn't give stable room to any but a quality registered animal. There is no reason to be caught in the middle of the controversy, but you should understand the philosophy behind people's opinions. My own view is that there is no point in having anything but a registered, well-bred horse of real merit. It costs just as much, if not more, to keep an inferior, nonproductive horse, and there is no way to get my money back if I wish to sell the animal.

My own horses are here to further the breeding program, to pay their way with foals every year, and to represent a breed of horses I respect and believe in. If I were more involved in using the horses as personal mounts, for commerce, to train for money for other people, or to use in competitions, I would have less concern about their parentage, their ability to pass on their qualities, or their soundness potential beyond the actual fact that they are serviceably sound while in my hands. In short, my personal interest in the horse would be a much more transitory thing. I would be inclined to pay less, I would invest less in their care, and I would expect less in return, in all likelihood.

Examining the Horse

Whether you buy a horse from his breeder, from a professional trainer who has horses on consignment from their owners, from a dealer who buys and sells horses for a profit, or from a hack stable, summer camp, private owner, or at auction, the actual method of examining the horse should be the same. Explain to whoever accompanies you on these visits that you should place yourselves on opposite sides of the horse, not stand together to admire the animal. The friend is there to observe subtle nuances of how the handler actually works with the horse, his hands, his whip, his grip on the halter or bridle. The friend should stand behind the horse and sight a line between the legs to see if all four legs are straight; the interior of the horse's stall should be examined for kick marks or evidence of wood chewing. The friend should be free to ask any question no matter how silly, and to test to see if the horse is frightened by sudden motion from behind or a strange object. By this I do not suggest that the friend bang a gong or wave a flag behind the horse and spook him over the handler's writhing body; but if a handkerchief suddenly pulled out of a pocket to catch a loud sneeze (from a safe distance of over 10 feet behind the horse) sends the animal into orbit, this may not be the horse for you.

You should be allowed to enter the stall, put on the halter and take it off, lead the horse through some doorways or stall doors, and over or at least up to a sheet of plastic or newspaper. It is all very well if the handler can put a chain over the animal's nose, pose him, and run him on the line for you; but if you yourself can't handle the horse from the ground at his own stable, how can you expect to cope with him in a strange place with new people? If the handler or seller will not allow this, forget that animal. You are not ready to take on problems.

Some farms put you in a fancy observation room and bring out only the particular horse you are to view. You have a wall or glass panel between you and the horse. You can't even reach out to straighten his forelock away from his eyes to see if he is head-shy or not. Only if you plan to keep that horse in the hands of a professional, and just go and observe him in the show ring, would you be able to accept such an arrangement.

If you are buying a horse to ride, you should *ride him* before you buy him. I can honestly say that fewer than 1 percent of the people who come to me to buy a trained horse are willing or even able to get on the horse, or into the cart to work the horse. I have to persuade them. In some cases, a trainer or owner will wisely put you up on a very quiet, safe horse before he lets you get on a young and lively one. Do not be insulted; he has an obligation to protect you from injury and to protect the horse from inept hands. If he feels that you are not ready or able to handle the horse you are considering, he will suggest riding or driving lessons, a different horse, or that you leave the horse for further schooling and come and work with the animal under his guidance. Three cheers for the conscientious sellers who insist that buyers do not take on horses that will end up in disasters! The cost of a month or two of continued education for both the horse and the buyer can be more than justified if you figure that mistakes and injuries, hospitals and veterinarians, are all expensive. If you live too far away for frequent visiting, perhaps the seller can recommend a trainer in your area, or you may already know some capable horseman who can help you. In that case, it would be wise to invite that person to come to see the horse and have a talk with the seller before you make the purchase.

You may already have decided on a particular horse before you read this book. It might well be one you have ridden at a stable or a summer camp. If the horse is good and well behaved at the stable or camp, and you are certain he is sound enough for the work you plan for him, this can be a fine choice. If he has some bad habits, such as heading back to the stable or pulling on his reins persistently from the constant succession of changing riders, ask the owner if you can rent the horse exclusively for a period of time, to see if you can overcome these habits with careful, consistent handling. Horses that have been soured from overwork or changing hands can be brought back sometimes, but not always. Again, if the owner will give you lessons with the horse, you will be far ahead. Take the time while the horse is "yours" on a rental basis to do his actual daily care, grooming and feeding, if you can work it out to suit the stable's time schedule.

All this may sound like a great deal of bother, but in the long run it will be a saving. I am sure you have heard the clichés "Fools rush in where angels fear to tread" and "Ignorance is bliss." Well, sad to say, children get seriously hurt with horses and horses can be seriously hurt by fools. You should not trust entirely to luck and instinct in acquiring a living, dynamic animal.

The "Expert"

It is sometimes difficult to come up with a real expert to aid you in your choice. Horsemen joke that an "expert" is anyone who is 100 miles from home. My experience is that an expert is someone who writes an article that gets published which someone else then quotes. That's all it takes. You don't have to know a thing; you just have to fool a couple of people into thinking you do. Years ago we had lots of expert horsemen around. Every man was his own trainer, vet, and blacksmith. Now, with the many good publications and fine graduate veterinarians to help us, we have a much better chance of getting good information. Still, I see many 4-H leaders, so-called riding instructors, and "professional" horse people today who have not progressed far from the dark ages. These people are full of advice and often are the ones chosen by the novice to help find a good horse. The seller finds that everything he says about his horse is belittled or somehow misinterpreted. When you choose an "expert," you would do best to choose a qualified one who will not try to confound and alienate every seller. Sometimes a breeder will actually refuse to sell a horse because he feels that animal will be placed in a bad situation. Often as not, it is the expert brought along for advice who sours the whole sale. Since the horse you buy should be suited to you and not to someone else, try to make these decisions intelligently yourself. Listen to what your friends and advisers say, but get enough real information to be self-reliant before the start of your horse-hunting trips.

Be Aware of the Costs

First, a warning: Do not buy a horse out of pity. It takes a lot of experience to bring back horses who have suffered from neglect, abuse, and ignorance. Unless you have ample money and a truly personal need to rescue animals, you will not get the full value of your money for quite some time and may never recover the losses if the animal is beyond your capacity to help it. The reclamation of horses who have suffered from illness, inadequate worming, or starvation requires special knowledge and may prove futile, even when properly carried out. It is reasonable to be suspicious of any horse that is kept isolated or handled in a different manner from the others.

It does not cost a "back-yard" horse owner nearly as much to raise a horse as it does a breeding farm. There are significant differences in the tax structure, bookkeeping, and personal evaluation between the two. If a family has a mare that they would keep for their own pleasure, regardless of having a foal, they can call a foal a profit if they sell it for anything above the cost of breeding the mare and feeding the foal after it is born. A breeding farm with hired help, a heavy show schedule, and fancy full-page ads in expensive breed magazines would not necessarily breed a better quality of horse, but certainly would have to get a much higher price! Many back-yard breeders with one fine, beloved, and well-cared-for mare take a long time selecting just the right sire for their foal. They make every effort to give that foal the best care and handling they can, and they endeavor to get it into just the right home. However, they are overshadowed by the big stables, who attract buyers with elaborate ads and fancy prices for animals not necessarily better suited to buyers' needs. There are also back-yard breeders who own inferior mares, use poor stallions, and give inadequate care to their horses. So it must be the individual horse that you select, and the seller must be something more than just well advertised. The price you will pay has to be based on some real understanding of the animal's value.

I can give you some idea of my costs, as a small breeder without hired help; but no matter what prices I quote now on the cost of raising a horse here, in this corner of New England, it will have gone up by the time this book comes off the press, and it will not hold true for other parts of the country anyway.

We do our own farm labor in caring for our horses. We buy everything we feed to the horses. Where we live, horses must be protected from hunters and harsh storms all winter long and from flies and extremes of heat in summer. So each horse must have a shelter, in our case an individual stall. This entails overhead in maintainence of the buildings, electricity, bedding, and feed, just for starters. We have fences that have to be maintained. Wire has become incredibly expensive in the past two years, rising from $16 per roll to $125 for a less strong wire in the same length. Fence posts, which were 65¢, are over $2, and they snap off if a horse leans on them. So just pasture alone has cost us more in the past two years. Pastures have to be fertilized, limed and clipped, cleared and maintained, too. Three years ago, if I figured the care of a broodmare, the price of a stud fee (or a portion of the maintainance of one stallion), and the overhead, not counting my own labor, a newborn foal cost me $700 the moment it dropped. If it stood and nursed, and the mare and foal both survived foaling, I could figure on maintaining that foal with its grain, vet and farrier cost, and advertising, and selling it at four to six months of age at a break-even price of $900. My cost of transporting it to its new owner or keeping it beyond weaning would not be included, but the price of registration (now $20) and transfer (now

$15) would. During the following year from weaning to yearling, the cost of caring for a horse escalates from $500 to $700 a year. People do not like to buy yearlings. They look awkward, act goofy, and are hard to evaluate. So we usually figure if we have a foal after weaning, it will stay with us until it is two and has started its training. Meanwhile, we invest in the horse at the same rate as we do a productive broodmare. By the time the horse is two, we start serious training to harness. If I send the horse to a trainer, this will cost from $200 to $300 a month (that will include his care and feeding, so I can deduct those costs from his cost at home for the year). By the time the horse is trained to harness and is about two and a half years old, not yet old enough to ride, he has actually cost me: $700 at birth, $700 for the next year, and about $1,100 for his training year—making a grand total of about $2,500! If the horse is a mare, I have a pretty good chance of getting that price back . . . that price, not a profit. If the horse is a good gelding, I have lost over $1,000, for it is hard to sell him for more than $1,500. If he is a superb stallion, I might make a profit at this stage *if* I have shown him successfully (add at least another $300 for showing). A show colt will cost me $3,000, but I might well be able to sell him for $4,000, if he is top quality. There are not many at any farm, in any year, that qualify for that price.

Now, the figures are not all in yet, but it looks as if the foals that are born on the farm this year will cost me over $1,000 by weaning time, because of simple inflation rather than any innovations.

Reading the Ads

There is no way to guess in advance where the right horse will turn up. You can look in the newspaper for animal-for-sale classifieds. There are classified ads in most horse magazines as well. Ordinarily, since the classified ad is far less expensive than a display ad, people assume that the horse sold thus will be less expensive than a horse in a full-page spread, and tend to stay away from display ads. Most display ads are used to promote a whole farm, or a particular show horse or stallion, and the little classified ads are counted on to move those horses that are actually for sale. In order to print a display ad of a given size, the copy usually has to be at the printer's two months in advance. A classified ad can be sent in up to a week before publication, in many instances; so the classified ad is often more current.

Learning to read an ad is an art in itself. Writing them is a constant challenge. The seller wants to whet your appetite and stimulate interest. He must be extremely careful of his wording for fear of misrepresenting the horse, so lots of ads allude to but do not state facts about a horse. When I send an ad into a classified section, I write it all out in words: e.g., "Morgan mare, chestnut, flaxen mane and tail, coming three, 14.2 hands, gentle, trained to harness, sound and pretty. Sire Champion Chief Red Hawk by Flyhawk, dam a daughter of Whippoorwill Duke." This ad will appear as:

Morgan M., Ch. Flax M & T, 3, 14.2, gtl., harness broke, sound & pretty. Sr. Ch. Chief Red Hawk (Flyhawk) x dau. Whip. Duke.

If all this means something to you, you rate a score of 10. Sometimes we read the ads just for laughs. They can be so abbreviated that it is hard to tell if you are reading the motor numbers of a car or the results of a basketball game. You will need a whole new vocabulary, which I have included below to help you interpret some of these ads. First, some abbreviations:

S is for Stallion. This means an uncastrated male horse over four years of age.

C is for Colt, a stallion from birth to four years.

G is for Gelding, a castrated male horse (any age).

M is for Mare, a female horse four years or older unless she has foaled earlier.

F is for Filly, a mare not yet four years of age or not yet having had a foal before four years of age.

Foal is a baby horse; it is rarely abbreviated.

Wlng is for Weanling, a foal after it has been separated from its mother.

Ylng is for Yearling, a horse from the middle of its weanling year (as of January 1 until next January 1). It is called a "rising" yearling from January 1 to the first birthday, and a "long" yearling after it is about one and a half but not yet two years old. The term "coming two-year-old" is the same thing. There are rising and long two- and three-year-olds. January is the annual "birthday" of all horses for the purposes of convenience for horse shows and races. Horses are considered mature at five years of age, although in fact some are and some are not really mature. They are considered in their prime at eight to ten, depending to some extent upon the breed. Many horses are "all done" by the age of ten, while some are still "youngsters"!

Height is given in hands—a hand is 4 inches. The horse is measured at the top of the highest point of the withers, with the head up. The horse is any equine *over* 14 hands 2 inches, written 14.2" or 14.2 hands. A pony is an equine at or under that mark of 14.2. A pony can be of any breed, including Thoroughbred, if it is under this mark. There are individuals of horse breeds that remain under 14.2, and a few ponies of pony breeding that achieve a mark over 14.2. In some cases these are ineligible for registration.

Thoroughbred is a breed of horse, *not* a term.

Purebred, or *full-blooded,* means that the horse's two parents are both recorded in the same register to which the horse belongs.

The terms *half-bred* or *three-quarter bred* mean half-Thoroughbred or three-quarters Thoroughbred. In other words, it is not correct to call a horse half-bred Arabian (unless the other half is Thoroughbred). Such a horse is called a half-Arab.

Crossbred is the term for a horse by a sire of one breed and out of a dam of a different breed.

Grade is the term for any horse that is more than half the blood of any registered breed, such as a grade Quarter Horse or grade Welsh. Sadly, this is one of the terms misused to such an extent that *grade* now is usually the term applied to any mongrel, and the named breed (such as grade Morgan or grade Saddlebred) may not appear in any part of the horse's actual lineage. If a horse is purported to be a grade, ask to see his papers to prove it. There is a registry set up to record these half-blooded horses, and any thinking breeder will take the trouble to get those papers when he produces a decent foal. Some stallion owners wisely insist on the registration of foals from their purebred stallion and nonregistered or other breed-registered mares, so that the foal will not be sold as purebred.

The breeds are abbreviated as follows:

Thoroughbred: T.B. or the number, given as Jockey Club No. _____, the name of the recording body.

American Saddle Horse: Called *Saddler* or *Saddlebred,* the number given as ASHBA (American Saddle Horse Breeders Association). Three gaited and five gaited horses and fine harness horses are *American Saddlebreds.* There are gaited ponies. The show equivalent of the three gaited Saddler in either the Morgan or Arabian breed is referred to as a *park horse.* There are no classes for five gaited horses except Saddlers. Horses shown in the same style as the fine harness horses in Morgan and Arab classes are called *park harness horses.*

Albino horses are recorded with the American White Horse Registry and are often called *American Albino* or *American White Horse.* They are not true albinos since they must have dark, not pink, eyes.

Quarter Horses are abbreviated *Q.H.,* and the number most often given is that recorded with the AQHA, but there are other Quarter Horse registries, such as Model Quarter Horse.

Standardbreds, S.T. for short, are listed with the ATR (American Trotting Registry), even when they are pacers. These are the harness racehorses.

Morgans are now recorded with the American Morgan Horse Registry (AMHR numbers), but until recently their numbers were often given as MHC (Morgan Horse Club).

Appaloosas are recorded with the *ApHC* (Appaloosa Horse Club), but the numbers are often given as T-_____ (temporary) or P-_____ (permanent).

The *Tennessee Walking Horse* is recorded as TWHA, and often referred to as a *Walker, Plantation Horse,* or *Walking Horse.*

Palominos are recorded with the Palomino Horse Association, Palomino Horse Breeders Association, or National Palomino Breeders Association, depending on their color and pedigrees. The PHBA is the largest, most formal and comprehensive in its rules.

Pintos also have two registries, the American Paint Horse and the American Pinto Registry.

Arabian Horses are recorded with the International Arabian Horse Association. Half-Arabs are recorded with this same body. An asterisk before a name denotes that an animal is imported.

Half-blooded horses of other breeds are usually recorded with the Part-blooded Riding Horse Registry.

Show Classifications

Roadster horses are shown either in harness or under saddle. The cart used for roadsters is called a *bike,* and is much like a regular racing sulky. The horses are shown at three speeds of the trot, and must maintain form and action as well as the distinctly different speeds of gait. They are shown with *stable colors,* which means a jacket and hat of matching color, usually silk or satin and belted at the waist.

Pleasure horses come in every breed and every color. In shows they are expected to be good examples of their breed, but not so highly strung or animated as the park or gaited horses.

Performance horses are now usually spoken of as working stock, reining, or roping horses.

Gymkhana horses and *game* horses are those for barrel racing, sit-a-buck, pole bending, and other games on horseback.

Stock horses are working cow horses, although years ago the term meant breeding horses.

Hack horses are those used for riding, often as riding-stable horses; but in the show ring the term is used to denote *hunter hacks* or *road hacks*. There are special classes for these horses, which include a *hand gallop* as one of their requirements. A hand gallop is a faster-than-usual canter, where the horse is supposed to be galloping "in the hand" and not simply turned loose to race. A real hand gallop is a controlled gait, balanced, and not especially tiring to the horse.

Trail horses are suitable for riding over rough terrain and obstacles, possibly but not necessarily in traffic, and in groups or alone. They should have a degree of soundness and training, but this is rapidly becoming a putdown term used by show people to denote any horse they consider too dull, unattractive, or plain to win in the show ring.

Competitive trail horses are those sound enough, fit enough, and schooled for actual competition.

Endurance horses are used for endurance racing, such as the twenty-four-hour 100-mile races held in many parts of the country.

Family pleasure horses are those suitable by their temperament and education to become pets and companions for a family. The term *back-yard* horse is often applied to this same kind. Show people mean to denote a horse that is not good enough for their chosen sport, but pleasure horse people take pride in such horses and believe them to be the backbone of the industry.

Temporary is a term used for horses that are registered on condition either of performance or of progeny. Some must meet a certain conformation requirement at maturity; some must race within a given time limit; while others must either develop a color or pattern or produce horses of the proper color before they are eligible for *Permanent* registry.

Cull is the term used for the removal from the herd of any individual which does not meet the criteria of that particular herd. Horses are culled because of color, disposition, soundness, conformation, pedigree, or any other quality that does not fit into the breeder's plans. A cull from one breeder's farm might be far more valuable than the best animal produced on his neighbor's, but the term *cull* is used in a most derogatory way as a rule. Breeders cull their herds in order to produce a uniform and constantly improving line. The reason the horse is for sale is often not mentioned, but is of importance. Some breeders try certain bloodlines, and if they do not happen to "nick" or cross well with their horses generally, the whole family is sold off (or culled), even if they are very nice individuals.

Sales

Sales are billed as *production:* selling of surplus stock; *reduction:* cutting down on whole herd size; *promotion:* gathering together of good animals to advertise and popularize a breed; *consignment:* where all the horses are sold for whatever reason the seller may have; and *livestock* sales: which include other animals besides horses, tack, and even tomatoes and TV sets. There are also *total dispersal* sales, where every animal on the farm is sold off. The quality of the animals varies from sale to sale, regardless of what a sale is called. Some breeds hold many auctions a year in various parts of the country, either privately or sponsored by groups of breeders. Some horses almost never turn up in auctions. In the Northeast it is very rare to see a registered Morgan or American Saddler go through a livestock sale, yet there are many of the Western breeds going through all the time.

Next come the terms which denote degrees of experience and training. A *novice* is anyone who has not gained experience in some particular field. Thus, I am considered by some to be an expert in farm management, breeding, or the like, but am a novice in innumerable fields, such as cutting horse, jumpers, racing, and dressage. To be called a novice is not an insult.

Beginners are people who are new to the world of horses. Experience cures this condition.

Amateurs are something to be wondered at. The American Horse Shows Association has become so intricate in its definition, changing it so many times within the past few years, that all I can say is that the term *amateur* is *intended* to define one who performs in a sport for fun, not for profit. I know professionals who have lots of fun in sports, and amateur card holders who are in the business entirely for money. However, the term *amateur horse* is supposed to denote a horse with manners that would be suitable for an amateur. The term *ladies' horse* means about the same thing. It denotes a horse that is not quite so bold or animated as an *"open" horse*—one that is able to compete successfully in classes open to professionals. Ladies' horses must be refined.

Limit and/or *maiden classes* are limited to horses who have not won a given number of blue ribbons at horse shows recognized by the American Horse Shows Association. These designations serve to make it possible to break up the classes into groups of horses and/or riders more nearly equal in ability and experience.

The terms *model, hand,* or *halter* horse refer to a horse that is shown posed in the style of the breed and judged on his conformation and sometimes on his way of going.

Honorable scars are those earned while the horse is in use, such as cuts on the legs from jumping.

Green is not a color in the horse world; it is a level of competition or degree of schooling. A *green hunter* is one that is eligible to show in classes limited to green hunters, and a *green broke* horse is one that is really just started in training of some sort and knows the basics but has lots of finishing work to do.

A horse with a *"hole in him"* has some sort of problem not necessarily evident on inspection; for example, one who shies violently.

Cold shoulders and *cold backs* refer to horses who will not lean into a harness or collar, or who hump up and sometimes buck when first saddled.

Stall courage is the frantic activity, sometimes bad manners and sometimes mistakenly called "spirited play," that a horse exhibits when taken from a stall in which he has been confined too long. It is pent-up energy, which is often explosive.

The classified colors are *black* (blk.), *bay* (b.), *chestnut* (ch.), *gray* (gr.), *brown* (br.), *dun* (dn.), *buckskin* (bu.), *white* (wh.), *paint* or *pinto* (pt.), *palomino* (pal.), *flaxen mane and tail* (f. m & t.). The shades of chestnut and bay may also be abbreviated, as in lv. for liver chestnut and bld. for blood bay, but this is not usual.

Colors

Generally, we call a *chestnut* anything that ranges from a red-gold shade down to a really black hide and black hair, but was chestnut as a foal. Light golden chestnuts are called *sorrel,* although the term used to signify a very dark chestnut. The very black-looking chestnuts are today called *black chestnuts* and are genetically chestnut horses. They can usually be identified if they are stood in bright sunlight and the hair about the coronets appears red or coppery. Chestnut horses frequently have dorsal stripes.

A *bay* horse is usually anything from a golden red to a brown body shade, with black mane, tail, legs, and points. If the body hair is black and the muzzle, flank, and hair about the eyes are sandy or light brown, the horse is then a true *brown,* not a bay or a black. Dorsal stripes are uncommon in true bay horses.

Blacks are a true rich black all over, including the muzzle and flank. Sometimes the hair inside the ears is sandy, but that is the only place. Blacks can be a true jet black or a fading or "fugitive color" which turns burned brown all over, in either the summer or the winter; but they are genetically black.

Gray horses are rarely born gray. They are usually bay or chestnut as foals and then gradually become gray in stages. There are many different kinds of gray: flea-bitten, rose, dappled, steel; some are so nearly white that people make no distinction and call them white. A true gray horse is born dark; a true white horse is born white. The Lippizaners, called the "great white horses of Austria," are actually gray horses; some never turn white.

Buckskins have a body coat some shade of yellow (gold to nearly brown) but not red. *Points* are black or dark brown. Dorsal stripes are not necessary.

Dun horses are shades of the same yellow, sometimes dull and sometimes nearly brown, with legs, mane, and tail that must be darker than the body color. In *red* duns, dorsal stripes must be present.

Palominos are golden horses with pure white, ivory, or silver manes, and tails and legs that are the same shade or lighter than the body color.

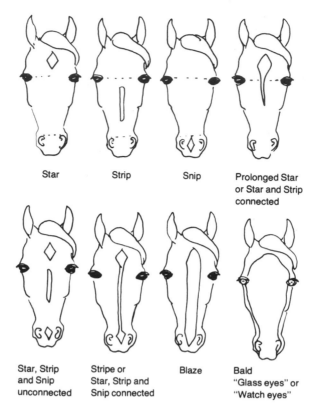

| Star | Strip | Snip | Prolonged Star or Star and Strip connected |

| Star, Strip and Snip unconnected | Stripe or Star, Strip and Snip connected | Blaze | Bald "Glass eyes" or "Watch eyes" |

Markings of the horse's face.

Markings

All of the above colors can have white markings. These markings have specific terms. A *star* is a white mark between and above the eyes. A *strip* is a mark between the eyes and nose down the face (the English call this a *race*). A *snip* is a white mark between the nostrils that may include the top of the upper lip. A connected combination of star, strip, and snip is called a *stripe* if it is narrow, a *blaze* if it is wide but no wider than the eyes, and *bald face* if the white does extend beyond the eyes.

White feet are designated as *white coronet*, just a thin bracelet of white; or *white spot* on heel or coronet. *Short sock* or *pastern* is limited to the pastern and coronet. *Sock* or *fetlock* includes the fetlock, pastern, and coronet. *Half stocking* is a white leg halfway up the cannon bone. *Stocking* is a full stocking, up to the hock or knee.

Markings that are uneven are further described as extending up the back or front of the cannon, fetlock, hock, or knee, depending on their shape.

Individual spots of white are called *body spots*. They are described as to shape and location.

Roan hair is white hair intermingled with the body coat. Sometimes the roan is a light sprinkling barely noticeable in the coat; at other times the roaning is so heavy that it changes the apparent color of the horse and can even be concentrated in what appears to be white spots. These spots can enlarge and increase with age, making a horse solid-colored at birth look pinto in old age. Bay horses heavily roaned are called *strawberry roan* and they look really strawberry pink. *Claybank roan* is a roaned palomino. *Blue roan* is a black horse with heavy roaning. Chestnut horses that are roan are called *red roan* horses.

The foregoing markings are those usually associated with the solid-colored breeds. Some colored breeds have special patterns and colors. Pintos and paints come in two styles of spots: *tobiano* and *overo;* Appaloosas have three main patterns: *blanket, leopard,* and *snow-flake.* Anyone interested in delving further into the color breeds should write to their breed registries for informative literature. The British use the term *piebald* for black and white spotted horses, and *skewbald* for any colors other than black and white. They also term the black spots on a white sock found on some horses' coronets *ermine marks.*

Lastly come the *man-made markings* and *accidental markings.* These are caused when the skin is branded—either by fire or by freezing—or when the skin is abraded or broken in an accident or by constant rubbing and pressure from ill-fitting equipment. No matter how the damage is done, the result is that white, rough hair, or hair of a different texture, grows in place of the mark. The hair-producing follicles in the skin are damaged, and while usually they do produce hair of some sort, there are times when new hair never grows and the spot remains bald.

Horses are branded or tattooed for a number of reasons. Farm or ranch ownership symbols have been a part of the American scene since the West was wrested from the Indians; Europeans brand their horses to indicate their breed. The Lippizaners have an L branded on the cheek and another brand under the saddle, while Trackeners have a brand called a double elk shovel. We brand horses to identify them as individuals, either by tattooing on the upper lip or by putting numbers on the neck, which are often freeze-branded. These sometimes include the horse's registration number or part of it. Some states are now branding horses found to carry a titer in their blood for EIA or swamp fever. These have an A somewhere in the brand, which indicates anemia, and such horses may not be shipped interstate. Army mounts used to carry a brand on the neck, but I doubt whether there are very many of them left now.

Let me finish with some relevant questions you should now ask yourself in order to get a better idea of the information you need from the seller.

Here is a check list to start you thinking.

I will use my horse mostly for _____
I may also use him for _____
I want a _____ [breed or type]
I prefer the colors _____ but know that these are not essential.
I prefer a size range of _____ to _____
I want an age range of _____ to _____
My price range is _____
I have had enough experience for a horse with _____ training.
I am/am not willing to take further lessons myself. _____
The horse must be sound to _____ degree.
I will/will not care for the horse alone most of the time. _____
I will/will not be riding in the company of other horses. _____

When the seller has volunteered this information, here are some more detailed questions for him:

Will the horse stand tied by a single rope? _____ In crossties? _____
Will he load into a trailer or truck? _____ And ride quietly? _____
Can I handle all his feet? _____ (How about on a trail where he can't be tied?) _____
Has he ever been alone in a stable or pasture? _____
Is he safe to turn out with other horses? _____
Is he good in company with other horses on a ride? _____
If I ride near a highway, can I expect him to be good about traffic? _____
Will he cross water, such as a puddle or stream? _____
Is he trained to drive? _____ Ride? _____ English; forward, saddle, or dressage; Western? _____

How many previous owners has he had?*_____

What kind of bit should I use on him? _____

What are his signals for a walk, trot, canter?_____

Has he any habit or vice that may cause trouble?_____

Has he ever been shown?_____

Is there a guarantee with this horse?_____ How long?_____

What terms?_____

Does his cost include transfer of papers and/or transportation?_____

Do I have to pay board on him until I can arrange to get him shipped home? _____

Does he need special shoes or other special considerations? _____

Has he ever stood in a box or tie stall?_____

(Some horses cannot be locked in a barn at all.)

Can I clean his stall while he is in it?_____

Is there any special thing that frightens him?_____

There will be other questions for specific horses, and you will doubtless develop a personal list of quite a few things you want to know.

*For registered horses, this is recorded on the back of the registration papers with each transfer.

CHAPTER 7

What Kind of Horse
Do You Want?

I AM A BREEDER OF Morgan horses and am therefore inclined to prefer that breed. It was not always so. I started out like any other horse-mad girl—anything with a mane and tail was perfection. Gradually, I realized that there were different breeds of horses and I developed strong loyalties to first one breed, then another. Raffles was my hero in my Arabian phase, and Man O' War held no equal while I was enamored of Thoroughbreds. I am still a fan of Cutter Bill, a famous Quarter Horse, and will always admire beauty, performance, and true perfection in any horse of any breed. However, with greater experience, often it is easier to find faults than perfection. I am not a wholehearted admirer of every Morgan just because it is a Morgan. My eye has become more selective, and my taste has narrowed the field to certain families and certain individuals within those families. The more you know about horses, the more you tend to focus on the kind that suits you personally. However, that should never interfere with an ability to appreciate the good in all breeds, nor with the pleasure in watching others enjoying the breed of their choice. People differ in temperament, physical abilities, and interests. Horses come in varities to suit everyone.

Horses usually are divided into four main categories: work horses, sport horses, show horses, and pleasure horses. Once you know why a breed was developed, you are more likely to understand what you want in a horse and how to go about finding your ideal horse. The problem for the beginner is that he is not truly aware of his own abilities, nor of the sort of horse that will help him most to develop his skill as a horseman.

The vast majority of horses owned in the United States today are maintained as personal pleasure horses. There is no breed which was originally developed solely for that purpose. It is perfectly possible to find a horse of any breed or mixture of breeds that suits you. This chapter will serve as a rough guide to help bring each breed into clearer focus. There are over 100 registered breeds of horses and ponies, innumerable crosses between the breeds, and mongrels with no traceable pedigree. Within the breeds, there are differing types again. No breed of horse just developed spontaneously and formed its own registry, standards, or rules for registration. Each was developed slowly to perform some specific function.

When settlers came to our shores in the sixteenth century, they brought horses with them—there were none here at the time. The horses they brought were draft horses to do their heavy hauling and carting, and saddle horses to ride. There were many strains of horses in those days, but only the Arabians and the Blood Horses, the start of what is now called Thoroughbreds, were of recorded ancestry, although the Welsh and Cleveland Bays are thought to have been documented. There was no American Jockey Club or U.S. Trotting Association. All the American registries for purebred horses have been formed since the Revolutionary War. The American Saddle Horse Breeders Association, for instance, was incorporated in 1891; while the first volume of the American Morgan Horse Register was published in 1894, with histories and recorded pedigrees of nearly 2,000 Morgans.

The horses brought to these shores were good animals. The risk and expense of importation over a rough ocean in small boats made it essential to limit the shipments to only the best. So selection for good qualities started before the new American breeding stock ever landed on our shores.

Many were war horses. Courage and soundness, hardiness and manageability, were all considered in the selection of animals to be used in the cavalry, where a man's life could depend upon his horse. Cavalry officers' mounts were almost the only horses used primarily for riding; the rest were harness horses.

Horse breeding was a profitable business. There was a tremendous demand for good horses to do many tasks and to move westward with the push into new territory. A man bred his mare in the locality where he lived. He could not ship her out to a stallion at a distance. Stallions traveled from town to town, servicing mares at the crossroads. It would be announced that a certain stallion would stand at one man's stable one week and another's the following week. Any mares that showed up at the stable to meet him were the mares he serviced; but it was not chance mating. The best stallions attracted the best mares, and their "get," the foals, went on to produce the next generations. The horses were not purebreds, as the animals were of all types and kinds. Only by gradual selection was there any differentiation between one family, then one strain, and then one distinct type and another. What we call American breeds today are all simply divisions of what those assorted horses produced.

Arabian horses and their close relatives, the Barbs, Andalusians and Turks, came to America and mated with English, Dutch, and French horses. The Spaniards added Jennets, Sorraia (which were buckskins), and Palominos. Without trying to establish superiority on the basis of which came first or did what famous deeds, let's take a look at *why* we have the Morgan Horse, the Standardbred, the American Saddle Horse, the Tennessee Walking Horse, and the Quarter Horse. They all started basically at the same time, from the same stock, and survived only because each fulfilled specific purposes. One was not then and is not now superior in any way, except for the purposes for which it was bred.

In the 1700s, the farmers of New England wanted a horse that was compact in stature, surefooted, and extremely hardy. He had to do anything and everything. The Morgan Horse was an obvious development of the time and place. This horse was never a specialist. He was a ride/drive/race/show horse right from the start. A farmer had to cut down the trees on a piece of property and haul the logs to the mill; he had to pick up all the stones from his rocky fields and drag them to the edges, where he made his endless stone walls. He had

Walking Horse.

to plow the rough soil in order to plant. His horse had to bend his neck into a heavy harness and work from dawn to dark, and he had to do it every day of the year except Sundays and muster days. Often that horse was the only horse the farmer had. He had to serve as a carriage horse to take the family to do the marketing and go to church, and then just for the fun and the pride of it, he often became a racehorse along the way. This same horse also carried his owner in parades, showed at the great agricultural fairs, and produced foals each year as well.

"Brushes," or impromptu races between friends and neighbors (even the ministers couldn't resist), were a diversion from the difficult and often frustrating lives of these hardy New Englanders. When a horse established some kind of reputation for speed, he gave his master a position among the townspeople. The ladies were impressed by young men who drove fast trotters, and racing in harness developed steadily as the major diversion for the area. Doctors, especially, valued the hardy, fast trotting horses for getting them from patient to patient in all kinds of weather. Remember, in those days everyone was a horseman, because everyone relied upon the horse for transport and labor. The horse who had ability was respected and was sought for breeding. Beauty was considered an added plus, but without the ability to work or race to earn his keep, a beautiful horse was dismissed as a useless frivolity and quickly shipped to the city market to become a carriage horse or hack. So the Morgan developed, with his varied abilities as well as his beauty.

As life became easier, farms were established, roads improved, and there was more leisure time. The craze for speed increased and those Morgan Horses which had become famous for their trotting speed were celebrated personalities of their day, much like the movie stars and super sports stars today. More and more of these good fast Morgans were used for breeding harness racing horses, and at one point

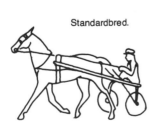

Standardbred.

American Saddle Horse.

in history, Morgans established and held every harness track record for speed in the country, records which remained in some cases for over a century. Then a homely-headed, evil-tempered Blood Horse named Abdallah was bred to a crippled mare who was far from a breeder's dream. The resulting foal, Rysdic's Hambletonian, was the butt of jokes, with his Roman nose and ungainly long hind legs. As a racehorse he was unimpressive, to say the least. But all of a sudden, he was catapulted into the spotlight as a sire of speed. Hambletonian was never sought to reproduce more horses just like himself; he was of value on Morgan mares of great speed, adding the long hind legs —set well back on the body—that gave the tremendous driving force to the trot and pace of the Standardbred, making them the undefeated harness racehorses of the world. So successful was he that the Standardbred is often called Hambletonian in his honor.

Riding on a horse's back in a race was considered decadent and immoral, and was actually even illegal in much of the Northeast. But riding horses for long-distance travel and for carrying messages and news was within the bounds of decency. The distance traveled on horseback in daily living is staggering to the modern imagination. Many of the trails were impassible with vehicles. There was an active trade in goods from the Northern states down the coast into the plantation states. The horses selected by the men who rode these long distances were easy-gaited, pleasant, and enduring. Even these had to be able to pull a light carriage and so were not exclusively saddle animals. They could be Arabians, Morgans, Narragansett Pacers, Blood Horses (ancestor of our own Thoroughbred), or mixtures. They were often identified by the name of their closest famous ancestors, such as a Black Hawk or a Diomed. In 1891, a registry was set up in Kentucky to record the names of horses best suited to this use while most nearly meeting their specific conformation standards. They chose horses of known blood or families, and designated them foundation sires for the American Saddle Horse. They aimed for a taller, finer, more elegant breed than any yet known. They regarded the amble, pace, and singlefoot superior gaits for comfort under saddle. They set standards for judging these horses in the show ring. That they have been successful in their aims is evident to anyone who hangs on the rail of a show ring and cheers for his favorite five-gaited horses who swing into that thrilling gait called the "rack."

The Tennessee Walking Horse, the "Plantation Walker," and the

Missouri Fox Trotter are Southern developments of Saddlebred, Narragansett Pacer, and Morgan ancestry. The foundation stallion of the Tennessee Walking breed was a Morgan named Allen F1. These horses are even more easy-gaited, their action less brilliant or precise, than the American Saddle Horse. They were bred to travel over large "soft-footed" fields where overseers checked the progress in the cotton fields. The Walker is a heavier, less elegant horse, but otherwise very like the Saddlebred. Properly built and properly trained, he does not trot at all, but travels in an unbelievably smooth, undulating "running walk" unique to this breed. The gait of the Walker is performed in a rhythmic, swinging style, often with a nodding head, clicking teeth, and flopping ears, as the horse floats along. In his own element, the good pleasure-type Walking Horse has no equal for smoothness, and the gait covers a remarkable amount of ground with seemingly no effort on the horse's part. The breed was known and being used during the Civil War although the registry was not formalized until 1935.

At the time when men were pushing back the frontiers, they valued the hard-working, rugged, tightly made horses of New England; but they also had a thirst for saddle racing, and so they took with them the best horses that could do a day's work under saddle, pull their weight in a hitch, and also turn on a good burst of speed on a quarter mile of roadway. The riders with their Morgans, Saddle Horses, Blood Horses, and "short racers" from Virginia colonies, descendants of a Blood Horse named Janus, met with horses brought to the West by Cortéz and other Spanish conquistadors. Many of these had been stolen by the Indians and were being bred selectively. Others had broken loose or had run off from battle when their riders had fallen, and were roaming in herds as wild horses. In 1940, ranchers and sportsmen gathered in a meeting to establish a breed of horse called the Quarter Horse. They selected horses of Morgan blood, Thoroughbred blood, and mixtures of well-established and proven short racers and working stock horses. They set up two stan-

Morgan.

Quarter Horse.

dards: one of conformation, and one of performance, and established the American Quarter Horse Association. The Quarter Horse type became fixed and recognizable as a breed with astonishing speed. Today, the "Quarter Horse look" is the standard look for several of the "color breeds." The same close-to-the-ground, heavily muscled build that got the racing short runners off the mark in Virginia is also the conformation that suited them ideally to stopping, turning, herding, and working cattle in the West. This same build, with the powerful legs well slung under the body, has proved good for jumping as well. So here you see the American breeds of horses fanning off the basic stock of imported horses like fingers off a hand, each finger growing in its own shape and each performing specific functions that gave rise to its existence. They are different, but they are all firmly rooted in the same palm.

As the fingers of one's hand radiate from one common palm, so the breeds of American horses spring from common ancestors. Each finger of one's hand is shaped as it is for a particular use, and each horse has developed in its own way to serve some special purpose for man.

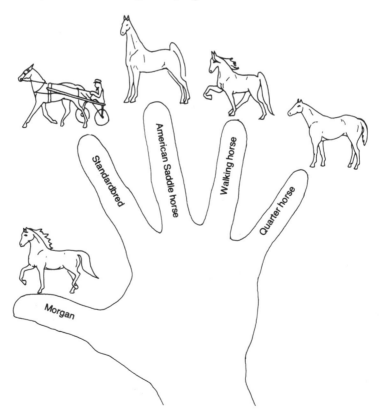

I have left the "color breeds" to the last, for they are really variations of the major breeds outlined above. While some claim historic
origins as far back as the Ming Dynasty in China or the first snowfall
in Norway, there is no solid link of blood to prove ancestry—only a
similarity of color or patterns. Probably the first "colored" horses
brought here in any significant number were the Palominos, the
golden horses with the silver manes and tails. These were a symbol
of wealth and favor with the royal family of Spain, for a Spaniard had
to either have permission to own a Palomino, or actually receive the
horse as a royal gift. Horses of most breeds can be palomino color.
Therefore, the Palomino breeders have wisely never claimed that
there is only one breed called Palomino. They have formed registries, so that every horse that bears this lovely coloration can be
recorded. The aim is to learn more about the genetics that produced
the color and the patterns of families that carry the genes, and to
improve conformation and beauty for all horses registered within the
stud books.

There are two registries which record pinto, paint, or parti-colored
horses. One is primarily aimed at recording spotted horses with
Quarter Horse conformation, and the other, an older association,
recognizes that there are many good types of horse that can have the
added "frosting" of the brightly colored pintos. Not all American
breeds can be spotted. In the Morgan registry, any indication of
Appaloosa or pinto marking, even stockings that are a little too long
or a single misplaced dab of white, eliminates a purebred Morgan
from registry. Quarter Horse registers do not accept pinto marking
either. Many good Arabians have an isolated spot on the side of the
abdomen; but these single white random patches do not make the
horses paint or pinto horses and, in fact, a horse can be refused
registration in both the spotted registries for insufficient white markings.

The Appaloosa people may be able to claim more of a true breed
than the other color registries, and indeed in America, years ago, the
Appaloosa was a blood-related and carefully established breed.
Horses with markings of the Appaloosa are recorded in history in the
Orient and in cave dwellings, and there are German, Dutch, and
other European horses with the same patterns of spots. But Appaloosa in this country signifies a strain of horses bred in the Northwest by the Nez Percé Indians on the Palouse River, and these horses

were cherished as fierce war horses. The Indians were superb horse-men and they wanted a horse so tough, enduring, and bold that if the Indian was killed, the horse would go on fighting. The spirit and strength of the horses they bred was so impressive that it was a long time before the Nez Percé Indians were finally defeated. Later, the breeding of these horses by the Indians dispersed and crossed on all other Western horses, so that now Appaloosas vary in size, shape, temperament, and color to such an extent that it would be impossible to say that they are all directly blood-related. It is still possible to register an Appaloosa who has only one Appaloosa parent and the other of a riding horse breed of any mixture. This register was started in 1938, two years before the Quarter Horse register.

The beautiful American Albino or American White Horse is an-other deliberately created breed. Ruth and Caleb Thompson started to breed white horses in 1947, from a pure white stallion who was of Arab-Morgan breeding. He passed on his color and his good traits of conformation and temperament, and they set about to build a band of pure white horses using him, a few other white horses, and a band of Morgan mares. The purpose was to breed a uniform-look-ing, highly tractable, pleasant-natured band of white horses which are marvelous as circus performers and parade horses. The register also maintains a separate section for off-white horses and for those that show no indication of their white breeding. The genetic infor-mation they store will be invaluable, since horse color is one area where no one has done a really significant amount of research to date.

In 1963 a new color group formed, the American Buckskin Regis-try Association. The color is an ancient one, the original color of all wild horses. There are two very old and well-documented breeds of horses, the Norwegian Dun, and the Spanish Sorraia. Most respected strains of dun-colored horses in America are supposed to have come from these sturdy equines. The West has spawned many legends and recorded many facts in its folklore about the toughness of the dun- and buckskin-colored horse, which is universally accepted among many of the working cowboys. Wisely, these people are again inter-ested in gathering information and trying to establish reliable ways of breeding good horses of this color, not in making any wild claims that all horses of this color are necessarily related. The dun and buckskin colors can appear, like the palomino color, in all registered

American breeds of horses, and in Arabians and other breeds of all nations.

Let's look at the breeds as they are today. They have all undergone some form of metamorphosis. The Morgan started first. His speed in harness was almost his undoing, for many whole families were swallowed up into the Standardbred registry and lost to the Morgan registry. The advent of the tractor, cross-country trucks, automobiles, and trains reduced the Morgan's value as a draft and commerce animal. Stage coaches and fine carriages became things of the past, and the Morgan, having always been a jack-of-all-trades, was suddenly considered a horse with no specialty. But the Morgan's endurance earned him a place in the breeding of army remount horses for the cavalry. The U.S. government bred Morgans to be a taller, better saddle type. A group of old-time Morgan men, fearing that the breed type would vanish, bought up much of the good stock available. They proceeded to establish what is now called the Old Type Morgan—a short, stocky, trappy-gaited type. Others who wished to preserve the Morgan started to show against American Saddlebreds and then gradually got classes for Morgans into the show ring.

Thirty years ago, if you traveled across the country, it was possible to find Morgans who looked like refined, long-necked Saddlebreds; short, squat, pony-like creatures; draft horse miniatures working on Midwest farms; tall, long-striding army horses; and stocky, fast-working cattle horses. On the West Coast, Arabian horses were being added to the Morgan strain. The Morgan identity was vanishing. And so, in 1948, the registry was closed. From then on, only horses with both parents fully registered with the Morgan Horse Club could be granted registration papers. A standard of perfection was published and distributed to all breeders. Everyone took a long and serious look at his breeding program and selected the best, most conforming stock to continue producing horses. The result was a tremendous surge back to the look of Justin Morgan and his famous sons.

The metamorphosis went on differently with other breeds. The Saddlebred was bred to be a long-distance horse, and he had to be a sensible, enduring horse who could negotiate rough roads and bad weather. As life grew easier, the horse's utility as a working animal became less important than his finesse and elegance. When he gained momentum in the show ring as the most perfect example of grace and style, he also developed a more high-strung and nervous temperament. The fad of setting tails, of showing the horses in an artificial manner, increased his image as a man-manipulated thing of beauty. Society, ego, prestige, status, and money all are part of the show ring world, and the American Saddle Horse became the most revered of all show animals. So stiff was the competition that soon only the wealthy could play the game, and gradually the American Saddle Horse became a specialist in the ring for the "very upper" of the upper crust in the horse world. Less affluent horsemen turned to showing Morgans, Arabs, and Quarter Horses. The numbers of horses that used to fill the classes for Saddlebreds diminished to the point where horse shows no longer held classes for them in many areas, while other breeds had whole divisions of classes. The Saddlebred people realized that they were losing popularity, and so they started to encourage the showing of Saddlebreds as pleasure horses. Now the Saddlebred Pleasure Horse division at shows is beginning to fill, and more and more Saddlebreds are being bred to look and act like their forebears, the long-distance, easy-gaited progenitors of the breed.

The pendulum has swung for the Quarter Horse also. He was a racehorse to start with, but with distinctly different overtones from his Thoroughbred ancestors. For a period, the style for the Quarter Horse was very short and compact. The term "Bulldog type" was applied to these rugged, useful animals. But racing money has a strong pull and horses must go faster and faster to stay ahead of their competition. The Bulldog Quarter Horse simply can't run as fast as the Thoroughbred, after all, and so gradually more and more Thoroughbred stock has been added to the ranks of the Quarter Horse. The breed is becoming a racehorse to reckon with, more strung out than it used to be (they like the term "streamlined"). Taller and more angular Quarter Horses now place in "model" halter classes, setting the style for more Thoroughbred admixture in the future. So a breed has come away from its former mold, full circle, only to return again.

All the horse breeds, like people, are taller now than they were centuries ago. Thoroughbreds, the tallest of all breeds, were a mere 14.3 to 15.3 hands in the 1800s; Secretariat is 17 hands tall. Saddlebreds have an average of 15.2 through 16.2 hands. Arabians can be found as tall as 16.3 on occasion, as can Morgans and Quarter Horses, although these three breeds have been traditionally 14.1 through 15.2 hands. Today, people are taller than their forebears and so there is a tendency to breed taller horses. However, children still start out short. There is a very active demand for horses barely taller than pony size (14.2), and it is not impossible to find Thoroughbreds, Saddlebreds, and Standardbreds no taller than 14 hands!

Some breeds are more uniform than others. There is less variation in Arabians, Thoroughbreds, and Saddlebreds, for instance, than in the Morgans and Quarter Horses. The Quarter Horse book is still open to the addition of certain Thoroughbreds, for there is a concerted effort on the part of many breeders to increase speed, height, and the comfort of gait. The color breeds have open books since in most cases only one parent must be registered.

But generalities must always be viewed with care. Each horse has individual personal traits, either inherited or environmental, which cannot be called breed characteristics. Up to this point, I have discussed mainly the physical differences between the breeds. Certain traits of conformation make certain kinds of performance possible. The more suited to his work the conformation is, the more likely it is that the horse will be tops in his breed. Through selection of the best-formed horse for the purpose, each breed continues to improve in its ability to perform its special function. This is the basis of selective breeding.

But conformation alone is not the whole story. The various tasks the horse performs require specific types of temperament too. Hence a certain type of temperament is right for each given breed. A racehorse is "hot." A show horse has "presence" and a certain brittleness of nature. A working stock horse is forceful, almost belligerent in his attitude, for he must stand up to stubborn and determined cattle. A versatile jack-of-all-trades must be flexible, rather easygoing, but at the same time energetic and willing to try new things. So we can clearly state that, as a generality, certain breeds are more likely to yield better horses for beginners than other breeds. Yet in every breed there are "mental misfits," which are not suited to anything at all. In every breed, there are "hot" individuals and "mild" individuals. And it must also be made absolutely clear that temperament (hotness or mildness) is not to be confused with disposition. There are many hot racehorses and show horses who are gentle, loving, and sweet-natured. There are many "dead quiet" horses who are actually just lazy and sullen, not sweet and gentle as they appear on the surface. These differences are not breed characteristics. They are disposition traits which are either inherited or the result of experiences—traits that are unique to each horse.

To say a horse is "hot" is not a criticism; to say a horse is ugly, mean, bad-mannered, or unmanageable is something else entirely. Hotness is not only desirable; it is essential in certain circumstances. But if you are a beginner looking for a first horse, it would be wise to look for one not quite so hot, and it might well be sensible practice to avoid the hot breeds altogether.

All horse breeders prefer their own breed, often to the exclusion of other breeds. Many people can only appreciate what they have by thinking no one else has anything good at all. I breed Morgans. I like them better than all the other great and interesting and beautiful breeds of horses, because they *suit* me. They offer what I seek in a horse. You may well like some other breed. I have no argument with that; that is why there are different breeds in the first place. This very difference is what makes America so exciting, interesting, and varied —our horses are truly American. The only horse that will ever suit you personally is the one that is right for you in size, style, temperament, training, and personality. That is something only you can decide. Don't let anyone else's prejudice keep you from looking at a horse that interests you. It might be just the right horse for you.

CHAPTER 8

Will This Horse Suit You?

ONCE YOU HAVE NARROWED the field down to some of the types or breeds that will suit your needs, you will be anxious to select a horse. This and the next chapter deal with certain aspects of personal variation among individual animals. Regardless of breed or kind of animal, it is an individual horse that you are buying, not the reputation of a breed.

Temperament

The horse must suit you in many ways. But first and foremost comes his temperament.

Temperament is the "hotness" or degree of spirit, liveliness, mettlesomeness, or boldness a horse has at birth. Some horses are born hot, others are born docile or placid; most horses are between the extremes. There is a certain kind of temperament that is right for a breed: Arabians, Thoroughbreds, Standardbreds, and racing Quarter Horses are among those breeds considered temperamentally hot. The next in line are the most highly competitive Saddlebreds, Walkers, and park Morgans. More temperamentally steady horses are the Morgans, which are bred for versatility, working-stock-type Quarter Horses, pleasure Saddlebreds, and the mixed-bred Hunters. There is a wide range of temperament in every breed. If you find a horse that is a top example of his breed, he will have the temperament which suits him to the work he was bred for. If you find a horse with all the physical qualifications of his kind, yet who lacks the "fire" to be a top show horse or racehorse, you may have a very good bargain for a beginner or for a noncompetitive owner who wants a quality animal. It is equally likely that you might find a horse who has the temperament to be a show or racehorse, but not enough of the other physical attributes to make him valuable. He is not likely to be of much value to you.

No matter how fine, well-bred, sound, trained, or beautiful the horse is, if his temperament is either too hot or too placid you will not be satisfied. Novices often purchase horses that are just too hot for their amount of experience, and the horse becomes a challenge. Some accept the challenge, become better educated and more proficient, but others find the horse a constant chore to control, an intimidating animal whose size and strength seem to increase with time. Yes, there is such a thing as a horse that is "too much for you."

Conversely, buying a horse that is dull, sullen, and stubborn can be just as discouraging. In some cases, a lazy horse is a danger; but you are more likely to get bored than anything else. Worried mothers who insist on a dull-as-dishwater mount for the ambitious and daring teen-ager often find themselves stableboy to an unwanted back-yard pet, while the son or daughter goes out looking for more exciting things to do.

On the other hand, horses who are lazy but firm-minded are sometimes wonderful for very small children, because the child is never really able to make the horse go faster than a jog, farther than a few miles, or longer than an hour or so. Then the horse has had enough and takes the child home.

Disposition

Disposition has nothing whatsoever to do with temperament. A horse can be as hot as a pistol and still have a perfectly sweet and cheerful disposition. Some show stallions who would seem to be unmanageable while they are strutting their stuff are children's playmates in their home stable. Racehorses are sometimes too valuable to be culled because of their dispositions, since speed is money, and the professionals who handle these horses know what they are about. There is no excuse to keep an ugly-natured horse for any other reason. Certainly, in breeding stock, disposition should be a prime consideration, for it is without doubt an inheritable trait.

NERVOUSNESS

Nervousness is another emotional trait that is often confused with temperament and disposition. (Nervous energy falls into a separate category, and can be useful or wearing; nervous energy may be the essence of temperament.) Nervousness, in the sense of being jittery, flighty, or what horsemen call "spooky," is a useless and dangerous kind of trait. A horse that is constantly shying, running away, or looking about for "tigers to jump out from behind bushes" is unreliable.

The nervous horse will dither and fret when he should just stand and relax. He will champ at his bit, not from eager spirit but from mindless worrying. He will be hard to keep, hard to condition, and hard to train. Nervousness may be a symptom of worms and discomfort, and sometimes is an indication of vitamin B deficiency, which can be completely cured by proper therapy. Some horses are "antsy" —they find it hard to stand still. It takes a little longer to get them to settle down and pay attention, but they are capable of doing so. They are usually smart, just a little bratty and irksome. Every horse will show nervousness if something new and threatening appears. Some stand, snort, or rattle their nostrils, quiver and bug their eyes, while others just dive for the nearest exit. Some are so bold that they look, arch their necks, and then go and sniff the offending object, and finally attack it with front feet. This kind of horse is not likely to hurt a rider in an emergency. He will stand his ground.

Manners

If you have experience and can move with the animal, grooming and saddling him on the fly, you may make some allowances; but most people prefer a horse to stand still on the crossties while they work on him. The veterinarian and farrier have too much to do to have to cope with someone's spoiled pet, and some refuse to work on a fidgety horse. Regardless of how high-strung they are, animals *can* be taught manners. A little moving about is excusable, but you should not have to try to land a saddle on a flying target or reach for a lead and find the withers where the head was a moment ago. The horse should be able to relax; if he can't, you may have a problem. Remember that if he is not relaxed in a familiar place, he will be much worse in a strange place with new handlers.

Manners should not be confused with temperament or disposition. A bad-tempered, sullen-natured, or hot horse can have perfect manners if he is skillfully trained. Manners are not inheritable at all, although some horses are far easier to school for good manners than others because of their willingness and ability to learn. A horse's manners are affected by everyone who handles him. One that is started out perfectly as a foal by a competent handler can very quickly be spoiled by poor handling. Except when panic-stricken, a horse can well control his behavior and suit his manners to the person handling him, being faultless with one and devilish with another. So manners are often tempered by disposition.

Manners encompass the total range of the horse's experience. The horse should be educated about the barn, on the trail or in the ring, in the pasture and in transportation. Many horses are safe enough as long as you have a line on them, but when turned out in a paddock will kick or run at you. Some horses are fine in a field but claustrophobic in a stall, tightening up, turning their haunches, or trying to hide in a corner when someone enters their stall. This is usually the result of a bad experience, but again, for the beginner, such behavior can be very dangerous. With experience, you can learn what moves are threatening to the horse and avoid them; but while everything is new to you, you are bound to make a few mistakes.

The Timid Horse

Let me put in a word for horses who lay their ears down when they want affection, food, or attention. All flattened ears do not indicate a mean horse. Some horses put back their ears defensively if someone comes near their stall, hoping to frighten the intruder and be left alone. It can be the bluff of a timid horse, not necessarily an aggressive action. Stand and observe, talking to the horse in a gentle tone, but stay well out of reach. If he is bluffing, he will often snap at the walls, rake his teeth on wire, or toss his head and snort. I always feel very sorry for horses who seem obliged to make such a display. They have been hurt or frightened sometime in their lives.

Other Clues

The expression in the horse's eyes is the best clue to his state of mind. If he stands in his stall with his head down, one foot cocked, and his ears at half-mast, he may be completely relaxed in his nice safe stall or even asleep. When he comes out of the stall he may still be groggy, still perfectly relaxed and content to be handled by people, even strangers. If he has no reason to be afraid, he may stay relaxed and placid while he is being groomed and saddled, but he should begin to wake up and start to look around as he realizes he is going to work. He should stand for hitching to cart or mounting and be ready to move off, alert for a command, but equally ready to wait until told to move. His responses should be quick enough to be satisfying, but not so swift or violent as to make you suspect nervous anticipation or fear. If his performance under saddle or in harness shows no more brilliance than in his stall or the crossties, you have a very dull horse to contend with. On the other hand, the horse who fusses and frets, rolls his eyes in his stall, shifts and dances about in the crossties, won't stand for mounting and then rushes into his performance, is not for the average horseman, either.

Some horses are lovely to handle, ride, drive, and care for, but are so herd-bound that they cannot stand to be alone. Separated from other horses, they fret and get so frantic that they become violent. Ask if the horse you are considering has ever been away from a herd. If you do buy one that hasn't been alone, make arrangements for the horse to be separated from the other horses for a week before you attempt to keep him alone at your stable. This is not to say that you should reject a horse because he has never been away from home; but you should bend every effort to make the transition to your ownership as easy and untraumatic as you can.

Some horses try out prospective buyers while the buyers are trying them out. They will check how alert you are, how good you are at discipline, how much they can push you around before you get really mad. I have a little mare in my herd that checks everyone out just a bit each day to see if he is with it or not. She doesn't bother with me, for she knows I am not one for her jokes, but she rattles everyone's cage if she can. She is not mean and has never hurt anyone. She just pretends to be wicked, then rolls her eyes and acts as if she is frightened if you scold her. She is not afraid of a thing. She wiggles and shakes her head to intimidate people and her antics are effective. No one likes to ride her, even though she is well trained and never does a thing wrong. So attitude on the part of a horse plays a great part in your pleasure in daily handling. Playfulness such as this is fine if you have a sense of humor and a good deal of self-confidence, and can see through the bluffing and shadowboxing. But for a timid handler, this mare could quickly take the upper hand and become useless. Her eyes dance and sparkle, and she has a sly expression that is a dead giveaway of her mentality.

Other clues to personality and nervousness are signs of stall weaving, pawing, and chewing in the stall. Observe how the handlers approach and handle the horse. Have them lead out more than just the horse you want to see, in order to find out whether all the horses are handled the same way. Some handlers put a chain over the nose of every horse they lead. We never use a chain on anything, except one stallion when we use him for breeding. Some handlers do not even own a chain shank, and others carry a whip or crop at all times. I visited a farm one day and the owner, before opening the first stall, took a gaiting whip off the rack and a chain shank. I was a little reluctant to enter the stall of his stallion until I saw he used the butt of the whip as he talked for making a point in conversation. Each time he made a final statement, he gently bopped the poor horse on the tip of his nose! It was obvious that the horses in that stable just accepted a whip as part of their owner's anatomy, not as a device for discipline at all. So the handler's manner will help you to determine the nature of the horse; but observe quietly and don't jump to conclusions.

You should be able to walk into the horse's stall alone. You should then be able to put a halter on his head, attach a lead rope, and lead him quietly out of the stall and into the crossties. He should permit you to lift his feet and handle him all over. If you can't do it in the security of his own home, how can you expect to handle him alone in a strange place? Do not convince yourself that with a little practice you will both learn together, unless the horse is under two years old. You should insist that you be allowed to lead the horse about, to see your car, look at a barrel or trash can, and to have him step on a grain bag or board or some other object under foot that is safe but unusual to the horse.

Sense and Courage

Bring a stack of newspapers, an umbrella, a sheet of plastic, or a trash barrel liner. You can lay some newspapers in a line on the ground so that the horse cannot side-step around them. Lead him to them, stop, then lead him over the paper line. An intelligent horse will look at any new object, sniff it, and then try it gingerly. A stupid horse will either go over such a thing without a look or else blow up and run. You obviously want a horse that has brains enough to check before he rejects an idea. Some horses are terrified of plastic and of snow jackets that rustle. I cannot go out in the rain in a plastic poncho and catch my old stallion—the noise of the rain hitting it frightens him for some reason. I do not pretend to know what makes a horse fear a certain thing, but I do know they all have one thing or another that will take their attention, and some are actually afraid while others are simply intrigued and curious. Try to judge the sense and courage of a horse before you bring him home.

His Education

Education is another variable in horses. Not every two-year-old is trained to harness; not every three-year-old is started in saddle work. In some cases, the horse has been an early or late maturer and training has been advanced or held off accordingly. In other cases, the horse has just been left because the owner has not had the time or skill to devote to training. Some horses have had too much training too early, driven as yearlings and ridden as two-year-olds, which can be the ruination of a good horse. No one should buy a horse that has been schooled too early, for it will contribute to early breakdown in his prime years. It does no harm to let a horse grow up completely, being four, five, or even six years old before he is put to work. The great Lippizaners are not trained until four. If he has been handled and gentled and kept wormed, the added maturity will make his training smoother, and he is less likely to have to take time off for cutting new teeth and other adolescent problems. We often breed our mares at two and let them grow up a bit before we begin serious training. This tells us whether or not they will be valuable to us in the broodmare band and pays for their keep with the foal. At the same time, it gives them the time for bones to harden and emotions to stabilize. Many people think there is something wrong with a horse that has had no training by three. This is not necessarily so.

Horses, by their natures, set some limits on how highly trained they become. If a horse is extremely responsive and quick, he may be trained to a very high degree indeed. If he is slow-witted or reluctant, he will soon reach the limit of the trainer's patience and stop at a point where he is just serviceable, but salable.

The horse you want should be trained to your level of understanding and use. A good horse who is thoroughly grounded in his schooling can be a great teacher, responding immediately when you get signals right, or letting you know when you get them wrong; but a horse that is sensitive and very highly trained can be overschooled for a beginner. Such a horse will get frantic with inept riding and clumsy hands. If a horse is purely a "push-button" animal who does everything right even when you fumble the signals, he will make you look and feel like a better rider than you are, and will be a tremendous satisfaction to someone who is not looking for a challenge in a horse. When I married and started a family, I temporarily left the horse business; but as I started to get active again, my husband began to get very resentful and envious of all the time the horses received. Every horsewoman's husband and horseman's wife is likely to face this problem. Since I am really not fonder of the horses than I am of my family, appearances to the contrary, I decided that what he needed was a horse for himself who would make his life more fun. I found him the perfect horse. She was a Palomino, and one of the most stupid but best-trained horses I have ever known. Any passenger could sit on her and look great. My husband has an eye for pretty blondes and this was a sure bet. Every time we went on a trail ride, everyone admired his horse and remarked that he was a fine rider. He began to like the people he met and have fun. Once he was hooked, I sold the "Solid Gold Cadillac," as we called her, and got him started on an intelligent young mare that he trained himself. They developed a bond which cemented his relationship with horses. He knows now that it was all a plot, but he has become a competent rider and has schooled two or three very pleasant trail horses. If that first horse had made a monkey out of him in front of people, or made a ride difficult, he would have lost interest and the whole tone of our lives would have been very different.

Sometimes a horse is suitable in terms of temperament, looks, and disposition, but not in terms of training. This is most likely to be the case where you find the perfect horse—except that he is a few years younger than you had in mind and he needs finishing. Such a horse would certainly be a better choice than one more fully trained that had bad habits, the wrong temperament, or an unsoundness that interfered with his use, for these are things which time, patience, and effort will not change. There is a great deal you can do about manners, training, responsiveness, condition, and general appearance of a horse. The perfect horse is rare indeed—and usually not available at any price. You might not save on the purchase price of a young horse when you figure that you may have to spend money in getting professional training for you and/or the horse, but you will grow and learn, and that is a positive consideration. Overcoming bad habits is usually more costly than training new habits.

An experienced rider will have some idea of what he can train a horse to do, where he can add polish or improve a performance. If both you and the horse are green or untrained, you have two choices. You can, if the horse has the right temperament and disposition, train him "by the book"; that is, you can get a few good books on horse training for the style of riding you want to do and lay out a plan. Go about the schooling in the most basic, simple system you can. *Go slowly,* and don't try every suggestion every passer-by has to offer. Shortcuts taken by those with experience can be disasters in the hands of the novice. The other alternative, if the horse and your finances make it reasonable, is to go through a training program with a professional. The pro may put you on a schooled horse, not your own. He may train your horse to a specific set of aids and signals and teach you on a horse that already knows them. He will teach you to feel the right responses when you give the right signals.

Comfort and Size

Size and stride are two physical attributes that must be considered. People have some strange notion that big horses are powerful and that they will look better on large animals. For a 6-foot 5-inch man weighing 200 lbs., this may be the case. For many long-legged people, a short wide horse may be just as suitable as a tall narrow one; for most women and children, a moderately broad and deep horse that is not too tall will very likely prove more comfortable. The length of a horse's legs is what determines his size in terms of hands high. But long legs do not make a horse a better weight-carrier than a shorter-legged horse. Indeed, quite the reverse is true. When considering size in relation to the people riding, remember that the Shetland Pony has long established the record for strength in propor-

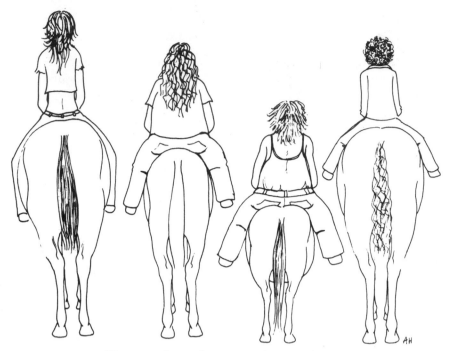

Horses and people vary in shape and size.

tion to size over all equines, even mules. Height in itself is not strength. For a horse to be suitable to carry weight, the proportions of his body must be substantial and sufficient to handle the load on his back. The carriage and attitude of the horse also markedly affect the size of rider he will suit—a high-headed horse can carry a tall rider much more attractively than a low-headed one.

Way of Going

A good ride is determined by the length and type of stride. If you have average legs in proportion to the size of your body, and are of about average size, you will be able to find both horses and large ponies capable of giving you a splendid ride. If you are short and overweight, you will do far better on a wide horse; you will have a more secure seat and the horse will be better able to handle your weight. If you are very thin and long in the legs, you can ride almost any kind of horse but will find that short, choppy-gaited horses are not your best mounts. You will, in all likelihood, gravitate toward a longer-strided, free-shouldered horse who has a springy or swinging

Your particular horse must suit your shape.

walk and trot. Again, a wide-barreled horse will take up a lot of leg, so that just because you are tall does not mean you are limited to tall horses. If the horse has a deep shoulder and wide rib cage, he will just as likely be able to suit you.

Shorter than average people, tiny children, or petite ladies have a problem with wide-backed horses and ponies; for them, a narrower animal is sufficient and comfortable. If you are short-legged and fat in the thighs, a shorter stride will be far more suitable and comfortable for you. A short, almost choppy pony gait is comfortable for some very short people. Some horses, such as the Thoroughbred, take a long stride and do so in a long, slow rhythm. They can cover a lot of ground since they are not traveling forward at a slow rate. Some horses, like the Morgan, take as long a stride, but take it at almost double time. This is most obvious at the trot. Their legs actually go twice as fast as the legs of a Saddlebred or Thoroughbred. Highness and lowness of action do not entirely determine the hardness or easiness of a gait. It is the manner in which the foot strikes the ground that will make the ride soft or hard. Each breed has a characteristic way of going because each is built differently. Not every rider likes the same kind of ride for exactly the same reason, for we, too, are built differently. We position ourselves differently on the horse's back and ride in a variety of seats and saddles, so that there is no one "right" seat, no one right kind of gait or length of stride for every rider.

Stallions and Geldings

A man's self-image often demands that he ride a powerful, impressive animal, which is at once a challenge and a servant. Women most often want a horse as a companion, and a challenge in terms of learning more refinement and precision; their image tends to focus on grace and beauty. There is one piece of masculine nonsense that must be shattered, and that is the myth that stallions should never be handled by women. I have been a stallioner for over thirty years and no stallion that I have handled has deliberately tried to hurt, intimidate, or bully me. My personal mount is an elderly stallion I have raised from a foal and have used at stud constantly and continuously since he was a two-year-old. I have seen many stallions who were too unmannerly and fractious for me to handle; they were also too much for most men to handle. Stallions such as mine prefer to be handled by women, and indeed mine will not carry a man on his back with any pleasure. Hundreds of women ride, drive, train, show, and breed stallions of Morgan, Arabian, American Saddlebred and Thoroughbred, Quarter Horse, and Appaloosa breeding. These are mannerly, gentle stallions, and the women who handle them are gentle, considerate people who understand and are aware of the instincts of a stallion.

When you seek your first horse, however, do *not* plan on keeping a stallion. They are not for the beginner. No one who is a novice with horses should start in breeding horses; there are too many complications. There is no reason to keep a stallion entire if he is not going to be used at stud, for he will always have to be confined and he will be barred from many activities a gelding can enjoy. The idea that a stallion is happier than a gelding and that castrating a horse is cruel is pure nonsense. Horses today are not kept in a natural, free state where they can roam in bands and mate when they choose. Horses love company and hate confinement. Stallions are confined, and often, simply because they are stallions, they are mistreated. Geldings are pastured with other horses, played with by children, trusted, and allowed to have company and freedom. They do not fret and grow anxious whenever they see strange horses. Since they have no biological urges that drive them to bad manners, they escape the punishment that stallions receive simply for behaving in a way that they find irresistible and natural.

The notion that a stallion is more spirited than a gelding and therefore a better show horse has also proved false. Stallions are no more spirited, just more anxious, nervous, and driven by instinct. The good show gelding is energetic, alive, and alert. His fire and animation come from true spirit and a will-to-do, and he can maintain his presence because he is fit and not fatigued by worries. Many racehorses cannot win as stallions and become top runners when gelded.

If you find a stallion that suits you in every way, he can be altered for a small sum. Breeders tend not to geld their stock for several reasons. Stallions bring higher prices than geldings. It is often mistakenly thought by buyers that a horse which is gelded is an inferior horse, but I have gelded a lot of colts which were far superior to many stallions actually standing at stud. Moreover, most breeders like to sell their colts as weanlings, and that is a little early for gelding them, as a rule. We like to wait until ours are at least yearlings. Of course, those with obvious faults, inheritable problems, ugly dispositions, and/or mongrel parentage or questionable bloodlines should be gelded without hesitation. So even if a breeder tells you that the colt is superior and "too good to geld," I would not take it too seriously. Good geldings are the best bet for the beginner and certainly the best bet for a family that will have only one or two horses. Many sellers will geld a horse for a customer, and keep the horse until he is fully healed. The operation takes about twenty minutes and ordinarily the horse is not upset or sick from it. New owners tend to hover, worry, and feel sorry for their pet. One of the saddest results is that they often feed the horse to "make him happy" and kill the poor animal with colic. Usually the horse hardly knows anything has happened to him. With proper care, he will be a little tender for a day or two and that is all.

Mares

Some people buy a mare because they feel she will be sweeternatured and more reliable than a gelding. From my experience, sex is no guarantee of disposition. Horses are individuals. Mares can be angelic or nasty, moody, hateful creatures. Mares' behavior tends to cycle with their heat periods. While some show no signs of change, others vary from nice to nasty or from calm to frantic. Breeds vary tremendously. The Morgan mares that we have generally show little or no change in their manner while in season. Thoroughbreds seem to be at the other extreme—they sometimes become erratic in their behavior and unpredictable to the point of being useless during their week of heat period. Some mares get crabby and everything seems to irritate them; others get affectionate and flirt with any person or animal they find. It can be a problem, it can be funny, or it can go entirely unnoticed.

Most breeders like to sell most of their colts out of every crop as weanlings. Mares can pay their way by producing foals if the mare has any quality and no serious faults. Breeders tend to hold on to their fillies until they are mature to see how they will develop. They are trained in case they do not turn out to be good producers, and are then culled or retained as the breeder evaluates them. Mares sell at a premium because buyers feel that if they have a mare, they can always breed her and raise a foal; or, if anything happens to her so that she can't be ridden, she can be used as a broodmare. With a gelding, a serious accident or unsoundness leaves you with just a pet. However, it is a fact that only about 40 percent of mares bred ever produce foals. Many mares are simply unable to produce. Many, if they can be bred, fail to carry the foal through, and some die in foaling; a few refuse their foals or kill them at birth. All is well if you happen on a good mare who is a good producer and also a good using horse, but there is no guarantee of this. Also, if a mare breaks down and goes unsound from normal use, she is unfit to be a broodmare because her weakness is inheritable and should *not* be perpetuated.

What About Age?

The final consideration in buying a horse is age. I buy very old mares or stallions who are proven producers, and I buy fillies or colts who might be fine breeding prospects; but I am a breeder and I am not buying a horse to use for riding. Many people ask to buy one of our "quiet old" mares for the children. Old mares who have earned a place in my broodmare band are the most valuable horses I own except for my herd sire. They are not quiet, worn-out discards. Some mares may wear out and calm down in old age, but my old mares are opinionated, tough, and spirited dames, with all kinds of life. The older they are, the more energetic they seem to be when we ride them. This is true of many Morgans. They simply do not, as a general rule, slow down as they become old horses—and I am talking here of horses in their twenties and thirties.

Horses go through certain phases of development from infancy through adolescence to about three years of age. They begin to mature at four and are considered mature by five. They are in their prime at eight to ten. They get to be senior citizens at fifteen to twenty, and are considered really old after twenty-five. Longevity is a characteristic of some breeds (Morgans, Arabs, Shetlands, Standard-breds), and the remarkable thing about horses that live long lives is that they are usually sound and active until the end, barring accidents, of course. Some breeds do simmer down with age. Thorough-breds and Saddlebreds mellow considerably and get "old enough to be sensible" as they mature. Other breeds change little with age, so the consideration of an older horse or a young one depends to some extent upon breed characteristics, but even more on the individual.

The best bargain in the horse world is a yearling colt, because no one really wants them. They are beyond the irresistible stage of foals, too young to put into hard training, and often full of adolescent peculiarities, confusions, and problems. They grow awkwardly, rear end first, and look all stretched out and scrawny. They are too young for much self-control, and are at the mercy of hormone changes. Yearling geldings are nowhere near so much of a problem as yearling stallions. It is best for a novice to get an education before taking on a yearling colt; but even if you are totally new to horses, if you select a colt with a really good disposition, tractable temperament, and intelligence, you can do a great deal of your own schooling and have a marvelous time at it. You may not turn out the perfect horse, with all the polish and finish that a pro can make, but your colt will be uniquely yours and something to be proud of. People who success-fully train a colt often become addicted to the sport. It is a facet of horsedom that many people never get to experience. If you have no patience and want a horse to get on and ride right away, do *not* buy a horse under three years of age.

If you really want to buy a young horse and school him, however, there are a few questions to answer first. How much time, every day, will you have to devote to the horse? How patient and firm-minded are you? Temper tantrums, frustrations, and vacillations rule out training a horse. Your desire has to be awfully strong to overcome these personality problems. But the horse must be selected with great care as well, for the wrong horse can defeat the whole purpose and demolish the ego of his trainer completely. If you buy a very young horse, buy an extremely well-bred one and train him with care, for you will invest hundreds of dollars in him before he is at a point where you can sell him if you lose interest. Only a good horse will be able to recover some or all of the investment, and only a good horse is worthy of your effort. If you can't afford anything but a cheap horse, buy a mature trained gelding of mixed breeding that is sound, tough, and ready to go.

A "Family" Horse

I have been talking here mainly of horses for a single rider, but often a family comes to me looking for a horse that can be used by several of its members. Only a truly flexible, versatile, and cheerful-natured animal has the ability to change his own performance to suit each rider. There are relatively few individuals suited to such a situation, and a horse with this ability is in fact most valuable.

I get most upset with people who come to me looking for a family pleasure horse, saying, "We just want a plain pleasure horse, we won't do much showing"—however, they do want an animal good enough to show—"and we will probably want to raise a foal or two" —so she has to be a breedable mare and can't have inheritable faults or conformation faults—"and we want something for Grandpa to be able to drive"—that's six months of training—"and gentle enough so Mom can handle her and do all the stable work"—well, at least they got that in the right perspective!—"and we like chestnuts or blacks with white markings. The only problem is, we have only $900 to spend because we have to have our boat hauled for the winter and Junior needs a new car." All I can tell such people is that I have a stable full of horses that can do all those things, but the price starts at about $5,000 for such a horse (mare) and goes up from there. When I tell them this, they say, "But we said we didn't want a show horse"; and my answer is that my show horses start at $800 because it is far easier to produce and raise horses to be good in the show ring than it is to train a horse that performs nine million different tasks and is the right sex and color too!

If you want one horse to suit every member of the family, that can in fact do the work of four horses, then you must be prepared to pay for more than a horse that can suit only one rider and perform only one kind of task. Remember, too, that people who breed good horses like to have them shown because it is an advertisement for their breeding program, and no one gives you a discount just because you are *not* going to show their horses unless there is something wrong with the horse.

These remarks arc just as applicable to unregistered horses as to purebreds. If a horse has had all the training and is sound and suitable as a family pleasure horse, he is worth a lot of money despite his lack of papers. You can pick up a riding horse in New England for $65 and a saddle that will cost you an extra $25, or you can buy a horse with no papers for $1,500 or more. Anyone who has a really good horse for sale is going to ask a reasonable or even a stiff price for that horse and get it if the horse is worth the money. The minute you start looking at registered horses, you should mentally add from $500 to $1,000 to the price. Horses proven in the show ring usually carry a higher price than ones who have not been shown. Showing horses costs money and is a form of advertisement.

When you fall in love with that particular horse and are sure he is right for you, you must ask just one more question: Am *I* right for the horse? Strange as that question might seem, horses have likes and dislikes, too. I once bought a horse, sight unseen, from California. She had all the requirements for my breeding program and I had long admired her parents. She was a winning show mare and had great promise. I was prepared for a new and exciting arrival at the farm, but when she backed off the trailer, it was instantaneous mutual hate. She was sweet and gentle to everyone else, but she immediately tried to kick me. She was loving and friendly to any stranger and fine with the people who bought her from me. But even years later, when I went to see her foal and looked into her stall, she flattened her ears and wheeled at me with her heels.

The reverse can also happen. A horse will take to a person for no obvious reason, and sometimes become jealous and possessive. That same California mare took a shine to the husband of the woman who bought her from me. He had never been much interested in horses, limiting himself to fixing fences, building stalls, and driving the truck; but this mare fell for him and won him over to horses by following him like a puppy. She "helped" while he worked, never leaving him for a moment. She whinnied and banged when he drove into his driveway until he came to her. She was jealous when he paid attention to the other horses in the barn, yet she didn't do this with anyone else in the family.

Personalities have to be compatible for real enjoyment. Some horses like men; some are afraid of men or dislike them. Some horses love children, but are unpleasant when handled by adults. My stallions all prefer to be handled by women. They are mannerly when handled by men, but obviously happy when girls and women are attending to them.

If the horse responds to you in a friendly, easy way and is relaxed when you handle him, you will no doubt get along. If your presence makes him nervous or upset, then you may never have the full pleasure and enjoyment you want in owning him. If he indicates a real dislike by flattening his ears and bobbing his head in a threatening manner or turning his hindquarters at you and switching his tail, take the hint. It may develop into a really dangerous situation when you try to do something complicated on your own with him.

He must be an animal you can truly love and care for willingly. His personality will be the most important factor. There is such a thing as love at first sight. And there is the love that grows with familiarity. But be absolutely certain that you buy a horse that "says something" to you when you first meet, or you may find that you never speak the same language.

CHAPTER 9

Take A Closer Look

THERE ARE SEVERAL WAYS to describe a horse's type. The term *type*, as it refers to kinds of horses, is a broad one; draft and saddle are the two main types. Saddle type can be further divided into English or Western. From there the distinctions become more specific: for example, pleasure, hunter, racing, and show types. There is also the very specific breed type. Within each breed there are at least two types—hunter or racing-type Thoroughbreds, bulldog and racing Quarter Horses, park or pleasure (sometimes referred to as saddle-bred and old type) Morgans, and so on. They should not look very different from one another in the all-over build, but there will be differences in head carriage, in weight in proportion to length of leg, in substance, refinement, and attitude.

Conformation is the way the horse is put together, regardless of the breed. All horses who have good conformation have correct legs, properly made joints, and a solid and sound body. The balance of the horse is important, too. He may look like his breed in type and he may have good legs and a good head, but his front end may be more developed and much larger than his rear end or he may lack enough girth to look correct.

Age will affect a horse's looks. An awkward, gangly yearling is obviously different from a cute, round foal or an aged and slightly worn-down old-timer. It gets harder to tell how old a horse is when the difference is between two or three and five or six years. Some

131

horses grow very rapidly and mature early; some look juvenile until they are six or seven; some hold their age well; while others look decrepit by the time they are ten.

Lastly, *condition* will affect the looks of the horse more than all else. Condition includes grooming, summer or winter coat, fat or a lack of flesh, health and skin disorders, muscle tone, and fitness or a lack of it. Only one of the components of a horse's looks can be controlled by the owner, and that one component is condition. You can do nothing about type, conformation, balance, or age. But you can improve on condition—or let it deteriorate.

Often the least important things assume the most important priority for the novice, who looks first at color and then at fat. If a horse appears pretty, fat, and polished, the beginner's eyes may go no further. If a horse is thin and dull, and looks like some leftover after the Christmas rush, it makes no difference what qualities the horse has, he may receive no further attention. It takes sharp looking and some experience with reclaiming poor horses to recognize what can be changed and improved by muscle tone, fat, and grooming, and what will remain faults in spite of restoring their condition.

Condition

Understanding proper condition is a key to recognizing good health. Yes, a shiny coat is one indication of good health, but the horse can have a long, shaggy winter coat, covered with mud, and be in perfect health. The hair should have a gloss which is not created by oil or washing and brushing but by internal good health. When the horse is well and properly groomed, it is difficult to tell by the hair, so look next for the expression in his eyes. They should be bright, calm, and relaxed, even if the horse is spirited. The eyes should not be dull and should be free of strain, anxiety, or pain. Next, look at the feet. They may be barefoot or shod, polished with blacking or covered with mud, chipped or smooth. None of this matters. You should be looking for the texture of the hoof wall, a smooth surface, a wide frog, and a springy, elastic bulb of the heel. Most confusing of all considerations in condition is fat. The majority of horses are kept either too soft and fat or too thin and run-down.(See Chapter 13.) People just don't seem to know what good, solid, healthy weight for a horse really means. Most horses that are to be shown have to be kept overweight because otherwise judges won't look at them. This is a sad state of affairs, and one that farriers and veterinarians deplore. It is no better for a horse to be fat than it is for a person, since the more fat you carry, the more strain you put on your heart and lungs. Horses kept fat as foals develop soft-bone disease, shortened tendons, and fat around the joints and organs. But since fat hides all manner of conformation and type faults, when a seller really wants to get rid of a horse, he fattens him up. So beware of the fat horse!

A horse in too thin a condition is no better, but this is easier to spot and makes a horse less salable to most buyers. In fact, I prefer buying a thin horse in whom you can see the bone structure clearly. After conditioning, such horses can be beautiful animals, well worth the effort. However, thin condition might indicate more of a problem than just a lack of food. There are some fatal diseases which make a horse thin. Most publicized is swamp fever or equine infectious anemia (EIA), although there are many forms of anemia, not all of which are infectious or incurable. Horses can become anemic from injuries that cause a slow internal bleeding. Broodmares often get "pulled down," as loss of weight is called, while nursing their foals. Horses who have nervous problems fret off weight at a great rate. Poor teeth can account for a thin horse, and even loneliness can keep a horse down. Any one of many low-grade infections or illnesses can rob a horse of fat.* So while building up a horse that is thin is rewarding and satisfying, it is not always possible or practical. Before buying a thin horse as a bargain, you should always get a veterinarian's opinion on the horse's chances of returning to health. You may be his last owner and pour hundreds of dollars into him before having to give it all up. Finally, good condition includes healthy-smelling breath, stool, and urine, all of which should be noted.

Age

Horses start out with small, soft bones, which enlarge and change just as ours do. A baby horse's face is just as baby-like as a puppy's or a child's. It can stay very young and immature and pretty for many

*Probably the biggest deterrent to gaining weight is parasites. These can be external, such as flies, lice, ringworm, and mites, or they can be internal, such as worms. Not all wormy horses are thin, but all thin horses should be suspected of being wormy (see Chapter 13).

years. As adolescents, horses have growth spurts that make the head suddenly get very long, the ears shoot up, and the neck look long and scraggly. The rear end gets higher than the front end. The slope of the croup changes sharply from a level, smooth line to a goose rump. Hind legs turn out and then go back in line. One week the horse looks smooth and "all of a piece," and the next he looks as if he's just been pulled apart and thrown back together again. Some horses are pretty all the time they are growing up, yet when they mature they get coarse. Their noses get too big, their bones get round, and they look clumsy and plain. Other horses never become strong and sturdy enough—they are called "weedy." They look as fine as deer when they are foals and you assume that as they mature they will develop more substance, but somehow they never do. They remain shallow, frail, and delicate. If you are considering buying a very young horse, you can get some idea of his probable looks at maturity by taking a look at his full brothers and sisters and at the sire and the dam. That is not always possible, but if it is, it should be a very important part of your examination.

The horse should look mature at five or six years of age, and remain basically unchanged for the next five or six years. Then, depending upon the breed, he may remain virtually unchanged on into his late teens or even late twenties, or begin to show his age by losing weight over the withers, through the neck, along the spine, and between the

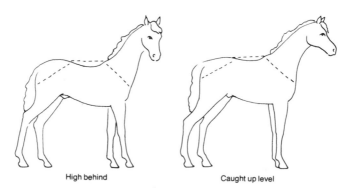

High behind   Caught up level

Foals and young horses grow first at one end and then the other. While they are "high behind" they often move awkwardly, look thin and out of proportion. When they catch up, the angle of the hip and shoulder actually changes and the back appears shorter.

legs. The old horse has soft, loose flesh, long slanting teeth, hollows about the eyes, and often gray hair over the eyes and around the mouth. The eyes of an old horse usually have an old look, just as people's do, although I know of one stallion who continues to look like a four-year-old. His eyes are bright and snapping, his hair is rich, dark, and gleaming, and he is firm and hard and always ready to go. He is over twenty years old, but no one, not even a veterinarian, could tell it without looking at his teeth and then checking his papers. Old horses who are fat tend to have rolls of fat with a soft feel to them and little muscle underneath. If a horse is kept in good muscle tone and good health all his life, he will not show age nearly as soon as if he is just allowed to drift into old age. The first and most obvious value of registration papers on a horse is that they establish the horse's true age. Without papers you must take someone's word for the age of the horse you buy. Teeth are a clue, but not an absolute guide; after age nine it is hard to be sure. Most dealers call everything eight years old unless it is obviously much younger. Many "eight-year-olds" turn out to be eighteen!

Balance

Balance is important because some horses tend to look larger, more developed, or better made at one end than at the other. This varies somewhat from breed to breed. The Quarter Horse breeders tend to emphasize strong hindquarters, big, muscular thighs and gaskins, and long croups. The horse works hard with his whole body, but the bulk of the thrust and weight lands on those hind legs. Sometimes such emphasis is placed on the rear end that the horse is bred with little consideration for the front end and is grossly out of balance. Arabian, Saddlebred, and Morgan fanciers put great emphasis on the front of their horses. They want a pretty head held high, with bold front-end action to show off in the ring. Sometimes this gets carried too far and the horse finishes up with a magnificent forehand tacked on to a slight set of rear quarters. Funniest-looking of all are the ones who are fine and upstanding in front, powerful and sturdily constructed behind, but lack any depth or breadth in the rib cage, so that they look as if they'd break in half if you sat on them. No special breed emphasis causes this sort of failure; it is just bad conformation. A weak and shallow body spells an inability to perform and sustain performance. The other lack of balance is one in which the body is too big for the legs or the legs too rugged for the body. A photograph of the horse often reveals such problems more clearly than seeing the horse in the flesh.

Substance and Quality

In talking about conformation, there are two sets of terms that people continually confuse: substance as opposed to coarseness, and quality as opposed to refinement. *Substance* means strength. It includes such factors as depth in the heart, density of bone, and adequacy of the tendons, joints, and attachments that make a horse able to endure hard work. *Coarseness* is thickness or grossness. It is a hindrance—coarse shoulders reduce motion; coarse bones in the nose reduce the air space in nasal passages; excessive thickness of the neck reduces flexibility and makes the horse heavy in the rider's hands. But coarseness, for all its drawbacks, is not nearly as bad a fault as a lack of substance. You should beware particularly of tiny feet, as they are highly prone to breakdown.

Quality means texture, and *refinement* means smallness. They are not interchangeable terms. Quality shows in horses in the suppleness of their hide, a clearly defined bone structure, chiseling of features, definition of tendons, and the visible blood vessels in the face and on the upper legs. The thinness of the nostril and ear cartilage, the consistency of hair, and the cleanness of the throat latch and the joints, all indicate quality. Refinement is seen in small features, daintiness, thin legs, tiny joints. It is the opposite of substance. Refinement is acceptable to a degree; it makes an animal more attractive to look at. Refinement is sought after in the show ring, but it can go too far, as can coarseness. Too much refinement in a Quarter Horse makes him look like a Thoroughbred; too much refinement in a Morgan makes him look like an Arabian or an American Saddle Horse. And generally speaking, too much refinement spells weakness.

Specific Conformation: From the Side

After judging condition, balance, age, substance, and quality, you are ready to look at *specific* conformation. Look first at the illustration indicating the parts of the horse. It shows a side view, which is the angle at which you should stand any horse at first. The horse must be made to stand *square*. It is fine to "view" him posed in a fancy stretch, or with the legs tucked under the body in the Quarter Horse pose; but when you settle down to really look at him, he will have to stand square, and stand still for quite a long period, for you to see him as he actually is.

Stretching a horse out, even a little bit, hides many faults very effectively, which is why it is customary in the show ring. When a horse is spread, posed, or parked, he is taught to flatten his croup. This gives the impression that he is stronger and shorter-backed than he is in reality. It makes detection of such defects as sickle hocks and camped-out legs impossible. But it does not cover up such faults as a peeked rump—one that is high at the spine and drops sharply down on the sides like a roof. Nor will it help a rump that is sharply tapered from wide hips to a pointed, narrow pelvic bone at the point of the rump.

The carriage of the tail has no bearing on soundness whatsoever. Tail carriage is an aesthetic consideration. It can, however, be an indication of mental or physical condition. Horses who flag their tails and carry them in an arch are showing good spirits, excitement, or good health. A horse who hangs his tail limply may not be in very good physical condition, and one who tucks his tail down may be intimidated, scared, or ill. Of course, a set tail, which has been nicked and/or kept in a tail set, will be carried high regardless of how the horse feels, and a "gingered" tail (carried high because hot ginger has been inserted in the anus) will sometimes fool the observer, too.

As I describe breeds, I will point out certain points of conformation and the most likely faults one might find in the breed, but bear in mind that faults of every kind can be found in individuals of every breed. The degree of fault is more important in most instances than the fact that it exists. In some cases, the presence of the fault in any degree should be cause for rejection. If you question a point of conformation or soundness and are not sure of its importance, a veterinarian can help; but write down your questions as you examine the horses, so that you can ask him to check specifically.

The *shoulder* refers to the shoulder blade itself. The *line of the shoulder* can refer to a combination of the shoulder and the relationship to the position of the withers—authorities differ on the definition here. The length and slope of the shoulder blade and its relation to the position of the withers have a very definite bearing on the comfort of the ride, the height of the knee action, and the shock absorption capacity of the front legs. The angle of the shoulder blade is supposed to be the same as the angle of the pastern, and hence the angle of the hoof. (See illustration, dotted line A.) The Morgan Horse should have the longest and most oblique of all shoulders, and the Quarter Horse the least by comparison. But the point is to determine which kind of shoulder you have in the horse directly before you, for that is what is important to you.

The *withers* are the top of a series of spinal bones, not the top of the shoulder blade, as many people seem to believe. They can be directly above the top of the shoulder blades or well behind them. In *low* or *mutton* withers, the spine does not stick up far enough between the shoulders, which makes for problems in mounting, as the saddle does not stay in place. Also, a horse with mutton withers is likely to be shoulder-bound, resulting in a short, stiff gait. Withers that stick up too high are called *knife* withers. A nice, cleanly defined or sharp wither is fine, but it can be overdone. White marks just behind the withers, scars in the wither area, and bare spots or swellings are clues to problems. These are usually the results of a saddle not properly fitted to the horse, but might indicate that the horse has

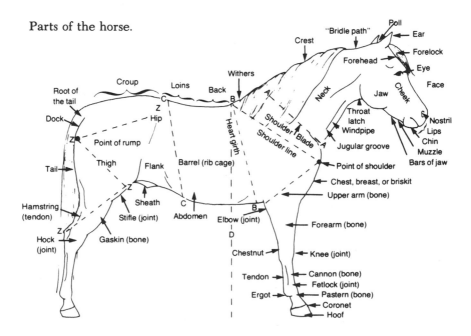

Parts of the horse.

a condition called fistula of the withers, which is a serious infection deep in the horse's body that can erupt as an incurable running sore and make the horse unsound. Run your hands gently over the horse's back to feel for warm spots and swellings, and pay particular attention to the withers.

A horse's back was not designed to carry man; we just happen to find it the most convenient place to put a saddle. The spine is a series of flexible bones in line. Connected through them is a very complicated network of nerves. When the horse puts his head down, he arches his spine; when he raises it, the spine hollows out. If he arches his back, it brings his hind legs beneath his body; and when he hollows his back, he pushes his hindquarters out behind him. We adjust his head set and, by so doing, change the bend of his spine. Natural head carriage places his spine in the strongest and most comfortable position for him to work. When we add weight to his back, he counteracts the pressure by lowering his head. As he gains strength in the back, he will gradually raise his head up to the normal position most comfortable for him. Natural head carriage depends upon the breed type and on the individual horse's conformation. Racing horses are bred to carry their heads well out in front of them so as to streamline their bodies. Harness horses carry a higher head. Working stock horses are encouraged to lower their heads as they face a cow. Gaited, park, and show/pleasure horses all carry their heads high and tucked in.

The horse does not have a collarbone. There are no bony connections between his spine and the legs until you get way back to the pelvic girdle. The shoulders support the spine and back with ligaments, tendons, and muscles. If these are stressed too young, the horse becomes *sway-backed* as he gets older. The results cannot be seen in the young horse, but they gradually break him down. Bear in mind that no horse you are considering should be trained to saddle by two, since he should never have felt the weight of a rider until at least thirty months of age, and a horse is not a trained riding animal in six months—he has only just started.

Depth in the body is measured in the heart girth and the flank. (See illustration, lines B and C.) Heart girth is measured around the body behind the withers and the front legs. In some breeds the lines should be nearly equal; in others, there should be a far greater depth in the heart than in the flank; but it should never be the other way around, except in a mare late in pregnancy. A short-legged horse, like the

Morgan, is one in which the depth of the body is equal to the length of the front legs. A line drawn from the floor of the chest to the top of the withers should equal a line from the same point on the chest to the ground. (See illustration line D.)

The *loins* of the horse are hard to define. This is the area behind the last rib and before the start of the croup—which in some horses is only the span of a few fingers, and in others, very long and slack. Short, broad loins are referred to as *close coupling* and are indications of strength and endurance. *Slack* loins indicate an inability to maintain stamina, to stay up in good condition, or to maintain body fat. The expression for a slack-loined horse is "a hard keeper." The *croup* is also a line you have to more or less imagine. It starts at the back of the loin and runs to the top of the tail. If a tail looks plugged into the body instead of following out in a smooth and continuous line, the horse is said to be "apple-rumped." The length of the hip (from the point of hip to the point of rump) is a critical one in terms of actual work. There should be a long Z from the point of the hip to the point of the rump, to the point of the stifle, to the point of the hock. (See illustration, line Z.) These long lines are tracing the lines of the major bones underneath. Length gives the horse drive and leverage. Muscle attachment gives him strength and endurance. The relationship in position gives the horse his particular way of going, height of action, and stride, and so is a part of the breed type as well.

One point which makes this book a little different from others is that I have tried to include some considerations that influence selecting a horse for breeding as well as for riding and working. Many people buy a mare intending to ride her first, but with the thought in mind that if she goes lame she can be bred. When selecting the mare, they are often willing to sacrifice certain criteria to get a good riding horse, but they are unaware that these criteria are essential for breeding. The world does not need more people breeding horses that are potentially unfit for work from a lack of substance, an inheritable predisposition to unsoundness, a poor breed type, or an inability to perform.

THE LEGS

All the old books on buying a horse tell you that a horse's legs must be straight, but what they fail to point out is that almost no horse is actually made that way. It is far more to the point to know which kind of crooked leg is preferable. The front legs and the back legs look alike in many ways, but they serve two different functions. The front legs support 65 percent of the horse's weight, absorb all the jolt of landing from a jump, and a lot of impact in running. The hind legs push and drive the horse forward. They are not subject to the same pounding pressure as the front, but they have to lift and propel the horse in jumping. In harness work, the load is divided between front and rear legs by virtue of the fact that the horse pushes his body forward with his hind legs and pushes his burden forward with his shoulders, thereby using both front and back legs to move his load.

Note that the front legs should be straight up and down under a horse's body in order to have the greatest strength, for a column standing perfectly straight can carry more weight than one on an angle or bent in its construction. The straight front leg will stay sounder than one that receives uneven impact and twisting due to an offset or crooked formation. The pastern and shoulder act as shock absorbers, which is why their angle of slope is important.

The hind leg is bent at the hock. It acts as a springboard, and works on a leverage principle. Hind legs are less subject to breakdown from impact, but more from twisting and straining. So what can be said of one end of the horse cannot always be assumed to hold equally true for the other end. While you stand off at a distance, you should check the horse first to see if he stands squarely on his legs. His front legs should be absolutely vertical below his chest, neither camped out in front nor back underneath him. If they are out in front of him, suspect at first that he is badly trained and posed, and second, that he may be foundered and crippled. If one foot is out in front of him, not supporting weight, he is said to be "pointing," and that is an indication of lameness, whether temporary or permanent. Note this

Normal

Camped

Standing
under

for the veterinarian to check. It is best simply to reject any horse who points unless you can get a signed veterinary certificate and written guarantee of soundness. I would also insist on an X-ray to diagnose navicular or other disease if I suspected it was present. (See Chapter 13 for more details on ill health.)

BUCK KNEE AND CALF KNEE

If the horse is standing firmly on both front feet but the legs are not perfectly straight, he may be either forward or behind at the knee. Here is where you start to make critical distinctions. The knee is designed to bend forward. Hence a knee which is flexed in that direction might be weak, but a knee which bends backward is in far more danger of permanent unsoundness. The expression "back at the knee" is interchangeable with the expression *"calf-kneed."* The result of stress on such a knee is a chipping of the bones on the front edges and bearing surfaces of the knee joint, and also bowed tendons. The *"buck"* or forward bend of a knee is nowhere near as bad, but looks far worse, particularly since some horses tend to shake and tremble with such legs. Bowed tendons can also result from this conformation, but are less likely than with calf knees. Buck knees are sometimes a temporary or correctible condition. As a young horse matures, his bones grow faster than his tendons, with the result that his knees suddenly buck. After a few weeks, the tendons stretch and the legs straighten up again. Then the process repeats itself until the horse either slows down in his growth spurts or matures. As long as he is not stressed while he is undergoing these rapid growth spurts, he will usually develop perfectly normal knees. Horses that are worked too young, ridden at two, driven too hard, and shod heavily for shows frequently end up with permanently bent knees. A mature horse with mildly bucked knees is not a hopeless case, for raising the

Calf-kneed

Buck-kneed

heels of the feet can often relieve the tendon stress and the horse can perform perfectly normal activities, even competitive trail riding, which is strenuous. It is far easier to spot a horse that is buck-kneed than one that is calf-kneed.

TIED·IN AND BOWED TENDONS

Examine the front cannons for the condition known as "tied in below the knee." The knees of any horse should be large, flat, and free of puffiness, and both should be alike! There should not be a sharp difference between the back of the knee and the tendon behind the cannon bone. The tendon running down the back of the cannon should be as wide at the attachment at the knee as it is at the fetlock. The tendon should also be perfectly straight, not bowed out. A bowed tendon may be the result of a severe accident or of break-down from normal use, due to poor conformation. Being *tied in* tells you that something will likely happen to that leg, for it is a serious weakness. This is something that will *not* improve with exercise and maturity, nor can it be cured by rest or treatment, as a bowed tendon might. Again, the lesser problem looks like the more severe one.

SET OF THE HIND LEGS

Have the handler stand the horse square. The horse's tail should fall at the back of the hind cannon bone, and the bones should be perfectly vertical. If not, you have a problem. It might be that the handler is not being cooperative, and is trying to impress you with how "pretty" the horse is. He may also not be able to get the horse to stand square, for horses are taught to pose and it is sometimes impossible to get them to stand still unstretched. But if he can get it all together and the tail falls in the center of the cannon bone or in front of it while the bone is vertical, then the horse's legs are set too far back or camped out. This is correct on a Standardbred, but not on any other breed. Legs which are camped out behind cause a stride, referred to as "dragging the hocks," in which the hock is flexed at its highest peak with the hoof under the hock instead of forward, where it should be, under the stifle joint. This is a serious fault, for it causes the horse to overreach, which in turn can cause an injury resulting in permanent lameness. Legs thus placed are most undesirable on a horse that is expected to use himself well while turning, stopping, and so on. The stock horse, polo pony, or hunter with such conformation would be at a very severe disadvantage, while a show horse or harness horse could get along fairly well with careful shoeing. For pleasure riding, the condition will affect the comfort of the gait to some degree. Camped-out hind legs are associated with a very flat croup and often with an excessively high, artificial head carriage. Hence this is more common on Arabs, Saddlebreds, and Morgans than it is on Quarter Horses and Thoroughbreds.

If the horse has the opposite problem—that of the tail falling way behind the cannon bone—then the legs are set in too far under the body. This looks worse and the gaits might be short and choppy. The horse will not have snappy hock action for showing and driving, but might be a better prospect for stock work and jumping. However, watch here for evidence of *sickle hocks.* This is a shape of the legs best described as too curved, both at the back of the gaskin and at the hamstring; also, the hock looks too bent, placing the fetlock forward of vertical. This predisposes the horse to *curbed hocks* (damage to the tendon sheath behind the hock), an actual pulling away of

When the conformation of the horse is proper, the action is balanced. Note that each horse has his front foot at the top of the stride. In the case of the properly balanced horse, the rear foot is well forward under the horse's body, but in the case of the horse "dragging his hock" the foot reached its peak of stride well behind the supporting hind leg. This is most commonly associated with a croup which is too flat, a hollow back, or a horse who is bitted too high.

Balanced   Dragging the hock

the small bones there, and also to a variety of injuries known as spavins (see below). Such a horse strains his hind legs continually and is weak and prone to breakdown. He might also crossfire badly and injure his front feet.

STIFLE

The *stifle* is harder to judge than the hock, but there is such a thing as a horse having too straight a hind leg. There should be a fair amount of depth in the stifle joint and in the gaskin. If this stifle joint is very shallow and straight, the horse will move awkwardly, without much flexion of the hocks or with an exaggerated snap. He will have too little leverage for jumping and may easily put his stifle out of joint or develop bog spavins. This is less of an evil than sickle hocks, but it is to be avoided in any horse used for barrel racing, pole-bending, polo, jumping, or handling stock. A horse used for hacking, horse shows, or harness work might never break down from this fault. Your use must determine how serious a fault is to you.

HOCK JOINT

The hock joint is one of the most complicated parts of the horse. It is made up of several large and small bones and can be adversely affected by a number of stresses. Most injuries to the hock are termed *spavins* and there are several kinds. Conformation causes some weaknesses, abuse and strain will cause others. Lack of conditioning before work and accidents can also cause breakdown of this joint. You

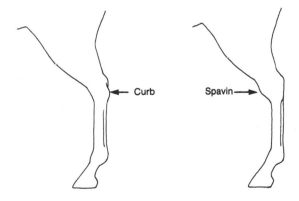

can assess two conformation points to guard against obvious failure of this joint. One is position, angle of bend, and height off the ground —in other words, the length of the cannon bone. The other is the size and texture of the joint itself. A horse is said to have well-let-down hocks when his cannons are short and his thigh and gaskin are long and properly shaped. This is important for any horse. Remember that the bottom of the hock should never be higher than the top of the knee. It is better if they are at exactly the same level, but that is rare.

The other major problem in hocks is that in an effort to refine horses and make them prettier, people breed for smaller and smaller joints, and a small joint is a weak joint, no matter how pretty it may look. Hocks and knees should be large, clean, free of puffiness and of heat or excessive lumps of bone. The two hocks and the two knees should be perfect pairs. The bones that enter them should do so in straight lines, and not be offset or twisted. It takes years of looking at hocks and knees to develop a good eye for problems, but practice on every horse you meet. Use your hands as well as your eyes.

Comparisons of assorted rear quarters. Please note these are compound problems for the sake of illustration. Any given horse may have combinations of such faults, or none, or only one, but frequently the faults as shown here will be found on the same horse, i.e., too flat a croup often indicates that the legs will be camped out. Steep, goose rumps are usually found with the broken axis and too-straight hock, while sickle hocks predispose a horse to curbs.

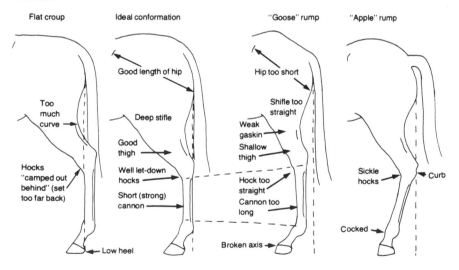

FETLOCK JOINT

The *fetlock joints,* front and back, should be clean, large, and pear-shaped (not round); all four should be alike. The rear pastern should be steeper than the front, but not upright. Pasterns vary from breed to breed. Upright pasterns make for speed and give horses used for racing an advantage; but they do not make for spring in a jumper or for comfort in a saddle horse. Rigid little pasterns may cause the horse to get puffy legs, and in the front legs will contribute to breakdown. Too long and sloping a pastern is just as bad a weakness, because it is subject to sprain and tearing of ligaments, and if the pastern flexes too far, the fetlock joint can be injured on impact with the ground. This is more of a problem in rough terrain than in flat,

Conformation of the leg indicates way of going, or the direction of foot travel.

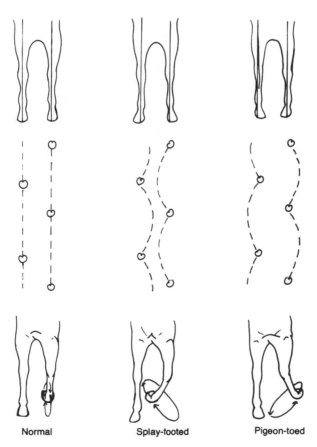

Normal   Splay-footed   Pigeon-toed

soft going. Hence the desert-bred Arab should have a longer pastern than the Morgan. It is more common for a horse to have more upright than too sloping a pastern. In the latter condition, the horse walks back on the fetlock joint, like a cat, dog, or raccoon (the horse with too sloping a pastern is called "coon-footed"). It is commonly associated with too straight stifle and hocks. Old broodmares get this way, but do not always pass it on. I watch for it in the offspring of the mares I own. I suspect that from the weight of years of foaling and the lack of strengthening exercise, broodmares may well be prone to this defect as a sort of occupational hazard. In a young horse, it would be fair reason for out-of-hand rejection.

Specific Conformation: From the Front and Back

This pretty much exhausts the examination you can give a horse from a side view, so now walk around to his front and, avoiding that pretty face, concentrate on the chest, legs, and feet.

The chest on any horse should be wide enough for the lungs and heart, and to give the muscles, ligaments, and tendons room for attachment and functioning; but width of chest is in part determined by age and condition and to a great extent by breed. The points of the shoulder should be wider apart than the top of the shoulder blades, so that the body widens out noticeably. This should be more obvious in a tall, fine-shouldered horse than in one of the shorter, more stocky breeds. On any mature horse, you should be able easily to insert your hand between the front legs at the chest. Less than that and the horse is lacking in substance. The expression "both front legs coming out of the same hole" is an apt and very descriptive phrase for such weak conformation. A broad chest is fine, and much to be desired, but the legs must be perpendicular under the body for strength, and the whole structure must be tied together with good muscle, ligaments, and tendons.

If the horse is broad-chested, the legs should be straight, and the feet ought to point straight ahead, but will more likely tend to turn in toward each other (pigeon-toed) to some extent. It looks awful, but it is far better than turned-out feet (splay-footed) for many reasons. If the leg "toes in" because the elbows are forced out by the wide chest, the horse will rock or wobble in his gait but will probably be comfortable. He may look awkward, but his chances of staying sound are good. However, if the legs are straight down to the knee and then the cannon bone starts to twist in, there will be greater strain on the joints and the chances of breakdown are present. If the twist in starts at the fetlock joint, the horse has even less chance of staying sound in very hard work. Being pigeon-toed is correctible to some extent by corrective shoeing, although the horse in motion will have a characteristic action called "paddling," which means that as the hoof is lifted from the ground, it swings outward in a circular motion, wasting the horse's energy.

Splay foot is a more severe fault. If the horse is young and the splay-footedness is a result of the elbows' being turned in, he may grow out of it with work and development of his chest and shoulders. It is common for narrow-chested horses to be splay-footed. As the toed-out horse travels, his foot rotates inward, which is called "dishing." If he is narrow or the rotation is severe, he will strike the other front foot. Sometimes these horses trip themselves, and they may actually drive holes into the inside of the other leg, often at the fetlock, causing severe permanent injury to the sesamoid bones. The lower on the leg the twist starts, as with the toed-in horse, the more severe the problem is likely to be. Splay-footed horses are very unsuitable for endurance work or for anything that requires agility— particularly jumping, which puts great stress on the fetlocks and pasterns.

Some horses stand base-wide or base-narrow, but with their feet pointing straight ahead. They will have a slight deviation of the path of travel, just as the splay-footed and pigeon-toed horses do, but to a much less marked degree. There is less likelihood of injury or breakdown than with the twisted lower leg. *Bench legs* are potentially the weakest of the malformed front legs. The column of the leg is straight from the shoulder to the knee as in a normal leg, but from

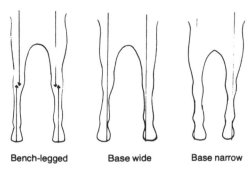

Bench-legged   Base wide   Base narrow

there down, the entire leg is shifted to the outside, because the cannon bone is actually attached to the knee off center. (This is similar to the effect of hitting a nail on one side of the head, which is bound to make the nail bend.)

Though you may not be able to see a crooked leg at first, you might be able to detect it through the feel of the horse's gaits. You can certainly learn to detect unevenness, such as a limp. But also each characteristic leg shape causes a change from the normal way of going. The base-wide horse and the splay-footed horse seem quite solid and straight when you ride them, while the pigeon-toed and base-narrow horses appear to waddle. They may sway and seem heavy in your hands. Such faults as bench legs assume far greater importance if the horse will be used for breeding purposes.

Now stand behind the horse to see whether he is either straight or crooked, just as you did in front. If he stands with his legs straight and his feet turned slightly out behind, that is *ideal* conformation. For most riding horses and all racehorses the leg has to come way forward, the stifle must get past the rib cage, and the hind foot must miss the front foot. Many horses go wide behind as they accelerate their gaits. If they did not, they would overreach and trip over their front feet.

Allowing for Growth

A young horse grows one end at a time. His hind legs grow first, and as they do so, they turn out at the toe, in at the hocks. Then his front legs catch up, and his rear legs straighten out. If you shoe, trim, and straighten a *very* young horse out behind, he will often hit himself and go short-gaited for fear of hurting his front legs. Yearlings tend

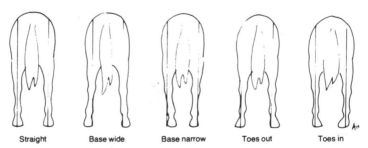

Straight   Base wide   Base narrow   Toes out   Toes in

Hindquarters from rear view.

to rotate out more than any other age, because they are the most likely to be very high behind and to do a great deal of seesaw growing. "Faulty conformation," then, may actually be a stage of development, not a permanent condition. Ask the handler to trot the horse away from you at a fast gait and see if he tends to go wider at speed than at a slow trot. If so, he probably has a long overstride and is protecting himself from injury. Although awkward-looking and probably rough at a fast trot, it will most likely be safe. Horses that are *bowlegged* or very close (base-narrow) at the bottom are more likely to get into trouble than horses that are base-wide or even cowhocked. As the base-narrow horse moves away, note how the foot tilts inward. The toe may actually touch the pastern or fetlock of the supporting leg. This is a horse that could injure himself by repeatedly assaulting the opposite leg.

As you examine the horse, note whether there is evidence of scuffed-up or short hair inside the coronet, fetlock, or even the knee. These are quite frequently *interference marks*—one of the signs used in competitive trail rides to judge the horse's physical condition. As the horse gets tired, he will interfere more and more. While you are looking, check the backs of the front feet for signs of *overreaching,* in which the hind toe, striking the front heel, often causes permanent damage to it. A well-made horse can be made to overreach by poor shoeing just as a badly made horse can be helped to overcome the problem with corrective shoes.

As you look at one leg, look at the other leg for a match. If there is an enlargement or a change of direction in one leg and not the other, then there is a problem in the odd leg, or foot. If both knees or hocks look rough and bony, they may just be bony joints and normal for that horse; but if one has large lumps and the other does not, the horse may have a broken knee or a spavined hock. Puffiness is an indication of strain and may not mean anything more serious than a bruise or contusion. But a hard, bony enlargement may indicate interference within the joint. X-rays are the only sure way to determine how serious such enlargements are.

Run your hands down all four cannons, feeling for little lumps of bone. This may turn up *splints*—small bony enlargements on the side of the cannon bone. Splints are considered a blemish, of no importance unless they are very large or high up near a joint. Those that are high in the joint or very large can interfere with the horse's action and actually cause lameness. Sometimes they are "hot" or "fresh," and the horse may wince when you touch them. A small splint is of no concern, but a horse that has several splints or one on each leg is a horse with problems. When numerous, they can be an indication of overuse, severe concussion, or poor quality of bone. Sometimes a colt will pop a splint while roughhousing in the pasture —or a horse might strike a stone and pop a splint as a result. Sometimes splints reabsorb and disappear. (See Chapter 13.)

Now from the side, study the leg from the fetlock down. Ideally, the line down the front of the pastern and the hoof should be one unbroken slant from the fetlock joint to the ground. If the pastern and hoof wall are not at the same angle, the horse has a *broken axis*. That is not a broken bone, but a broken line of force, subjecting the joints to uneven pressure, which can cause lameness. The pastern can be steep or sloping. The horse can have high heels, sometimes deliberately built up with pads or shoes to change the flight of the foot and enhance the action, and to relieve navicular disease. The horse may have too low a heel or too long a toe, due to neglect, poor conformation, or extra length of toe being deliberately built up to increase his knee action. This places a strain on the ligaments and tendons, and creates uneven pressures within the foot. Either way, too low or too high, the horse is in danger of going permanently lame. A veterinarian should be consulted before purchase if the feet are abnormally shaped in any way.

The Neck

The length and shape of a horse's neck will probably have more effect on the feel of a horse in your hands than any other factor in conformation. A long, fine, and curved neck will give the horse flexibility and lightness. The curve can be one continuous arch upward from the shoulder to the poll, as in Arabians, Saddlebreds, and Morgans, or a swanlike neck, as in the Paso Fino and some of the old Morgans who are descended from the Narragansett Pacers and Spanish Jennets. An arched and curved neck makes placing or "setting" of the head easy, and hence is very desirable in any high-headed horse. Less flexion is needed for the racehorse or the low-headed working stock or jumping horse as these horses use their heads and necks more for balance and leverage in changing direction. The neck must be light and fine for such horses, since an animal with a low head carriage and thick neck is well-nigh impossible to turn if he uses his neck against your hands. Also, a short, thick "bull" neck is undesirable in all breeds because it reduces the horse's ability to breathe and makes excess baggage to carry, thereby lowering his endurance. In certain breeds, the neck is wider from crest to windpipe, but a very thick or wide neck from side to side is not a characteristic in any breed. Breed character is probably best identified by the shape and carriage of the head and neck. Sex is also a strong factor in neck shape, for a stallion should have a much more crested and firm neck than either a mare or a gelding.

The Head

If the horse you are considering is adequately sound, has decent conformation, and is the necessary type for your needs, it is now safe to look at his head. If you have spent all your time looking at nothing else, you will have become mesmerized and failed to give either your horse or yourself a fair evaluation. People who look only at heads are called "head hunters." Some of the world's most famous horses have been poor-headed; Hambletonian, founder of the Standardbreds, holds the record here, but there have been many famous Thoroughbreds, Saddlebreds, and Walking Horses who were Roman-nosed and Lippizaners frequently are. Greatness does not depend on mere physical beauty—there are many pretty horses who are a total failure in all other respects.

Heads are, however, more interesting than merely as objects of beauty or ugliness. You should have a general idea of type difference in heads, but there are further variations which are more important. The three major kinds of profile are termed *straight, dished,* and *convex.* Heads can be wide or narrow; they may be tapered or not, depending on the proportion of the eyes and jaw to the muzzle. Eye placement makes a great deal of difference in head shape and in what is considered perfection. The length and set of the ears also have much to do with the attractiveness of the head. Lastly, the quality and chiseling of the features make a head fine or plain or homely. A good, clean head is referred to as "dry." A stallion should have a clearly masculine head, which will be less fine in the muzzle and fuller in the jaw than a mare, who should look decidedly feminine. Geldings fall somewhere between, depending to some extent upon the age at which they were gelded.

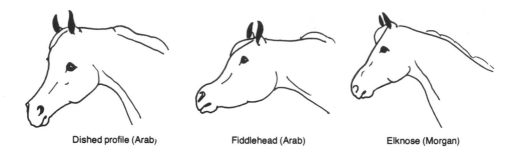

Dished profile (Arab) Fiddlehead (Arab) Elknose (Morgan)

THE DISHED PROFILE

The face of the Arabian type is a classic model for a "dished" face. It has a dome or arched forehead, which then narrows down sharply at the eyes to a narrow bridge of the nose, which is concave, and then straight down to the nostrils, which are fine and flaring. The jaw is round, the bars of the jaw perfectly straight, and the entire muzzle very small when the nostrils are not flared. The lips are very thin and soft. Few horses have such a head. Much more common is the "fiddle head," which appears Arab-like to the casual observer. The face is domed, but the nose is still arched between the eyes and even below them. The face then narrows down sharply to a small mouth. The jaw is large and round, but the bars of the jaw are frequently (not always) curving. Such horses tend to have flighty, unpredictable dispositions. That lump between the eyes is called a "mad bump." Another fooler is the "elk nose," also a pretty and Arab-looking head. The forehead can be domed or flat, and the face dished below the eyes; but the bridge of the nose above the nostrils rises in a curve and then drops off at the nostrils. If the nostrils are flaring and fine, the head is pretty; but if they are small and the mouth slightly pendulous, which is frequently the case, the head looks a little mulish. This head has no bad character traits, to my knowledge. I have had several and they all had a sense of humor and perhaps a determined nature, but never a mean or obstinate spirit. It is very common in the most famous of all Arabian lines, and many Morgans have this kind of head, too.

A head that is fast disappearing in American horses is the fully concave profile, associated with outlaw horses. The "dish" starts at the top of the head and is a continuous curve all the way to the nostrils. The eyes are tiny, set very high, and the ears are set on straight up and very close together. Such horses are generally so unpleasant and untrainable that they are not used for much more than rodeo work and dogfood. They are frequently lantern-jawed, and have a decidedly prehistoric look about their faces.

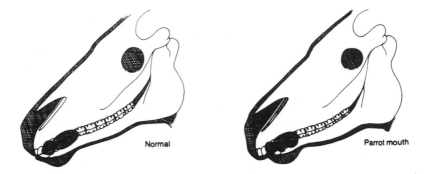

Normal and parrot mouth. Note the front nippers are useless for grazing. Such a horse would starve to death in the wild. Also, the space between the front and rear teeth is too small for proper fitting of a bit on the bars of the jaw.

Lastly, and sadly, an increasing number of horses are being kept and used for breeding which have a serious fault that gives them an attractive Arab-like face at first glance. This is the *parrot-mouthed* horse, in which the upper teeth protrude beyond the lower teeth. You can spot a parrot mouth from the outside, for the lower lip is shorter than the upper lip; but some horses who are not parrot-mouthed have a long, prehensile upper lip and some stallions suck in their lower lip when they are excited. So if you think you have spotted such a problem, open the lips and check. The teeth should meet perfectly. The parrot mouth appears at first to make the horse's head look dished and the mouth look small. It is the result of breeding for a small and delicate muzzle in imitation of the Arabian mouth. Needless to say, a parrot mouth should eliminate a horse from consideration for breeding purposes, although it need not interfere with using the horse unless the condition is too pronounced. The position of the teeth is important for grazing, but not for a barn-fed horse. The space in the bars of the mouth must be adequate for the fitting of a bit, but a hackamore horse does not have much hindrance if he is parrot-mouthed. So if this is the only fault you find in a gelding and you are willing to sacrifice perfect bitting or forgo using a bit entirely, he might be a bargain.

THE STRAIGHT PROFILE

In a classically perfect head, the straight profile starts right at the poll. The forehead is flat, the face is flat, and the nostrils come off the face high and well to the front of the nose. The jaw is large and round, the under line of the bars of the jaw is straight, the chin firm; the lips are also firm and meet square on. The head is tapered from forehead to muzzle. A clean, well-defined head is narrow below the eyes and down the nose to the top of the nostrils. One that is thickish, soft, and mushy-looking is called "plain" or "common." If a head is shallow at the jaw and has a large, square mouth and thick lips, the horse is said to be "hammer-headed." This, too, is being bred out as rapidly as possible in the breeds where it was quite common years ago. Hammer-headed horses are often difficult customers—stubborn, rough to handle, and frequently stupid.

THE CONVEX PROFILE

Roman noses are common to many breeds, including Lippizaners and Clydesdales. The true Roman nose starts right at the top of the head, and the entire face, forehead, and nostrils are curved in one smooth line. Stubbornness is often associated with this type of head. There have been many great performers with Roman noses. These horses have character and a solidness of nature that sometimes makes them better suited to nerve-racking work than their more sensitive cousins. The Andalusian profile has a flat forehead and the face then arches suddenly below the eyes. This head is common among Paso Finas and many western horses of Spanish descent.

Straight profile (Morgan)

Roman nose (Standardbred)

Andalusian profile (Lippizaner)

The horse doesn't need a long, huge head to contend with, but if he has got a big head, that is not the worst of faults. Mouths and noses, eyes and ears, make all the difference in the expression and look of a horse.

THE EYES

The eyes should be relatively large, particularly in the Arabian. The positioning of the eyes—out to the side or on the front of the face— is often a question of breed type, but the position of the eyes in relation to the ears, jaw, and mouth is important. The eyes should be well down in the head, never high up near the ears. A long nose can fool you here. Look at the eyes in relation to the lower edge of the jawbone and the ear, not the position in the head as a whole. The size of the eye is given various names. Large eyes which look like those of a cow are quite logically termed *bovine*. I have a strong suspicion that horses with bovine eyes are near-sighted and prone to shying. Normally large eyes are just called beautiful, full, and good eyes. Small eyes, if they are calm, prominent, and full enough, are not a problem, but little *pig eyes* are a bad fault. Pig eyes look just like their name: they have a selfish, evil expression. If the color is dark and the skin dark around them, and there is a fairly heavy eyebrow bone, they are not as easily spotted as light-colored ones, ones with pink corners, or those with mottled skin about them. Pig eyes are closely associated with poor vision and evil disposition.

Eyes that are sunken and dull indicate poor condition, or actual disease. Eyes that are bugged or nervous indicate temperamental problems. In show horses it is often considered desirable for the horse to be bug-eyed, which is fine if you do nothing but use the horse in the show ring. Such horses are not to be trusted on trails or with children. They don't like surprises. Horses can have white scleras and not be nervous in the least, but horses that roll their eyes and "show the whites" from fear are a very different thing. If a horse is frightened, he may do something irrational and violent. Panic is his worst enemy. Horses signal their feelings very clearly through the expression in their eyes. Pain makes the white show near the upper lid, while fear is usually indicated by white around the whole eye. The white shows for one of two reasons: either the horse has opened his eyes way up, or the eyeball has rotated in its socket. If the horse is looking behind him, a white edge will appear in the front of his eye from the rotation of the eyeball.

THE EARS

Ears are good indicators of quality, breeding, temperament and mood. The Morgan ears are set very wide apart; it is their breed characteristic. But they should be carried alertly and be active, sharply tipped, fine, and small. The Arabian and Saddlebred ears are longer, finer, and set closer together. They, too, are sharp and alert. Quarter Horse ears are short and stand more vertical than the Morgan or Arabian ears. While the Morgan, Arabian, and Saddlebred ears all turn in sharply toward each other at the tips, the Standardbred, Thoroughbred, and Quarter Horse ears often do not. They are sometimes held a bit wider at the top than at the base.

Ears sloped sharply forward and down may mean that the horse is concentrating on something directly in front of his face. Such ears may indicate a "spooky" personality. Ears which stand perfectly straight up mean trouble, either in excessive nervousness or unpredictability or both. Ears which lay out to the sides are "lazy" ears, and those which fall out and forward are "lop" ears. Horses with lop ears are generally calm and deliberate in their nature; cowboys say it is an indication of cow sense. Some are unflappable creatures and tend to be a bit more firm-minded than is completely compatible with willingness. Such horses rarely get into trouble or accidents. Long, thick, coarse, or shapeless ears indicate "cold" blood, probably draft blood. People will pay a tremendous premium for sharp and pretty ears. They will often prefer a horse with nervous, rotating, "antennae" ears over a horse with nice but lazy ears. If a pair of floppy rabbit ears is the worst fault you can find, nickname him Peter Rabbit, and take him home and love him. If they are really just disgraceful, call in a Doberman Pinscher ear-trimmer when no one's looking and keep the poor horse hidden for a few months. I know one breeding farm in Connecticut which did just that with an entire foal crop. I always wondered what the owners of those horses thought when their next generation began arriving with a touch of mule ears cropping up. I don't seriously recommend that you have the horse's ears trimmed. You can learn to live with such a blemish—they give the horse a wonderfully laconic expression.

THE NOSE

The nose is the only way air can get into a horse's lungs, since horses do not breath through their mouths unless they are under serious stress. If the nose is too short, the horse will have a problem with cold air. Desert horses get along fine with short faces, but Northern horses should have long enough noses to temper the cold air they inhale before it assaults their lungs. Air passages that are constricted by too deep a dish, or by coarse, thick nose bones, will diminish the amount of air reaching the lungs. The horse must be able to get a lungful of air of the proper temperature, filtered of debris by the hairs in his nose. So although we all agree that a short head is pretty, again it is possible to go overboard and horse breeders are tending in that direction now. If you plan to do competitive trail riding, racing, fast stock work, or anything that will require the horse to breathe hard for a prolonged period, reject a horse with too short a head, too deep a dished face, or too coarse a nose. Make it a point to have the veterinarian check the horse's sinuses if you have any doubts.

THE MUZZLE

Horses can have a variety of muzzle shapes. Small, narrow, flat nostrils are less than attractive, especially when they are set very low on a curving nose. They hamper inhalation. Flaring nostrils give the appearance of spirit. We like such nostrils both for the effect they have on looks and for the practical reason that they help the horse. Lips vary in breed type. The Arabian should have very fine, soft lips, and the mouth may have an almost pouting expression or pursed lips. The Morgan and Quarter Horse should have very square, firm lips, but they should be fine and thin, not thick. Many horses have a thick tip on their upper lip that makes it look as if it sticks way out, and the whole mouth comes to a point; some horses have a long, droopy, pendulous lower lip; others have a thick, flat chin and thick lower lip. This is frequently seen with the elk nose. The whole expression on the face is one of a wry sense of humor. A hanging lower lip is not an indication of old age or poor condition. I have had weanlings who were in great health that inherited this loose-lipped conformation. I have trained them to pull their lips up when I am there, but when my back turns, the lip flops down and flaps. This makes the horse look retarded, especially if he drools or retains a pocket of unchewed food. However, it is no functional problem; it's just funny-looking.

THE MOUTH

The mouth itself is of great importance both for the survival of the horse and for fitting him with a bit. A mouth problem can make eating, particularly grazing, difficult. A horse with a problem mouth can't be expected to be truly comfortable and cooperative. Take a good look at the shape of the mouth, and also have the veterinarian check inside for wolf teeth or malformations. Examine the tongue for cuts and indications of sores from sharp teeth edges. Horses' teeth must be checked and often these sharp edges need to be floated or rasped off. Sometimes wolf teeth (teeth which grow in the wrong place) must be removed. Horses shed their teeth and grow new ones during the first four or even five years of their lives. Any resistance to handling of the mouth or to the bit may indicate a tooth problem. (See the section on Teeth in Chapter 13 for further dentistry details.)

The length of the mouth from the front to the corner will have a great deal of effect on how easily a horse can be bitted. If his mouth is very short and there is too little space between the front and rear teeth (i.e., if the bars of the mouth are too short), he will need special care and training to get him to carry his bits and respond to them. Another problem with very short heads and tiny mouths is that the horse does not have enough room for his teeth. Many people resort to pulling teeth to make room for bits. You can pull wolf teeth, but not regular grinders and molars. If you want to do any precision riding and ensure that your horse is comfortable, check to be sure that the corners of his mouth are at, or behind, the back of the front teeth. Make sure, too, that the bars of the jaw are long enough and free of bruises, which appear as black patches or red marks. A horse with a short mouth may have a tendency to get his tongue over the bit frequently.

Breed Conformation or Type

So far I have been discussing good conformation in all horses. If you are looking for an example of one particular breed, the standards of ideal conformation become even more specific. What is considered an asset in one breed may not be desirable in another. Therefore, you should have a mental image of the best example of the breed before you make a purchase.

THE ARABIAN

Arabian type includes a small head with a dished face, and an arched neck, which is joined to the head with a narrow, upcurving throat latch. The neck is light and carried high. It meets the body slightly in front of the withers and high on the chest. The under line of the Arab neck arches clearly upward. Ideally, the Arabian back is short, the loins are smooth, and the croup is long and flat. The tail is set up high at the top of the croup and always carried gaily, even flagged up and often over the back. The Arabian shoulder is long and sloping, and the body is very rounded but not excessively deep. The ribs start out from the spine horizontally, never downward or flat at the sides. This roundness is what gives the Arabian his lung capacity, for he is not a very deep-chested or large-gutted horse. The legs of the Arabian are longer than his body is deep. The ears are of medium length, thin, very tapered and curving, set fairly close together, and always alert. The eyes are huge, very fiery and deep, and set out on the sides of the head. The Arabian's nostrils are distinctive, for they are very flaring and capable of tremendous distention. The flare and flexibility of the nostrils give the Arabian his advantage in getting enough air into his lungs. The windpipe is also a distinctive feature, for it is clearly large, loose, and free, less surrounded with fat than in some breeds. The Arab jaw is large and wide between, thereby making room for the windpipe even when the head is tucked in. The bars of the jaw should be straight, not curved downward. This, however, is a point of quality rather than an essential for good function. The Arabian mouth is very small, fine, and soft. Arabians have more refinement than the other breeds of the same size. They have long, sloping pasterns, which give their gait its cushion. The distinctive way the Arabian moves is a part of its breed type.

The Arabian was developed for travel on sand and over long stretches of level footing. The low, reaching stride and the long *period of dwell*—the length of time the supporting foot stays on the ground—are referred to as "floating." The foot reaches well out in front of the horse, pauses there a moment, and then is lowered almost heel first. The weight of the horse moves forward over the foot, with the knee straight, and the pastern flexed greatly. The foot then lifts to start into its next flight. There is relatively little snap or knee action. The rear foot also makes this long, low arc. Actually, the Arabian is more comfortable at a canter than at a trot, as this is a more natural gait for his kind of conformation. The Arabian is the smallest of the true breeds of horses; he stands from 14 hands to 15.2, and his weight ranges between 800 and 1,000 lbs. In an Arabian, watch for a tendency for parrot mouth, cow hocks, too short a shoulder, multon withers and too long a back. Any of these will reduce the horse's value considerably.

THE MORGAN

Morgans range in size from 14.1 hands and 900 lbs. to 15.3 hands and 1,200 lbs. The Morgan's most distinctive feature is his head carriage: he is very high-headed. The head is larger than that of the Arabian and not so tapered, for the Morgan mouth is square and firm. The ears are very short, curved, and set wide apart. The Morgan eye is large, dark, and prominent, with a gentle expression. The forehead is flat and the profile straight or only slightly dished. The throat latch is much deeper than the Arabian's, since the neck starts to arch upward behind the ears, and the windpipe is straight, attaching well down on the chest. The crested neck of the Morgan is often held nearly vertical, seeming to rise directly out of his back. The neck attaches on top or even onto the back of the withers. The shoulder is oblique, extremely long, and very sloping. The upper arm is short, which places the legs way forward of the body. The chest is as deep as the legs are long, since the Morgan cannon bone is short and the pasterns of only moderate length. The barrel and flank are as deep as the chest. A Morgan should never have a greyhound look. The ribs are well sprung and the barrel, back, loins, and hips are all very broad and rounded. The back is often so short that it is hard to imagine where you can find a place to put the saddle. The rump of the Morgan is distinctive, for it should be well rounded, never flat, with the tail set high, level with the hip bone, but not at the top of the croup. The hip and croup should be very long—giving the whole animal the appearance of being longer than it is high. The Morgan has a clearly defined but not very high wither. The shoulders and chest are broad. Altogether the horse should have a look of strength and power, but with enough quality and cleanness to look well bred. The Morgan should not look dumpy, or like a draft horse or pony, nor should it be lanky and rangy-looking. Badly made Morgans tend to be mutton-withered, the horse looking like a sheep. Finding a way to keep a saddle on such a back is a problem. Short necks are a fault in some Morgans, as is a downward curve to the windpipe, and with it, usually, a dip or hollow in the back. The family lines that carry these traits are rapidly being bred out with selection over the years.

A Morgan's proper way of going is as distinctive as the "floating" of the Arabian. The expression for Morgan action is "trappy." It is very rapid, elastic, and has a definite snap to the knees and hocks and fetlocks. The period of dwell is of very short duration, the foot barely touching the ground before it lifts into its high, round, wheelbarrow-like arc. Properly done, the gait is smooth and very quick, never choppy or short. The reach is quite great, with a free shoulder and a long stride. The Morgan park horse is shod and trained to have higher, more dramatic action than the versatile utility type of Morgan, but the trappiness and lightness of gait should not be greatly altered. It is a fault of action for the front foot to reach its zenith with the toe under the elbow; it should be more forward, with the cannon bone nearly vertical. The rear foot comes well forward under the body, and there is tremendous drive from the hind legs. The Morgan is happiest at the trot. He is capable of tremendous speed variation, from a very slow jog trot to a two-minute mile. The walk is also very rapid and elastic, and the canter is smooth and can be slow and collected or easy and free as a lope. Many Morgans are capable of a really fast gallop, too. Since the Morgan was developed as a mountain horse, he is a very sure-footed and "kippy-going" animal, who is not disturbed by uneven footing, deep water, mud, or rocks. He loves snow and is generally an eager swimmer, too.

THE QUARTER HORSE

The Quarter Horse is larger, heavier, and just as distinctive-looking as the Arabian and the Morgan. His range is between 14.3 hands and 1,000 lbs. and 15.3 hands and 1,300 lbs. The Quarter Horse has a smile on his face. His tiny ears and bright eyes are alert, and the ears are set quite upright on the head. The huge jaw is round and muscular. The whole effect of the Quarter Horse is of muscle and speed. The face is generally short and straight, with a square, firm muzzle. The Quarter Horse's neck is lighter and slimmer, less arched or crested, and is carried much lower than the Arabian or Morgan. He is a racer and is streamlined for greatest efficiency. Every horse uses his neck for balance, and a light, flexible neck makes a horse carry himself very differently than does a thick and rigid neck. The shoulder of the Quarter Horse is both shorter and more upright than that of the Arabian and Morgan. The legs are heavily muscled and the pasterns moderately short and upright. The withers of a good Quarter Horse are defined, but the shoulders are very broad and the back is also broad. Special Quarter Horse saddles are made (although they also fit Morgans and some Arabians as well). The Quarter Horse is not so short-backed as the Morgan, but the back is flat and strong and the ribs are as wide and well sprung. The loins are sometimes a bit longer, yet still very broad and full; and the croup is quite long, with a decided slope and a tail set on much lower than the Morgan's tail.

Most distinctive in the Quarter Horse conformation are his powerful rear quarters. Here the concentration in selection has been for a horse with tremendous thrust off the hind legs. This gives him his powerful starts, and his ability to wheel and stop with his legs braced firmly under his body. The Quarter Horse tail is beavered or pulled with care to emphasize the shape of the muscling on the inside of the gaskins. Some Quarter Horses tend toward sickle hocks, so this is a point to observe when the Quarter Horse stands perfectly square. The rear legs are sometimes longer than the front, making the rump higher than the withers. If, in addition, the horse is mutton-withered, he may appear to be standing with his front feet in a hole, although he is on level ground. The Quarter Horse standard specifies a definite V between the front legs; that is, the muscles of the forelegs should be full and nearly touching at the top. A chest that is too broad and flat is considered a fault. The Quarter Horse is bred to gallop, cut, turn, and stop; he is not bred to be a comfortable long-distance saddle horse. His gaits are workmanlike and practical for short-term, fast, close work. He is not bred for harness or to trot. Of course, Quarter Horses do trot and are used in harness, but don't expect to find comfort and easiness of gait in a horse properly bred for cattle work and racing.

When the Quarter Horse is ridden in a nice easy jog, he does well and his walk can be as smooth and free as any horse's. His lope can be slow or he can turn on a brilliant burst of speed. With the heavy admixture of Thoroughbred blood, the type is changing and will continue to do so. The taller, longer-shouldered, longer stride of the Thoroughbred-mixed Quarter Horse will make him a more popular horse for trail riding and hunters. The gaits should become more reaching, but he will almost certainly lose some of his agility and sturdiness. Beware of very small feet and extremely short, upright pasterns, and too straight stifles.

THE STANDARDBRED

The Standardbred is a far taller horse than the three foregoing breeds. He ranges in height from 15 to 16.2 hands and in weight from a surprisingly light 900 to 1,200 lbs. The Standardbred looks like the cross between a Morgan and a Thoroughbred that he is. He is bigger-boned, longer-bodied, and shorter-legged than the Thoroughbred, but otherwise he resembles the Thoroughbred very closely. Those Standardbreds that descend heavily from Hambletonian have his strong, convex profile, and many have far longer hind legs, with the legs set back in the quarters. Those that have a dominance of Morgan blood in their line look very like large Morgans. We had a bay Standardbred mare on our farm that would be hard to distinguish from the Morgan mares, from her pretty head and large eyes to her high and snappy gaits. The trot of the Standardbred is huge and reaching. It is circular, with the same wheelbarrow-like motion as the Morgan, but with tremendous use of the big, free shoulders and an enormous long stride of those driving hind legs. Standardbreds have longer ears, narrower heads, lighter necks, and more prominent withers than Morgans. The croup is quite sloping and often higher than the withers. The Standardbred is narrower-ribbed and lighter in the flank than the Morgan, more Thoroughbred in this proportion. Standardbreds both pace and trot. Theirs are harness gaits; the foot hits the ground with a certain solidness that is not really easy on a rider. The drive and force of the racing gaits are not meant to be comfortable—they are meant to get you there faster than the competition. Standardbreds make good jumpers and some of them are used as competitive trail horses; but the majority of those that leave the track are bought by the Amish, who use horse power exclusively for both draft and transportation.

THE THOROUGHBRED

Thoroughbreds have been around for a long time and they receive 90 percent of the news coverage of all horse events. Everyone has seen pictures of the more famous racehorses—Secretariat, Man O' War, Native Dancer, and others that have captured the public's imagination. A Thoroughbred is the streamlined, long-legged, low-headed horse who sets the image in many minds of what a horse should be. He is a smoothly turned animal with great quality. The ears are long and fine, the eyes set on the front of the longish, tapered head. The neck is thin and slightly curved, and it joins the body at a sharp and clean wither. The Thoroughbred back and hip are long and there is a slope to the croup less marked than in the Quarter Horse, but greater than in the Morgan. The body is clearly deeper at the chest than at the flank. The pasterns are long and the feet small by comparison to the Morgan. The hair of the Thoroughbred is fine and silky, never long or heavy. This is our tallest saddle breed, 15 to 18 hands, weighing 900 to 1,200 lbs.

THE AMERICAN SADDLE HORSE

The elegant American Saddle Horse is the same mixture of Thoroughbred, Morgan, and other, lesser-known breeds as is the Standardbred; but through selection for elegance, grace, and quality, the Saddlebred looks entirely different. The long, fine head is characterized by a straight or arched profile, and long, slender ears, set close together and carried at attention. The eyes are bright and eager, set on the front of the head. The neck is long, arching, and carried like a swan. The shoulder of the Saddlebred is laid back much like his Morgan ancestors, but the body is nowhere as deep and rounded. The croup is absolutely flat. The legs are long and slender, and the action of the American Saddle Horse is slow, high, controlled, and deliberate.

This is a horse capable of incredible collection and flexion. The gaits—two of which, the rack and the slow gait, are man-made and man-developed—are performed with precision and brilliance. All the Saddle Horse gaits are slightly syncopated and are comfortable to the rider. The action is high, but the foot should not strike the ground with great force. The high head carriage is enhanced by careful bitting rigwork, and the refinement and quality of the breed are emphasized in the clipping and grooming. Saddlebreds are taller and finer than Standardbreds and Morgans, but not so tall as Thoroughbreds, their range being from 15 to 16 hands and from 1,000 to 1,200 lbs. Here the look of refinement is perfected. There is little indication of the power or strength that the Morgan, Quarter Horse, or Standardbred exhibit, yet Saddlebreds are often capable of enduring long distances. The haughty, lofty air is their most striking characteristic. Beware of excessive weediness or narrow-chested and overlight bodies in both Thoroughbreds and Saddlebreds. When refinement is already near the limit in a fine horse, it can be easily carried to an extreme. For any real work the horse must have bone and substance, and this is the place where you would look closely for trouble in these two breeds. Excessive nervousness plagues some of these highly bred horses, causing a tendency to crib and weave in the stall.

THE TENNESSEE WALKING HORSE

The Tennessee Walking Horse is built on the general lines of the American Saddle Horse, but is heavier and has a thicker neck and shorter legs. The Walker often has a decidedly convex face, with long ears, and he clicks his teeth and nods his head, while letting his ears bob back and forth to the rhythm of his gait. His mane and tail are often heavy, long, and wavy like the Morgan's. There is a marked difference in the croup, for the Walker's is shorter and has a decided slope, setting his legs forward. This enables him to do his remarkable running walk. Like the American Saddle Horse, the Arabian, and the Morgan, his shoulder is well laid back, his head carried high, and his action high and circular in motion in front, while his rear legs take an enormous overstride, passing the front feet by several inches. Many of these horses have been "made" by artificial means in the recent past and a true, natural Walker may be difficult to find. Don't buy one with scars or marks about the pasterns.

Color

Color should be your very last consideration in purchasing a horse— except, obviously, if you are looking for a horse to be a matched pair with one you have, or plan to breed Palominos or join a mounted troop of all white horses. No color can make a bad horse into a good one, although colors do render horses more or less attractive. Color preference is such a personal thing that with some people it becomes a consuming passion. I have lost the sale of more than one horse on color or markings alone, when otherwise the animal would have suited the buyer perfectly. Recently I decided against buying a lovely mare because she had so much white on her that I was afraid her foals might inherit her markings and be ineligible for registration under the new rules of the Morgan breed (which exclude all white and too liberally marked horses). So color can both reduce the value of a horse and increase it. Many horse show judges are inordinately influenced by color, and will mark a horse down for having a light mane and tail or pin an inferior black horse over a better animal of light chestnut or bay coloring.

Horses inherit their coloring from their ancestors. One of the difficult things in registering horses is to be certain what color the adult horse will be by looking at the foal coat. Horses change color from summer to winter and often darken as they get older. The basic colors of horses are black, bay, chestnut, gray, dun, buckskin, palomino, and white. These colors are then enhanced by patterns. Dapples—which are dark, usually circular shades of the basic body color—can be found in all colors. They are usually an indication of good health, but dappled gray horses will remain dappled sometimes while in very poor condition. Other dark patterns include dorsal (spinal) stripes; zebra markings, which are stripes of dark color on the shoulders and forearms; black mane, tail, and points (edges of ears and nostrils). In some cases, it is difficult to tell a chestnut from a bay; there are horses who are on the borderline between the two. Usually a chestnut has a mane, tail, and legs of the same color as the body, but in some cases the mane and tail or the legs will look black and the horse will be taken for a bay. When just the mane and tail are dark but the legs chestnut, there is not much question; but when all are dark, then the deciding factor is the points, which are always black on a bay horse. We now have a bay colt with a mixed mane and tail and brown, black, and chestnut hair on his legs. He is a bay because his points are black. Many people get mixed up, and with horses as confusing as these, it is easy to see why.

Color is a tricky subject. If you run into a registered Appaloosa and discover that he looks like a Pinto, don't be surprised. It can happen. Most breeds that are based on blood rather than color will accept horses of black, brown, bay, chestnut, palomino, dun, roan, buckskin, and gray. Some refuse white horses; all refuse spotted horses, except those mentioned.

In the show ring, regional prejudices appear. Dark horses seem to win more easily in the East, and flaxen-maned and -tailed or other flashy-colored horses win more handily in the Midwest or Far West.

The genetics of color in horses has not had nearly enough study. We do know that it is very hard to base a breeding program on any single color, except chestnut. If both parents are a true chestnut, you can be sure the offspring will be also; but you cannot be sure what shade, or what the mane and tail will be. We find that in families where blacks are common, there is some connection to chestnuts with flaxen manes and tails and pure blacks. Palomino breeders have found that adding an occasional black horse is effective in enriching the gold color of their horses, but the black horse has to have bay horses in his immediate background. It is common for a bay and a chestnut to produce a black. That black may then go on producing blacks regardless of its mate, or it may never produce a black, even when mated to one. When a color gradually disappears out of a registry or family, it is said to "Mendel out." Gray horses *must* have one gray parent.

When you go out to look for your horse, remind yourself that color is only the surface of the animal and in no way affects its usefulness or value for most purposes. However, the color of the skin of the face can affect the color of the eyes. If the horse has a wide, white face marking, he will frequently have *watch* or *glass eyes*, which are either white, clear-colored, or blue. Glass eyes are just as good from the standpoint of vision, but they are statistically known to be subject to cancer, and many watch-eyed horses have difficulty in snow or sand. The color or pigment of the eye shields the retina from receiving too much sunlight. If you look at a light and then look away there is an afterimage, which is recorded in the retina. White or glass-eyed horses receive too much light and have problems with reflections. In a situation in which such a horse does not have to cope with snow, sand, or reflection from water, he is just as functional and comfortable as any other horse. However, some registries will not accept glass-eyed horses.

The three qualities which sell most horses to the beginner are color, fat, and animation. It sometimes takes years and years of making the same mistakes for buyers to learn to look beneath the façade. You can improve the color of most horses by feed and grooming if they look dull and drab when you buy them. You can certainly put on fat. Animation is a result of good mental and physical health. Remember that these three factors are adjustable or achievable, whereas making a crooked leg straight or a sour nature sweet is virtually impossible.

CHAPTER 10

The Moment Has Come . . .

BUYING YOUR FIRST HORSE marks both a beginning and an end—you have ended the search and begun an altogether new way of life. Of course, you must make payment for him and you have to be sure he is all yours. There are certain practices you should follow. If you have decided that this is *the* animal, and you have the cash and place for him, it can be as simple as handing over the money in exchange for the horse's lead rope.

But what if you are still not sure? You can ask for a trial period at home, or arrange to come and try the horse at the seller's a few more times; or you can put down a deposit to hold the horse for a specified period. If you do this, you are obligating the seller not to sell the horse to anyone else during your period of option. If you do not buy the horse, he gets to keep the deposit because he may well have lost a sale to someone else as the result of your indecision.

Paying for the Horse

If you know you want the horse but haven't all the money, or if, in the case of a foal, it is not ready to leave its mother, you can make a down payment. This means that you put down at least one third of the price, that the seller cannot sell to anyone else, and that you become responsible for the horse, his board, and his vet and farrier bills from that time. You remain responsible for them, even if you never pay for the horse. You cannot get your money back if you decide not to buy the horse unless you and the seller have agreed to this in advance. Most sellers will keep the horse until he is paid for in full, but that is an individual decision. If, for instance, you are buying a broodmare and wish to start breeding her before you finish paying, the seller may let you take the mare, but the mare will belong to the seller and the foal will become his property in the event that you do not finish paying. Sometimes the seller simply holds the registration papers until the horse is paid for in full.

I would advise that in all cases where a live animal is involved, dual ownership is *bad business.* Horses have a sneaky way of dropping dead or going lame when they are involved in such deals, and it can be very messy. By dual ownership, I do not mean a formal partnership or husband/wife ownership, but one in which the buyer and seller each owns a piece of the animal. There is no reason why the seller should have to act as a banker or loan agent. He is probably selling his horse in order to pay feed bills or to pay for another horse himself.

If you can manage to borrow the money or arrange financing and get the horse entirely in your name right away, you will avoid a lot of complications. People who own a horse are legally responsible for liability suits brought against the animal in cases of injury or property damage. If you take a horse home half paid for and he gets out of your pasture and into the road, the owner of a car that hits that horse can sue both you and the seller. If the horse is injured, the vet can charge both you and the seller for services, and if the horse dies, it is your responsibility to pay the seller his full price for the horse although you may not want to. Legal entanglements get very involved, and expensive, too. If the seller has failed to tell you that the horse jumps fences, pulls halters, or runs away, you may feel justified in not paying him; but when you have bought the horse (with all his faults), he will feel perfectly justified in forcing you to pay. It is far better to make as few "deals" as you can and to keep things simple. In leasing and lending, everything should be spelled out on paper, signed, and notarized to avoid any misinterpretation or hard feelings.

We sometimes sell a mare and reserve the foal she is carrying. Sometimes we sell a mare or a stallion and reserve breeding rights as a part of the payment for the animal. I cannot recommend the procedure to anyone. It takes a good deal of thought before you enter into these plans, and you must have enough experience to make the right decisions. You must be able to exercise control over the care the animal gets and its availability when you wish to use it. If I want a stallion for service to my mare and he has been sent to a trainer or off to a show, I am just out of luck. These things all seem so easy to work out, but in practice they are complicated.

Guarantees

Guarantees need careful consideration. If a horse is warranted sound or to have no vice, get that in writing. If the horse comes with a signed, dated veterinary certificate stating that he is sound, but you have some reason to suspect otherwise, have an independent veterinarian check on the horse *before* you make a payment, or before you accept delivery. Make it clear to the seller that if the vet you select finds the horse sound, you will not question further. If you have a horse delivered first, and then find out that he is unsound and have the horse vetted, it is up to you to pay to send the horse back, and unless specifically guaranteed otherwise, the seller can refuse to take him back.

Once that horse is paid for, he is your problem; if he kills himself as he is being loaded into the trailer, that is also your problem, even if the seller is delivering him to you. He is expected to take all reasonable precautions, and since he probably knows the horse better than anyone else he can be expected to handle him properly. But horses do weird things and accidents do happen.

If you ask to take a horse on trial, do not be surprised if your request is rejected. You may well reason that you should try the horse before committing so much money; after all, you might not like him. However, very few people feel that they can afford to let the average novice, or any stranger, take a valuable horse home. Once out of sight, the horse can be subjected to all manner of mishaps, overwork, improper feeding, accidents, abuse, and illness. He will have a change of routine and a stranger handling him, and there is no way the owner can protect him. You can always arrange to try the horse out to your satisfaction at the seller's stable, if he is reliable and reputable. You ride at your own risk when you try out a horse for purchase, but the seller will certainly do his best to protect both you and the horse from accidents. There are people who go from farm to farm claiming to be interested in buying a horse and "trying out" everything that is available. Word gets around, however, and these people are not popular with sellers, I can assure you.

It is wise to have the owner or trainer demonstrate a horse for you before you attempt to ride it, unless you are a reasonably good rider. Certainly, if he wishes to ride the horse first, you should not object. If, however, he works the horse hard in order to tire him first, you can be suspicious that the animal might be more than you can manage once you get him home. Be sure the horse understands the aids you are using for his gaits, and find out if he has any habits or likes and dislikes that could cause problems.

It is not unusual for a seller to offer assistance to a novice when he buys a horse. Sometimes he will just give the assurance that if there are problems, the buyer should feel free to call; sometimes he will actually go to the buyer's home and see that things are progressing as they should. This is the advantage of dealing with a reputable seller from the beginning.

When you buy a horse, be sure he is not already attached or encumbered in any way. If he is registered, make certain that the papers have been properly transferred and that they fit his description accurately. In other words, be quite convinced that he will be yours, free and clear. Lastly, you should ask for a bill of sale, and see to it that the horse, if registered, is transferred to your name exactly as you wish it listed, with your complete address.

Before you have the horse shipped home, remember to carry out the following procedures:

> Put the halter on the horse yourself and lead him out of his stall, up the driveway and back, into the stall again.
> Turn him out in a paddock and go and catch him yourself, without a bucket of grain.
> Put him in crossties and groom him all over, including picking up all four feet.
> Have a veterinarian check him thoroughly.
> Make certain he has been wormed and immunized for tetanus, Eastern and Western encephalitis, and rhinopneumonitis. (See Chapter 13.)
> Be sure he has a veterinary certificate for shipment if this is needed to take him into your state, and also a Coggins Test for interstate shipment.
> Write down what grain and exactly how much he is getting every day.
> Have the owner show you exactly how much hay he gets a day.

If he is on any medication or gets extra conditioners, find out what and how much.

Ask for a complete medical history in writing from the owner.

Find out what guarantees there are on the horse, if any. Get them in writing.

In the case of a mare or stallion, get a list of the registered offspring and their owners, if known.

If he has a show record, ask for a list of his major wins.

If he is not registered, try to get a list of previous owners, if any.

If possible, find out who trained the horse.

Getting Him Home

Unless you have access to a suitable vehicle, your next consideration will be getting your horse delivered. If the horse is purchased near your home, you might lead or ride him, if you can avoid highways and traffic. Short of this, he will have to be loaded and carried to your stable. In most cases, the seller can deliver the horse or advise you and help make arrangements with someone to deliver him to you. It is without doubt best to have the horse moved by people familiar with him and/or with transporting horses.

If you must make arrangements yourself, you will have several decisions to make. I have paid for horses to and from California, Connecticut, and Canada, and there is a tremendous variation in shipping charges.

There are commercial companies which are properly licensed and insured and, hopefully, equipped and experienced for the purpose of shipping horses from state to state. In many cases it is less expensive to ship a horse transcontinentally with such a vanner than to have a friend truck one a couple of hundred miles. Investigate if you have to move a horse over 50 miles.

There are state and federal laws regarding shipment of livestock. Professional vanners are licensed with a Public Utilities Commission license and governed by the interstate commerce commission. ASPCA rules for resting and unloading animals at intervals are more likely to be enforced with these drivers than with an unlicensed driver or shipper.

It is not unusual for a trucker to load at one end of the continent and never stop over to unload until he arrives at the other end. With horses that are hard to load, this may be the lesser of two evils, for more accidents occur in loading than during the actual journey, and the fatigue the horse sustains may not be as damaging as thrashing about in a loading fight would be. But most horses should be offloaded and given time to rest and relax. When we ship horses for a distance, we try to arrange for a stopover at the farm of another breeder.

Horses are transported by air in increasing numbers. This is still an expensive proposition, but may be worth it in terms of the reduced travel time and lesser risk of fatigue for the animal. This operation, of course, is handled entirely by professional shippers and is of greatest value to people who are shipping across the ocean or the continent, but it is also done for horses on race and show circuits with a limited time between events, where peak performance suffers from long trailering. Horses shipped by air are crated and loaded with a lift truck into the hold of a freight plane (which is pressurized just like a regular passenger plane) and attended by people throughout the flight.

Horses are often shipped about a great deal for a number of reasons, so you may feel it is worth buying your own vehicle after all. Many veterinarians prefer that their patients be brought to them at the hospital, where they have their equipment and can best serve the horse's needs. Some farriers are insisting on the same service from their customers, except where a breeder or stable has enough horses to make it worthwhile for the farrier to set up and work a whole day at one place. Sometimes our farrier comes here and has other customers bring their horses to our farm so that he is saved hours and miles of driving time. It is also necessary to have your own transportation if you plan to attend rallies, shows, and trail rides, or to use state forest trails that are beyond riding distance from your stable.

Buying a truck or trailer obviously entails considerable deliberation. I find that the trailer is more suited to my particular needs. I rarely have to take more than two horses anywhere at a time and can squeeze in two mares and two foals if I must. The advantage of a trailer is that you can park it at show grounds, leave equipment locked in it, or use it as a tack room and dressing room, and still drive to restaurants, motels, and meetings with ease. It costs more to license, insure, and maintain a van than a car or smaller truck and trailer. In most cases, a towing vehicle for a trailer burns less gas and oil than a large truck. I have often seen pickup trucks with camper bodies pulling trailers, but I find driving a trailer quite enough of a challenge. The horse's center of gravity is very high, and control in emergency situations is really often more by the grace of God than any mechanical advantages or skill you think you have. The biggest hazard on the road is other drivers, who have no idea what it takes to stop or maneuver a trailer without tipping over. You cannot slam on the brakes with a horse in tow. Some campers on pickups are lethal, even without a trailer. They obscure your view back into the trailer, so that you have no way of telling how the horses are riding and it is impossible to judge wind drag or the amount of shifting with such a big "sail" area. It should go without saying that the driver should learn to handle an empty trailer before loading up with live animals.

I strongly urge that two people always be present to ship a horse, even for short distances. I have had to ship alone any number of times and the problems that arise with a flat tire (you can't go off and leave the animals unattended to get help) or a fatigued driver (you can't pull off and park on the edge of a highway for a nap) are serious. Even with two people it can get to be a hair-raising experience if you have a problem horse in tow.

After all this good advice, I must admit that some horses have strong opinions about their transportation and will not ride in trucks, while others will not stand for trailering; so this may have some influence on your decisions and arrangements.

Have a veterinary certificate made out for any horse you plan to take from one state to another. Learn what shots are required or recommended both at your destination and in any states you have to pass through. Also find out if any "bug" is currently going around at your destination, and be sure to have the horse immunized far enough ahead for the shots to take full effect. Horses are tired after travel, and their resistance to disease is lower; further, the horse may not have been exposed to a particular strain or variety of virus or disease and may be more susceptible than a native horse. In some cases, such as a Coggins Test, this requires as much as three weeks of advance planning. Some states have recently closed their borders to horse transport during peak danger months when sleeping sickness and other diseases have proved severe. Places where horses congregate—horse show grounds, race tracks, and so on—are often closed because of disease, and sale barns and auction rooms are famous for the hazard of shipping fever. Even the motels which maintain stables so that travelers can rest their horses are a likely source of disease, since there is no totally effective disinfectant or sterilization method to prevent disease. But probably the truck or trailer itself is a bigger harborer of "bugs" than all the other places. Bedding, hay bales, hay nets, crossties, floor mats, and the walls of the stalls themselves catch bits of hair, dander, nasal discharge, and sweat. The next horse will steam up the trailer and inhale all the humid air, including the viruses. If your horse is being shipped as a part load of a group of horses, there is no way of knowing whether the other horses in the load are safe. Be sure your horse is up on his tetanus shots before trucking, for a scratch, puncture, or the like can go unnoticed on a trip and might cause trouble. It is often a practice to give horses a broad-spectrum antibiotic before takeoff. I am not sure that such shotgun treatment before the horse is exposed to disease is completely effective, but it makes the shippers feel more secure, and just on the chance that it works, it is probably worth asking the veterinarian about.

Blankets are another concern. We don't blanket most of the time. Horses sweat in trailers as it is. I sometimes put on a light sheet or a rain sheet if the weather is bad. We have no draft in the front of our trailer, but an open or drafty trailer would require a blanket if the horse is sweating and if it is cold, rainy, or windy weather. On very long trips we take a blanket along and put it on the horse at night.

Try to avoid tranquilizers if possible. They are illegal at a show, so you cannot use them before taking a horse to one. Horses that have been tranquilized are in danger of going berserk if they are hurt. They lose their self-control and get panicky, violent, and oblivious to their surroundings. Tranquilizers wear off and if you have a horse in tow who resents trucking, he may suddenly come alive in the trailer and thrash about so violently that he upsets the rig or swings the trailer out into traffic. In some cases, as with a badly hurt horse who must be taken to a veterinarian, tranquilizers can be a kindness; but have the good sense never to use them as a routine convenience.

Be sure that the vehicles you use in horse transport are as safe as you can make them. Any fumes from the truck that find their way into the trailer or up into the stalls of the van can sicken and even kill a horse. I have ridden in every trailer I plan to ship a horse in to find out first if this is a hazard. Floorboards, particularly those under the rubber mats, can rot, and must be checked. It doesn't take too long to check the most obvious things—including brakes in the vehicle, lights and horn, spare tire and jack, latches and safety chains, bolts and nuts, and the tie rings and breast bars. Check the trailer hitch every time you stop along the way.

Riding in a car is usually fun for children and dogs, but riding in a truck or trailer is no fun for anyone. For horses it is noisy, often terrifying, and always uncomfortable. I am never quite sure why a horse is even willing to set foot in a trailer once he has had his first ride, and I marvel at his good manners and willingness to be subjected to this form of torture. The least you can do is be sure that your horse is carried as safely and comfortably as possible.

Trailer Fear

Fear of trailering is particularly a problem with horses that have had trailer accidents. After the first bad experience, they tend to thrash and bang around every time they are loaded and often each trip further convinces them that they are in danger. It obviously takes great tact and patience to get such horses rehabilitated, and you must exercise constant vigilance to protect them from further accidents. If the first few experiences in a trailer are good ones, the horse learns that the trip is a finite thing with a beginning and an end. If it is somewhere near tolerable, or even pleasurable, then an accident may not make a permanent and lasting impression. He may accept the accident as just an incident in his life, unconnected with the trailering itself.

Last summer a pair of three-year-olds were in a trailer which had taken them to many rallies and shows. They were both veteran travelers, even at such a young age. They were on their way home from a rally when the trailer jumped the ball and both "safety chains" let go. The driver felt the disconnect, stopped his truck, and jumped out to catch the trailer. He could not stop it because it was running downhill backward, and he was not strong enough or heavy enough to halt its increasingly fast descent. He threw his weight sideways in a desperate attempt to swing the trailer. This was successful, and the trailer then backed off the road onto the shoulder. But instead of stopping when it hit the bank, it rode partway up, then tipped over on its side, pinning both horses in. The tailgate was against the bank, unopenable. The horses lay on their sides with the partition between them. The gelding was on the bottom, and the mare had got her front feet entangled in the bars of the head divider.

When help came, the trailer top was ripped off and the nose of the trailer removed. The two horses were very well schooled and had great trust in their trainer, who spoke to them as he struggled to get them free. The gelding was lying flat on his side and he was slid out of the trailer on his rubber mat. That left the entangled mare, alone and frightened. She had to be broken out of the bars with a sledgehammer. Each time they swung the hammer, her trainer said, "Whoa, Duet," and she lay still. Once she was free, the two horses were led the last few miles home. It was months before they were asked to load into a trailer again. Both had to heal from cuts and bruises, so they were not even hitched and driven for some time. Once the trailer was repaired, the trainer put grain in the two front mangers and led the gelding up, loaded him quietly, and followed up with the mare. They loaded, ate, and stood. Then he unloaded them and put them away. The next time, he loaded them and went for a short drive. To this day, neither horse has given any indication of fear in loading or traveling. Their trust in him is complete, and they had enough good experience in a trailer to disassociate the accident with the total experience of trailering.

Here are a few practical hints on trailering a horse. The first thing you need in loading a horse is time. The next is patience. I recommend tranquilizers here for the loader, not for the horse! You can train a horse in advance for trailering. Learning to truck safely is just as much a part of a horse's schooling as a slow gait or jumping. Hitch your trailer to the towing vehicle or to a solid "deadman" that will keep the trailer from lifting as the horse enters. Put the trailer in his paddock or ring, and leave it there for a week. Hold out his grain, in a familiar bucket, while you sit on the tailgate or in the trailer. Do not make any attempt to get him into the trailer on the first day. If he will stand outside and stick his nose in to eat, be satisfied. Gradually coax him in and feed him in the trailer daily. Your time and effort will be rewarded in proportion to what you are willing to give. His confidence in you, in the trailer, and in himself will gradually grow. We never truck a young horse alone if we can possibly avoid it. A good babysitter is a blessing when you must transport a sick or young animal. If we haven't a horse to use for company, we use a person, but in many states this is against the law. The only time we were ever stopped, I explained to the officer that the young animal was frightened and thrashing around in the trailer. His fellow passenger had calmed him down and therefore we could proceed down the highway in a much straighter line. He agreed we were much less of a hazard that way and let us go, but the laws are meant for protection and there is a good reason for them. I never let anyone ride in the trailer when it is empty or when there is no need.

When loading a trailer, put the heaviest horse directly behind the driver. In a three-horse trailer, but with only two horses, leave the center stall empty. It is dangerous to put a single horse on the right with the left stall empty, because the crown of the road pulls the trailer out of line and off the edge of the road.

Tie your horse properly in the trailer. I know that there are people who truck horses untied. We do not tie very young foals, but we close the trailer up tight so that they can't jump out the back. Many horses are killed every year going out of trucks and trailers onto the highway. There is no need for this risk. It is also a kindness to tie the horse, for he derives some support from his halter and rope if the trailer lurches. Use a panic snap on your trailer tie rope. Tie the rope so that it is snug enough to help steady the horse and there is no chance of his rearing and getting a foot into it. The tie rope must not be tight enough to make him uncomfortable or hold his neck in an unnatural position.

We always feed our horses in the trailer, hay and grain. Even a little will make the next trip easier.

For the actual loading, you must be calm. The slowest method of loading is to hurry the horse. The quickest way is usually the quietest, gentlest approach. Use bribery; don't be proud. If he'll sell his soul for a handful of grain, buy it and get on with it. But don't cheat him after he is in. Let him lick the bucket clean. If bribery fails, try persuasion. Have a leader who is familiar to the horse and of whom he is not afraid. Usually a hand gently stroking the horse on the rump will get him to step forward. We talk to the horse constantly, gently, and with reassuring praise, even if he is standing perfectly still. If he is inclined to pull, we tell him "No," and then praise him the minute he responds.

Endless patience, however, does not always work and not every-one has all day. Our next step is to have two strong people (who are horse-wise enough to avoid being kicked) grasp hands behind the horse's gaskins and pull his hindquarters forward, while the leader gives a gentle, steady pull on the halter. One rule we maintain is that no one is allowed to "cluck" to the horse, for this will most often make him back up. While his handlers are pulling the rump forward, the horse may sit down on them with considerable weight. He then braces his forefeet and is rigid. We lift the forelegs one at a time and place them on the ramps. Since you have to be something of a contortionist to reach both ends of the horse at once, it may help to tap the cannon bone with your foot. When the horse lifts his foot, everyone pulls. Often the horse will then hop in—and sometimes he will suddenly boom out again. We use a step-in trailer, with doors that we shut. Then we attach a rump bar and tie the horse's head. If you have a tailgate, you have to fasten the rump bar first in many instances, and this can be dangerous if the leader doesn't have the strength to hold the horse forward. If you have this problem, try fixing a chain or rope in the trailer that the leader can snap into the halter ring the moment the horse is in.

If the horse kicks, use a rump rope instead of holding hands behind him. *Do not wrap any rope around your hands, and don't allow anyone else to wrap a rope on their hands, either.* Sometimes the mere presence of a whip will work wonders, and some people find a broom a great persuader; but it is not usually possible to beat a horse into a trailer, and there is good reason for this. You can rarely over-come fear in a horse by getting him excited. Most horses refuse to load out of fear, not caprice. For the few who are just plain stubborn, a whip plied with very careful timing, used only as the horse pulls back, may be the answer. Excessive whip-cracking and actual flailing of the horse will usually cause trouble.

There are other methods. Blindfolds sometimes work—use a sweatshirt, saddle blanket, or towel, or any heavy material that will cover the eyes completely and allow no light in. Be sure it fits tight so that the horse cannot see the ground or behind him. Then turn him slowly round and round until he has lost his sense of direction. Lead him quietly and talk to him softly. The first step is the hard one.

Since many of these methods involve force and intimidation in one form or another, you must keep reminding yourself that panic is your enemy and temper is always a signal that you have lost the fight. When I suggest a whip, I do not mean a crop or quirt or bat. I do not mean this tool to be used as a club, but if a horse has been schooled to longe or drive, the whip is a signal to go forward. It is familiar to him and should not induce panic. The rope, on the other hand, is new and frightening to many horses, and a rope burn is slower to heal than even a real welt from a whip. Any method you use must be employed properly or it will backfire. Tentative attempts to "shoo" a horse, followed by weak clicks and tapping or nagging with a whip, and then scrambling and tangling with a rope, are of no value. If your horse is a real problem, seek professional help. Have him schooled to load. That is part of every horse's proper education.

What if for some reason you find you have to load a horse by yourself? The Westerners often use a *comealong*—much the same as the chest tie used to cure a horse who pulls on his halter. (See Illustration.) In this way, the loader stays on the outside of the trailer and can close the tailgate after the horse is loaded. The comealong is preferable to a rump rope because the horse is not so likely to become entangled. It can be left on him while he is riding if it is made fast to the halter so that it won't dangle at his feet.

Finally, when loading, always face your vehicle toward the sun. I have seen horses balk at loading because their shadow suddenly looms up in the trailer as they step in with the sun behind them.

Drive carefully!

Loading a horse with a comealong or chest pull. The horse is protected for shipment with a tail wrap, leg wraps and head bumper.

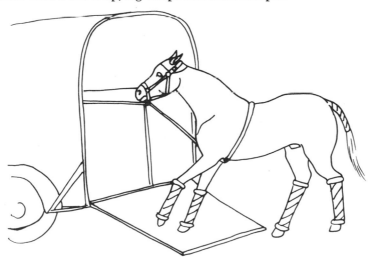

CHAPTER 11

Once He Is All Yours

The Day Has Come

The stall is ready with its fresh bedding, bucket of clean water, and cut-up carrots in the feed bin. His name is carefully inscribed on a plaque, and you've been gazing down the driveway and straining to hear the first sounds of the van. While you are waiting, take a careful look and see if everything is as ready as it should be.

The horse is leaving the security of his home, his familiar handlers, and his companions. You may love him, but he has no way of knowing that yet. He does not recognize his new stall as home. His past experiences are his only guidelines. If he has never had a bad experience and if he is a trusting and calm horse, he may be quite relaxed and take everything in stride. If, on the other hand, he has had a bad home or is of a nervous temperament, he may suffer mentally and even physically for quite some time. Your responsibility starts with making certain everything possible has been done to ensure his safety and comfort.

Look around you as if you were a state inspector hunting for violations. The line of flapping laundry, the yapping dog, the children's pretty toys—all so familiar and harmless to you—may be objects of terror to a newly transported horse. Are there a few remaining strands of wire in a heap in the corner that you intend to take to the dump? Were you planning to pick up that pile of shingles and those strips of tar paper? A horse could panic, pull away, and get entangled in these things. Wheelbarrows, old farm equipment in the pasture, boards with nails sticking up, and things that blow about in the breeze can all injure that new horse. I have delivered several horses to people who were still putting on the stall doors or shingling the roof, or who hadn't even gotten their pasture fence completed. People are in an awful hurry to get their horse, but they can be remarkably slow about getting ready for him.

If you have policed the outside area, next go into the stable and view it with the same mixture of care and healthy alarm. Are there nails protruding from the walls? Are the pitchforks and rakes along a walk where they can catch on the horse or fall on him as he passes by? There must be no projections, no hooks, no eye-gouging latches. The stall sides should be high enough and solid enough that he will not be able to jump out and run for home. The stall must be light, with good air circulation. If it is dark and stuffy, the horse will quickly become depressed and might also develop breathing problems.

Tell your friends and neighbors that no one is to be allowed to come into the stable or touch the horse until you are satisfied that he is relaxed enough. Post the veterinarian's number by the phone, and while you are putting up signs, put up a "No Smoking" one and enforce it. Also, post a chart with your horse's daily schedule on it.

For most horses, there is no trauma in moving. Generally speaking, a horse makes a trip of this sort without accident, but if he is hurt in loading or transit, the veterinarian should be available. The driver of the van may be persuaded to stay and help if the horse needs treatment. If all goes well, just pay the man for trucking the horse and plan to spend as much of the day as possible in the stable.

When the horse has been unloaded, he should be allowed to stand and look about him to get his bearings. He should be led about a little to loosen up stiff muscles and urged to eat a little grass and urinate in the tall grass, if he will. Don't turn him loose in the paddock right away or he might run through the fence and take off. Let him investigate the things that catch his attention. Speak to him in a reassuring and friendly tone. Then lead him slowly into his stall, turn him facing the door, and pull the door shut before you turn him loose. Leave his halter on in case he becomes excited and you have to catch him again. He will very likely urinate in the stall if he didn't do it outside. He may lie down and roll. Watch that he doesn't get cast against the side of the stall. Do *not* feed him grain the moment he arrives.

Take a little soiled bedding from the trailer and put it where you wish the horse to leave his droppings. Select the spot that is easiest for you to clean. Many, even most, horses can be trained to use the same spot, as they prefer to keep the rest of their stall clean. This is one of those simple things that can help you to get started right, but in the excitement of having a new horse, so many of us forget.

After you are convinced that he is relaxed, you can allow visitors to come and see him—but hands off for a day or two. For the first few days you own him, make certain no one opens his door or takes him out of the stall without your permission. When you lead him, put a lead on his halter. Don't take him out and pose him every time a new person comes to visit. Introduce other animals and objects to him cautiously. Watch his reactions, and if he is upset do not force the issue.

When it comes time to put him in a paddock, lead him around the fence and show him any water tank or other obstacle he might crash into if he starts running. Tie up all dogs or lock them out of sight. Stay in the paddock or right near the gate and watch him. He may settle down and eat grass, trot about and sniff at everything, or buck and play, roll and run. He might pace the fence whinnying for his lost stablemates; he might hang his head over the fence and stare at you. If he has not been out in pasture much, there are two precautions. One is that he should not be allowed to eat more than a little grass at a time. The safest thing is to give him his regular feeding with plenty of hay and water before turning him out to grass, so that he is not hungry. Limit his grazing to a half hour twice a day at first. If he digests that well and does not develop soft stool, increase the amount of time. The other thing you must avoid is too much running and a subsequent chill. If he is very excited and works up a sweat, you must walk him dry, and I mean walk. It is not sufficient to rub him off and put him in the barn. He may be better off if you tire him out with a ride before he is turned loose. Some horses cannot cope with pasture at all. I had a stallion here for two years who refused to settle down, relax, and eat grass; he paced the fence constantly. He was ten years old and had never been turned loose before. We never found any way to get him relaxed enough to allow him pasture freedom.

Some horses cannot stand solitary confinement. They will learn to be very dependent on a cat or dog or even a chicken or goat for company. The expression "Getting his goat" derives from horse racing, and refers to the practice of stealing an opponent's mascot goat before a race. This would upset the racehorse so badly that he would lose. If your horse will not relax and settle down, and particularly if he calls and calls for his friends, get him a companion right away, preferably another horse. You may be able to borrow a pony or a horse temporarily from some sympathetic neighbor. After your horse accepts his new home, he may no longer need equine company, but he should always have some living animal with him—although some horses will settle for a radio or television set going constantly.

If you are planning to introduce a new horse into an established herd, select an animal you know to be quiet and gentle, and put it and the new horse in a well-fenced pasture near the herd, preferably with more than a single fence between them. Allow the new and the established horse to become buddies, which usually takes a week or more. Then, either add one or two more horses to the pasture, or move the buddy pair nearer the herd or even with the herd; but stay around and watch. As a rule, once the horse has one friend, he will stick with it and not get cornered by the others. Gradually, he will make friends with the rest. One horse thrown into a herd, however, is sometimes kicked to death. It is particularly unfair to put a horse who has just traveled a long distance into such a position, as he is frightened and very unsure of himself; even the tiniest yearling can bully him. He will be desperate for company and will repeatedly try to get into the herd. He may be run in turn by each horse until he is exhausted or driven into the fences, whereas with a buddy he will be content to stay off to the side of the pasture and graze while the other horses advance and sniff noses with him.

It is very unwise to put a stallion or a gelding out in pasture with a bunch of mares unless they are fully acquainted and friends. If the mares have foals by their sides, they can be deadly—and they move very fast. It is hard to break up a running battle with several horses involved.

Strangely, people always seem to understand that a change of family is hard on a child or a dog, yet they expect a horse, who is a dependent, socially oriented animal, to take this experience without a qualm. Horses are also dependent on set routines. Their digestive system is particularly sensitive to change. The sounds of the night, the smell of the air, the taste of the water, and the voices and hands of the people—all are new. Some horses can accept this; others become nervous and irritable, and some can grow morose, go off their feed, even starve to death. You should certainly expect some changes in your new horse's behavior.

Your Horse's Food

The most important thing you should change gradually is his food. In the event that you cannot find out what your horse used to eat (as is often the case with a purchase at auction, for instance), feed him clean grass hay and small amounts of oats, which seems to be the one combination horses can go on without digestive upset. Oats should be given in quantities of not more than one 2-quart measure (or one 2-pound coffee can) per feeding at the start. If he is a big horse or a very nervous, active one, he may have to be fed three or four times a day; but do not give him large quantities of anything except hay at any one time for at least a week. Gradually increase the feed if he needs it, or gradually change to a different feed.

HIS DIGESTIVE SYSTEM

The reason behind gradual changes in feed must be clearly understood so that you do not make a fatal mistake.

Food is digested in several parts of the horse's digestive system. The grinding of food by the teeth breaks up the matter and exposes many surfaces to the action of digestive juices. The horse chews on only one side of the mouth for a long time, while the tongue moves the food within the mouth to mix it with saliva. The saliva breaks down starches into sugars, which are digestible by absorption through the bloodstream. The tongue also serves to detect and separate out indigestible material, such as bits of wire or stone. When the food is sufficiently chewed and mixed with saliva, it is swallowed. The horse's esophagus narrows down sharply where it meets the stomach, making it extremely difficult if not impossible for him to vomit. Once a horse has swallowed a substance, it continues through the system, whereas almost every other animal can discharge food voluntarily before it enters the stomach.

The horse's stomach is very small and very simple compared to that of cattle, for instance. The stomach contains gastric juices, including hydrochloric, lactic, and other acids. In the stomach, proteins are broken down to amino acids. Under normal conditions, a horse's stomach is hardly ever empty, even several hours after feeding. Digestion in the stomach is very rapid at the start of a meal, but it slows down markedly as the stomach fills. Foods do not mix in the stomach unless the horse is watered immediately after feeding, in which case a large portion of the food is washed out of the stomach into the small intestine, still in an undigested state, where it can produce indigestion or colic. This is why a horse should have water available *before* feeding, not withheld until after. The practice of feeding a horse in his stall and then turning him out to get water after a night locked inside is a dangerous one. There are many ways that colic can be caused—and colic can kill a horse. If fermentation in the intestine builds up pressure, it can bend and shut off the duodenum —the first section of the small intestine, which is U-shaped. In so doing, it traps the digesting food in the stomach and the stomach can rupture. It does not take a large volume of food to cause this to happen; one extra quart or two of feed, or any spoiled feed, can kill a horse in some cases. There are several secreting glands in or connected to the duodenum; these secrete enzymes and juices that break down food further into absorbable nutrients. The liver produces bile, which helps in the digestion of fat, among other things. In man and many other animals, the gall bladder stores bile and secretes it when needed. But the horse has no gall bladder, and the secretion of bile into the duodenum is continuous. Various enzymes present in the first section of the small intestine break down proteins further. After this the food passes on into more of the small intestine, which is about 70 feet long. Water takes from five to fifteen minutes to travel the whole length of the small intestine; food takes much longer. The large intestine is next in line: here in the caecum the digestion of cellulose takes place. Food does not reach the caecum for up to twenty-four hours after it leaves the stomach—and it can still be in the caecum as much as twenty-four hours after that.

When you consider all this, it should make you realize the implications of haphazard and careless feeding for a horse's health and comfort. A great deal of the horse's digestion takes place at the very end of his digestive system, in the colon and caecum. He therefore needs a considerable length of time after eating in order to gain the maximum energy and nutrition from his food. Sugar and starch, the instant energy foods, are digested early, but they do not comprise the bulk of a horse's diet. In order for him to digest his food properly, he must have small amounts at frequent intervals. Horses do not handle fats and oils in large amounts, so be careful not to dump in too much oil to make his coat shine. A little is good, but a lot might really do him harm. Minerals, vitamins, and water do not require digestion, as they are absorbed directly into the bloodstream.

Another digestive process is performed by bacteria in the intestines. The bacteria are specific for a particular feed. Horses that normally eat only hay and dry grain will get colic if put on a rich grass pasture. Horses taken off grass will die if locked in a stall and given huge amounts of grain. The same is true of a change of grain, such as putting a horse used only to oats onto a feeding program heavy in corn and molasses. The bacteria for a specific feed will develop in a matter of days, and the horse can learn to tolerate any feed which is healthy and appropriatë for his digestive system, but the introduction to one feed and the removal from another *must* be done slowly. When the previous feed is taken away, the bacteria for that feed will die off. Even if a horse has been on pasture exclusively all his life, once he is taken up and kept stabled without grass, he cannot suddenly be turned back onto it again without intestinal upset. The digestive bacteria, called intestinal flora, can also be killed by antibiotics. After heavy doses or prolonged use of these drugs, a horse will sometimes have a very soft stool or signs of colic. A freeze-dried enzyme to restore the flora is available through your veterinarian, or you can sometimes restore the natural flora with frequent feedings of plain, unpasteurized yogurt.

HIS WEIGHT AND METABOLISM

The horse you buy will do best on one kind of feed and one kind of feeding schedule. If at all possible, bring some of his own grain or buy the same brand and kind that he has had at his former home, even if his condition doesn't suit you. Then you can increase or decrease the amount to make him either gain or lose weight until he is right, or change him over slowly to a feed you prefer, but do so with an eye on his condition. You can tell when this is correct by noting a number of signs. Run your hand lightly over his rib cage; you should be able to feel his ribs. If you can't, he is much too fat. If you can stand back 50 feet and count his ribs, he is much too thin. Between these two extremes, he should look smooth, not hollow, just in front of the hip, not tucked up and shallow in the flank and abdomen. His belly should not bulge out to the sides wider than his stifles (unless of course it is a mare in foal). The neck should not be scrawny, with a deep dip in front of the withers. A light-necked horse with high withers might fool the eye, but if you can feel the spine through the sides of the neck the horse is way too thin. If the neck is thick and the crest hard, the horse is dangerously overweight. Each time I walk past one of my fatter horses, I check the crest. If it feels like muscle, fine; but if it is hard as bone, I stop all grain and take the horse off grass immediately. The hard crest in a mare or gelding or in an immature stallion is an early warning of founder. Many old stallions get crests like rock. I keep the horse off grain until the crest again feels pliable. So far we have not had a horse founder, but with Morgans this is something that must be watched all the time, for they gain weight rapidly on very limited amounts of grain and their own naturally rounded body shape conceals the fact that they are fat. Many people like horses fat despite their knowledge that it is harmful, even dangerous, for the horse. A little fat is not dangerous, but a fat horse is no better off than a fat person. Firm, trim bodies are healthy bodies; soft flab, hard rolls of fat, or a very underweight condition, rob the horse of his stamina and athletic ability and shorten his life. So for his safety and comfort, and for you to get your money's worth, he should be kept trim and smooth.

Every breed has a certain metabolism, or rate of burning energy (fat), and while our horses stay fat on 4 quarts of grain a day—even when nursing foals or campaigning in the weekend shows and training for them during the week—many Arabs, Thoroughbreds, and Saddle Horses would get thin on that amount of grain with no exercise at all. Use or exercise also burns up energy; the more a horse is used, the more concentrated grain ration and the less bulk and grass he needs. But how much and what kind of feed is needed will depend on the individual horse and how you use him. Two hours of conditioning for a competitive trail ride is far more work than two hours of work giving lessons to children under ten years old. Two hours of work for a hunter or jumper is a lot more strenuous than two hours in a cart on a country path.

Most grain for horses is formulated on research done on herds of horses kept for feeding experiments. They are wormed and pastured and fed high-quality hay along with the grain rations, as a rule. Then they are judged on their performance on certain feeding programs and schedules, under carefully controlled management. Their water, mineral, and salt intake are all adequate, and the amount of work (or stage of pregnancy) is known. When you buy a grain to feed your horse, it is assumed you provide all the other essential management that goes with dishing out a measure of grain once or twice a day. But for this you need an understanding of how and why, as well as what, you are feeding.

Horses do not handle urea well. The cow has a rumen in which she digests urea and it gives her the protein she needs, but the horse has no rumen. By the time the horse's body breaks down the urea, it is at the very end of the digestive tract, so that the protein goes out of the system and is never absorbed. Therefore, buying a cow feed at 16 percent protein for a cheaper price than horse feed at 14 percent protein is really no saving. The horse is not getting the extra protein you are paying for. Horses derive their best protein from soy. Rations that are high in digestible, available protein for horses are expensive. Many people think that since protein is essential to the horse, the more the better. Again, this is not so. Mares that are lactating, foals growing up to about two years of age, and horses under very stressful work do all require high protein. But most other horses will do well on 12 to 14 percent protein feeds, if the protein is derived from an available source. Protein does not make fat—carbohydrates make energy and fat. Horses that tend to stay thin need higher-energy feeds like corn. Those horses that tend to get overweight, on the other hand, should be kept away from corn. But in most cases, unless you feed your horse straight oats you will very likely be giving him a mixed commercial feed formulated for horses.

The choice of pelleted or non-pelleted feed depends on both the horse and the types of feeds readily available. Some horses choke on pelleted grains and some cannot survive on anything else. Between those extremes are horses who don't like them very much and those who prefer them to hard grains or whole-grain feeds. Mixed molasses or sweet feeds used to be the only kind of "horse feed" there was. My horses don't care for that; they carefully pick out all the corn and leave it in their buckets. Some horses will eat pellets only if they have lots of water; the minute their mouths get dry they stop eating. They take a mouthful of grain and a mouthful of water, alternately. I have several who do this. Rarely, horses get bored with a feed of pellets alone and need a little sweet feed or oats mixed in from time to time. But, as a rule, most horses do not get bored with a feed, and you should never assume that is the problem if a horse goes off his feed. Going off feed is more usually a symptom of illness, unhappiness, or discomfort. It might be sore feet, or the fact that a neighbor's cat got hit by a car, even though you never realized the horse and cat were friends. But most often it is a bellyache, sore throat, or tooth problem, and you should take notice of it. (See Chapter 13.)

Once you find the feed your horse does best on, stay with it. Don't run out and borrow some other kind over the weekend. And don't just assume you can get a bag of the same thing at a horse show. Take your own along. Your horse can't do his best with an upset digestive system.

HE NEEDS WATER

Water can be an awful problem when a horse moves. Some water supplies are so loaded with chlorine or sulfur that the horse will stop drinking entirely. If your water has a heavy chemical taste, before you bring the horse home ask the seller to give him a little vinegar in his water every time he drinks. When you get him home, put vinegar in his water also; it may make the transition far more comfortable for him. When you take him to a ride, rally, or show, if he is prepared for water with vinegar in it there is no problem. A cup of vinegar to every bucket of water will do many good things for the horse. First of all, it really does help to repel flies. Trail riders who have used this technique for years swear by it. Vinegar also ensures adequate potassium, which helps the horse to maintain his stamina.

We have just discovered a new way to get a horse to drink more water—put garlic salt in the grain. If the horse likes it, brown sugar also will persuade him to drink more. (The sugar goes into the grain, not the water.) Some horses relish Tang in their water.

There is a correct order in which to feed your horse. Water should be available at all times; but if it is not, the horse has to wait for you to fill his bucket. That is the first order of business. He should drink before he eats grain. Then he should be given hay and time to eat some of it, unless he is on a pelletted, so-called complete feed ration. Ten minutes is not too much time to wait. Hay should be fed at the rate of not more than 15 lbs. a day. Most "small" or string-bound bales weigh about 25 to 35 lbs., so less than half a bale of good hay should be adequate. Overfeeding is not very efficient, as horses who get a huge hay belly are often hindered in their movement. Many horses who know they will get grain right after their hay will not eat the hay but will wait anxiously. Then they bolt their grain. The hay is intended to reduce their appetite and their anxiety, and therefore to let them eat their grain at a more relaxed pace. Horses who bolt their food unchewed can choke. Chronic bolters should be fed tiny amounts of grain, either spread over a long, flat trough or with smooth, fist-sized stones placed in the grain box so that they cannot take huge mouthfuls of the grain.

QUALITY OF FEED

One of the first rules of good animal husbandry is to check each mouthful of feed you offer the horse to be certain it is the best quality you can get. Save moldy hay, dusty hay, or bedding for garden mulch. Give spoiled grain to pigs or chickens, or throw it out where wild birds can pick at it. They will not sicken from this feed. The average vet call for colic costs about $60 and the horse does not always survive. One bad bale of hay can start a case of heaves (emphysema) that will require several visits from the veterinarian and may prove totally incurable. So what savings you may have in feeding a bad bale of hay can be wiped out and tragedy can result. A missed meal is kinder than a spoiled one!

Poor-quality hay, low-grade oats, and other inferior sources of protein have to be fed in greater quantity than high-quality feeds, if the horse is to receive adequate nutrition. You as the horse's owner must determine if the feeds you offer are safe and of good quality. Grain must smell good, taste good, and be clean and fresh-looking. Hay must be bright and completely free from dust and mold. Vitamins must be fresh, not left open to deteriorate or exposed to high heat or humidity, as they lose their potency. For the average horseman, bulk buying of grain or vitamins is not only a waste but also a danger, for both can rapidly spoil and ferment, particularly during the humid summer months. One month's supply of feed or supplements should be the limit, and they should be kept moisture-free and covered.

Hay can survive storage for longer periods, but it too must be protected from excessive dampness. Hay that sits on the dirt will mold on the bottom. Mold—whether in hay, grain, or vitamin mixtures—can cause colic, which is often fatal, as well as eye irritations, heaves, and bronchitis.

There are some concentrated supplements, particularly Alber's Calf Manna and Agway's Bloom, which are high-protein and vitamin-mineral-fortified feeds. These are designed to be fed in small quantities in addition to regular grain. One pound a day of either of these good supplements improves a horse's coat and health in general, but a quart of either one can be fatal. They should be handled sensibly and never given in larger than the recommended allowances. Remember that if a little is good, a lot is *not* better. Calf Manna and Bloom, or any like concentrate, should be kept carefully closed up in a horseproof container, which should have a measure in it that constitutes one serving. I know personally of a number of good horses who have died from overdoses of these feeds and it was always because someone was unaware how critical the limits are. If you have small children or "Helpful Harrys" who come in and feed your horses as a favor to you, don't keep either of these feeds in your barn unless the grain room is locked.

SALT

Salt is an essential often overlooked by horse owners. Every horse should have access to a salt-lick. For some horses this is not enough, and loose salt must be available. Competitive and endurance horses sometimes require added electrolyte salts in their water; electrolytes are also given to horses under stress of illness. Again, these decisions are best made by the veterinarian, but at the very minimum, a mixed or *mineralized* salt-lick, not a plain white salt-lick, should be available to the horse constantly. Horses rarely, if ever, take too much salt on their own.·

HIS FEEDING REGIMEN

Many horse show exhibitors, professional trainers, and competitive trail riders have found that horses that work hard should have several feedings a day. The total volume for the day need not be increased, unless the horse is thin or losing condition.

A case in point is a young gelding we bred which is a versatile family horse for the parents and the children to ride as well as drive. The father probably works him harder than the rest of the family combined. The horse is by nature very willing and cheerful, and he is a capable working horse. But at one point the family found that when they worked him, he was sluggish and dull and he couldn't keep on performing for any length of time. The veterinarian checked him and they ran some tests. They then called me. My suggestion was to feed him a noon meal. His normal routine was breakfast at 5:00 A.M. and supper at 6:00 or 7:00 P.M. The family all went to school or work, and when they returned he was put to work. This meant that he was fed more than ten hours before working. All the sugars and starches would have been digested early in the day, and the horse would be working over his cellulose digestion by afternoon. My feeling was that he was experiencing a blood-sugar drop. In fact, with a feeding at noon the whole picture changed. His lively, fun-loving personality returned and he could maintain his energy level.

There are times when grain must be withheld or drastically reduced to protect a horse from ill effects. If the horse is normally an active, used animal, who has good muscle tone and is in good condition, and he is laid up on vacation because his rider is gone for a short while, or if the footing is too icy for him to go out, his grain should be cut *way* down. And when he is put back to work, it should be increased only gradually, not taken back to the full amount right away. This is to prevent a painful condition called "tying-up syndrome" (also known as *azoturia* or *Monday morning disease*). The horse may stagger, lie down and roll, or go lame, usually behind. He will often tremble and refuse to move, and may fall suddenly. His hindquarters and legs will become stiff and very painful; his urine will often be brown or coffee-colored. He should be covered with blankets, put into a warm and deeply bedded stall, and kept very quiet. The veterinarian must be summoned at once. You can prevent this painful and debilitating disease by making certain that his concentrated grain ration is reduced whenever he misses a day of normal work. Highly conditioned horses *must* be exercised daily, if only in a paddock.

Building Up Condition

MUSCLE TONE

Muscle tone is an essential part of a horse's condition. Some horses tone up very easily and maintain their muscle tone over periods of inactivity, while others go out of condition exceedingly rapidly. Sudden exercise can cause terrible stress and fatigue, which will slow down the conditioning process and can actually bring on lameness due to strain on ligaments and tendons. Horses that are ridden to the point of fatigue frequently hurt themselves seriously by striking the hoof of one leg against the bone of the other. If you do not know how much work a horse has actually had nor what his tolerance is, take your time and feel him out. Overweight horses can founder on a half hour of walking on a quiet trail. I had one that was leased for breeding and when returned was easily 400 lbs. too heavy. We led him for five minutes three times a day for a month, then gradually built up the time until we had him going under saddle. But on his first trail ride of not more than half an hour, he started to founder. Luckily the rider recognized the symptoms, dismounted, and led him home. The veterinarian came soon enough, with the right medication, to stop his complete breakdown.

Building up the horse's condition should be done systematically. Start each session slowly to warm him up. During this slow period, watch for stiffness, limping, or fretting, which might indicate pain in the mouth or muscles. The most important gait a horse can develop is a good, free, and eager walk. Most horses like to trot and will often tend to jog or jig rather than do a flat, free walk. Exercise the horse at all his gaits and over uneven terrain, if possible. Going up and down hills builds up different muscles from those used working on the flat. As the horse gets stronger in his muscles, his ligaments and tendons will also strengthen. He becomes less leg-weary after work. Increase the time of each ride and quit before the horse is showing signs of fatigue. With this sort of conditioning, he will become more and more eager to go out and work. If every ride ends in aching muscles, a feeling of exhaustion, and discomfort, he will soon sour and resent work. "Ring sour" is a common phrase for horses who travel with high action and their heads held in the proper position, but with their ears back and a dull or strained look on their face. Some horses get positively rebellious from ring-work boredom, and a quiet walk or a brisk trot through a shady woodland trail will restore their spirits and their pleasant attitude.

PULSE AND RESPIRATION

One way to check a horse's condition or fitness is by reading his pulse and respiration (P & Rs). Normally a horse at rest has a heartbeat of 36 to 42 beats per minute; he takes about 6 to 12 breaths per minute. With exercise, the P & Rs go up. The rate of recovery—that is, the time the horse takes to return to normal after work—indicates his condition. Trot your horse five minutes by the clock. Stop and check his P & Rs. If his pulse is between 60 to 100 beats while his respiration is between 30 to 60, he has a safe ratio (about 2:1). Wait fifteen minutes and check again. A horse in good condition will often have returned to normal. Then check again in one hour. If your horse is still not down to normal by one hour, he is in poor condition and should be checked by a veterinarian before being given any strenuous exercise. If, after five minutes of trotting, his ratio is close to 1 breath to 1 heartbeat, he may also be sick. Horses can experience what is called an *inversion,* which is an elevated P & Rs with more breaths than heartbeats. There is also a painful and dangerous condition, caused by strain, called the "thumps," where the diaphragm, instead of operating smoothly in and out, seems to snap rapidly, like gigantic hiccups.

SWEAT

The horse's sweat is another good indication of condition. A horse should sweat while he works, although some normally sweat far more than others. There is a marked difference between healthy, clear, watery sweat—which is salt, water, and a little protein—and the foamy, sticky, strong-smelling sweat that indicates a great loss of protein. A sticky foam or froth warns you that the horse may not be in condition for much strenuous work. Take your time and give him a chance to develop his lungs, circulatory system, and condition so that he can sustain his energy and work efficiently. He will stay sound a lot longer.

COOLING OUT

Be sure to groom and cool your horse after every workout. If you haven't the time to walk him out and groom him after a workout, then you do not have the right to use him for so long. Shorten the ride and be fair.

Why is walking so important? There are two reasons. One is that a horse gets hot when he works. Then if you just stop and let him stand still, he will get stiff and sore and possibly catch a chill. Muscles build up power as they work; blood flows more rapidly through the system, building up lactic acid and other wastes. In walking a horse after work, you are preventing him from cooling off too fast. The muscles have a chance to *depotentiate,* wastes are discharged, and oxygen is restored to the myoglobin molecules which store oxygen in the muscles. If the horse cools off too quickly, he is very likely to have stiff, sore muscles all night and the next day—what we call a "charley horse." Also, the weight of the rider on the horse's back compresses the blood vessels; if you yank the saddle straight off his hot back and release those compressed blood vessels suddenly, they will swell up and become very tender. So loosen your girth, dismount, and walk the horse with the saddle still on his back. Put a cooler over him and walk him until he is cool to the touch between the front legs. Then take off the saddle, towel off his back, and walk him until he is dry. Now he is ready for his thorough grooming. Sounds like a lot of work? Caring for your horse in an intelligent and thoughtful manner has many rewards, but it is not easy.

His Grooming

There are three kinds of grooming—preparatory grooming, after-work grooming, and cosmetic grooming—and they are done for three different reasons. *Preparatory* grooming is the brushing down a horse should have before a workout. This is done to be certain there is no mud or sand, nor burs, sores, or rough spots, that will chafe. After the horse is brushed, he should be gone over carefully with your clean, bare hand to feel behind the elbows, all along the back and girth line, and around the poll and ears. Grooming *after work* is his most important grooming—done to relax stiff muscles, stimulate circulation, check for swellings or sores, and remove every trace of bridle, harness, and saddle. *Cosmetic* grooming, alas, is what most horses get. It is done to make him look pretty, and what gets brushed is what shows. Worse, this grooming is usually a bath, not even good hard brushing and currying.

HOW TO GROOM PROPERLY

First, place the horse in a clean, light, comfortable work area. His feet should be picked out and examined for any signs of bruises or soft, oozing spots about the frog. If the foot smells it should be treated for thrush two or three times a week, depending on what treatment you use. (See Chapter 13.) To treat the hoof, lift it so that it is sole up and level. Clean the foot deeply with the hoofpick and pour a little Clorox, Foulex, Kopertox, or iodine into the affected area. Hold the foot a moment, then put it down. After the bottom is clean, feel the hoof surface. If it is muddy, brush it off with a stiff scrub brush and water. If the hoofs are dry, wrap a facecloth soaked in water around each, and leave it on while you groom the horse's body.

Examine the head, checking the skin around the eyes and mouth for sores or lumps. Then use a soft brush or towel to clean the face. Put your hand over each eye as you brush above it, so that you do not dislodge dirt that could irritate the eye. Handle the face and ears gently. Most horses enjoy having their faces groomed if you are careful not to poke or jab. Starting behind the ears, use a curry comb in a circular motion, backing the hair up to scrub all the dirt to the surface. Then, with a stiff dandy brush, flip the dirt out of the hair and away from the horse. This is done by laying the side of the brush against him and snapping the wrist while whisking the dirt off. Work the dirt out of the skin all the way down the horse's neck and spine, back and rump. Then start in at the front, and work back along his sides. Next, from his chest, work around and down the front legs, belly, and hind legs. Particular spots to check are where the leg bends at each joint, and where legs rub against the body or equipment lies against the horse. After you have done this rough grooming, you are ready to use a towel, again from the top down. Rub, don't pat. Then a soft brush should be used to lay the hair, which should always be brushed in the direction it normally grows.

If the horse has botfly eggs on his hair or legs, scraping them off with a dull knife works best. Burs are easily removed with a little salad oil or mineral oil where the hair is pulled back toward the horse out of the bur clump. Don't grab the burs and rip them out of the horse's mane or you will get lots of hair with them.

If your horse receives this kind of grooming daily and after every workout, he will not need gobs of oil smeared all over him, nor special feed to bring out a healthy glow. He will feel clean and healthy after grooming, because his circulation will be stimulated and his appetite improved, and his digestive system will actually function more efficiently. Remember that daily grooming is a must for horses that are sick—it is actually a substitute for exercise. Bear in mind, too, that a horse which is stabled most of the time needs a lot more grooming than a horse on pasture. Pastured horses (which does not mean horses enclosed only in a small paddock area) need grooming just enough to stay ahead of the botflies and burs and to check the animal for cuts and bruises. Overgrooming a pastured horse can rob him of a certain amount of the oil in his coat, which weatherproofs him.

BATHING

Horses should not be shampooed often, as this dries the natural oils from their hair. Sponging with cool water occasionally is adequate. However, you may want to give your horse a bath, especially if he is white, gray, or palomino. Start by heating the water in the sun or bring warm water from the house. Use a wrung-out sponge to go over the horse lightly at first, so that he is not shocked or made uncomfortable by running water dripping down his sides, legs, and belly. Dampen him once and then just a little more. Use a soap that will wash out in cold water, or a castile or baby shampoo; lather him up all over, then sponge again. This time you can use a little more water. If he will stand for it, you can turn a hose on him and flush all the soap off. Use a sweat scraper or the back of a Shed 'n Blade to scrape off the bulk of the water. Rub him with a towel, walk him until he is dry, then brush the hair flat and smooth and blanket him to keep him clean. Don't walk a wet horse uncovered in the sun—wet hair bleaches and burns very quickly. Some horses love baths and enjoy a hose; others are very upset by the whole process. Remember, you should never use a bath as a substitute for a good grooming.

SHOW GROOMING

Grooming for a show requires some special tools and cosmetics. First, each breed or type of horse has its own distinctive style of hairdo: some have pulled and braided manes, and some are clipped partway down the neck; some are shaved entirely down the neck and halfway down the tail; some tails are "broken" (actually they are cut and kept in a tail set); some have the tailbone cut off, or "docked," about 8 inches from the top, similar to the operation on poodles, boxers, and other dogs. Then horses may have more hair removed—eyelashes, muzzle whiskers, and the protective eye whiskers, too. Such horses should never be turned out in pasture at night, for they have no way of protecting their eyes from foreign objects. The hair that keeps flies and rain out of the ears is shaved out from the show horse as well, and usually replaced with a smear of oil to make the inside of the ear look darker. The hoofs have all their protective layer of periople sandpapered off and replaced with a layer of black lacquer, which inhibits normal respiration of the hoof wall, often resulting in contracted hoofs. Then the horse is greased from head to foot with a waxlike preparation and the owner stands back and admires his handiwork. What the poor horse thinks of all this we don't know. Since many of these practices are time-consuming and bad for the horse's health, there is no reason why you should ever get involved unless you become hooked on showing. It is certainly not the kind of grooming that should be encouraged for the family pleasure horse.

BLANKETING

I never blanket horses to prevent them from growing a winter coat —I don't believe in it. Man covers himself up warmly when he goes outside in winter; yet he blankets his horse in the stable to prevent the horse from developing protective covering and takes the blankets off when he goes out to use the poor animal. His horse is probably not conditioned well enough to prevent working up a huge sweat during a workout, and it takes a long time and a lot of grooming to cool out and properly clean a horse in a heavy winter coat once he gets hot. People like to rationalize and say we are doing all this for the horse's sake, but common sense will tell you that a horse will be cold if his blanket comes off and he is made to stand about out of doors with a rider on his back.

Some people simply don't like the looks of a shaggy fur coat and prefer to clip or blanket their horses, despite what is actually best for the animal. If in the late fall or winter you buy a horse who has always had a blanket, you should continue the practice until spring. Wean him away from the blanket slowly, and the following fall just don't get around to dragging the thing out. His skin will thicken, his coat will become luxurious, and he'll be happy. If you decide to show him in the spring and clip him all over, as many impatient owners do, bring out the blanket and keep him covered.

Cleaning His Stall

After you have mastered the art of feeding, have conditioned the horse properly, and done your honest best at grooming, you have one more important chore to address, which is the art of being a good stablehand. Stall cleaning is as much an art as any other part of horse management. It is also a major part of the management of the horse for the sake of his health. Obviously a clean stall contributes to his looks and comfort; deep and proper bedding will help him relax and sleep soundly; clean air in the stable means he can breathe better. But cleaning the stall also gives clues to the horse's health.

When you first enter the stall, observe the condition and odor of the manure. If it is strong-smelling, sickly sweet, soft and greenish, or crawling with worms, you have a problem. A strong urine smell may mean the horse is not drinking enough water. A sweet-smelling stool sometimes means *diabetes* or *ketosis,* conditions which require veterinary attention. Rank manure sometimes is a first clue to a viral condition. A soft stool can tell you if a horse's diet has changed, he has worms, is coming down with a disease, or his digestion was disturbed for some reason. All these are warning signals to be recognized. Unfinished grain in his bucket should also alert you.

If all looks fine in the stall except that it is filthy, you should select the driest corner, pick up the driest bedding, and place it there. Then remove the soiled bedding, piles, and wet spots. Put the remaining bedding, still too good to throw away, into another corner. Then rake the whole floor clean, pick up all the leftover wet and manure, and if the floor is a dirt one, try to level it out as much as you can. Sprinkle the stall with ground limestone if it is very wet or smelly. Rake the not-so-dry bedding all over the floor. Then spread out the drier bedding you have saved, and lastly top the stall off with a little more fresh bedding if needed. If you follow this procedure every day, the stall will never get ahead of you. You can get by with picking up the stall and adding fresh bedding to cover wet spots for a while, but gradually the bottom of the stall will deteriorate and become smelly and slippery. It will also promote the growth of bacteria causing thrush and ringworm. If you pick up the stall daily and then once a week give it a thorough cleaning, you will have to throw away most of the bedding because it will become saturated. My method saves bedding—and with prices the way they are, any savings help.

Cleaning should not be limited to the stall floor. Sweep down cobwebs and clean out the feed and water buckets or fountains at least once a week. If they are detachable, standing them in the sun will do much to reduce the bacteria growth which is inevitable in the collected grain and scum that forms in feed buckets. Clorox and a scrub brush will help to keep your horse's feedbox clean. Be sure you rinse everything well. Cobwebs collect dust, which is bad for the horse's lungs, and they also present a fire hazard. I hang a sign in my barn saying: "You are not done with your stall until you have cleaned the hall." Fire hazards are everywhere and hallways are the best avenue for flames to spread.

Lastly, what separates the really good horseman from the average horse lover is a thorough understanding of the workings of the horse's mind, body, and social structure. Your alertness to signs of change or indications of minor discomfort can prevent suffering. A horse will sometimes go off his feed because his feet hurt. He can have a headache and just a slight change in the expression in his eyes will signal his distress. Nervousness or discomfort can make a normally neat horse turn his stall into a pigsty. His frantic lugging on the bit or tossing of his head can warn you of a problem tooth. Only by exposure to the horse and his ways can you become an experienced and observant horseperson. You will find that you actually spend more time caring for your horse than using him, and the satisfaction increases. You will take a genuine and well-deserved pride in a horse who is shiningly healthy and vibrant with good spirits, all because you are a good and generous horseman.

CHAPTER 12

The Horse *Is* Different

THE INDIVIDUAL HORSE YOU SELECT is unique because you chose him and will expect him to fulfill your particular needs. I have made comparisons of breeds and types of horses, explained some of the differences between individuals, and tried to show what makes one more fit than another for a given task. But there are also certain psychological things about the horse—all horses—that you as a horse owner should clearly understand when you make a purchase. If you really know what makes a horse tick, you can make your life with him a joy and his life with you fun from his point of view. All too often, people think of the horse as either a furry person or a large dog. We are familiar with people, dogs, and cats, and we tend to try to make a horse "fit" our mental image of them rather than distinguishing what makes the horse a distinctly different species. The horse's vision, herding instinct, self-protecting behavior, and mental ability are all very different from those of other domestic animals—and particularly from man.

When psychologists study animal behavior, they are doing so from the perspective of "gatherers and hunters"—that is, they themselves are descended from hunting primatives. The things we consider signs of intelligence, even to this day, have to do with getting what you want (food, money, power, or "the good life"), protecting your own pride (family), and satisfying biological and emotional urges. We are not herding animals, dependent upon food where we find it. We do not require a large range for a constant food supply. The experiments set up to study so-called animal intelligence all have to do with food or sex. The primary method used to find out how smart an animal is, is to tempt him with one or the other, and then see how long it takes him to satisfy his needs. But the horse is a grazing animal, who either eats what he sees in front of him or walks about until he sees something edible. He does not hunt for his food; he doesn't bury it and come back later to find it. The hunter eats a meal, then waits for days for the next one to come along; the grazer must eat a little all the time, and cover a huge territory to get it. He is not lazy. He is athletic and he loves to move from place to place and see new sights. He is hardy and doesn't mind the elements. The horse is hunted by other animals, and so he is therefore a genius at avoiding capture.

But the main thing about the horse's "intelligence," which is not studied, or even considered, is that he is a loyal and obedient member of a society. He has a rank in his herd, a leader, a buddy, and a commitment and rules to do as the herd does. When one horse runs, they all run. They don't "love to race"—they are following a primitive self-preserving instinct. In order to become swift, the horse has to develop his legs, muscles, and lungs. Only by learning to run well will he be able to flee from predators. So when a foal is young, part of his play pattern is to race about as fast as he can go. The instinct to stampede is what makes a racehorse outrun the competition—yet his instinct is *not* to outrun another horse. We have to train the horse to go on *after* he passes his buddies; many a racehorse tries to drop back and stay with his group. There is safety in numbers. He has to be made to run faster yet by judicious application of whip, spurs, heels, or the encouragement of his jockey. Horses will work hard for a jockey they respect. This is instinctive obedience to their leader, part of being a herd animal. It is this willingness to obey, even when stressed to the limit of endurance, that makes the horse valuable at all to man. Think how utterly useless a 1,000-lb. cat would be! The cat has no loyalty or willingness to put himself out for anyone unless he feels like it. If horses were as independent and self-sufficient as cats, we wouldn't get a lick of work out of them. The horse is dependent, frail in many respects, and it is this vulnerability and his dependence upon us that make his strength, spirit, beauty, and personality all so compatible with our desires.

Why Does a Horse Learn?

A horse is very easy to train. This is due in part to his willingness to obey, and in part to his fantastic memory and sensitivity to what his leader wishes to communicate. The horse pays strict attention. When I was giving a talk at a university recently, a student asked me what was the most complicated thing I had ever taught a horse. I answered that I had never taught a horse anything complicated, for the horse learns only one step at a time. He is then able to put what he has learned in order very rapidly and the end result can be a very complex set of maneuvers. But the training is step by step.

Some trainers explain each lesson to the horse as if the horse could understand the conversation. They are gathering and ordering their thoughts in order to present the lesson to the horse simply, and in fact horses do seem able somehow to read our minds. Most really good animal trainers do this so automatically that they are completely unaware of it. A muddle-headed person who thinks in circles, worries over how he is doing and tries first one thing and then another, only confuses an otherwise perfectly trainable horse. The horse will resist and fight any lesson if he is afraid, confused, or in pain, or if he does not have trust in his trainer. If you are upset, angry, or afraid of something, you sweat, you feel warm and keyed up. The horse is highly sensitive to this. It changes the way you smell and the smoothness or jerkiness of your motions. Even a very slight stiffening of your muscles is discernible to the horse. The odor of fear is distinct enough that I can smell it. So if you are nervous, the horse is made nervous. And when a horse is nervous he becomes hard to handle, for he is getting prepared to flee for his life and restraint makes him worse. Since, from birth, the horse is taught that man is the boss (the leader) and the one to follow, he is logically ready to be afraid if you are. So when you are uncertain or ill at ease, the horse's mind is not on what you are trying to train him to do, but on self-preservation. You do not have his undivided attention.

This is why many horses who work calmly and smoothly at home become maniacs at a show. The handler, and many of the other people about the grounds, are keyed up and nervous. The excitement infects the horse and he gets high. As the horse gains more experience at shows, he begins to realize that he's not going to get hurt and he responds to the excitement by getting more competitive and keyed up, instead of frantic and unmanageable. In short, he becomes a better performer, and people think that he is getting to "like" shows. Horses do like an audience and admiration, and they have a sense of pride when their handler is pleased with their performance. They learn how to please—and the experience is rewarding to them. If they make a mistake and are punished after the performance, they do not understand why they are being punished and they get sour and rebellious. Some horses are punished because the judge didn't pin them, not because of any act or mistake on their part at all. These horses become failures because they cannot please their owners. Any horse that is asked to do something he is incapable of doing and then punished for failure will become more and more of a failure. Horses learn by being praised and caressed at the moment they have succeeded. They understand a firm reprimand (just the word "No" is enough) when they have erred, but it must be immediate. The reward can be just a lessening of the tension in your hands or legs on their sides. They do not need a carrot or a sugar lump to know that they have pleased you. Most horses are very smart, very tuned in and sensitive. If they regard you as their respected leader, it takes almost no effort to let them know when they have done the right thing. A horse will try to repeat every successful move that he has made; he will try to avoid the ones that will cause pain for him or displeasure for you. The more subtle your method of communication becomes, the more responsive and eager to please he will be.

It is this order and respect for leadership that makes the horse so useful. Many people view such behavior as stupid or simple-minded, but it is not. Independence and aggressiveness are for hunters and killers; cooperation is essential for grazing herbivores. It is pure self-preservation to run first and be curious about what frightened you only after you have put enough space between you and that object. This has nothing to do with intelligence or thinking ability. The horse's failure to find food that is hidden in boxes also has no relation to his intelligence. He has no instinct to hunt or search—indeed, it is totally foreign to his nature to find food in this way. Grass is not found under rocks or in hollow logs; it does not fly from one spot and land in another. Also, unlike the dog or hunting man, the horse does not regard food as a reward for an effort. To make a gift of food to a dog that has done your bidding is completely within his frame of reference. Horses like handouts, too, but they have to figure out that it is a reward, and then they have to figure out that it is a result of something they voluntarily did for you. They find this out by repetition, and if you are consistent they will learn. But they will be just as willing to do your bidding for a kind word and a pat on the neck. This they appreciate more readily, for they are receiving approval from their leader and that is very much a part of being a good herd member.

DOMINANCE THROUGH LEADERSHIP

It is important to understand the theory of herd dominance, for you accept the position of dominant member when you take on a horse that is to be your dependent, servant, and companion. You are to provide his food, shelter, protection, and leadership. A *dominant* trainer will set up some situation in which he has complete control and can keep the horse from getting hurt, but at the same time can get him mad enough to try to fight back or rebel. He then proceeds to convince the horse that obedience is both more pleasant and easier than fighting. Usually, only one or two lessons are enough for a smart horse with a reasonably willing nature, although some horses take much longer and there are those who can never be dominated.

COOPERATION THROUGH TRUST

The approach most horse people will find most successful is the establishment of a *cooperative* relationship, with the person calling the shots. This is based upon careful groundwork to convince the horse that the leader is reliable. It is done by going slowly enough to give the horse time to think and at the same time moving ahead with sufficient determination to convince him that you know what you are doing. If you truly don't know what you are doing, you might have a hard time getting the horse to let you be the leader! But if you remember that a horse can learn only one thing at a time, it will also help you to think out clearly what it is you are trying to get across to him.

The Effect of Vision

There are other things about the horse that it is essential to understand. First, and most important, his vision is not like ours. A horse has a *ramped* vision: what he sees with the bottom of his eye is quite different in apparent size from what he sees out of the top of his eye. He can look down over his nose at the grass and select just what he wants, leaving the rest. The grass appears to him enlarged and in great detail. When he looks up to identify something in the distance, he looks out of the lower part of his eye. If you hold your hand 2 feet in front of his nose and then raise it up perfectly vertically, it appears to him to jump in suddenly closer and enlarge. He will raise his head to get it back into focus and keep it the same size as it was. This is why horses duck or shy or even rear when you wave your hand suddenly above their eyes. The horse can also see all around his head, directly behind his body. He sees a different image with each eye. He may only recognize an object with one eye, for if he has never seen the object with the other eye it never made an image on the corresponding side of his brain. That is why it is essential to do things from both sides of the horse. It is also why, when handling a new horse, you should take care to approach and mount only from his *left* side. This requires an explanation. The traditions which have built up about the uses of horses stem from the days when men wore armor and swords. Since most men are right-handed, the sword was worn

Because of the ramped vision of the horse, objects which rise up in front of the horse seem to him to enlarge or come toward him. He will try to raise his head or back up to keep objects in their proper perspective.

on the left side. When mounting the horse, the sword hung by the supporting leg that lifted the rider into the stirrup. If he had hung the sword on the right leg, it might have struck the horse as the rider threw that leg over. This is also why the mane is traditionally worn on the right side of the horse's neck. When the rider gathers up his reins on the left side of the horse's neck, he does not get entangled in the mane. It has become so ingrained in our culture to follow these traditions that it is actually sometimes dangerous to ignore them. Some horses spook violently and even kick when mounted from the right. Such a kick is just like the kick you get when you touch a sleeping horse. It is not a deliberate but a reflex action, entirely automatic on the horse's part. It does not indicate a bad disposition nor anger. If you do the wrong thing and get kicked for it, it is a failing on *your* part. Good horsemen don't get kicked or stepped on or run into walls very often. They are aware of what will make a horse jump or shy and they keep alert. The horse uses all his senses to stay out of harm's way. The only things that concern him are comfort and safety. He wants to eat, he needs to sleep, and he wants to stay in his place in his herd. If you are his "herd," he will make every effort he can to please you. The rest of the time he will defend himself as best he can, and he will be alert for dangers all the time.

THE EAR FOLLOWS THE EYE

You can judge just how alert a horse is by his ears and his eyes. As he passes something strange, he rolls his eye toward it, lowers his head or tilts it slightly, and "drops" an ear to catch any sound. He may also extend his nose and sniff the thing, or try to face it and back away until he can identify it. If he is a brave and trusting horse, he will be aware but not necessarily shy of something new. If he is stupid or dull, he may not even be aware. If he is timid or has had bad experiences, he will be cautious. Here is where your horsemanship comes into play. Some horses are near-sighted and have to get very close to something to recognize it. They may even touch it with their nose and then jump backward as if stung. Allow a horse to look, but help him to keep his self-control. Use your voice to steady him in a firm, positive way. Keep a steady hand ready to stop his panic flight. Never punish or inflict pain in connection with anything that has frightened the horse. You can't beat sense into him; a beating works only if a horse fully understands that he is being punished for a conscious act of his own, such as biting, striking, or some other act of aggression or rebellion.

How His Brain Works

The horse's brain is actually a different shape from that of a dog or a man. The different compartments of the brain control different aspects of an animal's existence. The brain does a great deal more than just "think." It works all the time, even while the animal is sleeping. Each species of animal has a different brain. In some the ability to think and reason is very well developed; this is credited to a portion of the brain called the *cerebrum,* which in man is very large by comparison to other animals. The *hypothalamus* is the part of the brain concerned with thirst and hunger, temperature and emotions. This explains why people often substitute food for happiness and why you perspire when you are angry or nervous. The *subthalamus* is in control of coordination. The horse has a comparatively small cerebrum but he has an exceptionally large *hippocampus*—a section of the brain still not fully understood. It is believed that in man it has to do with sense of direction, map-making, and the ability to relate to one's surroundings; horses have this capacity to a marked degree.

Horses remember where things belong. A jacket on a fence post is out of place, and to a horse this may be cause for real concern. Your life may depend upon your understanding and your powers of observation.

They remember things they have seen and where they belong to such an extent that they are truly upset by things' being out of place. A horse can always remember where he found food or water, and can return to that same spot even years later. If you hang a bucket in the left-hand corner of the horse's stall and feed him there for a month, he will look in that corner first, even though you move the bucket to the right and he can clearly see it. Horses who cover hundreds of miles in free-range grazing know when to return to a spot that had good grass, and they can get there even in the dark. They know what time of year and what time of day it is. This is one of the reasons why you should try to feed on a regular schedule. Horses get very upset by changes in their time schedule. Some are also terribly disturbed when they are put in a stall other than their own, even in the same barn. Their security depends upon things being in the proper place. Horses that pass a certain spot and see a school bus parked there every day will become frantic if the bus is absent or even a few feet down the road. People are unaware how much the horse takes in. The horse does not understand that the bus can be driven away; he only knows it is in the wrong place. We can only guess why change upsets a horse so much; possibly he feels that predators have moved things. If you are aware, you can save yourself from accidents. I clearly recall a mare that was giving a dressage demonstration at her own farm. There were hundreds of spectators, cars, and activity, none of which disturbed her. But she suddenly froze in the middle of her performance, and until her owner finally figured out what was out of place she remained motionless. She had spotted a plaid jacket hung on a fence post several feet from the rail. To her it could have looked like a lurking wolf or puma. The moment it was removed, she continued her show as if nothing had happened. A more excitable horse might have shied violently or even turned and run. Your ability to spot things that look different can save you from a wild ride, or a roughly shortened one.

COMMUNICATION

As you ride or drive the horse, he will communicate a great deal to you. Remember that horses speak to one another silently and convey a great deal of information using attitude, gesture, and tenseness. Their eyes and ears are your biggest clue. The tenseness and swelling of muscles are also a reliable guide to the horse's mind. In other words, you can feel a shy before the horse makes the jump. You can tell which direction and pretty much how hard he is going to go. You can tell when he is going to slam on the brakes, for he bunches his shoulders and tightens his haunches under him. You know when a horse is going to throw a foot at you because he clearly warns you by a squint in his eyes, a snarling lip, a shake of his head, and a decided flick of the tail. Horses never intentionally do anything without some signal which you can learn to read. They do make totally instinctive, reflexive moves with no warning because they themselves don't know they are going to make them. When you are on the horse's back and he sees something that is strange, he will raise his head at first. He will then focus his eyes and ears, and tense his neck and those muscles directly under the saddle. This should be all the warning you need to make you pay attention and try to identify the object. Once you know what he is seeing, you can either prepare to stay with him if he leaves, or you can reassure and steady him, and help him to accept the thing as harmless. If the object does not move, you can usually convince a horse that he is safe. But if it does move suddenly (whether it is a leaf or piece of plastic, a snake or a rabbit), hang on! Many horses pass something that frightens them as if the thing were not there, and then bolt and run. A steady, restraining hand and firm seat will be required on such horses. Usually, in harness, if the horse is made to trot a good fast trot and keep his head perfectly straight, he will continue on his way, leaning on the bit for stability and communication. It is often safer to keep the horse in motion than to stop and let him investigate, but that depends on the horse and your relationship with him. Remember, too, when the horse tenses up, that if you also tense up and make a mental image of a runaway, you have just told the horse what you expect of him. You must project your authority, security, and knowledge that the thing in question is not a tiger waiting to pounce. You are not stronger than the horse, so you had certainly better be smarter. Your safety depends upon your own self-control.

SENSE OF TERRITORY

The horse's sense of where he is in the world makes him different from other animals in another way. The horse is a nomad and does not "own" a territory. He shares his grazing land with all other animals. He protects only his own body and his/her own immediate, dependent offspring. The horse's sense of territory or "own space" covers an area of only about 15 feet from his body. He thinks in terms of that limited area one way; things outside it do not concern him unless he thinks they will enter his area. So you can usually ride a horse past a fearsome object if you make a wide enough space between it and his body. A dog or a car that rushes toward an animal is threatening to enter his sphere of concern. A person who enters his stall or approaches him rapidly in pasture is closing in on him. If you keep frightening things 20 feet from a horse and do not make him go toward them, he will usually just look, try to identify them, and then go on about his business. Gradually, a horse with any intelligence will investigate, providing he feels he can flee if necessary. Bearing this in mind, you can introduce the horse to anything he fears with time, patience, and a minimum of restraint or force. If you want a horse to look at something that has spooked him, take a lengthy piece of line such as a longe line, and snap it on his halter. Then walk up to the object, letting the horse stand way back. Touch it and lean against it. If it is metal, do *not* bang on it to make a noise. I see people do this all the time, but it will only worry the horse more. Stroke or pet the thing as if you like it. Walk around behind it but without vanishing out of sight. Call the horse to you with a firm command, making sure there is no suggestion of anger in your voice. Don't "coo" at him, either. He should not pick up any clues from your voice that he should be scared. Let him touch the object with his nose and back off. Stay where you are and let him come back again until he is satisfied.

People get into terrible fights with horses over puddles. The horse will try to avoid putting his foot into a hole. A puddle that reflects the sky or is black on the bottom looks like a trap to him, and he will not walk into it until he knows and understands that it has a bottom. There is no point in creating a huge fuss over walking through a puddle. Give the horse time to look at such things, then, if you really want to convince him it is safe, walk through it yourself first. Once he sees you do it, he is much more likely to go through himself.

VIBRATIONS

Horses sense vibrations through their feet. Many horses that are good on trails and in harness alone suddenly become runaways when another horse charges up behind them. This stampede reaction is evident in very young horses and gradually fades as the horse becomes accustomed to working with others. Vibrations from a train on a track or heavy trucks on a highway can sometimes trigger a run; people who hear these sounds can identify them and then discount them as ordinary and harmless, while the horse is thoroughly alarmed. When you learn to sense that the horse is tensing up, try to listen as well as look for something that might be causing his anxiety. He will probably not be anywhere near as disturbed by a gunshot in the distance or some other loud noise that does not send shock waves through the ground. Helicopters, which vibrate the earth, are much more likely to disturb a horse than a far noisier airplane. The horse can be trained to have self-control in such situations as long as you know what he is reacting to.

Lastly, if you can hear a horse breathe, be alert. Horses normally breathe noiselessly, even after hard exercise, unless they are winded. They make no breathing sound whatsoever if they are relaxed. The moment a horse "huffs and puffs," he is trying to identify something he is scared of. He will look and listen, stiffen his muscles, and prepare to bolt. Rattling in his nostrils or a fear snort is a clear declaration of intent to run.

Training

In teaching a horse, you must realize that he learns only if he makes the right connections, that is, if he is rewarded or punished at the moment he consciously acts. One moment later he is doing something else and reward or punishment then will teach him only about the thing he is then doing. Since "reward" and "punishment" can be very subtle, requiring no more effort on the part of the trainer than a stiffening or tightening for punishment and a relaxing or giving with the hand for reward, there is no excuse for this cue being given too late. The mistake we make in training is often that we feel we have to hit or feed a horse—and that takes time. Even your tone of voice is a cue to the horse of your pleasure or displeasure, and that is what he is working for. I use my voice as a whip and as a caress and my horses know what I have in mind. They do not understand the vocabulary necessarily, although they can learn certain single words delivered in a specific tone of voice, such as the commands "Whoa" or "Stand," the reassurances "Easy," "Steady," or "Shhh," and the praise "Good." These they will respond to very quickly. They learn the words "Walk," "Trot," "Canter," and "Back." The rest of the conversation we hold with horses is mostly for our own benefit. As we speak, we have a mental image of what we mean. The horse reads our image more than he hears our words—he senses the "body English" we use as we utter the words. Think of your communication with the horse as being strictly personal; no one else should be able to see or hear you giving your horse cues. Once you have mastered this art, you will be communicating properly with him.

Communication, however, has to go both ways. You must learn to recognize the horse's slightest inclination to do your bidding, even if he does not get it all right the first time. If you pull on the reins, he might only nod his head instead of flexing his neck and relaxing his jaw. That is the first step in his learning and must be reinforced and rewarded. If you want further flexion and relaxation, another gentle pull and another reward will do more to gain his cooperation than a stronger pull. When you ask a horse to collect himself or to bring his legs in under his body in order to stop, turn, or take a proper lead, you must have the sensitivity to feel his muscles under the saddle when he tries. All too often a rider gives a signal and if the horse fails to give a total and proper response, he is snatched in the mouth or belted with heels. Many horses start to canter or lope by taking a plunge forward, and the rider, instead of giving a little on the reins and leaning forward, yanks back for balance or slows the horse down and actually pulls him out of the gait he was asked to perform. Development of this give-and-take and quiet communication is the first step in learning to think like the horse.

Horses are also right- or left-"handed," as we are. It is not at all unusual for a horse to turn easily to the left and become rigid if you try to bend him to the right. This has more to do with coordination than with thought, but you can train a horse to bend, and the earlier in life you start, the easier it will be for him. We lead our horses from both sides, but since I am right-handed I find it much easier to lead from the left. So, naturally, they get led from the left far more often. When you turn a horse, you should walk him around to the right instead of letting him pivot around you to the left. It is safer, for he is less likely to step on your foot and also he will stay in better balance as he turns. But most of all it should be a regular habit with you because you will be helping him to become more flexible. A long row of pylons, stone heaps, wastebaskets, or other markers are a great thing to work with. Weave the horse "in and out the window," making full circles first one way and then the other around each marker. It will be hard at first, but eventually the horse will get the point and become far more willing to turn. You may find it a real lifesaver to have the horse bend and respond to you instead of becoming rigid and resistant.

Overcoming Some Problems

Training a horse to change his habits is a little different from teaching him something new. You have to overcome an idea that is already in his memory bank. You cannot wipe it out, so you have to reschool him to respond differently to the situation. Even simple things like learning to accept the position and signals of a new rider will take a little time. In fact, horses are quicker to change their habits than people; a horse will learn a hunt-style signal to canter, even when he was trained to saddle seat signals, a whole lot quicker than a person can learn to give saddle seat signals when he has previously ridden only hunt seat. But it does require a little time for a horse to learn to walk through a doorway if he has been allowed in the past to rush. Horses learn to hurry through narrow passages because the people who have led them have banged them against walls, allowed doors to slam on them before they are through, slapped them on the rump, and so on. You can change such a dangerous habit only by stopping the horse before he enters, letting him relax, and then proceeding directly in front of him, using your back against his chest if he starts to run. That can be dangerous with a horse who is badly scared of being struck or trapped. But the key is to gain the horse's trust, and to work quietly and without anger if the first few attempts are not successful.

Reeducating a horse with a serious hang-up such as fear of an accident in harness should be done with the help of a skilled trainer. Some habits, such as rearing, are truly unbreakable. A rearer can be made to refrain for some riders but the tendency will never be completely overcome; such horses remain dangerous for every new rider. Since learning in the horse is based almost entirely on memory or experience and almost always on one single lesson that made its impression, when you try to rehabilitate a horse you should try very hard to determine what caused the problem. This is not always obvious, and of course when you buy a horse that has developed habits before you got him it may be impossible. The system for reschooling the horse is to put the animal in a situation close to the one in which he developed wrong responses, and then to keep that situation under control so that you can help him to learn the right responses and prevent him from getting hurt or frightened. If you can repeat this lesson successfully and reward the horse for the proper response, he will make the connection. He may revert back to his bad behavior with the previous owner or with someone who reminds him of the earlier experience. This is why an owner, having hurt or spoiled a horse, can send him to a professional trainer who will reschool him and have no trouble; but as soon as the owner handles him again, the horse reverts back. That is not the fault of either the horse or the trainer.

Horses that jig constantly are extremely badly trained. It may be a horse that has been spoiled or one that was never educated in the first place—that nervous jig is a positive clue to poor horsemanship somewhere in his past. It is one of the hardest of all vices to cure. There is a difference between a high, prancing parade gait and the jigging of a nervous or uncomfortable animal. Bring the horse to a standstill from a walk and from a trot, and count slowly to twenty-five before you start again. If a horse jigs, turn him in a very tight circle and start off at a walk again. Speak softly to him and relax your legs. Since he may do it from distress, check his mouth for sores or loose teeth and his back and girth for raw spots. If you ride in company, insist that your fellow riders do not go off and leave you behind. If you fall back, have them stop while you walk to catch up. Do not let the horse jog or trot. Develop as fast a walk in your horse as you can. Reward him with praise and a scratch on the withers, even if he only walks for a few steps at a time. Keep your legs and body as relaxed as you can.

Discipline

Since horses vary tremendously in their level of sensitivity and their reaction time, it is impossible to lay down rules on how much or how little discipline is required to maintain control. Morgan horses seem to require a minimum of force as long as they are not frightened or hurt. Even when they are scared, they usually show pretty good sense and will rely on their handler for leadership. There are some breeds which are so resistant to training and discipline that people joke about having to teach them everything with a two-by-four. In some cases, the horse that is awfully nervous or energetic takes a long time to train because he is not paying attention but dithering in his own mind. Overdisciplining can breed resentment—Morgans are well known for their intolerance of abuse. They will accept control, but if they feel that they are being wrongly treated they will fight back.

ROUGHHOUSING

There are horses that make a game of roughhousing with people. They like to nip or bump you with their heads or shoulders, or step on your toes just to get a rise out of you. If you ignore this, often they will stop because it is no fun. Others will try even harder until they get a slap or even a beating—they have then managed to get a rise out of you and will continue to push you until you get angry. Remember that horses are very rough when they play with each other; they bite hard and kick hard. If you allow a horse to entice you into a game, you may well get seriously hurt. You must make it clear to the

A plastic bleach bottle tied to a braid in the tail is one method of training a horse to stop kicking at things that touch the rear legs.

horse that you are very angry for even a small nip. A halfhearted slap or, worse, a squeal will encourage him to try more nonsense. If you hit a horse, be careful that you hit him well below the eyes. A blow on the head is dangerous for many reasons, but it also might make the horse rear and strike back at you. If he bites, bring something hard or rough, like the bristles of a stiff dandy brush, up from under his chin and hit him in the mouth. If he doesn't know where it came from, he can't duck. But remember, if you can't do this right away, don't do anything. Just be prepared for the next time and let him know you won't tolerate such behavior, ever. Do not get carried away and keep hitting the horse; do not hold a grudge. Get all your steam out with one hard blow and then drop the matter.

KICKING

Kicking is a defensive action; biting and striking are offensive behavior. It takes a little thought to reschool a horse that kicks. If the horse makes all sorts of threats and gives plenty of warning that he intends to kick, you can be sure he is trying to be boss or is defending himself because he thinks you are going to bully him. If he kicks only under certain circumstances, such as when his girth is being tightened or when you are mounting, you know he has a memory of pain from a past experience and is trying to defend himself. Obviously you can't allow him to go on kicking and obviously you don't want to hurt him if he is frightened. So you have to be sure you know the reasons before you can know how to correct this particular behavior.

We have had horses who would kick at anything touching their hind legs. One mare, in particular, was not safe to groom. She had been raised in a pasture with a low, hock-high electric fence, and I suspect she had made contact with it a few times. We were trying to train her to harness and the lines and traces made her frantic. Our solution to her problem was not discipline but reeducation. We braided a strand of her tail and tied a plastic bleach bottle to it, where it could bump her hocks and rear cannons. We put a chain shank over her nose and led her into a safe enclosure before letting the bottle hang down. Then when the man on her halter was ready and the gate was closed, we lowered the bottle gently and he started to lead her about. He had his hands full for quite a few huge jumps and some frantic spinning. Once she knew running wouldn't help her, she walked and jumped and kicked for a long spell. We then left the bottle tied to her tail and let her live with it for a few weeks. Finally, she realized that it would not hurt or shock her, and then accepted other things around her legs. She never kicked again while we had her here.

I have seen horses "sacked out" for kicking. If the person doing this does not get angry and does not allow the horse to get hurt or to run away, it has always proved a permanent cure. Sacking out is done by holding the horse by a rope, not a chain, on his halter, and then gently flapping a sack, blanket, or some other large, nonpainful object against him. My farrier uses his leather apron, which makes a loud whooshing noise and lands with a slap but does not sting. The point of sacking out is to create noise and sights that will frighten the horse but at the same time convince him that he will not be hurt. This is why you don't use a chain on the nose. It is essential that no pain is connected with the experience. My farrier gets the horses so used to the apron that he can bop them right over the head, up under the belly, and all about their legs and they just stand and stare at him. He never ties a horse, but holds it on a line and allows it to back up. He follows it quietly, talking to it and swinging the apron slowly, with no force behind it. It is remarkable to me that a horse will learn from such a frightening experience and be far less jumpy about anything flying up, bumping him, or moving suddenly after proper sacking out. He also will have a much greater respect for the farrier and his voice. The farrier never allows the horse to back into something except a solid wall. He never dumps a horse over backward or yanks on his head. He just keeps at him until he quits flinching, and speaks gently to him to let him know he is not angry.

Before you get into discipline with a horse that kicks, have the veterinarian check his vision. Blind horses kick involuntarily. If you can be sure it is just a case of nastiness and trying to bully you, then stay far enough away to avoid his heels and let him have it with a whip; but remember once again that the discipline must be immediate to be effective.

RUNNING AWAY

Running away is a symptom of pain or panic, and once more it is not a punishable offense. First assume that the horse either is in pain because of an overharsh bit or an ill-fitting saddle or harness, or has had an experience that triggers panic and he bolts to escape injury. Obviously, neither of these problems is cured by inflicting more pain. To stop a runaway, the safest method is to turn the horse in as tight a circle as you can under saddle. To stop a harness runaway is far more difficult, for the horse may run as long as the cart is chasing him. Often it is possible to run a harness horse into a wall or a fence corner that he can't jump, but let me warn you that a horse in a cart can jump a whole lot higher than a horse with a rider on his back, and a horse tangled in a fence with a harness and cart attached is one awful mess to get unscrambled. Once a horse has run away, it is not safe to assume that he will not do it again. Very few horses run in order to scare their riders or because they learn they can "get away with it." With those that do, the solution is simple. You find a long enough road or a big enough field, then make the horse run until he wants to quit, forcing him to continue until he simply can't. That usually stops the habit once and for all. Reeducation is a must for most horses who run away. There is no sure cure until you have found the cause.

Lastly, let me stress that negative training does not work on a horse because the horse does not comprehend it. If the horse does not come running to you when you call him, and you decide, "Well, to heck with you, I won't speak to you," and walk away, the horse does not know he is being deprived of your company or that he is being punished—he has no faculty in his brain to make that connection. The horse will not understand your withholding food if you are not pleased with him. The only discipline he can comprehend is that which happens at the moment he has deliberately and knowingly done a misdeed. Therefore, you must win his cooperation by communication and reward his good efforts. Reserve discipline for those specific times when you are certain it will be effective.

More Psychology

Some books on horse psychology would have you believe that the horse that runs fast does so because he knows he will then be kept and used by his master for racing and that he is preserving his species as a conscious act. These books also would have you believe that the horse is myopic and sees things only when they are in motion. There are a lot of strange myths about horses that prevail in spite of much effort and research proving them false. Horses do see colors and respond to them clearly. They have preferences and strong dislikes. Our horses all react violently to shocking pink. They will actually avoid a person wearing a shirt or jacket of this color, yet they are not particularly disturbed by international yellow or electric blue or bright red. All these are "unnatural" colors, usually found only in plastic raincoats and nylon windbreakers.

RECOGNITION

Horses clearly recognize photographs of other horses and respond to them. I first experienced this with a stallion I leased. He responded to a photograph of my old stallion. The photo is a black-and-white head shot, which was a full-page centerfold used in the *Horse Of Course!* magazine some years ago. I have it framed and hanging above horses' head height in the entrance to my barn. It is much smaller than lifesize. This stallion stopped, whinnied, and nickered, then started to flirt with the picture. I called my husband and we watched him put his nose to the photo to sniff breath. He arched his neck, struck, and squealed, and went through the whole mating dance. When he later saw my old stallion in the flesh, he acted as if he recognized him as the one he had flirted with. I thought this was just one unusual horse and incident until another stallion I have just bought reacted to this photograph in exactly the same way. I have since talked to a trainer who has a stallion in her barn that flirts with the pictures hanging beside her crossties. Now, these are small pictures of horses with riders on them, and horses in groups, not a single large head shot at all.

I have had equally dramatic proof of horses' seeing and recognizing each other over a great distance. I had a mare once with only one eye. She had a colt which was a light chestnut with a wide white stripe. I weaned a group of foals with hers and kept them separated for two months. When I was sure the mares' milk had dried up, I waited until the mares were way out in pasture on top of a big hill. I put the foals as a group in the barn, then slid open the door to the pasture where the mares were and let the foals out very quietly. The one-eyed mare heard the door open and looked up. When she saw the colt with the white stripe, she did something quite remarkable.

She ran to each mare in the pasture with her that was light chestnut and she looked directly at their faces. Once she was sure all the white-faced, light chestnut mares were there that belonged there, she knew the new horse was her foal. She ran down to the meadow where the foals were grazing and took possession of her weanling son. There was absolutely no wind that day, so she could not have smelled him from that distance. The foals did not make a sound, so she could not have recognized him by voice. Since it was obvious that she was counting white faces among her band, she had to have made that distinction in her identification of the colt.

ATMOSPHERIC CONDITIONS

We have a rule here that no one teaches a horse something new, frightening, or potentially dangerous on a windy day or prior to a storm. Atmospheric conditions have a decided effect on horse behavior. Wind makes horses very skittery and they don't pay attention. Brewing storms make them extremely nervous, and we have had some terrible accidents because horses panicked while a storm was brewing. Mares frequently foal early or even hold up a few days in order to foal at night while it is raining. The reason for this is that hunters cannot see in the dark and cannot smell their prey in the rain. When a mare foals, she is helpless for a period of time; a rainy night is the safest time for her to deliver. I doubt that there is a conscious effort on the part of the mare—it is far more likely that the foaling process is triggered by the right atmospheric conditions.

AFFECTION

Some people truly believe that horses are not capable of affection. They cite the fact that the horse does not run up to you, jump on your chest, and lick your face. Thank heaven they don't! Horses also do not show submission to their master as dogs do by throwing themselves at your feet and exposing their throats. Horses greet their friends by a whinny, by nuzzling the nape of their neck, and by blowing gently into their nose and sniffing their breath. Some gently nip along the back of the leg or smell the shoes with great care. These are all methods of recognizing and exchanging greetings with their own kind. If you are included, you should respond by blowing gently into the horse's nostril, scratching his back, withers, or neck (he may scratch you back with his upper lip or even with his teeth), or just stroking his neck.

YOUR OWN SELF-CONTROL

Horses do not do things for you because they like you or refuse to obey because they don't like you. They will avoid you entirely or they will actively reject you, even threaten you, if they do not like you. They will obey any command that they fully understand if they trust you and respect your leadership. Control of a horse has nothing to do with mastering him. He is bigger and stronger than you. If your signals are clear and unambiguous, consistent and appropriate, and if the thing you are asking the horse to do is within his grasp and his capabilities, he will try. If you meet with resistance or rebellion, your first questions should be: What did I do wrong? What hurt the horse or confused him? What am I asking for that he cannot give? Frequently, a tiny child can handle a horse that baffles and confounds an adult. Children are fearless, clear-thinking, and honest; the horse can respond to that kind of leadership.

Some horses are stubborn, some are lazy, and some are mean. But if a horse is not normally any of these things, there is no reason ever to assume that his refusal or rebellion stems from these sources. Keep in mind his vision, his sense of orderliness, and his feeling of personal safety within a very limited area of his body. If you inspire his trust, respect, and confidence, you can win his cooperation.

CHAPTER 13

Your Horse's Doctor

THIS CHAPTER IS INTENDED to acquaint you with the essential care every horse requires as a regular preventive-medicine program, with some of the more common ailments you may encounter, and with general procedures of first aid. In no way is it intended to encourage you to dispense with the services of a qualified veterinarian.

Routine Care: Prevention Practices

Immunizations are available for a number of diseases and in most areas of the United States the following are given annually: tetanus toxoid, Eastern and Western equine encephalomyelitis, Rhinopneumonitis and influenza. In some areas Venezuelan equine encephalitis and rabies shots are also given. Your horse's immunization requirements depend upon several factors, including his exposure to diseases, your geographic location, and the regulations of the various sport activities in which you and he participate.

Worming should be done at regular two-month intervals throughout the year. Every horse has worms and no reasonable amount of stable management can prevent them. The point is to identify the specific types of worms your horse harbors and use the remedies that will be effective against them.

Encephalomyelitis

The three strains of so-called sleeping sickness are abbreviated EEE, WEE, and VEE—for Eastern, Western, and Venezuelan equine encephalomyelitis, disorders within the central nervous system that are transmittable by insect bites. Once afflicted, the horse staggers, leans dejectedly on walls, walks in circles, or shows other signs of noncoordination. Death soon follows, all three types being fatal; they are incurable once the animal is sick. Horses do not carry EEE or WEE or pass them on from horse to horse under most circumstances; they are carried in an alternate host, usually a bird, such as a pheasant, pigeon, or cardinal. VEE can be passed from horse to horse.

Sleeping sickness can be prevented by annual immunization, though immunization against one type does not protect the horse from the other two; there are, however, combined shots containing two or all three. The E/W immunization may be given in two shots spaced at specific intervals, two weeks to two months depending on the recommendations of the manufacturer. A new vaccine became available this year combining all three, and there is a single-shot vaccine for E/W. There is also a vaccine which combines E/W and tetanus in a single injection. Since encephalomyelitis is caused by a virus, it does not respond to antibiotics. Immunization is the only rational preventive. The shots are usually given in the spring before the mosquito season begins and they take time to build up an immunity—the necessary antibodies in the bloodstream—to be effective against the disease. E/W vaccinations are effective for only the one season. Immunity used to last only six to eight months and had to be timed accordingly. Two injections each year were required. In New England we usually aimed for March through the end of May. In early 1977 one drug company, Haver Lockhart, got government clearance for an E/W vaccine requiring only one injection each year. Immunity is good for twelve to sixteen months thus enabling vaccinations to be given at any time of the year. Consult your veterinarian.

Tetanus

Tetanus, or lockjaw, is another fatal and preventable disease, to which horses are particularly susceptible. The causative bacteria, clostridium tetani, is abundant in horse manure. There are two injections for tetanus and many people think their horse is protected when it actually is not. *Tetanus toxoid* gives lasting immunity, usually considered good for one year. *Tetanus antitoxin,* given at the time of an injury, confers temporary protection or reduces a horse's chances of contracting the disease, but it lasts only about ten days. Lockjaw gets its popular name from the stance or attitude of the sick horse. The muscles become rigid, with the neck extended and the jaw locked in a closed position. The tail extends out and the third eyelid, the nictitating membrane, covers most of the eye. The victim becomes unable to move about or swallow. Death is slow and painful and only rarely is it possible to save a horse in the advanced stages of the disease.

Immunization can be administered at any time of the year. Foals are frequently given antitoxin at birth. Toxoid immunization is started at two months of age with a two-injection series the first year followed by a single annual booster. Mares are given a toxoid booster thirty to sixty days before foaling to give them time to build up a high antibody level. These antibodies will pass to the foal in the first milk, colostrum, and protect the foal against tetanus for approximately the first two months of life. The mare is also well protected at foaling time. No amount of care, cleaning of a wound, or doctoring will prevent lockjaw once the toxin produced by the organism has entered the bloodstream. Immunization is the only rational preventive.

Respiratory Diseases

Respiratory diseases have many causes, including viruses, bacteria, and such mechanical factors as dust or mold, to which some horses are allergic. Those respiratory diseases that are spread from horse to horse are a primary concern to horsemen, because so many horses are shipped about from show to show. Some can be prevented by immunization and some cannot. They generally have similar symptoms, so that evaluation of each horse's case requires examination and often cultures and blood samples to make a definitive diagnosis.

RHINOPNEUMONITIS—EQUINE VIRAL ABORTION (EVA)

Although the term "viral abortion" might make you think this disease is limited to pregnant mares, it most certainly is not. Its other common name is "the snots," and it afflicts horses of all sexes and ages. Symptoms may be mild or severe. It is caused by a virus, as the name indicates, and there is a preventive vaccine that is effective. In breeding-farm situations, abortions, stillborn foals, and breeding difficulties may be encountered. Where the virus is suspected or the exposure considered high, injections, as frequently as four times a year, may be indicated. Similarly, animals on the show circuit, which may be exposed to horses with the disease, may also have these immunization injections repeated throughout the show season. The symptoms of this disease often include a heavy nasal discharge and cough. Runny eyes are sometimes but not always associated with rhino. As is the case with all virus diseases, treatment is symptomatic; you relieve discomfort and prevent further stress until the body fights off the disease. For this reason many horses lose a whole season of showing if they are not protected. If done carefully, the vaccine may be used in treatment. Vaccination against rhinopneumonitis in foals is started at two to four months of age with a two-shot series, then repeated as indicated by the individual situation on the brood farm. A minimum of one immunization per year is recommended for horses that are not ordinarily exposed to other horses or do not participate in competitive sports. Immunization during pregnancy is safe if proper care is taken to time the shots in relation to the mares' breeding and foaling dates. The vaccine given intramuscularly is a vast improvement over the old intranasal vaccine of past years.

The *adenovirus* group is a series of respiratory viruses that cause a disease clinically indistinguishable from rhino and flu. A definitive diagnosis of this disease can often be made through the use of blood samples taken at proper intervals during the course of the disease. Titers for various viruses can be taken and the causative agent detected. Treatment is symptomatic as for rhino, but there is no immunization vaccine for this disease group.

INFLUENZA

Influenza—similar in its symptoms to human influenza—is a virus-caused disease for which there is a vaccination. Flu is not curable through the use of any specific drug but is seldom fatal except in weakened horses. Treatment is basically supportive, giving the body strength to fight off the infection. Horses being shown or trailered about should be immunized one to three times yearly.

STRANGLES—EQUINE DISTEMPER

Strangles is a disease caused by a bacteria: *Streptococcus equi*. The symptoms include swelling of the glands under the throat, which sometimes grow large, and if they do not rupture by themselves must be lanced. Strangles is not as common a disease as it was some years back, when nearly every horse had a case of it sometime during his life. It hits mostly young horses because once a horse has had a case of it he becomes immune for many years. Now, since it does not go through every herd each year, older horses may be afflicted with it. It is seldom a fatal disease and not considered very serious or incapacitating, though it may be disfiguring if the abscess leaves a scar; further, the scar tissue and damage to the throat and associated nerves may leave the horse with permanently damaged wind. Strangles vaccine is available and the disease can be treated by specific antibiotics. Many horsemen do not elect to use the vaccine, for some horses seem to get an adverse reaction to the immunization that is worse than an actual case of the disease, providing they are given adequate treatment. The immunity conferred by the disease itself seems to be very long-lasting, whereas immunization through injection must be repeated. In the event of a serious outbreak of the disease in your area, you should be guided by your veterinarian's decision.

ADDITIONAL RESPIRATORY DISEASES

Many other bacteria also cause respiratory diseases. Staph and strep infections are common. Viruses besides those mentioned also cause respiratory infections. Additionally, fungus infections can occur in the respiratory tract. The important thing is to try to make the proper diagnosis of the specific causative agent and then determine which, if any, drugs will help. This can be done in a number of ways. I have already mentioned the analysis of blood samples for viruses. Cultures of nasal and/or pulmonary discharges can be taken, grown in a laboratory, and analyzed. By growing the culture and then treating sections of the growth with various drugs, it can often be established which drug should be effective against the specific disease. In this way you do not waste money treating everything randomly with penicillin. Since viruses and many bacteria are not touched by penicillin, you may actually mask the real problem and allow it to take a firmer hold. Certain diseases respond to streptomycin, sulfa drugs, or one of the scores of new antibiotics being developed constantly. Fungus infections are far more difficult to diagnose and treat. Any cold symptom should alert you to isolate the horse from other horses, call the veterinarian, and take the disease seriously. Early diagnosis can prevent spread of the disease, unnecessary suffering for the horse, and costly medications, which may prove ineffective or even harmful.

Rabies

Most people are familiar with rabies in dogs but fail to realize that other animals can be affected by this dread killer. In many areas of the country rabies has become a very real threat to horses. It is preventable by immunization and if you have any idea that it is a problem in your area it should be included in your regular vaccination program.

This pretty much exhausts the diseases for which you can immunize at the present time. Many laboratories all over the world are working toward more immunization against diseases and even against parasites, but these are not available as yet.

Immunization is created by actually giving the patient a small dose of the disease organism. This causes the horse to manufacture antibodies in his blood stream to fight disease, which stresses the system. Horses should not be worked for a period of days after receiving immunizations.

Heaves, Allergies, Asthma, and Chronic Bronchitis

The ailments in this group are usually preventable by good stable management. Humid barns, confined spaces, mold, dust, and untreated colds are the major causes of heaves and bronchitis. Heaves is much less common now than it was fifteen years ago. Once a horse has heaves—emphysema—it is controllable but incurable. You can keep the horse comfortable with careful management and bronchial medications, but the disease stays with the animal, for the damage to the tissues of the lung is permanent. Heaves is evidenced by a cough and by a characteristic pumping action of the abdominal muscles. This is a double bellows-like action of these muscles below the flank at the end of the rib cage. Often the ribs suddenly are plainly visible through the hide. The horse has difficulty getting air into and out of his lungs. Most "heavey" horses can be seen to heave while at rest, but some show distress only after exertion. It is generally very difficult to get a heavy mare in foal. Horses so afflicted often lose weight dramatically and are very difficult to maintain. There are specially formulated grains on the market for these animals and they certainly do help. If a horse has any kind of cough or breathing problem, wet his hay thoroughly before feeding him. Give only as much hay as he will consume in a short time so that it does not start to ferment or mold. Better yet, eliminate hay completely from the diet. Antihistimines and/or steroids can help a horse with heaves or the related problems.

Laminitis—Founder

Laminitis or founder is another often preventable disorder. It has a number of other names—seedy toe, dropped sole, chest founder—all descriptive of the victim's appearance. Founder has many causes and experts are by no means in agreement as to a single most important one. Allergies, inheritable metabolism and predisposition, stress, and other factors have all had their share of the blame. I have listed this problem among the avoidable diseases because the largest propor-

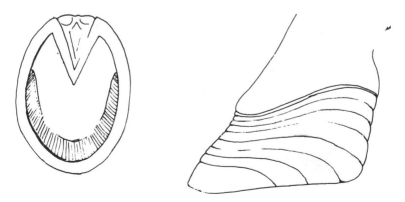

The exterior of the foundered foot from the bottom showing the tearing of the laminae. The side view shows the founder rings, dropped sole and contracted "dished" surface of the hoof wall. This is a very advanced case.

tion of founder cases are considered management-originated. Over-feeding is probably the most common mistake we make where foundering horses are concerned. Some horses burn up their grain at a great rate due to a high metabolism, while others seem to gain weight just thinking about food. Thyroid dysfunction is suspected to be a problem in these horses. Ponies are particularly subject to founder and Morgans probably rank right behind them. You can prevent overfeeding founder by checking the horse's condition daily. Run your hand over the ribs, squeeze the crest of the neck. It should be pliable and feel like normal muscle, never hard like bone. Feel the feet whenever you groom. Excessive heat in the foot is a clear warn-ing signal that there is fever, infection, or founder starting. Some mares founder while foaling. Horses may founder as a result of colic, overwork while in soft condition, stress while shipping—and un-known causes. If prompt diagnosis is made, and proper treatment instituted much founder damage can usually be stopped in time, but in the case of a horse foundering while sick with some disease that causes an elevated fever, it is often not discovered that the horse is foundered until after the symptoms of the disease have passed.

Signs of founder include a particular stance assumed by the horse to relieve pain in his toes. He places his feet out in front of him and rocks his weight back onto his rear legs. The chest often appears caved in, hence the term "chest founder." Inside the foot much has

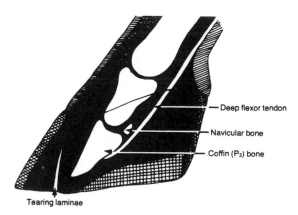

— Deep flexor tendon

— Navicular bone

— Coffin (P₃) bone

Tearing laminae

The interior of the foundered foot. Compare this with the drawing on page 252 and note the downward rotation of the coffin bone (3rd phalanx) and the short pastern bone, and also the tearing away of the laminae from the hoof wall.

occurred. The blood supply to the foot is disrupted, the temperature rises, and the laminae of the hoof are damaged. The foot bone (pedal bone or P_3) actually leans away from the hoof wall. When this happens, the sole drops and the pedal bone rotates downward. Viewed from the bottom, there is a widening and often a reddening of the white line, most pronounced at the toe. Horizontal rings appear around the foot later on as a result of abnormal hoof growth. It is most common to founder only in front, but an occasional horse founders in all four feet.

Treatment for founder varies, depending upon the cause and the stage at which it is detected. First aid consists of standing the horse in cold water to reduce the temperature in the feet. Then the veterinarian will administer drugs he deems advisable. Founder is an extremely painful ailment which renders the horse lame. If caught in time, it can be arrested before it progresses too far. It can be helped to a great extent by proper shoeing and hoof trimming and a regimen of proper diet and exercise. In advanced cases this can take a year or more. Teamwork by the horseman, the veterinarian, and the farrier are required to restore a horse to a normal and useful life. It is better to be aware of the causes and symptoms and do all you can to prevent the disorder.

Parasite Control

WORMS

There may well be no such thing as a worm-free horse. Good management of pastures and stable facilities and a regular program of worming can keep the population under control so that the horse never has to suffer severe worm damage. Worms are believed by many authorities to be a major cause of colic. They can certainly contribute to malnutrition and unthriftiness in foals. They can cause blockage of the blood vessels and intestinal tract, damage to the lungs, rupture of the stomach and blood vessels, and death. They should be taken seriously. All the different kinds of worms have specific life cycles and susceptibilities to particular wormers or vermifuges.

Wormers are poisons. They are effective because they poison the parasites. Careless use of wormers can kill the horse. They can also cause problems when used in conjunction with certain other chemicals or drugs. So make it a point to really understand what the wormers do and how they work. Use them only in the proper dosages. Ideally the way to worm a horse is by examining a stool sample under a microscope to determine the specific worms involved by identifying their eggs and administering specific worm preparations for that given infestation. Frequency of worming depends upon the age of the horse and also, like immunization, depends upon the exposure at the particular farm. Where horses are kept in permanent pastures and in large numbers over a period of years, and where herds of horses are frequently very young, such as at a breeding farm, the exposure to worms is far greater than in a stable in which horses are kept isolated in stalls and receive all their exercise under saddle or harness. Young horses should be wormed a minimum of four to six times a year. Older horses can often get by with three-month worming.

The worms that afflict horses most commonly are bloodworms (strongyles), roundworms (ascarids), pinworms, and bots. However, once in a while a horse will get a tapeworm or some other uncommon worm which will require careful diagnosis and special treatment.

Ascarids (Roundworms) are large white worms that resemble spaghetti with pointed ends. While they are immature they look like strongyles or pieces of thread, but at maturity they can reach as much as thirteen inches in length. Though they are a particular problem in young horses and as horses mature many seem to build a degree of immunity to them, they can be found in older horses, too. I purchased an eleven-year-old mare that was thin and near death. She was wormed at the veterinary clinic and the doctor was so astounded at the worm kill that he had the stall bedding screened; he found over fifty pounds of roundworms. We have one mare who delivers a satisfying number of mature worms every time she is wormed. She is fat and slick and never gives the slightest indication that she is such a carrier, but she tolerates the worms well and seeds the pasture constantly. She is wormed every time the foals are wormed, to keep the population down. Ascarids succumb to several wormers which are not very toxic to horses. (Some are highly toxic and must be handled with extreme caution.) Piperazine, pyrantel pamoate, dichlorvos, mebendazole and cambendazole are all drugs effective against ascarids. These are sold under a variety of brand names. Now,

I have said we get a very "satisfying" number of worms from one mare. It is often possible to worm a horse that needs to be wormed and never see a single worm as a result of your efforts. There are three possible reasons: one, the worming was done at the wrong stage of the worm's life cycle so that it was not affected; two, the wrong wormer was used and/or it was not properly administered; and three, they were so immature you couldn't see them.

Of course, concrete evidence of effectiveness is gratifying, but what is really important is the condition of the horse, and within a week you should begin to see a marked improvement in his looks and attitude if he was badly in need of worming and the procedure was indeed successful. If there is no evidence of worms killed and no marked improvement in the animal, worm him again, with a different wormer. Worms can become immune to the effects of any given wormer. After a worming some horses get sick. This can be from an overdose, a bad reaction, or a large kill of worms passing through the system and causing pain. Under most circumstances the effects are short-lived and the horse is fine in a day or two. Reaction to some drugs seems to vary with different breeds. Morgans seem particularly sensitive to some and can die from a dose that would not even sicken a Thoroughbred or Arabian. Again, metabolism varies from breed to breed and should be considered whenever medication is administered.

Strongyles or bloodworms are regarded as the worst enemy of the horse. They are believed by many to be the major cause of colic. They can completely block the arteries of the hind limbs, inducing paralysis. They can stop the heart and can rupture blood vessels, causing internal hemorrhage. These worms are small, thread-like creatures. They are susceptible to many of the same wormers that kill ascarids, but by no means all of them. Phenothiazine, fed in a low-level worming program, can reduce the fertility of strongyles so that they stop reproducing. But consult the veterinarian before embarking on any program of this nature. Many horses who are irritable, rebellious, crampy, distressed or appear mentally retarded, are suffering from strongyles. Some faint, stagger, and appear to be suffering from other ailments, such as sleeping sickness. Some go bald over large areas of their body and look as if they are infested with external parasites, but close examination does not turn up signs of any.

Pinworms are irritating to the horse but not nearly as severe a threat to his health as ascarids and strongyles. They crawl out of the anus and lay eggs about that area, making the horse itch and rub his tail. Evidence of pinworms is usually only a slight yellow secretion. The worms themselves look like immature ascarids. Stool sample examination is a good way to determine which worms are present.

Bots are not true worms. They are rather the larvae of the botfly, which does not sting, bite or feed while in the fly stage. Thus it lives for only a few days or less. During this time it lays tiny yellow seed-like eggs on the horse's legs, neck, mane, and body. These are scraped off by the horse's tongue and teeth. They are then hatched in the mouth and begin their journey to the stomach. Once in the stomach they burrow into the mucous membranes. A large infesta-tion of them can cause digestive disturbances and sometimes perfo-rate the stomach lining. It is best to worm for bots in the fall after the first heavy frost and through early spring. Worming during the warm months such as July and August is not recommended. The wormers that kill bots are the ones most likely to be hard on the horse, so use caution. Of these, the orlanophosphates such as trichlor-fon, and dichlorvos may have side effects which resemble a colic attack, but the treatment for this is quiet (not walking) and an injec-tion of atropine.

This is not something that the average owner is prepared to han-dle, so when you set up a worming program, here are a few things to keep in mind:

1. Wormers are all poisons. Dosages must be figured carefully. Horses are wormed by weight, keeping in mind their metabolism, age and condition.

2. Worms multiply rapidly and mutate to build up resistance to the various wormers. You must change wormers, not use the same one each time. Also remember that different wormers are specific for different worms.

3. Timing is essential for effectiveness. The worms migrate through the horse's body in a life cycle. Sometimes they are in the lungs or throat, sometimes in the bloodstream or digestive tract. The wormer can kill them only while they are in the intestine. Thus a horse that is wormed with no effect can two weeks later be wormed again with an enormous kill.

4. Other aspects of timing are important. As stated before, bot flies should be exterminated during the winter months, not during warm

weather. December and February are the most usual times to bot-worm. Timing is also important in broodmares. They should be wormed several times during pregnancy so as to minimize their foals' exposure to worms. Foals eat manure and soiled bedding. Still another timing consideration is the fact that the bloodworms a foal has picked up from his mother are not susceptible to worming until he is four to six months old.

5. Since wormers can make a horse very sick, you should be sure to worm on a morning when you will be around to watch the horse for ataxia or other signs of a bad reaction. It is frequently difficult to get the doctor if a horse sickens during the night.

There are three methods of worming: tube worming, syringe application, and placing the wormer in the feed or water. The method depends upon (one) whether the horse will eat a wormer in his food and get all of it, and (two) the fact that certain wormers are far more effective with tube worming. Your veterinarian can tell you his preference. You should make it a habit to weigh your horse with a tape measure, available from several feed companies and at most grain stores. Dose exactly as labeled for the average horse in good health. Give lesser doses if the animal is very old, weak, or debilitated. Tube worming is the most positive way of being sure the horse gets all his wormer, but it can be traumatic and a lot depends upon the horse's own reaction to tubing and to the veterinarian. I have had horses so badly frightened by tubing that it took literally months to regain their confidence—and my doctor is a particularly gentle, tactful, and careful man. If you can be sure that the horse eats every bit of his wormer, there is no advantage to tubing the horse at all. Syringe application is not injection but dosing the horse via the mouth with one of a variety of syringes. I use a large disposable catheter made of plastic. Sometimes I fit a short piece of surgical tubing or rubber hose on the end. There are wormers that now come in a gel or paste form in their own applicator. They are very effective, are easy to administer accurately, and the horses don't get excited by them. Some wormers and some medications are so palatable that you can put them in the horse's drinking water and they will be readily consumed.

The choice of wormer first should be based on a stool sample examined by the veterinarian to determine the offending worms. Then upon the most effective and least traumatic method of administration. The wormer's own palatability will have a lot to do with this decision. And finally, remember that you must use alternative wormers. Don't stick loyally to one because it worked so well before.

You may find that a few days after you have wormed the horse he won't eat. Just be patient, for he will return to normal eating within a few days. A very large kill may be upsetting him or he may have had cramps and upset stomach from the wormer, causing him to distrust his feed bucket for a while.

It is important to note that when a horse learns what is good or bad for him he has a specific mechanism to prevent himself from being poisoned. In nature, every new thing a horse eats he will eat only in a very small quantity the first time. If he has no ill effects he will try a bit more. If he gets sick he will remember the last new thing he ate and will not touch it again. We interfere with that instinct when we stable horses and feed them mixed hay and grain, but still the instinct persists. Once a horse has a bellyache from his grain he will proceed cautiously for a while.

When you read the label on your wormer—which you should always do with great care—you may come across the unsettling message: "Do not administer within x number of days of a cholinesterase inhibitor." Since you are unlikely to find the definition of cholinesterase or information about what inhibits it in any book in your bookshelf, unless you have a biochemist in the family, I offer here a very abbreviated description. Cholinesterase is an enzyme. It is a normal constituent of blood serum. When the brain signals a muscle to flex, it does so by sending an electrical impulse through a nerve to the muscle. At the point where the nerve touches the muscle, a substance called acetylcholine exists. It is involved in the process of nerve firing. Each time the nerve fires, more acetylcholine is generated. Cholinesterase hydrolizes or eats up the acetylcholine. If it does not do so, the nerve fires again. As the nerve fires more and more, the muscle flexes more and more until it goes into spasm. If this continues, the animal is overcome by flaccid paralysis. Therefore, if a substance is introduced into the horse's system which destroys the action of the cholinesterase, the horse can die of convulsions and paralysis. Thus, do not worm the horse at the same time you delouse him or spray with repellents and insecticides. A doctor who is going to anesthetize a horse for surgery must be told if you have wormed it recently. If the horse shows signs of spasmodic muscle activity, paralysis, or convulsions after a worming, call the doctor and tell him. Try to find out if he has been exposed to any substance which might have interfered with his normal metabolic activity. Tranquilizers are to be avoided in conjunction with wormers and with delousing unless the veterinarian gives them.

EXTERNAL PARASITES

The external parasites that are most commonly a problem to horses are flies and mosquitoes. There are hundreds of fly repellents available and some seem more effective than others, but none of them really repels deer flies effectively enough that you can ride your horse in the woods during the hot summer months. The best protection you can give your horse is a thorough grooming and a wipe-on repellent before a ride and a thorough grooming to rid him of sweat afterward. Shelter from direct sun and flies in the heat of the day is essential. It is our practice to keep the horses in during the day and ride or pasture them in the evening, then leave them out all night.

Mites, lice, and ringworm are the other external parasites which commonly plague the horse. *Lice* can bite, which is very irritating, and they can also suck blood and actually debilitate a horse from blood loss. They are usually at their most active in the early spring months while the horses are stabled and shedding. Lice infection causes itching. Lice are grayish white and look like tiny hayseeds; they are most easily found along the sides of the neck and in the base of the mane. Lindane is one of the effective pesticides for lice on horses. There are several delousing materials, such as organophosphates, which are not always safe to use on horses. I recently bought some louse powder for cattle and was astonished to read that it could be used on all except Brahman cattle. I asked my veterinarian about its safety for horses and he said throw it out! Delousing should be done three times at ten day intervals. Brush the horse, bathe or dust him with the pesticide and if he wears a blanket, wash it also. Hang the thoroughly brushed blanket inside out over the fence in the hot sunshine all day long every day you can.

Mange, caused by mites, is much harder to get rid of than lice and it would be wise if you suspect it to have the doctor take a skin scraping and give you a prescription.

Ringworm is not a worm; it is a fungus, sometimes called rain scald, which can cause total hair loss. Like lice, ringworm is normally a springtime problem. It is not itchy. It is most particularly severe with pastured horses during drizzly, cool spring days and nights. If you run your hand over the horse every time you pass him, you will pick up such problems as ringworm very quickly. Little scabs or tufts of hair on the back are usually the first sign. If you pull one of these the horse may flinch. The tuft will come off and there will be a small, circular bare spot. We have found our most effective treatment for this to be two or three injections of vitamins A, D, and E, spaced at weekly intervals. Some people treat their horses very effectively by sponging a solution of Clorox and water all over the horse. Keep this out of the eyes. Use one cup Clorox to one quart of water; do not substitute just any bleach. Some of the thrush remedies are used against ringworm. Since I have not used these, I cannot make any recommendation, but I do warn that skin is sensitive to chemicals and overdoing any caustic or harsh chemical may cause permanent damage, such as the hair not regrowing, or coming in white. Sterilize all your grooming tools if you find the horse has any parasites; these are all transmittable from one horse to another.

Other Diseases

Recently we lost a foal, born two months prematurely, but an apparently normal fetus out of an apparently healthy mare. We suspected rhino but upon autopsy found no evidence of this. Further tests revealed a high titer in the mare's blood for a disease called leptospirosis. This problem has no clinical signs, but can cause blindness and abortions. Horses may contract this from deer or rat urine in their feed supply, pasture or water. Though no treatment will prevent abortion, blindness, if recognized in time—and it comes on slowly—can often be limited in its extent. In one of our mares, we first recognized it as a pool of yellowish blood inside the eyeball, first in one eye and then in the other. This condition came and went, with the eyes cloudy one day and clear the next. Of five mares of ours who contracted this disease, only two lost their vision, and it was gradual, over a period of several years. Leptospirosis requires prompt diagnosis and extensive treatment.

Swamp fever, or equine infectious anemia, is a disease that has

Funquest Wallisa, a mature Morgan mare at the time of purchase. Note the ragged coat, big wormy belly and shallow neck and croup.

Funquest Wallisa, one year later. Her teeth were floated, she was wormed, her feet were trimmed and her nutrition was improved. The dapples in her coat, alert attitude and change in her head shape clearly show the effects of proper treatment.

Albinos, a color breed bred
for disposition and versatility.
Here the White Horse Troupe,
circus performers par
excellence, in action.
(Courtesy American White
Horse Registry)

High Bar, an Appaloosa
stallion. Appaloosas were
bred to be war horses by the
Nez Percé Indians in the
Northwest. (Photo by Johnny
Johnston, courtesy ApHC)

Yankee Doc (Doc's Benito Bar X Blond Gold). This is an excellent example of the Quarter Horse type, even at the tender age of 6 weeks. Note the well-developed rear quarters, head carriage low and forward. (Photo by Foster)

Rondout Belle Linda and colt Whippoorwill M'Lord by Whippoorwill Duke at 5 weeks. Morgan type horses, high head and tail carriage, well-laid-back sloping shoulder. Yankee Doc and Whippoorwill M'Lord illustrate the different conformations of the Quarter Horse and Morgan.

Quarter Horse working a calf. He is a Buckskin color. (Artist: Randy Steffin, Courtesy American Quarter Horse Association)

Hi-Lo Klondike, a Palomino Morgan by Keomah Scot out of Salisbury Lee. Shown as an English Pleasure Horse and a Road Hack by owner Andrea Laubach. (Photo by Winifred Laubach)

Whippoorwill Anfield, Morgan mare by Whippoorwill Duke out of Broadwall Mayfield, ridden by Paul Winslow. This young pair are setting out on their first competitive trail ride.

Thoroughbred Hunter, Blue Hour by This Evening out of Beverly Blue. Harry de Leyer up in perfect form over a fence. (Pettinger photo by Nina Brandsema, courtesy Peggy Jett)

Whippoorwill Starling by Bald Mr. Black Cloud out of Whippoorwill Melody, being trained by Nancy Zizka. This is a young Morgan mare being ground driven in a biting rig.

Whippoorwill Cardinal Morgan gelding by Chief Red Hawk out of Whippoorwill Melody. Owner Rudy Herbst demonstrates the use of a brush drag. This pair also compete in dressage, in harness, sleigh rallies, etc.

Whippoorwill Suzuki and Amy Welch, both three years old. Age is not what determines a horse's value as a child's pleasure horse. The temperament and disposition that are bred in from the start are the qualities that will count in the long run.

Whippoorwill Cardinal driven by Linda Salwen. This versatile gelding is demonstrating a Carriage Rally Obstacle Race judged on time and skill of both horse and driver. (Photo by Rudy Herbst)

Whippoorwill Morgan broodmare drill team. Our mares earn their keep raising foals, but they also put on a precision display of teamwork for our annual versatility events. (Photo by Linda Salwen)

Those same Morgan broodmares are also *fun*! After the drill team practice, Andrea Laubach, Cynthia and Diana De Wolf take their mares for a splash in the lake. Note they are riding in halters and leadropes only.

been known for a long time and affects only about 1 or 2 percent of the horse population. There is no vaccine yet for the disease and no cure. However, a test was recently discovered that determines antibodies in the blood for this disease, which indicate that the horse has at some time in its life been exposed to it. (Some horses never show any signs of having had the disease, while others sicken and die.) The Coggins Test is required by many states for shipment across state borders and some states mandate compulsory testing of all horses. Most shows and race tracks require proof of a negative Coggins Test before horses are permitted on the grounds. There are differing opinions on swamp fever and the best methods of handling it. Many favor testing and destroying all horses who have positive test results, while others argue that it is wrong to kill perfectly healthy horses. There can be no question that since the test was discovered more horses have been put down because of the use of the test-and-slaughter procedure than have died of the disease itself. Many horses are now branded and quarantined instead of being destroyed. There will be great controversy over this issue for some time to come. Research to find a safe and effective vaccine is under way at many laboratories, but there is no encouraging news about its development at this writing.

Colic is abdominal pain. It can stem from several and varied causes. Colic due to fermented feeds, too much rich feed, change in the diet, or sudden overeating of grass are all perfectly preventable. Colic due to worms is also preventable and some veterinarians feel that worms cause colic more than any other factor. Colic due to impaction is a little harder to blame on management and colic in pregnant mares is sometimes due to the shifting of the foal. Most forms of colic have similar outward signs. The horse looks and acts distressed or depressed. He will stamp or kick at his belly, turn and look at his sides, and sometimes run his upper lip up in the air. Most horses try to lie down and roll to relieve the pain. Colic should always be treated as an emergency. The horse need not be walked fast, but should be prevented from rolling. Sometimes it is easier to keep the horse walking and at other times it makes more sense to allow him to rest and stand or lie still. I often see horses force another horse to get up in pasture and make him walk about, and upon close inspection I will usually find signs of colic discomfort.

We have had our most dramatic recoveries from colic with the administration of a gallon of pure mineral oil, an injection of Butazolidin, and sometimes antihistamines and other drugs if our doctor feels the case warrants them. He follows the mineral oil with warm water, which seems to give almost immediate relief from the cramping pain. Horses can get colic from not drinking enough water, which can be a serious problem in a bad winter. Our old stallion does not like very cold water. It may well bother his teeth or give him cramps, too. It doesn't really matter to you or the horse what sort of colic he is suffering from, but it will make a difference to the doctor, for impaction, poisoning, gas built up from fermentation or other causes, can be variable from case to case. Obviously if the colic is from worms, it is futile to treat the colic symptoms without a follow-up of proper worming. Our veterinarian administers the mineral oil and warm water by stomach tube. If you must give mineral oil by bottle or dose syringe, let me warn you that it is difficult and messy, and mineral oil stains fabrics permanently. Use a plastic or rubber dosing bottle or a regular dose syringe. Elevate the horse's head and extend his neck, but remember that you want him to swallow and it is hard for a horse to swallow if his head is too high. Put the oil on the back of his tongue but take care not to squirt it into his mouth with force, for you might shoot the stuff into his windpipe and cause mechanical pneumonia. I have mineral oil and dose syringes on hand at all times, but I always call the doctor for a colic case and will treat this problem only if he is unavailable.

I find I most often spot a case of colic at suppertime. The horses all come in and rush to their food, but one will then turn away and stand dejectedly. He may show no other sign than a lack of appetite, but that is my signal to stay in the barn and quietly observe his behavior. Some colic attacks are brief twinges that go away and then the horse will resume eating. We have noted with several young fillies between ten months and two years that they exhibit colic-like symptoms which appear to be connected to their heat cycle. They are brief but sometimes quite severe cramps. There are a few clues you can observe. Loud rumbling gas in the abdomen, strong odors of evergreens, skunk cabbage, or wild cherry, a wild expression in the eyes but no wild behavior, and sweat around the ears and eyes are all things that alert you to stand and watch the horse awhile. If he shows no active signs of colic but is off his feed and looks somehow just not right, take his temperature. Anything over 102 degrees would warrant a call to the veterinarian.

Fever, regardless of its cause, can damage brain cells. But fever is also the body's defense against disease. A low fever which is brief in duration simply makes the horse's body less hospitable to its attackers and helps to kill bacteria and viruses. High fever or a very prolonged fever should be dealt with promptly. There are a number of medications, such as aspirin, which reduce fever, and soaking the victim in a mixture of alcohol and water will lower his temperature. We stand horses in buckets of cold water to prevent founder in the hoofs, then cover the horse with a sheet, over which we pour the water and alcohol mixture. This keeps the body wet and we then set up fans to blow directly on the horse from all sides. In the case of one mare we did this continually for four days. We did get her fever down several times, but as soon as we stopped treatment it would spike back up to 105. So several friends took turns day and night to save her. She lost her foal and she went blind in one eye, but she did not founder and showed no signs of brain damage.

Lowering a fever and reducing congestion in the feet. This mare stands quietly in rubber buckets filled with ice water. Her hay net keeps her content and occupied. The attitude of the ears and the light showing at the top of the eyes indicate the horse's pain or distress.

To take a horse's temperature, use a rectal thermometer. Insert it well in the anus but hang on to it very carefully, for if you let go and it gets taken in the anus it is a very difficult matter to remove it. This has happened often enough that the regular veterinary thermometer is made with a loop at the end to which you attach a string, and many horsemen take the precaution of wrapping the string firmly around their wrist. I do not encourage that practice because the horse may dance about the stall and it can get difficult to detach yourself and the thermometer from the horse in one piece. There are new disposable plastic thermometers on the market which might reduce the chance of breakage. Once you have the horse standing quietly, keep the thermometer in place for a full two minutes. I have found with experience that I can guess the horse's temperature by the feel of the underside of the tail where it rests on the back of my hand as I hold the thermometer in place. If you have no thermometer, sometimes this is a good way to estimate a fever's presence. The horse can have quite a range of "normal" temperature, from 99 to 101.5 degrees. Very young horses tend to run higher temperatures than adults. Exposure to hot sunshine will raise temperatures as well. Morning temperatures tend to be lower than afternoon readings.

Wobbler Syndrome

Some horses are born with incurable malformations, which are not recognizable in the foal but which develop into a debilitating disorder. Also injuries or strains can sometimes cause damage to the spine, which shows up in other parts of the body. The horse's spine runs the entire length of his body, and through it goes a bundle of nerves which carry the signals and responses of the central nervous system. Damage to the nerves or to the bones in the spine, which then pinch the nerves, can cause paralysis, ataxia, and lack of coordination. The horse can compensate to some extent, or may show only mild symptoms; but he may also be rendered useless in a slowly progressive affliction. *Wobbler syndrome* is the term for such uncoordination. There is reasonably good evidence that the problem is inherited; certainly, there is no question that it can also be caused by trauma to the spinal cord, and that such trauma can be the result of either external damage (as in an accident) or pressure from abscesses that impinge on the cord.

Wobbler syndrome can be detected by clinical signs, radiograph and autopsy. There are other methods of detection in the experimental stages now, and these may help to identify those horses that have the problem but do not show the classic clinical signs. A horse that staggers or loses control of his hind legs may be suffering from something quite different, including a contagious disease. Any unevenness of gait or lack of stability should be noted with care. Do not ride a horse that stumbles or has problems negotiating corners or cannot back up. Have your veterinarian watch the horse in motion and ask him if he thinks the horse might be a wobbler.

Teeth

Horses need dental attention as a regular part of their health care. Their teeth are not quite like ours. They do not suffer from cavities and rarely have painful toothaches, but their teeth do grow long and the edges of them get sharp. These sharp edges cut the tongue and the inside of the cheek. Sharp points may be rasped off, a process called *floating*. It is not painful or difficult to do, but some animals get very upset over the noise and sensation. Though many horses need to have this done only once a year, some individuals have to be floated as often as every two or three months. A horse's teeth continue to grow all his life. A grazing horse picks up a certain amount

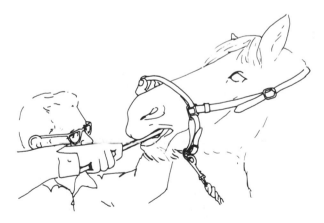

Floating the teeth is done to remove sharp edges and points which can cut the inside of the horse's gums and the edges of the tongue. Regular dental attention is an essential part of horse care.

of sand and grit and the teeth wear down. In stabled horses fed on soft feeds, the teeth wear unevenly and frequently cause the animal to suffer when he eats or when carrying a bit.

Recently a colt we had in training began to limp when circling to the right but not to the left. He had some sharp points and a couple of wolf teeth—which are vestigial teeth that were once in the course of evolution useful grinders or molars—which our doctor removed. His mouth was still tender and he continued to limp, trying to escape the pain he felt when the overcheck of his bridle tightened as he led forward with his right leg. There was nothing wrong with his legs; we did nerve blocks and tests of his feet. When he wore a halter he could go in any direction without limping. Once his mouth healed, the limp disappeared. Several horses have exhibited lameness in the hind legs from mouth trouble. Many become rebellious and even dangerous because they need to have their wolf teeth pulled or their grinders floated.

Checking the teeth takes the veterinarian a few minutes and requires no special tools. Generally, horses stand quietly and are cooperative. However, removal of wolf teeth requires some form of restraint and/or tranquilizer or sedation to hold the horse still. As a rule, wolf teeth come out easily and the horse does not seem uncomfortable after their removal. Some soreness may exist and it is a kindness to let the horse recover a day or two after a bad extraction. Flushing the mouth out with salt water, most easily done with a rubber ear or bulb syringe, will help to clean the hole and prevent food from accumulating there while the gum heals. Sometimes horses break their teeth and occasionally a tooth will decay and need removal.

During the first five years of life horses shed their baby teeth and grow a second set, as we do. While the teeth are shedding, the horse may be quite frantic and difficult to bit. Get in the habit of watching the horse while he eats. If he tilts his head sideways, his mouth hurts or he has a sore throat. If he stretches his head forward, drops food out of his mouth while eating, or exhibits any difficulty in chewing or swallowing, have the doctor examine his mouth. Any bobbing of the head, tossing it up and down, or "yawing" on the bit should make you suspect tooth problems.

The term *coopering* or *copering* or *bishoping*, found in old horse books, refers to the fraudulent practice of filing down a horse's teeth and putting new "cups" in them to make the horse appear younger than he really is. This trickery is not so prevalent now, since most horses carry registration papers. But there are still many "eight-year-olds" that are well into their teens going the rounds of the dealers.

Eyes

Horses' eyes are subject to the same disorders as people's. They can get cataracts, detached retinas, internal infections, scratches or punctures, and reactions to irritants. Horses can have poor vision or an inability to identify what they see. They may suffer from allergies, which frequently manifest themselves as red and running eyes. Also, face flies irritate the eye and then live on the resultant discharge. You must learn what a healthy eye looks like and then take the trouble to look at your horse's eyes to detect any signs of discomfort or injury. Remember that the expression in the horse's eye is a good diagnostic tool for early identification of many diseases. Eyes can water because of blockage of the tear duct and from the irritation of the horse's own forelock hair sticking to the eyeball. Any excessive tears, swollen eyelids, a dull expression, a white or cloudy appearance, or pus in or around the eye should prompt a call to the veterinarian. If you wish to wash the eye, flush it with pure clean water. Never use boric acid or any eyewash preparation unless it is given to you by the doctor. Do not scrub or rub; if there is a thorn or a bit of glass or some other sharp object lodged in the eye or eyelid you may force it farther in.

Ophthalmic medications come in drop, powder, and ointment forms. Each has specific uses and prohibitions and it is decidedly unwise to use anything in the eye without a concise diagnosis of the problem. Some drugs contain steroids, which must always be used under a doctor's advice and with great care. One system of treatment entails the alternate use of two ointments; one opens the pupil and the other makes it close again. This is done to prevent scar tissue from forming and holding the pupil in a fixed position. While the horse is undergoing this treatment he should be kept in dim light, not allowed out in daylight at all. Light is often very painful when an eye is injured. Some ointments that are used to counteract internal eye disorders can cause ulcers when used on surface problems. A thorough examination is in order if any eye problems are encountered.

The veterinarian has an instrument called an ophthalmoscope, with which he can look deep into the eye. He has a paper strip impregnated with dye that he can touch on the surface of the eye to help show up scratches or indentations. He can dilate the pupils in order to see the retina in the back of the eye. Do not make the mistake of putting any substance in the eye to "clear it up" and make it look healthy. If it isn't healthy it must be treated. If the veterinarian tells you to put ointment or drops in the eye three or six or eight times a day he means that often, not occasionally, at your convenience. If you are unable to do the job, send the horse to the veterinarian's clinic and have it done by him and his assistants. The eye flushes itself constantly and once-a-day medication is in most cases a waste of time.

Some training or behavior problems are actually vision problems. Horses that suddenly act nervous, become startled easily, stop abruptly and look down at things at their feet which they would normally cross, or halt in doorways and balk, are sometimes experiencing difficulty recognizing what they are seeing, or adjusting to changing light. Remember always that it is to the horse's best interests to be cooperative and most horses truly want to please their handlers. Any sudden change in this attitude should make you think of teeth, eyes, pain, or a misunderstanding of what you had intended. Never just assume that a normally cooperative animal has developed a stubborn streak or is being mean.

Ask your veterinarian to show you the technique he uses for putting medication in the horse's eye when unaided. (If you have help, it is not so difficult.) I run my hand up under the noseband of the halter, until the heel of my hand is against the cheekbone to hold the head still, while with that same hand spreading open the eyelid, I apply the medication with the free hand. I roll back the upper or lower lid of the eye and place the ointment on the inside of the lid. It's advisable to hold the tube parallel to the eye surface—that way you are not so likely to poke the eye itself with the point of the applicator tip. Rest your hand against the horse's face so that if he jumps he will push you away rather than ramming his eye into your hands.

Sometimes I get my feet into the act by attaching a lead rope to the halter and standing on the end to prevent the horse from tossing his head. You may find it helpful to put the horse in crossties and stand on a box, then place his head on your shoulder and force it up high enough so that he is restrained for the time it takes to get the medicine in. If he is a real stinker, you can use a humane twitch (the kind that clamps over his nose), run a lead rope from this over your elbow, and hold it firm in the crook of your arm while you use both hands on the eye.

If a wound is on the face near the eyes, or on the front leg where the horse will rub his face, take care not to use anything that he could get into his eyes. Sometimes a powder or spray is preferable on a certain wound, but again you should leave that decision to the veterinarian. Some highly effective drugs contain steroids, which are powerful but have side effects that are complex and varied, depending upon their application, form, and duration of use. Some medications are soothing, some cause burning or stinging sensations; some have the effect of drawing out the infection and others a drying effect. In order to understand all this, you must study each drug, getting to know its properties and its limitations.

Lameness

Lameness, as I have pointed out, can result from a systemic disease, such as founder, from pain in the teeth, from parasites damaging nerves and/or impeding blood flow, and from other causes which are not confined to the feet or legs at all. If you have determined that none of these are the problem, there is a systematic way of examining for lameness in the feet and legs. First have the horse led at a walk and a trot to locate the affected leg. The horse nods his head with the limping leg, lifting his head up to relieve the weight on a sore front foot and nodding it down to throw his weight forward on the front legs when lame on a hind leg. The nod or bob comes just before the lame leg is to take the weight. I find that I can hear lameness more easily than I can see it. If I lead a horse behind me on a hard surface, I can hear the odd footfall or lighter step. I often know a horse is limping by the feel of the lead line when I lead him.

Once you determine which leg is in trouble, stand and observe the way the horse holds the foot. If the leg is in front of the body, resting on the toe, he is trying to protect his heel or the sole of the foot. If both feet are way out in front of the horse and his weight is thrown back, he is trying to relieve his toes. Feel both legs. If you detect heat in any part of the sore leg, that is usually the site of the problem.

Include the hoofs in this heat test. Always compare both feet and both legs at the same time. Remember that lameness can be up as high as the hip or shoulder, so don't neglect to feel these areas, too.

If you cannot detect heat in the leg, examine the bottom of the horse's hoof. Start with the hoofpick and clean the entire sole, well into the lateral clefts and the cleft of the frog. Scrape hard along the white line and feel and look for evidence of gravel, nails, or wire embedded in the sole. Sniff the foot. It should smell like normal horn

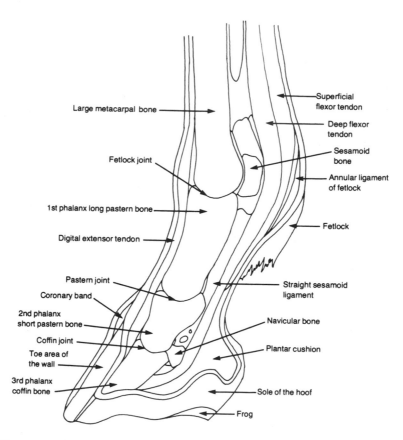

The internal parts of the foot.

or hoof and not have a rank, strong rotten odor. There should be no sign of ooze, blood, or pus. The frog may be ragged, but that does not always indicate a problem; it is normal for horses to slough off or shed the surface of the frog from time to time. If there is no evidence of punctures, thrush, or bruises on the surface, rap the sole sharply with a hammer. Remember that there are sensitive bones and tissues inside the hoof, so don't hit so hard that you cause a bruise. What you are looking for is sensitivity, and a rap on the hoof may cause the horse to flinch. If you cannot detect any problem in the hoof, you would do well to call the veterinarian for a diagnosis, keeping the horse quiet until he arrives. Squeezing the hoof with his hoof tester will help locate internal damage or abscesses. He can block the nerves in the leg at intervals with injections of anesthetic to find precisely where the pain is located. His experienced hands and eye may well pick up swelling in a tendon or joint that you didn't spot.

If you find a nail or other object embedded in the hoof, do not just pull it out. Soak the foot until it is soft and clean. Epsom salts and warm water are the best combination for this. When you pull out the object, note carefully where it is located, for often a small puncture will close so completely that it cannot be located again. The surface of the hoof should be pared away around the wound so that it will not close and build up pressure from an abscess. The horse should have a tetanus toxoid booster and antibiotics to prevent infection and the foot will probably have to be soaked to draw out pus if an infection has already started. Give tetanus antitoxin in horses not previously vaccinated.

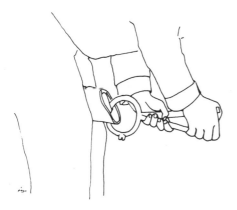

The hoof tester shown here is used to locate internal pressure and pain. It pinches the foot, and when the horse flinches, the area is either probed to find evidence of abscesses or gravel or the foot is X-rayed to locate fractures.

If his foot smells or oozes, the horse has either an abscess or thrush. *Thrush* is a fungus, much like athlete's foot. It is cured by paring away excess frog or sole where the thrush has taken hold and then treating with a fungicide. We use Clorox, though there are a number of effective thrush remedies on the market. Remember that these are strong, harsh chemicals, designed to dry up the hoof and kill the fungus, which thrives on moisture and filth. It is unwise to use these remedies daily, and dangerous to use them "just in case" the horse gets thrush. Employ them sparingly and only when a positive case of thrush is diagnosed. We pour about an ounce of Clorox into the cleaned thrush pocket and hold the foot up three or four seconds. This is done once every other day and the treatment is continued until there is no more evidence of softness or smell. Thrush can affect horses that live outdoors on dry, clean pastures, as well as those that are stabled. Some horses have a chronic case of thrush in just one foot. I have seen animals so lame from thrush that they were unable to stand and they were resistant to treatment because of the pain. Since thrush can be passed from one horse to another, make certain if you have a horse with the problem that you do not use his hoofpick on another horse's feet.

Lameness in the joints can come from arthritis, various forms of trauma, and fractures. When joints are inflamed, there are a number of medications that can be injected into the joint space and/or painted on the outside of the joint to reduce swelling. Rest is usually required to allow the joint to return to normal. Strains and sprains are as painful for a horse as for us. Treatment must relieve pain and also reduce inflammation and swelling. When an injury is fresh it is treated one way, and when it is chronic it requires nearly the reverse treatment. Liniments that create heat should not be used on fresh injuries, which are already quite hot enough. Cooling and soothing a new injury with cold water washes, ice packs, and alcohol reduce the swelling and pain. Once the injury has cooled, if the pain remains it is sometimes useful to rub the injury with liniment to increase heat which will stimulate healing circulation. The right treatment at the wrong time can actually prolong the problem. So do consult the doctor before embarking on a time-consuming liniment treatment. Often alternate applications of heat and cold are necessary to cure a problem and sometimes doctors resort to actual blistering or firing an old injury to bring the swelling down. Remember, too, that no amount of liniment will cure a broken bone, and if this is a possibility, an X-ray might have to be taken to make a positive diagnosis. Fractures are not uncommon and many horses heal broken bones with no permanent disability, but the treatment for a break is complete rest and sometimes immobilization of the injured part and the joints above and below as well.

Injuries to the hock are called *spavins,* of which there are several different kinds. Bog or blood spavins are soft swellings within the joint. Bone or jack spavins are hard and usually on the medial side of the joint. Thoroughpins and windgalls are soft filling along the tendon at the side of the hock; capped hock is an injury to the top of the back of the hock. Curb is not actually on the hock but immediately behind it and it is a rupture or injury to the tendon sheath. A blind spavin is internal and not visible at all from the outside. Osselots are a bone problem in front of the pastern joint. Sesamoiditis is inflammation of the sesamoid bones. Enlargements of the splint bone, lying along the cannon bone, are called splints; boney enlargements around the coronet band are called ringbone; while enlargements that extend up from inside the hoof on the sides of the pastern are called side bones.

In many cases, a horse is lame only while one of these problems is "hot," and once it becomes cool or chronic he is serviceable again. But if the enlargements, which are often actually a build-up of extra calcium, interfere with the joint, the horse may be permanently lame or may become lame after use. Since the tendency toward arthritis is thought to be inheritable, a horse that is afflicted is questionable as a candidate for the breeding band. Have a careful evaluation of such a horse if you are considering breeding.

Navicular disease, a bursitis and/or degenerative arthritic condition involving the navicular bone, is buried deep within the hoof and has no outward signs except lameness. It can be caused by a number of things, including trauma, such as trotting hard on pavement, jumping, cutting the feet down and fitting them with undersize shoes to make the hoofs look smaller, and not resetting the shoes—even normal-size ones—frequently enough. The disease in itself is not inherited. That is, a horse is not born with an eroded or calcified bone, but a tendency toward it or a prone disposition is inherited. Obviously you can prevent the hoofs from being cut down and shod with too small a shoe. You can also refrain from pounding the horse down a hard road and jumping too high and too often. Of course, a bad landing on a stone is harder to anticipate and prevent. Navicular disease is detected by X-ray in most cases but by no means always. There is a characteristic way of placing the foot very carefully in walking that an experienced horseman can detect. The horse with navicular stands pointing the toe, with his weight off the heel. Certain types of bar shoes and other treatments can help to relieve the pain. The condition is arrestable though not curable. The horse is considered unsound if he shows lameness. However, some horses that appear upon X-ray to have damage to the navicular bone do not become lame at all. The navicular is a small bone that lies directly behind the coffin bone or P_3 and acts as a pulley for the deep flexor tendon. (See illustration.) The problem develops at the point of contact between tendon and bone. It should go without saying that a horse suffering from this disease should not be used for jumping or hard riding of any sort, and of course not for breeding.

Grease heel or scratches is a problem that seems to plague some horses and never bother others in the same stable that are given the same care. Like thrush, it has always been referred to as a disorder caused by neglect and filth, but this is simply not borne out by the cases I have seen. Scratches look like wire cuts along the back of the heel, pastern, and even sometimes up as high as the fetlock joint itself. They are hot, inflamed, and sometimes oozing. Clean the area with a soft clean towel and examine the injury. It may indeed be wire cuts and need suturing or a veterinarian's attention. If the swellings appear to be raised and irritated lines, clean the foot well and apply daily a soothing ointment such as Bag Balm, toilet lanolin, petroleum jelly, or A and D. We have found that switching the horse off sweet-feed to straight oats and increasing his intake of water clears up the problem quicker than any external applications.

Open Wounds

When a horse is cut, try to determine how the injury happened. If it was on a dirty nail or wire, a tetanus shot is a must. If the injury is through the first two layers of skin, and muscle or tendon is showing, summon the doctor and do nothing to the wound at all. Do not apply water to any cut and keep all medication away from it until the doctor has had a chance to examine it. If it is over three inches long he will probably want to suture it. A wound with a great deal of contusion or swelling and bruising is going to be harder to repair than a neat slice. If you do feel you must wash it, do so with a saline solution—1 teaspoon salt to 1 quart warm water. Use a large wad of sterile absorbent cotton. Do not rub hard but rather flush out the wound; you do not want to force any foreign matter farther in. Rubbing hard will also damage the edges of the wound. Do not apply iodine, blue lotion, or red oil lotion to an open wound. These three old-fashioned remedies can be put on the skin well away from the edges of the wound to help repel flies, but they will all interfere with healing if applied directly to the wound. Nothing should be applied to any part of a wound if it is to be sutured.

Horses rarely lose much blood from an injury; their blood clots very rapidly. Unless bright scarlet blood is gushing in spurts—indicating a severed artery—leave the wound alone until the doctor arrives. If there *is* spurting blood, a tourniquet can be applied, but remember that it must be put on, then released, retightened and loosened continually. It cannot be put on and left there. You can sometimes stop blood by pressing hard with your finger on the artery or blood vessel just before the wound.

Our veterinarian usually cleans the wound with antiseptic, gives the horse antibiotic and tetanus boosters if needed, and also squirts some antibiotic directly into the wound. If the wound is to be sutured, he shaves the skin around it, cleans off the area again, and then trims away ragged or damaged or hanging skin, which would interfere with healing. If the wound is not to be sutured, he cleans and then bandages it with the ointment of his choice. Usually we use one containing Furacin and change the bandage daily after the first two or three days. If proud flesh, which is superfluous granulation or healing tissue, forms, it must be treated with a caustic powder or ointment to burn it back. This requires care and judgment to prevent scars. The important thing about any wound is that it must heal from the inside out, never close over on the surface, trapping infection inside. If this happens the pressure will build and rupture through the wound, find or make another hole in the skin to break out of, or go into the horse's bloodstream, where it can sicken and even kill the horse.

Bandaging horses is not an easy task and they can be devils about removing bandages. Your veterinarian can show you how to apply bandages and then it will be up to you to change them and medications according to instructions. Kling gauze and Elasticon bandage have made the job far easier now than it used to be with ordinary gauze and adhesive tape. We use tin snips to remove bandages; they are very difficult to cut off with scissors. If the horse removes them for you, you will probably have to invest in a bib or neck cradle. Horses will constantly rub and work over a wound and keep it from closing. That is nature's way of preventing an infection from becoming trapped under a scab. But horses will tear out stitches and work dirt into a wound, which will then heal more slowly and may form much more scar tissue. In the summer, flies lay eggs in wounds. These develop into maggots, which live in the wound and eat the tissue. They irritate the horse and make a mess. Bandages and repellents do help reduce this risk. Cleaning the whole area and smearing petroleum jelly over the surrounding surface will also do some good. Serum, which is part of the blood, often oozes out of a wound, and pus and serum both can scald or irritate the skin and make the hair fall out. An effective treatment our veterinarian has used for summer sores and injuries is one of the worm preparations, thiabendazole, which, mixed into a lotion, helps kill off flies very well.

Doctoring

Bandaging a horse's leg is much easier with someone else on hand to help hold him. If the horse fusses, the friend can pick up the opposite leg, making the horse support himself with the leg you are working on. But if you must work on a horse alone, here are some methods and precautions to make it safer. Cross-tie the horse securely in a place where he will be calm and not distracted by noise or activity. You will need good light and a place to set things so that they don't all land in the dirt. Gather together your snips or scissors, ointments and bandages, perhaps in a pail, to keep them clean and so that you can move them quickly if the horse dances about. Open the ointment and apply it to a Telfa pad so that you can put it directly on the wound when you have it prepared. Do not kneel beside the horse, but squat so that you can get away from him. Talk quietly and remember that fear and excitement will make him harder to handle. If he will not stand quietly, you can make a Scotch hobble with a stirrup strap. Wrap a small towel around the cannon bone of the leg opposite the one you want to treat. Loop the stirrup strap around the towel, cross it behind the leg, and bend the knee. Bring the ends of the strap over the forearm, and if it is long go around the forearm once and buckle the strap. You want the foot right up tight under his elbow. If this does not keep him still, tie a rope to the hobble and run it up over his back to your hand, and when he jumps pull on the rope with a sharp jerk to let him know that you want his attention. Do not yank so hard that he is knocked off balance and flies backward. Scotch hobbles can be used on the hind leg, but that is not something you should do without expert instruction, for if the horse really resents it and starts to thrash, you will be unable to get him untied before you are both hurt.

If the Scotch hobble doesn't work, a humane twitch is the next alternative to try. Place the twitch over the upper lip, twist the cord around the handles so the twitch is very tight, and then snap the snap to the side ring of his halter. This usually occupies most horses enough to let you get done before they start to fidget. If you leave the twitch on too long, however, the circulation is cut off and the

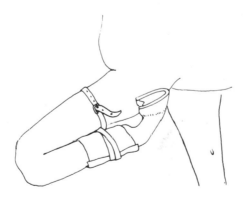

Scotch hobble. Note the carefully wrapped and protected leg. The straps must be placed close to the fetlock joint and well up on the forearm, near the elbow, in order to hold the leg effectively.

upper lip gets numb, so work as quickly as you can once the twitch is applied. Some horses resent a twitch and will fight even more than without one. In this case, run a chain shank through the side ring of his halter, under the upper lip along the gums, and back through the other side ring. Hold the long end of the shank in the crook of your elbow or in your teeth while you work on the leg, and jerk *lightly* on the shank if he wiggles. Go easy and be prepared for him to react violently. Some horses stand perfectly for this method, but again, each animal reacts differently.

In many cases a horse and a handler can work out a routine for dressing wounds. If you must work on a hind leg with no help and no restraint, and if the injury to be treated is on the inside of the leg, stand on the opposite side and take a firm hold of the horse's tail. While you are bending down to reach over the leg, pull a hard, steady pull on the tail to shift the horse's weight to the foot nearest you. This means that he can lift and kick and stamp with the foot you are treating, which is a nuisance, but he is less likely to hit you with the foot nearest you and also less likely to cross-kick toward himself, and so at least you are relatively safe. To work on the outside of a leg, stand beside the hurt leg and again pull the horse over toward the leg nearest you. He may kick, but if you are balanced correctly you can move away and keep a hard tug on the tail to bring the foot down so that it receives his weight before he falls down. If you have to work in the area of the flank or hip and the horse is likely to kick at you, stand very close, actually leaning up against the horse with your back to his head, but tie up his head so that he cannot reach around and bite your back. If he does decide to kick you when you are close, you can shove him hard and send him off balance, at the same time pushing yourself far enough away to escape his foot. However, if you stand near him but not really hard against him, he can get his foot up and smash it into your leg or groin before you even see the muscles in his thigh twitch. Always try to keep a free hand or arm on the horse's body. This way you can feel a kick starting before you see it, which may give you an extra tenth of a second to avoid serious injury.

The most vulnerable place for you to be is at arm's length, which is where most novices stand to do anything the horse might resent. That puts you at just precisely the right spot to receive the full force of a hard hoof. You are off balance because you are leaning forward and will fall against the horse if he hits you in the knee or leg, and his next kick can then be directed toward your head. *Never* stand at arm's length to a horse and lean toward him, even for grooming. You would be courting disaster. This is most important when you are going to do something that might pain the animal.

Injections

Injections are administered in different ways because the speed with which the animal absorbs the medication is often a major factor in the effectiveness of the treatment. Intravenous injections are those given directly into a blood vessel, which places the chemical in the horse's system as quickly as possible. Intramuscular injections go straight into a heavy muscle, and thus take a bit longer to get into the bloodstream. Intradermal (between the layers of skin) and subcutaneous (under the skin) injections administer a drug at an even slower rate. These injections are usually used for vaccinations, in which a very slow absorption over a prolonged period is desired.

Obviously, if a substance is supposed to be administered subcutaneously and it is instead put directly into the blood vessel, it can really jolt the system and its effect is considerably altered. Likewise, a drug that should be given in the vein can lose its effectiveness if given intramuscularly. There may be a time when your veterinarian would prefer to have you give injections to your own horse, as in the case of repeated daily doses. Have him show you how to fill the syringe, how to draw back to make sure you have not hit a blood vessel, and how fast to depress the plunger so that you do not create a huge lump. Learn exactly where in the muscle to apply the drug so that you do not hit a nerve, such as those in the spinal column. It is highly unlikely that he will ever allow you to give anything but an intramuscular shot unless you are a doctor or nurse yourself. Horses can react to penicillin just as people do, and unless you have the proper antidote to administer, you may not save the horse. Even if your doctor does trust you to inject your own horse, do not try to do his job and help out a friend. If the horse reacts badly, you have no legal protection.

A Down Horse

Horses may sleep standing or lying down. Sometimes they lie down because their feet hurt, because they have an illness or have had a heart attack. If you find your horse lying down, do not rush over and get him up. If he is enjoying a peaceful snooze he has a right to enjoy himself. If he is sick it may be best not to disturb him at all. Stand and observe him quietly. Call his name and watch his expression. If his eyes are calm and his body relaxed, offer him a wisp of hay. He is probably o.k. if he takes it from your hand and eats it. Just wait or rattle his grain bucket and see whether he jumps to his feet. If he looks dull or is showing white around the top of his eyes, stoop down near him and feel his ears. Very cold ears and sweating around the eyes and ears are signs that you should take his temperature. Look at the insides of his eyelids and mouth to see if the mucous membranes are very pale. Listen to his breathing. Very shallow, rapid breathing should get you to call the doctor. Deep breathing and loud snores sound a lot worse but are normal when a horse lies down.

If you want to get him up, slip on his halter and attach a rope. Pull his front feet out from under him and stand back, tugging lightly on the rope. If he makes an effort to get up but is unable to do so, leave him alone. In case he can hardly lift his head, get a few towels or an old pillow and prop it up a little to help him breathe and to protect his eyes from bedding and debris. If he is sweating or trembling, lay a light sheet or blanket over him and close any door or window that

A very weak foal in trouble. The extended head and the limp body are characteristic of weakness. In this case the foal was suffering from open heart valves, which closed gradually. She was confined and needed complete rest in order to recover. She was born active and very lively. This drawing shows her three hours after birth. She would have died of exhaustion if her problem had not been correctly diagnosed.

might cause a draft. Then sit still and keep things quiet until the veterinarian arrives. Observe him, counting the number of breaths per minute he takes. Look at the stall for signs of violent struggle or for a change in the consistency of manure or an absence of any if you would normally expect to find some in his stall. Look at his water and grain buckets to see if he ate and drank normally. All these observations may help the veterinarian to make a diagnosis. If there are any jerking, convulsive movements in his legs, head, or stomach, watch these closely. The veterinarian will want to know if he is prone, all the way flat out on his side, or lying up on his sternum, with his head raised and his legs tucked under his chest.

Horses do not lie on their backs like dogs and cats. An upside-down horse is stuck and in trouble. If he is cast against the side of the wall, try to get someone to help you. To free a cast horse you must stand behind him, grasp the tail, and swivel him on his forequarters, turning his head and neck toward the wall and his hind legs away from it. Once he can kick himself back away from the wall he will usually force himself back and get right up. Do not stand between the horse and the wall to try to roll him over. Kicking, he could break your legs and smash you against the wall. You can't help him much if you are both in trouble. Should his head and forequarters already be too close to the wall, put on his halter and a long rope and try to swivel his forequarters. Don't twist his neck in the process, however.

Sometimes a horse will jam a leg into a gate or between stall boards and be really trapped. Trying to free themselves, some horses struggle until they break loose even if it means breaking the leg, while others soon give up and lie perfectly still. I found a filly lying with her neck stuck out of the stall under her gate and her eyes glazed. I lifted the gate off its hinges and tried to get her to respond. She looked as if she was in shock. Her breath was so shallow I could hardly see her sides move. When the doctor came he examined her with great care, then stood up and gave her a tremendous slap. She came to with a start and jumped to her feet. She was perfectly all right but had given herself up for dead. I have seen sheep do this but never a horse. She must have been stuck for quite a long time. Of course, many horses will stand perfectly still if they get a leg caught in a fence and just wait patiently for someone to come and cut them loose. They sometimes even call for help.

If the horse is down and stuck in something where thrashing will cause more injury or make it hard to free him, you should first get him to stop his struggling. Obviously you have to remain calm yourself, so keep voices quiet and reassuring. Place a jacket or towel under his head and then hold it down on the ground while someone else cuts him free or pries off the trap he is in. To hold him down you must lie over his head. Place yourself behind his head and neck, not where he will hit you with his front feet. Put your body over his jaw and eyes, but take care if you are wearing a belt buckle that you don't injure him with it. Best to take off the belt and bend up one of his front legs and tie it in a Scotch hobble, if you can. Horses can bite while they are lying down, so be aware that he may get frantic; keep your fingers away from his teeth. As long as his head is down on the ground he cannot get to his feet, but a horse's neck is very strong and he can lift a full-grown man with his head. Be prepared to really bear down. If he has a halter, take a firm grip on it and hold his nose down. Many horses will cease to struggle if you hold their head down.

Surgery

Certain kinds of surgery require that the horse be thrown and put under a general anesthetic. If this is the case, usually the veterinarian has all the equipment and will bring along a reliable assistant. More and more veterinarians have proper tables for large-animal surgery and prefer to have horses brought to their clinic and kept there for a few days for preparation, operation, and recovery.

Old Soldiers

Horses are mortal. This is a fact many people do not wish to face, as if somehow by not believing it we can prevent the eventuality. Yet animals have a comparatively short life span, and unless you were old when you acquired a very young horse, you will probably have to make some decision regarding his last years. The horse is at your mercy, for he cannot make that decision for himself.

To be honest, when a horse is old and arthritic, lame or disabled, can't chew food or any longer enjoy life, it is cruel to keep him hanging on just for the sake of saying you still have old Dobbin. He'd be far better off going to the local mink farm and being used for food. You even get paid for his weight and many an old horse brings his highest price the very last time around. However, few pleasure riders who have enjoyed hours of a horse's company can bring themselves to this conclusion. The disposal of old horses presents many problems nowadays. City dwellers are in many cases better off than people who have several acres, for in the city a call to the humane society is usually enough to have a trailer sent to pick up the horse, and that is the last thing the fond owner has to do. Suburbanites can contact their veterinarian and leave all the details up to him. Farmers usually end up not only having to bury their own horses but also those belonging to the kids in the neighborhood as well.

But what of the horse who is not yet too old to enjoy life, but is also not sound enough to be of use? In many parts of the country there are old-folks' homes for horses and other large animals. The ASPCA and The Humane Society can often help to find a retirement home where old or useless horses can be boarded.

If you have room for an old or useless horse who has served you well, perhaps you will feel you want to keep him until the last. In this case, there are special factors to be considered. His inability to chew effectively will likely be the first sign of aging. There are many soft feeds—pelletted alfalfa; various meals such as corn, ground oats, soybean, wheat germ, and bran, which are ground finely enough so that no chewing is required—and these should maintain an old horse in good flesh. Be cautious about adding minerals, such as large doses of calcium salts, for this may tend to make his bones more brittle. Avoid beet pulp, coarse hays (chopped hay is fine), and whole corn or oats; they are too much for an old horse to grind, and will irritate his gut and do him little good if swallowed whole. Old horses have difficulty staying warm in the winter and cool in the summer. They need fresh air, exercise, company, and their share of barn room and grooming. When you retire a horse from service, you are not really putting him "out to pasture," for if you do he will simply suffer and die. You save some money by pulling off his shoes and not having him reshod regularly, but you will probably have to spend those savings on having his teeth floated and tended. If the horse is in good spirits and good health, he will be useful in keeping another horse company as well as being good company himself. However, if arthritis and a weak heart, poor teeth, failing vision, and nervousness start to plague the poor creature's last years, it is far kinder to find a quiet spot for a grave and have him put to sleep. This is no longer a painful or frightening end. Modern drugs are excellent.

HAS HE STILL GOT GOOD MILES IN HIM?

Ponies that have been outgrown, or horses that have taken their riders as far as the horse is capable in advanced work, can find a ready market among new riders and children. Even horses with minor unsoundness can make a family happy for light use and loads of affection, or can be used to educate a novice in the care of a horse. Sometimes the best solution to the problem of a horse you do not need but that still has good miles in him is to find a local breeder, a professional trainer, or a 4-H leader who might know of just the right sort of home. My blacksmith is the source of such horses around here, for he is frequently in and out of everyone's barn.

Advertising in a local paper or an area horse magazine will get lookers, but if the horse means a great deal to you, personal recommendations as to the suitability of his next home will be important. Don't be afraid to ask for references and for payment. The people who pay handsomely for horses usually treat them with more care than those who get them free. I have found this out painfully, and will not give animals away except under very specific circumstances.

You certainly will not make a profit on a horse you bought as a sound, healthy young animal and used (or abused) into old age or unsoundness. No one will pay you for having years of fun on that horse; that must be considered a certain amount of your profit. But in the case of good, purebred, registered animals that have had proper care and training, there is a fair chance of making money *plus* having those years of fun. If you decide to sell the horse, make every effort to put him in tiptop shape.

Ask the veterinarian to give him a thorough going over to be sure you are representing him honestly, as you can be sued for false advertising and misrepresentation. If you have no idea what a fair price is, you will have to get expert advice from someone familiar with your horse's breed and type. If you cannot stand behind the horse, an auction is the obvious answer. Horses are sold at auction with all their faults, and without any guarantee or warrantee. People who buy at auction should be clearly aware of this. You may also want to consign the horse to a brokerage or a sales stable. If so, be certain that you clearly understand the terms and the commission fee.

PUTTING HIM DOWN

If, however, you make the decision to have a horse put down, you must follow through and see to it with your own eyes. You really cannot pass that unpleasant task on to anyone else except the vet. Even he will be reluctant to put down a horse that is in good health. Often veterinarians end up keeping unwanted pets for themselves because they can't bring themselves to kill animals that aren't suffering.

When any registered animal dies, the owner should return the registration papers to the register to be officially stamped and recorded. (This is in fact required by some registeries.)

Your horse may make a real contribution if you donate him to a school of veterinary medicine (you may be able to claim him as a charitable deduction on your taxes). You must give him free and clear for whatever purpose the school intends. Some horses are used for X-ray studies to determine causes of gait defects and lameness; some are kept for controlled breeding experiments; some for nutritional experiments or behavioral studies. Research has many forms. The animals are treated humanely, not put to death uselessly. All horses and the people who care about them benefit from what is learned in these studies in terms of better understanding of veterinary problems. To be perfectly practical, it is much less costly to donate a horse to a veterinary school than to hire a veterinarian to put the animal to sleep, and far less of an emotional strain. I have buried several horses—those too badly injured to ship away—but I will never bury one that can further man's knowledge of horses.

If you find such a decision hard to make, appeal to your veterinarian. He can give you a pretty fair estimate of how happy a life a horse can lead in his condition of age or soundness, and perhaps some estimate of the costs involved in his care.

Old or sick horses, like old or sick people, need and deserve more care—and in most cases that care is expensive. If you take on the responsibility, do so with this clear understanding. Personally, I find it very depressing to see an old friend failing, becoming weak and unsure. I enjoy seeing horses in radiant good health, and would far rather spend my time and money on them.

You and the Horse Doctor

The veterinarian is the single most important person in your horse's life besides you, his owner. He is a professional man with many years of education, a heavy investment in the tools of his profession, and a practice that takes him into the stables of many people in the area. In most cases he works for himself or for a small professional group of veterinarians. Doctors are called at all hours of the day and night, sometimes for real emergencies and sometimes for imagined ones. It is better to call if you think there is a real problem than to wait until the horse is in dire straits. But pestering or calling for false alarms can wear very thin. If the doctor is put off by your attitude, he may be disinclined to come when there is a real emergency. Make an effort to learn the things he will want to know when you call him. Learn to be observant, but don't try to make a diagnosis for him. Once you and the doctor have established a working relationship, you will learn more with each visit. You will be a better assistant to him and a better nurse for your horse.

Animal lovers tend to get very emotional about their animals, so that a veterinarian often comes in for very unfair criticism when a pet dies, even when the death was no fault of his or was actually the result of the owner's waiting too long to call or having already tried to treat the disease himself. Most such problems derive from an owner's desire to save money, the decision to seek help being delayed beyond the powers of the veterinarian to save the patient.

You will be frustrated and even angry when you call for the doctor in an emergency and he is not available. Remember that when you make an appointment with him you must keep it; be there with the horses ready and make certain that you told him when you called for the appointment all the things you wanted done. If he goes to you expecting to give one shot and ends up having to do a half a dozen other things, he will be late for his next customer. His schedule will be thrown off for several calls after that and he may not get back to his office to handle new calls. Do your part to help him so he will be able to schedule his time with advance notice and his visit to you will not be a rushed affair. In the end your horse will benefit from your consideration.

CHAPTER 14

Your Horse's Farrier

THE MAJOR CAUSE OF LAMENESS in horses is people. People cause illnesses, injuries, and stresses which break down the feet and legs of the horse. People breed horses without regard for structural strength and straightness. They use horses that are not sufficiently trained or properly conditioned for the tasks, and the horses suffer fatigue and injuries. People change the natural habits of horses without regard for or understanding of their physiology; and some people are simply careless about having horses attended to with necessary frequency or competence.

The responsibility for an animal is real. You may never learn much about the human body and its needs and may rely on how you feel and on visits to a doctor to stay alive and well, but you have to know more than that to care for a horse. Mismanagement of feed, exercise, and professional care can cripple the animal. Horses are large, active, and strong, but they are also sensitive to sudden change, and they can't take care of themselves in confinement.

The farrier who is responsible for the feet of your horse should be a highly skilled professional. You must rely on him, his experience and judgment, to guide you and safeguard your horse's soundness. Even a slight miscalculation or carelessness on his part can lay up a horse for months. There is no regulatory agency that controls who may become a farrier. Some states are beginning to set up licensing, and in Connecticut the farriers themselves have established an organization to set standards, with levels to upgrade and improve the trade. There are men who have learned the trade by apprenticeship to a great farrier and then have extended their own knowledge by keeping abreast of the latest techniques and ideas. There are serious students of horse anatomy and farriery who take extensive courses in farrier science and go back to school to keep on learning, but there are also "ninety-day wonders" who take a course for six weeks and promptly hang out a shingle, and then entice as many horse owners as they can to use their services. You cannot recognize a good farrier just by talking to him or to a few of his customers. Before you can judge his abilities, you must arm yourself with the knowledge of what a horse's foot should look like, and then go out to see some of the man's work at a variety of stables or on different horses. Your veterinarian might be the safest guide in choosing a farrier.

Horses may be born with normal or abnormal feet, with straight or crooked legs. While they are growing, many things influence how straight and strong their legs will be. Nutrition and exercise, which affect the soundness of the horse all his life, are most important during the growing years. Much can be done to help a horse with problems while he is very young. Colts can be corrected for longer than fillies because they mature a little more slowly, but the cut-off point for any dramatic changes is twenty-three months for fillies and twenty-seven months for colts. Until a horse is three years of age, the farrier, with diligence, can help to straighten and change the direction of bones. After that he can change the level of the hoof, its pitch or angle, the length of the foot, and the weight and shape of the shoe to improve performance and maintain soundness.

So if you buy a horse with a serious problem and he is fully mature, the farrier can help you, but only to a certain degree. The factors that he can affect are (1) the actual growth and shape of the feet and legs up to two years of age; (2) the way of going, action, stride, and straightness; and (3) rehabilitation of a horse that has suffered injuries including founder, navicular disease, breaks, or strains. These three areas of horse care are very different, and some men are more qualified in one field than another or specialize in only one type of horse. Therefore, you must select a farrier who is able to deal with your particular horse or horses.

The Normal Foot

The standard procedure consists of trimming the foot (done whether the horse is kept barefoot or shod), then shoeing it with new shoes or resetting with old shoes until they are worn out and need replacement. It is rare that a pair of shoes doesn't last for at least one resetting. Of course, if you do a lot of riding on pavement, they will wear out faster than on trails or in a ring.

The more the normal horse can stay barefoot, the better his chances of remaining sound. But shod or not, the horse's feet will grow too long if left alone. If he is barefoot and able to scramble over rocks and gravel and take plenty of exercise, he may go as long as two or even three months without any foot work. If shod, he may not need more than a reset and a little leveling once every eight weeks or more. When you race or show a horse, the care of his feet is absolutely critical for his performance, whereas if you just hack lightly, he may have loose shoes or even lose a shoe and not have a problem for a week or more.

It is important to arm yourself with a clear image of a normal, healthy foot. A horse's foot should follow a straight line down the front of the pastern directly to the ground. The angle of the pastern and hoof should be between 40° and 50° in front and 50° and 55° behind. The hind pasterns and feet are slightly more upright, but

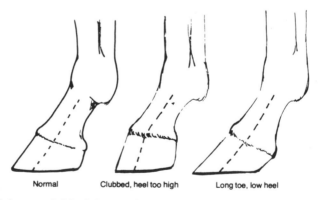

Normal   Clubbed, heel too high   Long toe, low heel

A normal foot, a clubbed foot and a foot with a too-low heel. Dotted lines indicate the axis. In the normal foot the hoof and pastern lie in the same line. With either too high or too low a heel the axis is broken.

there is not a marked degree of difference between front and rear. The shoe should be flat and the same shape as the hoof, but about 1/16-inch wider at the heels to allow for expansion; this is to avoid the pressure on the sensitive heel area that can cause corns. If the foot is padded, only one thin pad should be used. From the bottom, the foot should look nearly round, with a wide V of a frog that is full, with clearly defined clefts on both sides, and strong bars of the hoof. The white line should be very narrow and the same thickness of width all the way around the hoof, never more separated at the toe. The sole should arch upward, or be concave. The frog should be very springy or elastic, like gum rubber. Press on it with your thumb—it should not be dry, hard, or stiff, nor should it be mushy or smelly. The hind feet are narrower than the front feet, but should be as wide at the heel and frog. They are simply more oval in shape. The surface of a clean and healthy hoof is dark unless there are white stripes on it, and it should be moist and smooth, without ridges and irregularities, for they spell potential unsoundness.

Look carefully at the heels. Many horses suffer from feet that have been allowed to become dry, narrow, and contracted in the heels. This can be caused in a number of ways, and you will have to make some observations to tell whether or not the contracted heels can be corrected. If the horse has been kept confined in a clean and dry stall, his feet will dry out unless he has had regular care to restore moisture. A foot left long for any reason will tend to contract at the heels because the frog and the hoof wall do not receive enough flexion, pressure, and expansion. The good farrier and able horseman will guard against this by making certain that padding in the hoofs is

This instrument measures the angle of the hoof wall in relation to the sole of the hoof. The angle is read in degrees. Raising or lowering this angle will change the stride of the foot.

adequate and of proper material, and that the shoes are reset often enough so that the heels remain open and springy. You can test for dry feet and contracted heels by pressing against the back of the bulb of the heel. It should feel bouncy and fairly soft, much like a rubber ball or crepe soles on shoes. If contraction continues for a long time, the inside of the hoof becomes deformed (the hoof can contract in all dimensions). Look carefully at the illustration of the normal hoof. Make sure the horse's hoofs are pairs—i.e., that both front feet are alike and both back feet alike.

Signs of excessive filing and filling with plastic wood or acrylic indicate hoof problems. Sometimes this is done because the horse has been brought in, after having been barefoot, to be shod for show or work; the filled-in spots may simply be surface chips and the foot is made to look smoother with the plastic wood, which also prevents gravel and sand from entering the toe. But filling can be a sign that the horse has shelly (poor-textured, weak) feet, or quarter cracks which have been pinned and covered. Pinning or covering a quarter crack or toe crack is perfectly ethical; indeed, it is the prescribed treatment to prevent the crack from worsening. But while the foot is receiving such treatment it cannot be considered sound, and the horse must be watched for evidence of the crack's spreading or new cracks.

RINGS ON THE SURFACE

The surface of the hoof may be perfectly smooth because it is healthy or because it has been sandpapered and filed. It may have ridges because the horse has a high fever or founder, or has had a sudden change of diet. Nutritional or dietary rings are of no concern, as they happen to horses every time they go from dry hay and concentrates to pasture. Some get rings from the change in the weather, but these rings look slightly different. Nutritional rings are slight, circle the foot, and are level. Founder rings are usually deeper, and drop sharply lower toward the heels. With severe founder, the surface of the hoof dishes and the sole drops down at the toe edge. Foundered horses can be helped by the careful trimming of the hoof at very frequent intervals, and they are often shod with bar shoes. Horses with navicular disease are usually shod with a spring bar shoe, which should look like a bar shoe to the casual observer. Any horse wearing a bar shoe is suspect as an unsound horse since there is no need for a bar shoe on a normal foot.

Inside the Hoof

When I was a child, I thought horses stood on one toe. I visualized a single digit, surrounded by a hard sole and a wall of bone. I thought the hoof was made of bone, not realizing it is actually horn, which is no more or less than thick layers of insensitive hair. Beneath that horn, which is both flexible and porous, lies a complicated structure composed of a sensitive network of blood vessels and nerves (called the laminae), connected to bones, tendons, ligaments, and soft tissue, and including, too, a blood-pumping system and shock-absorbing facilities.

The top of the horse's foot is not the top of the hoof. The whole foot is comprised of the following bones: proximal sesamoid, long pastern, short pastern, pedal (also called P_3 or coffin), and the navicular bones (also called the distal sesamoid). These bones are suspended in the foot and through the hoof by ligaments and tendons. The coffin bone lies in a pad called the pedal cushion, whose function it is to protect the bone from shock and stress and also to act with the frog as a blood-pumping unit. The leg is activated by tendons; one of these— the deep flexor tendon—passes under the tiny navicular bone, which acts as a pulley. The whole hoof is held together in the hoof wall, which protects the sensitive laminae and other delicate internal structures. The coronet is like the cuticle of your finger, and it is from here that the new material for the hoof is formed. The foot normally grows at a rate of ⅓ inch a month. Certain diseases cause a speed-up of growth. Stimulation from heat can increase the growing rate, and hoofs grow more rapidly during the summer than in the winter.

Moisture is essential for the hoof, as the fluid acts as a shock absorber. Anything that dries out the hoof starts a process of degeneration and atrophy. The outside of the hoof is protected by a thin layer of material called the periople, which is a delicate and essential structure. It controls evaporation and allows the hoof to breathe. Rasping of the periople, sanding it off, covering it with blacking, or smearing the hoof over with grease or hoof dressings, all interfere with the functioning of this vital surface.

The hoof is designed to circulate its own blood, since there are no valves to handle this in the legs of the horse. The pumping is accomplished by the interaction between the pedal cushion—squeezed by the weight of the horse on the coffin (or pedal) bone down from the top—and the frog—squeezed up from below with contact on the ground. When the hoof is raised, the pressure is relieved and blood flows into the hoof again. As the horse wanders and grazes, his feet are constantly lifted and lowered, and the blood is pumped up the legs. The motion is constant and circulation is regular. When the horse runs, there is a much greater pressure and the blood is pumped more rapidly, just as the heart pumps blood faster when stimulated by greater activity. If a horse works hard for a period of time every day, the blood vessels enlarge in order to facilitate the greater flow. When the horse then stands still for a prolonged time, the blood and fluids tend to pool, and the horse's legs "stock up." This condition clears up when the horse again takes exercise. Stocking up, in itself, is not a serious problem, but when the condition becomes chronic or the distention too great, the pressure starts to break down tissue. So horses that do fast or hard work should never be made to stand in straight or small stalls; if at all possible, they should be free in a paddock all the time they are not working.

Blood which pools in the foot and increases the heat there starts the breakdown of the laminae—a tearing away of the hoof wall from the sensitive inner surface. The tearing pressure in turn initiates a letdown of the pedal bone, which then rotates downward, increasing the tear of the laminae and causing the collapse of the hoof wall. The horse has the classic dished and ridged hoof, with its dropped sole, of founder.

Proper Shoeing

Racehorses and jumpers suffer more frequent ruptures of tendons and breaks than other horses, but show horses with their long feet suffer from unsoundness, too. Proper shoeing for the show ring need never cripple a horse. The usual shoe worn by high-stepping show horses is toe-weighted, has a wide "web" (wider along the toe edge than along the sides or heel), and is normally padded. The difference in weight between an ordinary shoe (about 14 ozs.) and a weighted one (about 20 ozs.) is not that great. Too much weight makes a horse labor and land too heavily on his feet, so that the addition of weight alone is not the route to good show action. However, even an additional pound of weight on the foot, including the pad and show shoes, should not disturb a normal mature horse as far as soundness goes. What does have a deleterious effect is the additional length of foot, and/or a radical change in the angle of the hoof. If the hoof is allowed to grow slowly with no major change or angle, and the length of the foot is strictly limited, the show horse can be maintained in sound and usable condition for years. With the long show foot, special precautions must be taken to prevent dehydration and atrophy of the frog and heels. Pads must be applied under the shoe with sufficient resilient material beneath them to maintain and assist frog pressure and ensure proper circulation. The material should be treated or saturated with a nontoxic fungicide of some sort, for once the shoe is nailed on, air and light can no longer penetrate to fight thrush and hoof rot. The shoes of a show horse *must* be reset frequently, never allowing the growth to be so great as to necessitate a major cutback and hence change the angle of the foot.

With a horse, all changes—whether in diet, exercise, hoof trimming, or training—should be done gradually. It should be a rule that no horse is allowed to wear his show shoes and long feet for more than six weeks without resetting. After the show season ends, the horse should be allowed to relax, his condition let down somewhat, and his feet cut back slowly over two or three sessions. Then he should be permitted to go barefoot for a month. Such a program enables the horse to regain the original healthy texture of his hoofs, restores the proper functions of the frog, and expands his heels. It will also greatly lift his spirits, help his body to regulate its normal functions, and get him set for a new season in fine spirit and shape. Horses that show extensively need, and deserve, a vacation just as much as harried business executives. They may enjoy their work, but it takes its toll nevertheless. They will perform better if their feet don't hurt.

Trimming

When the farrier trims a foal's feet, he calculates what effects this trimming will have on the bones all the way up the leg. A change of a fraction of an inch at foot level can start a chain reaction. The growth of bone takes place in response to the pressure applied: if you add pressure to one side, that side will grow longer. Such pressure is added by cutting away on the other side. But horses can overreact, so that the results of each trimming must be carefully observed and analyzed. We had a filly born with very sloppy knees. She stood as if she were cross-legged, but actually she was just very knock-kneed. We trimmed her feet in the prescribed manner to get the legs straighter, but in the process her foot suddenly dished. Then she had to be trimmed to overcome both the dishing and the knee-knocking. She grew out of most of it by the time I sold her at weaning, and I cautioned her buyers to have the farrier keep an eye on the foot and be sure not to let it regress. One of the treatments for her weak knees was enforced activity, since bones grow only if a horse has exercise. With her mother, she was put in an open paddock and stall, where they could go out of doors all the time and run around. She was a peppy foal and spent a good deal of time running and playing with her exuberant young mother. Had she been lethargic or out of a much older dam, she might not have made such rapid improvement.

Between their first and second year, horses grow unevenly. The rear legs grow first. Then the front end catches up; next, the rear end shoots up again. While his hind legs are longer, the young horse will tend to stand toed-out behind. This is an indication that he is growing and should *not* be corrected with trimming. If the rear feet stand perfectly straight behind the front feet and the hind legs are long, the horse will step on himself. With the feet rotated out from the stifles, as they should be, and the whole leg turned during growth, the hind legs will by-pass the front ones on the outside and avoid injuries. Horses should stand straight all their lives with their front feet. If there is a deviation here, it should be corrected from the moment it is observed, but beware of overcorrection.

Shoes to Correct Problems

Some farriers always put toe clips on a horse—that is, the edge of the shoe is led up over the toe to prevent the shoe from sliding back; or there may be side clips to prevent them from twisting sideways. The heels may be built up slightly with additional leather pads to raise them and so affect the stride of the horse. The shoes may also be padded to raise the front of the foot, counteracting too high heels. These are the usual methods of correcting simple and natural variations of the horse or the rider's preference for a particular way of going.

More severe faults include toeing out in front, which makes a horse dish in or swing the foot in a circle toward the supporting foot. This is corrected by trimming away some of the outside edge of the hoof so that the foot is tilted inward. The pigeon-toed horse is trimmed inside to prevent his winging or paddling outward. Sometimes, if the condition is severe, the horse is shod and the shoe wedged or thickened; or one side of the foot is padded more than the other to make a greater difference between the two edges of the hoof.

Long extensions of an inch or more out the back of the shoe are called trailers. Long extensions of the toe where the shoe is forward of the foot are designed to correct clubfoot and contracted tendons. If the horse's foot is dished, the standard procedure for shoeing is to hold back the shoe from the front edge, dub off the toe, and extend the shoe behind the foot.

Calf-kneed horses have a snappy, choppy action. The foot is yanked up from the ground, which has the same effect on way of going as too high a heel. The motion is shortened and elevated and also made rough. Stiff, upright pasterns cause the same stilted action. If it is desirable to shorten the stride in order to reduce overreaching,

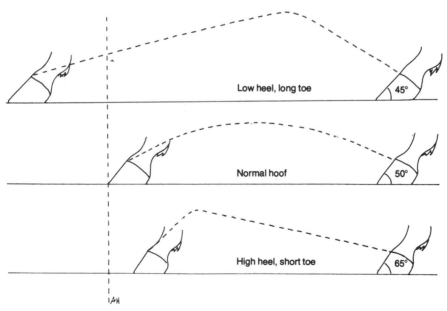

Low heel, long toe   45°

Normal hoof   50°

High heel, short toe   65°

The flight of the foot is determined by the angle of the hoof and the length of toe and heel. Note, too, that both the arc of the stride and the length of the stride vary with the conformation of the foot.

then the technique would be to raise the heels and cut back a bit on the toe. But since this will increase the impact of the foot as it hits the ground, it can be potentially damaging or at the least fatiguing to the horse. Remember that fatigue is a factor in breakdown. The problem might be better solved by rolling the toe of the front shoe so as to allow the front foot to break over faster and hence be out of the way sooner. This will tend to extend the reach of the front foot somewhat, but it will make the action softer, rather than more choppy. Sometimes both corrections must be made.

When you raise the head of the horse, you hollow his back and flatten his croup. This in turn rotates the hind legs out back and creates the problem of forging or overreaching. Sometimes the solution to the problem, therefore, is to give the horse a freer use of his head. You and the farrier must study the conformation of the horse and your method of riding or driving to find out whether the problem is caused by legs set too far back, hips that are higher than the withers, too flat a croup, too high a head, or some abnormality of the legs and feet themselves. It does little good to start making all sorts of corrections without knowing what causes the problem.

A friend recently spoke to me of a horse he was "reschooling." The animal would buck each time he started to canter and he would cross-canter—that is, canter on one lead with the front feet and the other lead with the hind. He was worst at this when ridden on a loose rein or when going uphill or on a rough path. He could be prevented from bucking by being whacked with the crop, and he would canter perfectly while held tightly, head up and very collected. My suggestion was that the problem with the horse was not physical but mental. He had been started under saddle while still growing rapidly, and he

Over-reaching, forging and scalping: three faulty ways of going which can cause injury to the horse. These are commonly corrected by adjustments in shoeing and trimming of the hoofs.

had been ridden by small children. In all likelihood, he had hit his front feet with his rear feet several times in starting to canter and this was very painful. He must also have learned that by cross-cantering he could avoid striking his heels, so when he had the freedom of his head or while negotiating a rough trail he would cross-canter to prevent the overreaching. My friend experimented for a while with changes of balance in the saddle, gradual takeoffs at a canter, and other measures to get the horse more secure about cantering. It was only a matter of weeks before he found a dramatic improvement. The horse had to relearn how to canter and get over the fear of injury; no amount of "corrective shoeing" would have helped his particular problem. If your farrier watches you ride your horse, he may be able to suggest corrections other than shoeing.

You must be aware that the farrier has no way of divining how a horse moves. He has to see him go, or you must describe to him what the problem is and what you wish to accomplish. Remember, too, that he sees the horse once a month at the most, while you see him every day. He can trim and he can shoe, but he cannot give your horse the daily hoof care he must have. If the horse is kept in a dry stall or paddock, you must add moisture to his feet. Make it a practice to soak four washcloths in water and wrap them about the horse's feet during grooming. (It helps to sew a shoestring across the top of each to secure them on the feet.) After grooming, wipe the feet off with clear water and inspect them. I had a friend who had the most healthy, shiny feet on her horses and she never had to black them for shows. I asked her the secret and she said, "Onions." She rubbed the feet with a cut onion each day and they stayed in excellent shape.

Problems can arise within the foot that the farrier can detect and relieve. Gravel can work up the white line inside the hoof. Sometimes, if caught in time, the hoof can be trimmed, allowing the gravel to descend. If not, the gravel will work on up and out the top of the hoof at the coronet, which makes the horse severely lame for a while. Corns, which are like blood blisters, can be caused by ill-fitting shoes and also by bruises. They can be protected by proper shoeing.

Your Responsibility to the Farrier

If your farrier shoes the horse and you then turn the animal out in deep mud or into a pasture where he is constantly pulling off his shoes in the fence, don't blame the farrier and expect him to rush back to reshoe him. Since the farrier, like the veterinarian, is essential to your horse, when you find a good one, have the sense to keep him happy. Hopefully, you will never have to have the veterinarian and farrier work together on your horse; but if you do, it helps tremendously if they respect each other and get along.

If you want the farrier to do a good job for you, you must give him a decent place to work. It is impossible for him to see whether a horse has a perfectly level foot when the animal is standing in a stall knee-deep in bedding or in mud up to his fetlocks. You would not want to go to work where you had to stand all bent over to work in a driving rainstorm with an animal ten times your size fidgeting above you, or to have to labor in the blazing hot sun while the horse dances frantically to escape flies. The farrier can't do a good job if he can't see, either. There is no reason why you should not have adequate lighting set up, even if it is just a pair of portable droplights hung where they will shine on the horse's feet. Make the farrier comfortable with a fan and a cold drink in hot weather, plus a place to sit and relax for a few minutes between horses if you have several. Keep your appointments with him.

The horse should be caught by you, have a strong halter put on, then led by you to the crossties and secured. Many people have the nerve to leave written instructions for the farrier and the horses out, without halters, in a big pasture. He is expected to find the right horse, catch him, haul him in, and fend off the other horses. Needless to say, such people keep having a harder time getting a farrier to come at all.

Lastly, if your horse is an absolute beast to shoe, don't blame the farrier if he beats the horse or refuses to shoe him. Bad manners are excusable in a very young horse who has not learned to stand for the blacksmith and balance his weight, but there is no excuse for a lot of bad manners in mature horses who are spoiled. If you don't want your horse punished for yanking, kicking, rearing, and plunging while the farrier is bent over and trying to do a careful job, train the animal to stand and behave while the farrier is at work. Keep dogs, cats, and kids out of sight and hearing. Your farrier is a professional. Have the courtesy to recognize that. More and more farriers are insisting that horses be brought to them, where they have a good setup and all their equipment. If you are fortunate enough to get one who will come to you, be grateful, and remember that anything you can do to make his job easier and more pleasant will give him a chance to do a better job for you.

CHAPTER 15

Breeding Your Own Horse

BREEDING HORSES IS A fascinating occupation. It poses a challenge to try to produce the best individual from the horses that are available. Like does not always produce like, regardless of what the old saying would have you believe; as for "blood will tell," another favorite expression, sometimes it tells you things you do not expect.

The Investment Involved

Breeding a mare and raising a foal is an investment. You must figure the cost per day of boarding the mare, the cost of trucking and of veterinary examination, added feed supplements if needed, and the booking and breeding—or stud—fees to the stallion's owner. If you want to breed your mare to a given horse and plan to bring her in a particular month, the stallion's owner keeps a stall available for her. Should he have other people who want to breed at the same time and no stall for them, and then you change your mind, he would lose money. Thus many stallion owners require a nonrefundable deposit —the booking fee—which is applied to your stud fee when you do bring the mare. Before your mare has even seen the stallion and decided whether she likes him or not, you have embarked on quite an investment in time and money.

If the mare is good and has no inheritable unsoundness or severe fault, and her mating is based on real knowledge of the blood behind her and the stallion to which she is put, the chances of a successful foal, worth the investment, are reasonably strong. Of course, there are risks involved. Mares do not always conceive. As a matter of fact, recent statistics indicate that of all the mares bred in any year, fewer than 50 percent conceive and carry a normal foal to full term, have a normal delivery, and nurse the foal successfully. All along the way there are obstacles. I try to discourage people from breeding their family pet if they are very involved emotionally, for the mare can die and leave you with nothing but a lonely stall. It is far better to keep that mare for pleasure and purchase a carefully bred and properly started foal.

The Importance of the Mare's Background

But if the mare has some special trait that you wish to perpetuate, and you are willing to take the risk, then the next step is to learn as much as you can about the horses in her background. All the conformation characteristics a horse has are inherited through the sire or the dam. Traits acquired through training and upbringing cannot be produced by breeding. Speed is inheritable, but the winning of show ribbons is acquired. With a clever and skillful trainer, even a poorly built, bad-tempered, crooked-legged horse can find a place in the show ring. Racehorses simply must have the speed, the physical conformation, and the competitive spirit needed to push to the finish line ahead of the others.

Most people, unfortunately, look at their horses with love-blind eyes. Even those of us who try to be objective and critical sometimes have to call in help when it comes to finding out where our own horses need improvement. The expression "barn blind" means that after you have looked at any given horse or band of horses, your eye becomes so used to their look that you see only the features you like. Their crooked pasterns or longish backs somehow seem perfectly in proportion. Allow someone with a fresh eye to scrutinize your animal and evaluate it honestly, even if it hurts your feelings or proves somewhat embarrassing to your self-image as a good horseman, for it is a necessity for every breeder to protect the quality of the stock from deterioration. A person with but one mare has as much obligation to breed intelligently as a breeder who produces horses in large numbers, for every horse is a potential influence on the whole population.

Systems of Breeding

First let me explain about so-called pure breeds of horses. Each true breed is the result of careful selection of animals for particular traits found in their parents and grandparents. A famous name four generations ago in a pedigree will have little real effect on the individual if that influence is overshadowed by mediocre animals represented on all the other lines. A good pedigree is one that shows horses of similar type or traits, which exhibit good qualities and have no faults *in common*. If the horses are not related by direct family lines (all horses within a "pure" breed are related to some extent), the pedigree is said to be "open." This means that though all the horses had similar desirable traits, those traits were inherited through unrelated sources. A horse can be "line-bred" or "inbred" to increase or intensify the chances of getting desirable traits. Line breeding is the mating of related horses such as cousins, aunts, and uncles. Inbreeding is an even closer breeding, as that between siblings, father and daughter, or mother and son. Such intense inbreeding does preserve good qualities, fixing them in the bloodline so that they will show up with remarkable frequency. But faults are concentrated just as good qualities are, and unless the animal is nearly faultless, the practice of inbreeding is a very hazardous one.

My Morgans are line-bred to three different horses: Mansfield, Jubilee King, and Ashbrook. These stallions have produced "get" (as it is called) which have proved to be compatible with one another. In other words, the get of Mansfield have proved good crosses on the get of Jubilee King. Jubilee King–line horses also cross well with Ashbrook, and Ashbrook crosses with Mansfield have proved very satisfactory, too. From each of these famous sires I am looking for specific traits that I wish to incorporate into my bloodlines. This is the way a family is developed; it is then established by judicious inbreeding, so that it will breed more or less consistently to produce certain desirable traits.

All breeders use one or more of these systems of breeding if they are serious about raising good horses. A totally random, or "open," pedigree, based on the matings of individuals as judged on their own obvious characteristics, is fine where you want to produce a single animal. Usually such a horse is of little value, however, in a breeding program aimed at a specific kind of product. So when you study the pedigree of your mare, try to ascertain what was in the breeder's mind as he made the combinations which produced each generation. It is to be remembered that most horses are not the result of one breeder's work for several generations. It takes years to get a family line established, and even longer to have more than two or three generations of your own breeding on both sides of a horse's pedigree. There is a minimum of three years between each line or generation of the pedigree—in most cases it is far more spread out than that.

Breeding for Color

There are breeds in which color is the prime consideration. Here it is possible to find horses which have no two ancestors even remotely alike in pedigree, conformation, ability, or type. In many cases, a registered horse's pedigree will have one line of registered blood-bred horses and all the rest of the pedigree can be blank; or the horse can have one line which is half Appaloosa and half Thoroughbred while the other line is half Quarter Horse and half blank, so that when you try to figure out what the horse has to offer in genetic terms, the answer is color—if he happened to inherit the color. It is even possible to find a registered Appaloosa that is pure Thorough-bred except for one blank line, from which the color must have come.

ONE-TO-ONE SELECTION

When you breed for a particular color or pattern, you are of necessity forced to breed on the basis of the individual horse you have before you, and the known ancestry is only part of the consideration. You must then weigh factors on a one-to-one basis. Look at the mare and write down all the faults she has. Then have the veterinarian tell you everything he can see that he would change, if he could. Ask your farrier to give his own honest analysis, too. Then select a stallion who can overcome the faults that the mare shows. Take a long look at every available foal that stallion has sired (and at the mares who produced them) to see what contributions he has made.

After you have gone through this process, you will have some idea of what you should be able to expect from any given mating. The discouraging thing is that even in purebred horses, full brothers or sisters can be totally different in looks and even more different in what they have to pass on to the next generation. It is much harder to breed good individuals in a wide-open pedigree situation than in a breed where the bloodlines have been concentrated to establish traits. So it is impossible to state, for instance, that a particular color breed has any characteristics (other than color) that it will pass on without fail. And there is no color registry which makes the claim that their horses will pass on color without fail. Some stallion owners can claim this for individual sires, however.

The Mare's Contribution

The genetic inheritance of any foal comes half from the sire and half from the dam. While the mare is 50 percent of the foal's inheritance, she is 100 percent of its environment throughout the gestation period, and most of its environment for the suckling period of the foal's life. Carrying the foal from conception to parturition involves a great deal more than being a simple incubator. Nutrition of the foal is the most obvious influence the mare can have on the fetus. The foal can be well fed, or it can be hindered in its development by the mare's inability to assimilate and utilize her feeds. Some mares grow very fat and slick while they are pregnant and then give birth to foals with rickets. Some have fine fat foals but are unable, themselves, to produce enough milk to feed the foal when it is born. In some cases there is a factor, much like the Rh factor in human beings, in which the foal is actually allergic to antibodies in the mare's first milk, or colostrum. Unless this is diagnosed and the milk withheld, the foal dies within hours of birth. Even if a mare has a normal pregnancy and feeds her foal well, other disasters may occur. She may be stupid and run the foal into fences, step on his legs and break them, teach him to be afraid of people, or keep him awake so much of the time through her own nervousness that he fails to grow normally. I know of two mares that were kept in stalls and were so large and moved so little that their foals did not shift inside them. As a result, the foals stayed in the same position for months of development and when born were both so badly deformed that they had to be destroyed. Some mares reject their foals and even kill them; some are good mothers from start to finish. There is no way to predict how they will act unless you happen to know how their own dam was, since daughters sometimes follow their mothers' tendencies. There are also problems in actually giving birth, but fortunately, less for horses than other domestic animals. Twins are rare and not usually successful, although Arabian horses seem to twin more often than other breeds and a fair portion of them survive. It should be clear, then, that the mare you use for breeding is of more importance than the stallion in terms of the particular foal you are about to produce.

The Stallion's Contribution

Most people think of the stallion as being the major factor in a horse's genetics. This is not so. It *is* true that the stallion should be as perfect as possible, because stallions can produce several times the number of offspring in a lifetime that a mare can. A stallion has more impact on the breed than a mare, but less impact on the individual foal. Once you become a student of bloodlines, it is easy to see that only great broodmares produce great foals, and the stallions who have been bred to hundreds of mares have not reproduced hundreds of top-quality foals. Well-bred, well-publicized stallions produce more foals than do unknown ones. Generally, they attract better mares and have a better "record" of reproduction in the end. But the stallion does not, necessarily, have a good or strong influence on every foal he has sired.

Conception

WHEN TO BREED

Although it is customary at breeding farms to breed mares to foal as close to January as possible, so as to get a jump on the competition in shows and races, it is easiest to get a mare in foal between April and August. The closer to August, the easier it becomes. The process from breeding to foaling takes about eleven months, which means that many people try to breed their mares in February. This is one of the reasons there are so many failures. Mares are hard to breed as long as they have their winter coats, and they have more problems feeding their foals when they do not have grass. Grass makes the conception rate shoot upward. What actually regulates the ovulation cycle and hence the chances of conception is not grass but hours of daylight. You can fool nature with lights, blankets, feed supplements, and hormone stimulants, but getting a mare bred earlier than her normal season has drawbacks at foaling time. I suffer for every winter mating because I sleep in the barn during foaling season, and even in a snowmobile suit, with a sleeping bag and an electric blanket, I am miserable for most of the early spring months. If I feel sorry for myself, I just remember how the poor mares and foals must feel. They have to stay locked up in stalls when the ground is slippery with ice. There is no grass. There is not enough sunlight for the foal's bones, and he cannot possibly get the exercise he needs for the development of his lungs and circulation. If you want to raise a foal as a replacement for its dam and you plan to keep the horse all his life, there is no need to rush the season and try for a January foal. Your chances of a live and healthy foal will be greater, and the foal and mare will both benefit, if you wait until April at least before you breed.

YOUR CONTRIBUTION

While you are waiting there are many things you can do to help the mare conceive and carry a healthy foal. First, have the veterinarian do an internal examination to see if she is normal for breeding. Some mares are immature even at five years old. Some are closed from scar tissue, and some are lacerated or have growths that will prevent conception. Have him also do a culture to make certain that she has no infection. Start her on a program of regular grooming and give her wheat-germ oil or meal to help increase her fertility. I know you will hear arguments against vitamin therapy for pregnancy, but it has been the experience of thousands of horse breeders that something in wheat-germ oil does indeed affect conception. Even if all it does is to get the mare to shed out and grow a beautiful coat, you will have gained. The mare should be neither too fat nor too thin. She should have regular and consistent exercise to be in good muscle tone. Take her away from home and lead her in strange places. Get her used to being handled by strangers. When you leave her at the stallion's stable she will be in a new situation, and some mares are so bothered by change that they will not settle down and cooperate. If she is not really well halter-broken start now, because not only will it be hard for the stallioneer to handle her during breeding, but also you will have a bad time with her when she has a foal at foot if she is not genuinely nice to lead.

HEAT CYCLES

The standard procedure for breeding is to try to establish when the mare cycles in her regular pattern, if she has one. Record the days of a few of her cycles before you plan to breed her. Arrange to take her to the stallion two or three weeks before she is due to come into heat, and plan to leave her there until she has been bred and then passes one heat-cycle time without showing evidence of heat.

Mares vary in their evidence of heat cycles. Some urinate frequently, particularly when introduced to another horse. Some change their behavior or apparent disposition. But many mares' heats are undetectable without actual "teasing" by a stallion.

THE COURTEOUS STALLION

From experience I have found that mares and stallions have preferences, and that even when you force a mare to stand for service, if she really hates the stallion she may not conceive, though that is unusual. If the stallion owner is skillful and the stallion himself a proven and capable horse, it rarely ends up in failure. But if the horse is a noisy bully and the owner a roughneck, it is not at all unusual for the mare simply never to show any heat at all.

We have had several stallions. Our oldest and most experienced one is a gentleman and a very courtly lover. He asks the mare if she is interested. He prances and arches his neck and makes himself as attractive as he can to her. Then he does a great deal of nuzzling and talking and gentle nipping. He pushes her with his shoulders and checks to see how she is reacting. If she does not smell ready to him, or if she acts uncooperative, he walks away and eats grass. Even when we cannot tell by the mare's actions if she is ready or not, he can, and he acts accordingly. His success is phenomenal in settling mares who are normally hard to breed.

Another old stallion of ours has as many foals on the ground as the first horse, but his technique is quite different. He is a flirt; more important, he is a clown. He plays the fool and entertains his lady with a show. He prances and trumpets and sometimes brings her a mouthful of grass or leaves as an offering. If the mare is reluctant, he stands by her and talks for long periods. He rests his chin on her back and rubs it back and forth with a dreamy look on his face. He, too, pushes the mare with his shoulder. The object of this maneuver is to get the mare to spread her hind feet and brace herself so that she will be in a position for him to mount without problems. If she threatens to kick him, he screams at her and stamps a foot. He will try to bully a mare if he thinks she is faking and just teasing him, but he gets kicked more often than quieter horses.

A third stallion is an absolute klutz. The mares don't like him. He comes out of his stall shrieking like a demented idiot, rears, and tries to breed the mare without even smelling to see if she is in heat. For this he gets kicked. He pays little or no attention to anyone handling him for the first few minutes out of his stall, so he gets yanked down and scolded until he becomes settled. Then, once he has decided to ask rather than demand, he takes so long the mares get bored and irritated and they start to fidget. When he finally gets himself organized, he has been kicked so often he tries to mount the mare at the head and then walk back along her side to avoid being belted again. This is fine, but he bangs the mare's handler and the mare with his front feet. Once he is in position, he slams his feet together on the mare's ribs and tries to keep his balance by holding onto her neck with his teeth. I don't need to tell you it is hard to persuade a mare to stand for too much of that. They won't even show heat to him, so we have to use one of the older stallions to check the mare for him. Obviously, we get more results from the older and more intelligent stallions than we do from this spoiled roughneck. Since he is by no means a young horse, by now he is a bit too old to learn manners, and besides, he is also a big strong horse. If he were not an exceptional producer, he would not be worth the effort.

Stallions can be trained to have a technique and manners if they are handled right in the first place. This is particularly important if your mare is nervous and thin-skinned, hard to find in heat and easily frightened. Sadly, many of the privately owned mares that are sent out to be bred either fail to come in heat because they are so upset by the new surroundings or are hurt in breeding accidents. Part of this is due to a lack of preparation, and part is because mares are sent to a cheap local stallion and the mating is based on his stud fee and convenience, rather than the quality of his proven get, his handlers, and his stable. But sending a mare to a fancy stable with a long string of show ribbons is no guarantee of success, either. The horse and his handlers will make the difference. If you have a friend with an unproven colt and both of you want to see what he can produce, fine. Make sure he is handled properly and be there with the mare to help steady her. Some colts are rank, hopelessly confused, and funny in their adolescence; others are instinctively smart from the beginning.

Now, what about those one-shot deals we hear about, in fact and fiction? Lots of foals are produced when a mare comes in season, either she or the stallion gets out of the pasture, and they meet and breed only once. How about the old-timers who brought a stallion to a crossroads and stood him there to all the mares that showed up that day? He could be there for hours and breed several mares. Then he would move to another town and breed many mares in that town. They got foals. None of the breedings were recorded and no one knows how many mares those horses settled in comparison to the number they serviced. There was a Morgan horse named Gifford Morgan, who at the age of nineteen was shown at a state fair with 124 of his weanling foals. That means he serviced more than that number of mares in one year in this fashion. He also was kept at hard work throughout the time, which kept him in top physical condition. In all these situations where mares were bred but once, it must be clearly understood that they were bred at precisely the optimum time for conception. They were probably in excellent working condition, not overfat, flaccid in muscle tone, or suffering from malnutrition. The farmers really knew their mares, as they were in intimate working contact day after day. If the mare was not ready for breeding, she was not taken to the horse. No foals were born in the cold weather, so the mares were bred during the optimum seasons. Mares were led, driven, or ridden to the point where they were serviced, rather than being vanned or trucked to strange places or left on a changed routine with strange people. Few, if any, of these mares were hobbled, twitched, or forced to stand—no one had the time or patience for that nonsense. So the mares bred when they were good and ready, and there was not a great deal of trauma or distress. That is a far cry from today's methods.

MANAGEMENT OF THE STALLION

Remember that the owner of a stallion may be the nicest person in the world, but the people who handle your mare and the stallion are the ones who will determine how much skill and patience goes into your mare's breeding. They may be experienced, true horsepeople or stable bums and brutes. Check that out before subjecting your mare to their care. This is not a matter of sentimentality. I have known of mares sent out to be bred who never came back. I have had mares so badly frightened from a bad experience that it took months of patience and vet care and handling to get them to the point where they could be tried again. I had a mare here who had had her leg broken and her skull caved in from stupidity on the part of the breeders who were supposed to get her in foal. Once I sold a colt to some people who had sent three mares to a well-known stable to have them bred. The mares stayed there all summer, at considerable expense, and came back not even serviced, let alone in foal. The stallion owner said they never came in heat. One month after they bought the two-year-old colt from me, all three mares were safely in foal. In some cases, mares actually do not show heat away from home. But it is always to be suspected that either the manager is not careful or intensive enough in his "teasing" of the mares, or the stallion might actually intimidate them. In some stables there is little doubt that showing a horse is more important to the owners than breeding visiting mares. If the stallion becomes agitated and will not show well, the mares are simply overlooked.

When you read the ads for stallions standing at stud you will see a number of notes: live foal guarantee, with return, private treaty; purebreds one price, grades another; registered or approved mares only; and so on. These are the terms under which the stallion owner will accept mares. Some will take any mare, breed her for a fee, and that's that; some will take only the mares they feel will produce good foals, and refuse to breed a mare with inheritable problems because they wish to protect their stallion from siring poor foals; some breeders want to encourage people with unregistered stock to get involved with their breed in the hopes that they will someday want a purebred; some are sure their stallion will produce a live foal but feel that if a mare is bred and does not produce, then the mare owner should not have to pay the full price. Most of these owners are paid half at the time of service (which is about the same as for a horse standing without a live foal guarantee but with return privileges) and the other half when the foal is born. "Return privileges" means that if you send the mare to be bred and she comes home and then returns into heat for any reason, you can take her back to the stallion without paying another fee. Most stallion owners limit this to return within the current season; if you bred the mare in March and brought her home assumed in foal in April, and she aborted in July because you jumped or raced her, or she got sick, you could take her back to the stallion for rebreeding that same year. Some horses stand only from January 15 to July 15, and that is the limit of their season. Some stallion owners are smart and will breed your mare and then keep her until she has a foal. That means you pay board for eleven months and do not have the use of your mare, but she will have a foal under their supervision.

MORE ABOUT HEAT CYCLES

In most breeding farms the routine is to check each morning all the mares expected to cycle. This is done by teasing the mare with a stallion or sometimes with a gelding. If there are several mares in heat at the same time to be bred to one horse, they are staggered to try to breed each mare two or three times throughout her heat, trying always to breed on the last day if possible. It is evident that the majority of mares actually ovulate toward the end of the heat. Some are tricky and ovulate after they finish showing heat. Some ovulate only once in a great while and still show heat. If there is one mare to be bred, she will sometimes be bred each day of the heat if both she and the stallion are easily managed. If the horse is rank, has several mares, is old, or is servicing a mare who is a problem, he may service only on alternate days. Some breeding establishments have veterinary examinations every day while the mare is in season and the mare is serviced only once, on the day the follicle ruptures. Sperm from a normal, average stallion will be viable for about seventy-two hours. If the mare's tract is of normal acidity, she can be bred the day before the follicle ruptures and still conceive, or be bred the day after and still conceive. If the stallion's fertility is low, the motility of the sperm is low, or, if the mare's tract is less than ideal, the chance of conception is reduced.

Some mares carry low-grade infections or get manure trapped in the vagina, which will prevent conceptions. There are also a few diseases that cause abortion, but both mare and stallion should have been checked for these prior to breeding. The mare may receive a follicle-stimulating or luteinizing-hormone shot if necessary, and there are mares who will not take without them (I owned such a mare once). Some will not accept a stallion if they are held, but will breed readily if turned loose with the horse in a paddock. Part of this has to do with how relaxed the mare is.

Some mares seem to come in heat the minute they arrive in a strange place, but the heat is not a true one and they will not conceive if bred. Other mares come in heat and stay that way for weeks. This long heat is usually "not good," and besides, the stallion owner has better things to do than spend all his time on one mare. Ordinarily, a mare that does this is given a manual exam and a shot to put her out of heat, and then rebred on her next cycle. Mares can conceive on one heat, and return to a standing heat two or more times after they are in foal. If the stallion is a smart one, he can usually tell; but if he likes the mare, he is likely to service her anyway. There is no harm in this, as a rule, for if the mare will stand, it is not painful or hazardous for her. Normally what happens is that once she conceives on a service, she forms a mucous plug which prevents further introduction of sperm into the tract and her hormones change so that she loses her desire to mate. Sometimes the mucous plug forms normally but the hormone activity doesn't shut down right away. Oddly enough, such activity seems to be endemic in one area of the country at the same time; several breeders will have mares returning to heat over and over, yet the following spring they give birth at a time that corresponds most nearly with the first service.

Heat cycles are controlled by more than just the internal workings of the mare. They are somehow subject to atmospheric condition, and a correlation to the moon has been noted in many studies. There is no doubt that mares respond to longer daylight and that they tend to foal during storms. We find that in spring our mares show irregular heat patterns, as would be expected, but as the summer wears on they tend to come in heat all at once, which means that we will have three weeks without any mare in heat and then seven mares in at the same time. Needless to say, this is a nuisance, but it is so common that we learn to judge when one shy mare is in heat by watching the other mares. We have a mare that will show heat if we tease her while all the horses are in the barn and things are quiet, but if we put all the other horses out she is so anxious to be with her cronies that she has no interest in the stallion. It takes time to get to know each mare and her personal foibles. No wonder some mares are sent off to be bred and come home unserviced!

FALSE HEATS AND SILENT HEATS

It is important to remember that some mares can ovulate without showing any signs of heat. This is called a silent heat. Such mares are naturally hard to settle unless you have a wise and experienced stallion that talks a good line and is persistent. Such a one can determine by smell if the mare is in a good stage to breed. Some mares show a false heat and do not ovulate at all. My old horse will not breed a mare who is just showing heat unless she is ready to conceive. His father was the same way and he would not breed a mare who had even a low-grade infection. If he sniffed a mare and turned away, the vet was called, the mare was cultured and was palpated for a follicle. The old stallion had made the right decision every time.

With a mare in silent heat, the stallion can sometimes talk her into standing even if she won't "show." The veterinarian can feel how developed the follicle is. This condition is inheritable and should disqualify a mare from a breeding herd. When a mare goes for more than thirty days without showing heat, it is to be suspected that she has silent heats. The veterinarian can make regular checks on her manually, then when the follicle is ripe and ready to rupture, the mare is forced into standing for service. It may take force, hobbles, and a twitch, but it can be done. Once the mare has stood for service, she will sometimes come into a strong heat and stand willingly. We had one we couldn't shut off again. We also have a mare who does not ovulate while nursing her foal. She can be bred only on alternate years.

ARTIFICIAL INSEMINATION

The practice of artificial insemination for horses as well as cattle is a growing one. Some of the breeds will not recognize the get of artificial service at this time; but when regulatory measures can be set up to establish honesty in breeding procedures, they will probably consider the practice acceptable. Artificial insemination has many advantages: Only a small amount of semen need be transported, not a horse, or worse yet a mare and foal. It reduces the spread of disease. Only viably fertile stallions are used (which is not always the case today), since semen is examined when it is collected. And it eliminates the risks of injury to man and animal, as well as being likely to result in more normal, healthy foals. The problem is that not all horse people are as honest as they should be and there are too many opportunities for pulling a fast one.

When the techniques of blood typing and identification now developing have been perfected and brought into reasonable price ranges, it will be an easy matter to demand that any foal which has been produced by artificial means must be positively identified as the get of the sire listed before being registered. This will make an enormous difference, for even now, with the mare and stallion both having to be present on a farm where the mare is bred, there is still no guarantee that the specified stallion was the one who covered the mare. Many stables use stallions to tease mares and then cover the mare with another stallion. This saves the older or more excitable or valuable horse from strain. Some good sires are poor lovers, and if left to their own devices couldn't persuade a mare to stand. There are times when things get out of hand and the teasing stallion gets the mare. There are also a few mares serviced by the teaser in order to keep him happy. Since the foals sired by the more valuable stallion will sell for more money, his name is sometimes put on the papers. If the two horses are similar in looks, it would be hard for most people to identify the father in the foal.

I know of a Quarter Horse breeder who sent her mare to be bred, choosing the less expensive and less well known stallion they had at stud. The foal she got was clearly by their expensive, valuable sire and a perfect example of the breed. The owners of the stallion would never admit that they had used the wrong horse on her mare, so she had papers for the less valuable stallion and paid the lesser stud fee, but got a superior horse out of it. The problem, however, was that she was honest and felt that since the horse's pedigree was inaccurate, she could not use him for breeding with a clear conscience; so she had him gelded. I know of another farm where a horse stood for years at stud and was sterile. "His" foals were always by another stallion in the barn, which was referred to as the family pet. There is a stallion standing now who has sired but one foal in his life at stud, which spans nearly six years as far as I know. Take heed to investigate this aspect before booking your mare.

Pregnancy

If all goes normally and you send your mare early enough for her to relax and settle down before her due period, she should be able to be bred and then checked through by thirty days from the last day of her service. Then you should bring her home, and in another fifteen days have her vetted either manually or by blood test to see if she is pregnant. If she is, you can start making plans for a foal in from 315 to 365 days from the last date of service, with 344 days being about average.

CARE OF YOUR MARE

While you are waiting, don't just sit back and think how well nature works. You have an obligation to the mare and foal to be sure that they come through this experience in good health. Pregnant mares do not become delicate or fragile. They should go on being used at their normal work. Some mares will abort in a natural and spontaneous manner. The theory is that this happens because the fetus is in some way malformed and it is nature's way of protecting the species from misfits. I'm not too sure this is always the case, but it is a comforting thought. More likely a disease or a chemical or hormonal malfunction triggers abortion in a normal mare. Of course, many shots and chemicals introduced into our horses can cause abortion. Every time you have the veterinarian work on your mare even for a swollen foot or a case of ringworm, *be sure* to remind him that she is in foal. Steroids, cortisone, iodides, certain immunization preparations and worm medicines are not to be used on pregnant mares unless the doctor is positive that the foal is safe. He has hundreds of animals to work on. Never take it for granted that he will remember your particular mare is in foal, even if he himself did the exam and pronounced the good news.

Besides spontaneous abortion, there are mechanical abortions. Slipping on ice, being overworked to the point of exhaustion, or straining from jumps can cause a mare to lose her foal. Mares are tough and strong and the baby is pretty well insulated by his sac of fluid and his mother's strong ribcage, but a well-aimed kick from another mare or a bad accident can bring on loss of a foal.

PROPER NUTRITION

Assuming the mare carries the foal normally and does not abort, you are not off the hook yet. For the mare to raise a healthy foal, both she and the infant must have proper nutrition. Calcium and phosphorus must remain in balance, vitamins and minerals must be available through high-quality feeds and/or supplements. Protein levels of 14 percent or higher should be maintained, but don't get carried away. I know of people who are feeding not one, but two cups of calf manna, on the theory that if one is good, two must be better. Don't do this. One is sufficient and practical. One is going to help the mare, while two might upset the balance of the diet, creating super-vitaminosis, crooked bones, deformities, and strain on organs. Use vitamins and minerals in a standard mixture recommended by your veterinarian. One major warning here: *Don't* feed your mare anything with antibiotics in it and don't give the foal any, either. There are products on the market that claim to make "healthier," more disease-resistant, and larger foals. What these fail to tell you on the package is that animals develop intolerances to such drugs. Antibiotics over long periods can predispose the horse to problems that you then cannot cure with other medications. You are not raising this foal to slaughter, I presume. If all you care about is the first three or four years of the horse's life, go ahead and force him to grow and gain weight at a faster rate. Race him at two and can him at five. Show horses are judged on fat, finish, and size, so a horse destined to a life in the show ring can be pushed by such tactics in terms of being a winner. But if you are raising a foal as a pleasure animal and a companion for long-time use, read the labels carefully and leave the antibiotics to the veterinarian when they are needed for specific problems. You can get changes in the foal's growth and size with hormone shots, too, just as caponizing chickens and castrating steers make them grow bigger and fatter. But you are better off keeping things in close harmony and balance with nature, and letting the mare and foal come along naturally.

HER GENERAL HEALTH

Your mare should be in superb health when she is pregnant, for all her systems are at peak performance. Her nutrition will improve, as her digestion and all her body functions are geared to pregnancy. It is often possible to rehabilitate a "down" horse by getting her in foal. For the first few months, you probably won't see any outward signs of a foal on the average mare. Some bloom right away and you can tell they are pregnant even before the first check period, but most show no radical change.

Pregnancy is divided into trimesters of about 115 days (figuring on a 344-day average). Reabsorption or spontaneous abortion occurs most often within the first trimester. After this time the mares are pretty resilient and normal in all their functions. In the last trimester the mares are most subject to complications from medications, colic upsets, changes of any kind, and a viral abortion from rhino-pneumonitis. Exercise must be maintained throughout the pregnancy; if you normally work the mare hard, continue to do so up until the last month. If she is going to foal in the spring and you live where there is snow and ice, you will very likely have to cut down somewhat because of the weather. In the last month it is well to let the mare down all the way, but not to lock her in a stall. She should be out of doors in the sunlight because sun is a source of vitamin D and important to her health. She should move all the time, walking as she grazes, playing and romping at will. Even if she just paces the fence out of loneliness and boredom, that is better than standing in a stall, but it would be a kindness to give her company. If she will not take exercise in some form, lead her for a mile or two a day. She will enjoy your company and you can tell her just what you want to produce. We tell all our mares to "think pink" because we want fillies. I sold a mare to a woman who wanted the mare to have a filly, but she also planned to show the mare. As we closed the deal I told her to think pink and she looked shocked. "Oh, no!" she protested. "Pink is fifth place. I want blues." Needless to say, she got a colt. Seriously, taking the mare for walks and talking to her serves a very useful purpose. If she thinks of you as a companion and a friend before she foals, when the foal is born she will be less apprehensive about your presence. Should she have problems and need your help, it will be easier for her if your voice is familiar and pleasurable to her.

NAVEL ILL

The mare should receive her annual tetanus booster about three weeks *before* foaling. This acts as a preventive to increase her immune response to the disease called navel ill (though in fact there is no known direct link between tetanus and navel ill). Navel ill is a crippler which is introduced into the foal's body at the moment of birth. The reason you should put iodine on the navel is to close it up, so that germs do not enter directly into the bloodstream of the foal through the umbilical cord. Remember that the shots the mare gets go into her bloodstream and thence into the foal she is carrying, for his bloodstream is a continuation of hers through the cord. For this reason, extreme caution should be taken in feeding and medicating a pregnant mare. There are only certain medications the foal can tolerate; he will die if the mare is given shots that are adverse to his system.

EDEMA

Mares who are very heavy in foal often have trouble with fluid accumulating in the lower part of their legs, more so behind than in front, as a rule. This is called edema. There can be a number of causes and they should be systematically eliminated until you find the answer, and then treat it with proper remedies. First, if the mare looks filled when she is in all night and the filling goes away when she has been out in pasture, it would be the kindest thing to arrange her stall and paddock so that she can go in and out at will to relieve this pressure. If exercise does not reduce the filling, watch when she urinates. If she strains or grunts, if her urine is dark amber or smells very strong, she needs a vet posthaste. Some mares always grunt when they are eliminating; if this is normal for her in a nonpregnant state, then it is certainly no cause for alarm when she is pregnant. Never attempt to treat *any* internal problem of a pregnant mare without competent advice. Electrolytic salts may very well be the answer if the mare shows signs of imbalance, but she could as easily have an infection that must be cleared up with the proper medication first. A change in her diet may be all that is necessary to clear up edema, but always consult the veterinarian. The fluid can distend the tissues in the legs so badly that they never completely recover.

Watch particularly for heat in the feet, because founder during pregnancy and delivery is not uncommon. A small amount of fluid that comes and goes is not anything to get upset over. Just keep an eye on the situation and be aware of the possibilities.

THE EMOTIONS

You should be aware that your pregnant mare will undergo emotional changes as a result of hormonal influence. The mare that has always been loving and friendly may become restive, suspicious, and even aggressively defensive as she nears parturition. She may change from a spirited, gay, and playful animal to a lethargic, placid, even seemingly dull-witted one. She has not really changed; she is simply responding to the instincts of motherhood and preparing for foaling. There are people who breed mares to "settle them down" and sometimes it does indeed seem to have a gentling influence on a high-strung animal; but I had one who changed for the worse and became more treacherous with each pregnancy. Once her foal was weaned, she became her own sweet affectionate self again. The hormones which stimulated her to produce milk also excited her defensive nature so that she was prepared to protect the foal. Some mares get extremely worried; make excuses for them and try to eliminate all the things that cause them to be ill at ease.

THE FOALING STALL

If she is to move to a foaling stall, transfer her at least a month in advance and let her make a nest for herself in which she feels secure. If she insists on lying in a pile of manure and messing up her grain bucket because she always faces the window to watch for predators, perhaps you can darken the window or else move the feeding utensils to accommodate her. She should not be spoiled and babied in the normal sense, but her anxiety is not put on to get attention. She is not the master of her emotions or her actions in this case. Nervous mares are hard to handle and often inadvertently injure their foals and the people who try to help them. Fear makes delivery difficult and frequently causes tearing and straining in the mare, whereas if she were calm, she could deliver with less trouble.

Pregnant mares should never be left standing tied up. Even early in pregnancy it is a mistake to tie them, walk off, and leave them. If they take fright and pull back hard enough to break the halter, they can fall and hurt themselves; and if the halter holds, they can pull abdominal muscles, which will cause delivery problems. Near the end of pregnancy the mare should not be kept in a standing stall, for if she should foal early and without the advance signs, she might get jammed in the stall, killing herself and/or the foal in the process.

There should be no drafts, and no heat is necessary unless the foal is born in the winter or in early spring. An ordinary heat lamp suspended in a cage high enough so as not to singe the mare's back will provide enough warmth and the foal will quickly learn to sleep under the lamp. Do not seal up the stall or make it snug, for you will trap humid air and cause the stall to be damp and clammy.

Hay and water should be available at all times during delivery, for eating is often a soothing and calming activity for a mare who is extremely nervous. They get very thirsty after delivery, and unless the mare is really drenched with sweat she should be allowed to drink as much as she desires. There should be no radio left on nearby, no visitors or onlookers, and no horse in a neighboring stall that will intimidate or pester the foaling mare.

You will hear all sorts of advice about cleaning and sterilizing the stall before birth. It is virtually impossible to sterilize a barn stall completely and probably not necessary to do so. It should be clean, of course, and you can spread ground limestone under the bedding, sprinkle the floor with creolin or diluted iodine, and wash down the walls with disinfectant. Remember that you can easily get carried away with chemicals and create problems of poisoning and skin irritation, so ask the doctor about this and use your commonsense.

Lights often bother a foaling process and can actually interrupt it, causing the foal to suffocate. So if you feel you need light, have a night light in the stall for weeks in advance and let her get used to it. If you were to leave the lights off until the mare produced the head and front legs, then a light would not stop her, but if you suddenly switched on the overhead lights she might jump up and tear herself badly. Therefore, get the mare used to your coming into the stall every night and shining a flashlight at her belly and her dock. The best light is one you can stand in a corner or hang on a wall that will stay still and give you just enough light to move about the stall if you must help the mare—but not so much that it upsets her. Indirect lighting with a rheostat is ideal. Lighting after a foal is born is also a consideration. We had the lights on for a young mare with her first foal, then when she and her colt were all fed and dry and settled for the night, we turned off the lights and prepared to go home to bed. She yelled and carried on because she didn't know how to find her foal in the dark and we had to leave the lights on for the rest of the night. Of course, the heat lamp gives enough light to solve this problem if you have a winter foal.

It would actually be best of all for the mare if the foal could be born out of doors in a clean grassy paddock, with no other horses in the same lot. The one problem is that if the mare lies down against a fence or a door which is open at the bottom, the foal may be born on the other side of the fence or door, and the frantic mother will be separated from her helpless newborn.

The choice of bedding is up to you. I like dry shavings and sawdust, or straw if it is not terribly long. As a rule, straw is nice and clean and soft. I have recently seen mares foaling on poorly bedded stalls. The mare goes through a lot of pain and getting up and down; she will appreciate a soft bed. Also, while the process of foaling itself is a remarkably nonbloody procedure, there is quite a lot of amniotic fluid and the mare may urinate heavily, too, so that in order to have a dry place for the foal, the bedding should be deep enough to absorb all this. Since foals take a certain amount of bedding into their nostrils and mouths as they struggle to get up, it might make sense to invest in one or two bales of really undusty shavings that you save for the day your mare starts to foal. You can't rush in and clean the stall or spread the bedding after foaling begins, but if you can judge readiness fairly closely, you can give her the bedding. Try to keep the floor of the stall level, because the foal will have problems enough getting up without coping with mountains.

THE LAST TRIMESTER

During the last months of her pregnancy, keep your mare's stall clean and dry and put her in a paddock, also clean and dry, where you can watch her during the day. She may lie down a great deal. She may also roll, and she may colic slightly, after meals. Divide her feedings up and do not make any sudden changes in feed. The practice of giving mares a huge hot bran mash before foaling is about as sensible as giving a child a large dose of Epsom salts before an appendectomy. If you want her to have bran, give her a little at each feeding. You do not want to induce diarrhea, and most mares adjust their stools perfectly naturally without your interference.

Before foaling the mare will start to shed, even if it is January. The area over her croup may gradually sink in slightly, and the foal—who may have been carried high and forward, hardly showing at all—will slowly descend into the back and lower part of the abdomen. She will suddenly look as if the foal is huge. Indeed, it has grown more in the last few months than you imagine. The foal is preparing to get into position and in so doing may engage in lots of activity. The mare may experience some discomfort if the foal is very active. Her milk veins will fill and her udder swell. Some mares look as if they will have no milk at all and worried owners try all sorts of things to try to stimulate milk for the baby.

THE UDDER

I doubt that massaging the udder does anything to increase the mare's milk, but it will get the mare used to having her udder touched and her belly bumped. Some mares are so ticklish that they actually kill their nursing babies. It is a good idea to stroke the mare gently all about the belly and over the udder. But *do not* tickle, milk, or manipulate the udder prior to foaling. The very first milk in her udder is colostrum, which contains all the essential antibodies and immunities she has built up. They are for her foal and absolutely essential to his health. Even when a mare dies in foaling, it is wise to try to get some of this milk for the foal and bottle-feed him with it first. Some mares do not have milk for their foals. This may be because they have not had the proper nutrition, or they have a metabolic problem and are unable to convert their food into milk, or else they are just not ready yet and the milk will come when they are stimulated by the foal. There is a pituitary-stimulating hormone that the doctor can give the mare if necessary. Some mares will have milk but not enough, so that you must get the foal to eat grain and milk replacer as quickly as you can. Other mares will reject their suckling foal entirely. You cannot tell anything at all about this by looking at the outside of the mare's udder. You will just have to watch the foal's condition after it is born.

SIGNS OF GETTING CLOSE

Before she foals, the mare's bag will fill and become firm. The nipples may be large or small, let down or way up. It is usual for a mare who has foaled previously to have a full bag and large, let-down nipples, and for a maiden mare to have a small, firm udder with the nipples almost hidden. The foal can usually cope with any sort of udder except a truly malformed one, and mercifully that is rare in horses.

Just before the mare is about to foal, she may show a deposit of waxlike, pea-sized droplets. She may also have very tiny droplets of wax all over the nipples. Some mares wax up and then drip milk for weeks or even months before their foals arrive. You may not see the wax but may find evidence of milk having leaked out on the mare's legs. These wax drops can appear and disappear, which is normal.

Another sign of imminent foaling is softness around the birth canal. The flesh may sink down along the spine and get flabby around the top and sides of the tail. Again, there is no set timetable, but it will

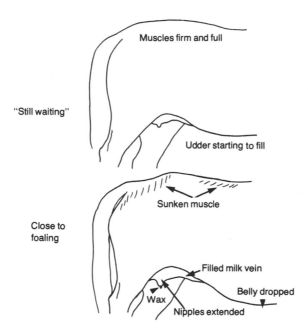

happen before the mare foals, so if she is firm and resilient she is not yet ready. You can check this by *gently* vibrating your fingertips on the muscle just along the side of the dock, but don't poke or jab the mare, as it won't tell you anything. When the hormone called relaxin is released in a mare's body, the flesh will bounce like jelly; until then it bounces like rubber. A marked difference is perceptible once you get used to checking mares. However, some mares are always flaccid compared to others, as muscle tone varies with condition, age, and use.

The Foaling

YOUR FINAL PREPARATIONS

Most but not all mares foal at night; often they do not finish all their grain at supper. Don't urge them. Check the feed and make sure it is not spoiled or dirty. If the grain is fresh and she is restless and nervous or very droopy or irritable, she is close. Braid or bandage her tail, and then leave her alone in as clean a stall as you can manage without disturbing her. Throw everyone out of the barn and keep things quiet. If you plan to be on hand, prepare your foaling equipment: one clean pail; a sterilized cup and baby bottle; a bar of Ivory or green soap; several clean towels; a large plastic bag; a flashlight; a baby-food or other wide-mouthed small jar; a bottle of 20 percent iodine (veterinary strength); a pediatric Fleet enema; and a blanket for the mare. Then get a cot, blanket, and pillow for yourself, and settle down quietly at a good distance from the mare's stall to wait silently. Post the veterinarian's phone number by the nearest phone and if you have any reason to suspect trouble, alert him that the mare is about the foal. In case he is going to be unavailable, ask for the name of an available doctor or call someone experienced with horses who can help. A dairy farmer who has delivered calves can spot trouble in a mare; if horse people are scarce in your area, the veterinarian will probably know of a cow man who could come if you need him. In all likelihood, you will have no trouble.

As a matter of fact, you will probably go to sleep and wake up to the sound of the mare nickering to her foal. Mares can tell when you are awake or asleep and they will outwait you if they possibly can. Most horses do not want help, company, or interference—and most of them don't need it. Some mares resent interference so much that they will waste all their energy fighting or will hold up their foaling to the point where it is actually a much more difficult delivery. If your mare shows signs of discomfort from your presence, have the sense to depart and wait, outside the barn if necessary. Be content to check on her at half-hour intervals. After the foal is born, the mare may suddenly take offense at your presence and even become dangerous. This is no time for discipline. She is doing her job as she sees it, and no amount of punishment or force will make her accept you. This protective stage usually lasts a few days—sometimes until after the foal heat, or after the foal follows her about.

DELIVERY

The actual foaling is usually a very brief and routine procedure, starting with the water breaking, the arrival of the front feet, followed by the nose, and then a pause while the mare gathers strength for the push to deliver the shoulders. The hardest part of the delivery is about to take place—and this is the only time you might need to be involved. You can clear the sac off the foal's face and front legs by tearing it open at his nose. Wipe off the face and front feet with a clean towel. When the mare starts to strain, gently, smoothly, and firmly pull the front feet out and downward toward the mare's hocks. Pulling in any other direction will tear the mare. It is essential that you *help*, not force her, so you must pull only while she is straining. If you get too enthusiastic and pull while she is resting, you can do her serious harm. It is hard work to deliver a large foal and sometimes two people are needed with a really big one. A mare may get so exhausted that she seems to go to sleep after the foal is out to the middle. Let her rest as she needs to. The rest of the foal will follow with little effort on her part.

If there is a problem during delivery, the mare will be distressed. If one foot and the nose appear, one leg may be turned back. If both feet come out up to the knees, she strains, and there is no sign of the head, the foal is a malpresentation and the mare is going to have a hard time. Sometimes foals come hind feet first—a breach birth—and sometimes they come upside down but front feet first. Anything but the normal position should get you to the phone for the doctor, but remember that he almost certainly can't get there in less than fifteen minutes. You can get the mare up and lead her quietly to try to hold off delivery somewhat and give him a chance to arrive. But once the delivery starts, the entire placenta pulls away from the inside of the mare, so that if the foal doesn't come in a short time he suffocates. With other animals, the placenta stays attached to the mother, and the fetus has oxygen until the placenta is fully delivered. A foaling mare is really about the only thing my present veterinarian considers an emergency.

AFTER DELIVERY

Both mare and foal will rest for a few minutes after delivery, talking to each other. Then the foal will struggle to get up. Sometimes the foal is the first one up and sometimes the mare. When one stands, the umbilical cord usually lets go and they are separated. At this point, you should apply iodine to the foal's navel to prevent infection. (Pour iodine into the baby-food jar. Place it firmly against the foal's umbilical cord and roll him on his back to douse the cord. Watch out for his hind feet.) The mare may lick the foal all over or even take an ear into her mouth. All told, it takes about fifteen to thirty minutes for the foal to be delivered and as little as five to twenty minutes more for the mare to be up. Sometimes the delivery takes longer; the longer it takes, the less likely the mare is to be up right away. She will want to rest. She may get up and lie down several times, walk about, change position.

The normal foal lies sprawled, wet and jerking, behind the mare. The jerking is like small currents of electricity, as if all his circuits are checking in. His ears will hang down ludicrously by the sides of his head. He will gurgle and sneeze fluid out of his nose. As he develops more control of himself, his ears will start to stand up. I have watched for years and find that until a foal's ears are up, he can't stand. Acually, if one ear is up, he is beginning to have control of the legs on that side, and when the other ear is up he will have control of the other. You can mop up his face and clean out his mouth and nostrils, but do not clean his rump, as it is instinctive for the mare to lick the foal and her licking of his rump and tail is her way of guiding him to nurse. We rub a foal with clean towels to stimulate circulation from the loins forward.

HELPING THE FOAL TO NURSE

The foal may suck on walls, the mother's tail and front feet, all over the feedbox, or anything else he bumps with his nose. Gradually, he will locate the mare's udder and try to find a nipple. He is guided by instinct and by smell. Between the mare's nipples there is a soft, smelly substance that guides the foal. *Never* remove this substance. In fact, do not wash the mare's udder at all or the foal may not nurse and may starve to death. When a foal is not up and actively searching for food in the length of time I feel is appropriate, I pinch his rump. He immediately makes an effort to get to his feet, and the sucking motions of lips and tongue and the extension of the neck all shift into gear. The foal may nuzzle his mother too high on the sides and not put his head down low enough to find her udder. Sometimes a nip from her or a pinch from you will get him oriented. This pinch is not a sharp, painful one, but rather an imitation of a mare's bite, which obviously does not hurt her foal.

What if the foal does not get up? You have a problem—and it is not one you can linger over. First, call the doctor, because a foal who cannot get up and nurse is in serious trouble. Next, rub him vigorously with warm towels. Rub particularly along the chest, back, and loins to stimulate circulation. Get a few drops of the mare's milk on your fingers, put it on the foal's lips, and smear a little under his nose. If he is still too weak to rise, get the mare's milk into a bottle and feed him her first milk. That is a lot harder than it sounds. You milk her into a clean cup, then pour the few ounces of milk into a baby bottle. You will probably need a Davol lamb nipple, but may be able to get away with an ordinary baby nipple for a few days. Open up the hole so the foal can get milk without too much strain, but not so that it runs out in a steady stream. If the mare is good, you can hold the foal up or prop him until he can nurse for himself. It is harder to lift and support a foal than you think. Actually, two people are needed, unless you are very experienced and very strong, because foals buckle in the middle and wilt. You will have very little success pushing down on the foal's head to get it under the mare's belly. Here again you are confronted with a reflex. This one makes the foal respond to downward pressure on the forehead by tilting the head up to find the nipples. So if you push down, the foal pushes up harder.

You must get some of the mare's milk or the odorous substance between the nipples on your fingers and lead the head down. It takes patience, but it pays to get the foal nursing, because milking a mare and bottle-feeding are unbelievably difficult if correctly done. Foals nurse every fifteen minutes, twenty-four hours a day, for the first few days, and then every half hour for weeks. I've nursed just enough to know I don't want to do it anymore.

We once raised a horse in our dining room when it was a case of survival for a premature orphan foal. An old rubber-backed rug was folded in one corner of the room, and two stall walls were made out of sheets of plywood wired together. She had to drink formula every fifteen minutes for the first few weeks, so I got up and held her bottle all day and all night. As soon as she could go longer periods of time between feedings, we rigged up a large plastic bottle with a nipple and suspended it with a bracket fashioned from coat hangers. Her head was so small I had to make her first two or three halters, and her feet were crooked and wore badly because they were soft, so our farrier made her a pair of leather sandals out of the hides he used to make pads for horse shoes.

Sometimes the foal is fine and eager to nurse, but the mare is a problem. Some mares won't stand for nursing until the afterbirth has dropped. The nursing of the foal creates contractions which help to deliver the placenta. Some mares are afraid of their foals or too ticklish. Some are so curious that they keep turning and sniffing the foal so that the poor thing can't get back to the udder. Others are nervous or too exhausted to get up because they are in a state of shock, which is fatal if not treated. If the mare is in shock she needs prompt veterinary attention and there is little you can do for her yourself. If the stall is cold, put a warm blanket over her, hang a heat lamp, and place a bucket of lukewarm water nearby for her to drink.

Mares can get a disease called eclampsia or milk fever, in which the calcium from the body concentrates in their milk. Years ago when we had a dairy herd, I remember a cow with milk fever. The veterinarian put a bicycle pump on her udder and literally pumped her milk back into her body, restoring the calcium. Recently, I had a mare with the same problem. This time the calcium was pumped into her system a lot more effectively with an intravenous needle. The mare was given other injections, we milked another nursing mare to feed the foal overnight, and by morning the mare was up and nursing her foal normally.

If the mare is physically sound, you must do something to keep her still and let the foal nurse. We hold the mare against one wall of the stall so that she cannot keep turning. Sometimes this is all that is required. At other times she has to have a chain over her nose or a twitch; often she can be held by lifting one front foot off the ground, and that is sufficient. Some people routinely tie a mare up and lift a front foot if it is her first foal. Usually, after a foal has nursed and the mare understands what it is all about, mare and foal settle down and get along fine.

THE AFTERBIRTH

The mare's afterbirth should drop within two hours of birth. Remove it from the stall and make sure it is all there, as any that remains attached inside the mare will cause hemorrhaging. If the doctor is on his way, save it for him to see. Dogs love to eat placenta and will dig it up, so bury it deep in the manure pile.

If the mare does not pass her afterbirth, she must have competent help. Do not make any attempt to remove it unless you have a real knowledge of what you are about. It must be pulled gently and carefully and no infection should be introduced into the mare. If the afterbirth is retained more than two hours, the mare should have an antibiotic—either a bolus placed inside her uterus or an injection. Obviously, this is no job for a novice. Mares who retain their afterbirth should not be rebred until they have been checked by the doctor. Many breeders skip a year on such mares because they may have complications and it is very hard to get them to conceive. In any case, never rebreed on the foal heat with a mare that has this problem. You will not get a foal and you are very likely to lose the mare. A veterinarian at a lecture recently stated that a mare should not be rebred on the foal heat if the placenta weighs over 16 lbs.

THE FOAL HEAT

Breeding on the foal heat is not recommended, both out of consideration for what is best for the mare, and for the likelihood of not getting a healthy normal foal. The chance of conception is less than half that of the "thirty-day" heat, and the chance of abortion, even if conception takes place, is somewhere near 80 percent. Since it also places a risk on the mare's life, it is rarely practiced by intelligent and informed breeders, and then only under carefully controlled conditions.

The mare will usually come into foal heat five to ten days after the birth of her foal. When she does, it is likely that the foal will get scours (diarrhea) or have very loose stool for the duration of the heat. This should clear up when the mother goes out of heat and should not return during subsequent heats. If the foal has loose stools for a prolonged period, it will suffer from dehydration and can die. If the stool is any color other than the normal yellow-orange, keep a close eye on its consistency. It will not be formed into individual balls for a few days or even weeks, but it should never be watery or squirt out of the foal. Once the foal starts to eat grass, the stool will change color, to brown-green, as a rule. If the stool is loose, it may be because the foal is getting too much milk, and you can cut down a little on the mare's grain to see if that helps, but go carefully. The mare makes milk in response to demand. She usually makes just enough and her udder is not a storage tank. If the foal gets sick and can't nurse, the mare will dry up.

We used to give every newborn foal and its dam shots of antibiotic. Although this was supposed to protect them from infection, it created more problems than it solved. The foals almost invariably got diarrhea, and the more we tried to clear it up, the worse it got. The antibiotics were actually killing the bacteria in the gut that were necessary to digest the foal's food. Now we have a new veterinarian and a new system, with no further problems with infections.

It is a good policy to interfere as little as possible and to let the animal build up its natural resistances. Save your money and everyone's time for real problems. Get the necessary inoculations, but avoid other medications until there is a proven need for them.

Your New Foal's Well-Being

The newborn foal must pass a black stool called the meconium very soon after birth. This is the waste from its nourishment while inside the mare. It is thick and sticky, and at least 4 to 8 inches of the substance should be passed. If the foal does not pass the stool, he will be dull and lack appetite. Indeed, some won't nurse at all. A simple remedy for this situation is an infant Fleet enema, available at any drugstore. (Do *not* use the kind with mineral oil.) The foal may pass the first meconium but still be somewhat constipated and need an enema more than once during the first few days of life. He can be given as many as three Fleet enemas at a time. You can also administer a plain warm-water enema with a bag and tube, but do so slowly.

If the foal is active at first and then starts to get weak and stagger, there are at least three possible causes. The first is that he has an open heart valve, which, if he remains very quiet for a few days, should close. The doctor can determine this with his stethoscope. A second possibility is that the foal may be allergic to his mother's milk; this means he must be weaned promptly and fed some other way. The third cause may be that he is impacted; for this he will need help.

REJECTION

Mares will generally not injure their foals, but if they are upset by people or other horses and made to chase about, they do sometimes step on their foals or knock them down. Some mares reject their foals completely, in which case the foal must be removed before its mother kills it. This is one reason to be around, but there is no need to interfere or help unless there is a problem. Just observe and keep out of it if you possibly can. Uneducated help is often worse than no help at all.

Some mares reject only their first foal. Some don't seem to have any mothering instincts at all, whereas others are natural-born mothers, even though they have never had a foal. I had a pair of maiden mares, one bred and one unable to breed. They were raised together and were inseparable. One day the unbred mare came running up to the gate from pasture, screaming for me. I ran out and she ran a short way down the pasture, then back to me. I followed her to the field and down to a stream. The other mare was calmly grazing in the field. The calling mare led me to the center of the stream and there, just above the surface, was the nose of a newborn foal. I hauled him out and rubbed him down, with the unbred mare helping and licking the foal frantically. The foal followed the mare back to the barn, while the mother never stopped grazing. When we brought her in, she would not let it nurse. She kicked and tried to get out of the stall. We bottle-fed the foal and the other mare adopted it. After about two weeks, the real mother suddenly started to produce milk; chasing the adopting mare off, she nursed her foal, and kept him by her side from then on.

EVALUATING YOUR FOAL

Once you have bred your foal and handled him for a few weeks, it would be well to consider if you have bred a good one or not. How do you tell? A foal is judged on exactly the same basis as an adult horse, but with an eye to those things which change with maturity and those which do not. His color will surely change, for all foals are born a soft neutral shade of gray, tan, or cinnamon. Don't get too excited or disappointed about shades of color, because all this will change as the foal sheds. All newborn foals are funny-looking, with unbelievably short necks, dished faces, and lop ears that appear yards long. They have ewe necks and goose rumps, and stand firmly on their fetlocks while their knees buckle. It takes a few days for some of them to get coordinated and stand up on their feet, and weeks for the croup to level out, the neck to extend, and the eyes to darken and show their true expression. As they get fat, they get cute and their personalities become evident. A foal of less than one week has a characteristic sawhorse stance, but after that he should have his legs straight up under him where they belong. His back will be short, so he may have spectacular action, and many foals pace instead of trotting for months at first. Some foals mostly trot and some mostly canter. Some buck and kick energetically or stand on their mother's ears and bang about on her back with their front feet. Most foals tend to be somewhat cow-hocked at first.

What you should be able to tell from a foal is the length of the shoulder and its position. By two months, the front legs should be straight, the chest should have broadened out, and the rump should be rounded and level. I find I can better judge the adult prospects at three to five months than I can after that until they are three years old. There is a point where they suddenly look like miniatures of their adult self. The foal's cannon bone at birth will be its final length, but the pasterns will lengthen and change their angle. The upper arm, forearm, and depth through the heart will all change. If the foal is, at the knee, on a level with his dam, at maturity he should be as tall as or taller than she is. All foals are cute but some are obviously superior right from the start, while others are late bloomers. It takes experience to judge. Quality is usually evident in foals very early; they either are coarse or fine right from the start.

HIS PERSONALITY

If the foal looks narrow and pathetic at one month of age, there is something wrong. If he gets a ragged coat which looks dull and his belly is big, he has an infestation of worms which should be cleaned up right away. If he is dejected or too quiet, he needs help. Foals are full of mischief and if they are not active, they are in trouble. They should sleep a lot, then get up and roar about until they are sweaty, then flop down and sleep some more. They should race until they are panting and puffing, and go leaping up in the air for no particular reason. They should run until they fall over and splash in mud puddles and roll in sand if they want to. They should be out in the snow as long as it is not too windy and the temperature is moderate. Running, leaping, and falling down expand the foal's lungs, stimulate the circulation, and teach him coordination. He must have freedom to do all these things in order to mature and develop normally.

If a young horse is confined, his bones will be weak, his lungs underdeveloped, and his circulation and coordination below par. Without mental stimulation, he will become retarded. If you want to meet a really stupid horse, find one who was raised to be a show horse, born in January, and kept up to be fat and showy by the first spring shows. Foals will get a certain amount of bumps and bruises in the course of learning about life. Children do, too. You can only try to avoid exposing them to real hazards and to keep an eye on their condition so that nothing gets by you.

CHAPTER 16

Your Foal:

Newborn to Weanling

A FOAL IS BORN WITH certain essential reflexes that give him his protection—his ability to find nourishment and his instinct to stay with his dam. He does little "rational" thinking for the first few days, but he has a fantastic memory for every sight, sound, or sensation he encounters. His first few moments of life can shape his whole subsequent relationship to human beings. Thus, a basic understanding of what his special needs and responses entail will make your job of befriending him much easier.

First, be careful to observe his mother and her response to your presence. If she is hostile and afraid, she will teach him to fear you. Should you attempt to force yourself on her and her foal, she may become violent and defensive, even going so far as to attack the foal to keep it away from you—inflicting pain as he looks at you in order to instill fear, for he will associate the pain with you, not his mother. You must win her confidence and cooperation before you attempt to handle the foal. If she is receptive, go into the stall slowly and quietly, in a relaxed frame of mind. Squat down in front of the mare and reach up and scratch her chest and neck to keep her standing facing you. Let the baby look you over from whatever distance he deems advisable. Do not attempt to touch him at all. He will be curious. The degree of shyness will determine how fast he will come to you, but come he will. Allowing him to sniff at your face and hands, talk quietly to his mother and pretend he does not even exist. If you focus your attention on him he may suddenly depart, perhaps even throwing his heels at you on his way. Use your usual tone of voice with the mare, not a high-pitched, baby-talking tone, for you want the foal to get used to you as you are.

Foals who are bold will nibble on your nose or ears or pants and will often stamp on you, so be ready. Don't jump or yell or slap him if he strikes out at you; it would take weeks to overcome his fright. If he is bold and you can scratch his chest, keep your hands very low and rub and scratch as hard as he will let you. If he strikes, you can shove him to arm's length or off to one side gently to defend yourself, but it is better to just receive a couple of blows. He won't do much harm at this age. He may nip while you scratch him. This is reflexive action; your scratch causes him to express one of the social-grooming reflexes that horses use in greeting and in communicating with one another. Just make certain he does not get his teeth into your face or ears. He won't hurt you if he pinches your arm. This is not biting, so it does not call for punishment.

In another defensive reflex reaction, most foals will kick if you move too fast or touch their rump. The rump or buck reflex, as it is called, prevents horses from running a foal down. The foal normally runs directly in front of his dam, and he is programmed to buck and fling his heels into her chest to warn her when she is too close. If you trigger that response you will get both heels, and if they hit you in the groin or in the knee you will have learned a valuable lesson. Many people think it is cute to make the baby buck. It is not. It can instill

To approach a new-born foal, stoop down to his eye level or below. Note the ear and eye of the foal are both directed toward the man's hand as he comes to investigate.

the buck reflex as a fixed reaction which will make the horse buck whenever anything touches him on the back. If left alone, the reflex goes away within a few weeks.

Halter Breaking

We like to put a tiny halter on our foals at a very early age. I usually do it while they are lying down, and there is no problem. You halter a foal exactly as you should halter a horse. Squat or stand beside the foal, on his left side, facing the same direction he is. Hold the halter under his neck and get it adjusted in your hands. Move it forward under his face, and flip the noseband up over the nose while you slide your hand under the neck and flip the long crown over the head. Hold the halter in place with your right hand along the right side of the foal's face, while you catch the end of the crown and buckle it on the left side. Never should any part of the halter or either of your hands move forward into the horse's line of vision. Keep your hands behind his eyes, and you will never make him head-shy. No part of the halter belongs in front of the eyes, and there is little excuse for putting it there.

When you halter-break the foal, you are going directly against his instinctive behavior. You must tactfully overcome his natural instincts and replace them with the habits you wish him to have for the rest of his life. These are very influential months in his life. His proper reaction to a lesson must be immediately rewarded. His attention span is exceedingly short. The lessons must be brief and gentle, and he should be expected to learn only one thing at a time.

Never attempt to lead a foal by his halter when you first put it on. He will be terrified. If the halter is too big, he will try to get it off, for it will fall back on his neck and make him frantic. He may throw himself and get injured. If you cannot find one small enough, do not take a chance and put a large one on him. Proper early handling of the foal is essential to establish the trust and response to human beings that will make him a useful and valuable animal. If you can't do it right, leave him alone. When you do start to train him to lead, do it with a light rope properly snapped into the lead ring of his halter. Let him walk about the stall as he will, and make no attempt to lead him forward or hold him still. Your first lesson is to get him used to the weight of the rope and your hand applying slight sideways pressure as you bend his neck to the side. Do not pull him sideways. Simply get him to respond to gentle pressure and flex his neck toward you. Pet him and tell him he is good when he responds. All lessons should be done from both sides. If he runs, go with him; don't pull back.

The second day, get him to let you actually pull a little and teach him to step sideways with one front foot. You can use your other hand on his withers to rock him a little. The third day, if there has been no uproar about the first two lessons, see if he will turn on both front feet and move closer to you. Still make no effort to lead him forward. When he turns, it is time to teach him to stop. Do this by allowing him to follow the mare. As the mare stops, say, "Whoa," and pull back and a little downward on the foal's halter to tuck his chin. You may have to put a restraining hand on his chest to stop his forward motion. Have him stand, and reward him with petting and congratulations. Then allow him to start as his mother proceeds, and say, "Walk" in a firm, gentle tone. If he does not go forward, put your hand behind his rump, below the hip, and push gently. You are probably going to have to switch hands on the lead; don't jerk his head as you do—he might take off with a jump or just sit on your hand. If he bolts forward, go with him and do not pull him up and over backward, as this could cause a cracked skull or twisted spine. If you can't hold him, ask the farrier or an experienced horseman to give him his first halter lessons.

Leading

Once the foal can lead behind his dam, you will want to lead him first alongside and then ahead of her, then away and on his own. For quite a while after the foal is born, you will not actually be leading him. He will follow his mother most places, but when you want to get him into a stall or trailer or through a narrow gate, he will surely decide it is time to play games. If this happens, you must catch him in a "chest-and-rump" hold and push him where you want him to be; avoid being hit in the head or having your toes trampled. Since foals aren't very heavy, they do not usually inflict serious damage, but it hurts enough so that you may let go. The usual way to hold them is to place one hand in front of the chest and the other firmly on the back of the thighs, below the tail but above the gaskins, and push forward. If you "hug" a colt against you or between your front and back arms, he will struggle. The trick is to learn only to push forward and to keep the front hand ready to stop wild leaps and charges.

If you must handle the mare and foal alone, do not attempt to lead the mare and have the foal follow if there is a chance he will get on the wrong side of a wire fence or run off into a road. Grab the foal and hang on to him. Usually the mare will follow you. If not, you can hold her lead rope while you push her baby around. If you treat the colt as a hostage, you can usually manage his dam.

The best system for leading a foal in a halter is to use a rump rope. You can use a single rope from the halter, up the left side of the neck, crossing over the back, down on the right side of the rump at the level of the gaskin, and back up to your hand on the horse's left side to your right hand. The left hand guides the horse at the halter. This is fine while the foal is small. By the time he is weanling size, one rope would be too long and cumbersome, so we use two separate lead ropes, one in each hand. The right hand always controls the rump rope, and the left the lead rope.

After the foal leads well without a rump rope, get him to lead behind you as quietly as he does beside you. You will find that you have to go through stall doors, narrow paths, and between parked cars single file. If the horse insists on walking next to you, he may run up on your heels or crowd you badly. Also, be sure to lead him from the right as well as from the left. Horses remember a thing only on the side on which it was taught to them. You are a strange and exciting sight the first time you show up leading from the right. Some horses are so uncomfortable they refuse to move, or they duck be-

The rump rope as we use it to assist in moving the foal forward. Both sections of the rope are held together in the right hand while the left hand is held gently in front of the foal's chest to prevent him from bolting forward.

hind you and try to get back to your right. An awkward situation is created when you try to lead two such lopsided horses.

When a horse is properly trained to lead, he will follow you into a trailer, a dark, strange barn, or under sheets of flapping laundry. He will cross streams or bridges quietly and trust you to take him past machinery. Few horses are well trained to lead and this is a pity, for there are three years of the horse's life in which he can learn this before he is put to useful labor. Once these simple lessons are learned, he will forever be a more reliable and useful animal.

While the foal is small he will follow his mother anywhere she will go. If she is a good trail horse, he can be taught a good deal simply by being allowed to tag along on trail rides. If she is nervous, it is better to lead him after a calm horse or take him for walks and have him follow you over strange obstacles. Remember that if you refuse to step over an obstacle, the horse will do so, too. They are imitators to a great extent, and if you are careful to walk directly through puddles and prove to them that it is safe, they will very likely follow you without protest. Most people do not use enough imagination in schooling a horse; they miss the opportunity to expose the youngster to things while he is still small enough to be held if he panics.

His Vocabulary

We teach the foal his name from the first day. Horses learn a huge vocabulary, and their name is the first thing you want to impress on them clearly. They will learn to come if they are rewarded by a scratch on the chest.

The other important word to learn is "Whoa." When you open his stall door, say "Whoa," and do not let him past you. He must stand quietly at the door. Pet him and talk to him and then close the door again. Horses should never be allowed to step out a door just because it is open. If the horse forces his way out, punish him. Make him return to the stall and stay there. Use the word "Whoa" whenever you mean stand still and can enforce it. If you mean slow down or relax, or change from a trot to a walk, use the words "Easy," "Walk," or "Steady."

Keep in mind that you are teaching the horse a vocabulary that he will use for the rest of his life. Make sure the words he learns are not some obscure language or secret signals, for if he changes owners he will not be able to understand what is wanted of him and may well end up being mistreated for "refusing" to do as he is told.

His Manners

Manners and attitude are established within the first three months of a horse's life. You have an obligation to train him to be gentle and mannerly—this goes for nipping and biting, which start when a foal is newborn. Do not confuse this with a scratch reflex. You should not hit a foal in the head to prevent him from nipping. Push him away every time and scold him. If he actually bites, then he must be hurt in return so that he gets the idea that inflicting pain on human beings receives instant retaliation. Do not hit his head anywhere but on the mouth, and only hit the mouth up from underneath. If you can't contact his mouth, hit the chest. Never hit a horse high on the neck or head, and particularly never up near the eyes or ears.

His Handling

When handling a foal, you want to get him used to being touched gently all over his body. It is especially important that he allow his belly, legs, eyes, and ears to be handled. Start at the chest every time, and gently rub and scratch him over his body. He will come to enjoy it. You will find spots he especially likes—we call them itchy spots, and it is good to know where these special places are. In times of distress or fear, it is quite possible to calm a horse by vigorously scratching his favorite spot.

In picking up a foal's feet, many people err by lifting the foot too high and holding it too long. Start by just holding the foot lightly on the ground. Make no attempt to lift it. He will sometimes lift the foot for you. If so, keep your hand on it, but do not attempt to lift it up higher or hold it in the air. Just keep contact with it until he puts it back down. When he has accepted your hand around his foot, lift it ever so slightly, no more than an inch or two off the ground, hold it just an instant, then put it down. Do not let go of it, but place it on the ground. When you lift, say, "Give me your foot," and when you put it down, say, "Put it down," so that he knows this is your intention. When you work on a foot or leg with clippers, you do not want him to lift it, and he should understand that he is to keep it still while it is touched. It is very hard to apply medicine and bandages to a foot in a raised position.

The reason for not raising the foot too high is that the foal has not yet learned to balance on three legs, and if he loses his balance he will become frightened. You never want to associate fear with any routine grooming or working procedure with a horse. The only time you will ever want to frighten a horse is if he tries to attack you. Then you should fly at him, yelling and waving something such as a plastic bag or towel. You do not want to hurt him but to call his bluff. Don't carry a whip around a nasty colt. He will learn that if you do not have it, you are defenseless. Use the end of a lead rope for discipline if it comes to a confrontation. Snap it sharply on his hind legs if he kicks, but never hit a horse in front of the girth with anything that could snap up and get at his eyes.

Try to handle the foal as much as you can while he is lying down, for this will greatly aid him whenever he is sick or injured. It will relieve his anxiety if he knows that you will sit with him for quiet moments and talk to him gently.

Teaching a foal to stand tied should be done as gradually and quietly as possible. Many people set a day to "have it out" with the foal on tying, with the result that the foal is hurt. When you groom the foal, he should stand quietly near his mother, wearing his halter. Loop the lead rope over your arm, or let it just hang from his halter, so that if he starts to walk away you can check his exit. After he gets used to the fact that the rope stops him from leaving, slip it through a ring in the wall and hold the free end. Use a rope that is long enough to allow you to walk all around grooming him while still holding one end. If he tries to pull away, resist and speak to him, but don't set up a struggle. Let him back off, then bring him right in place again and proceed to groom him as if nothing happened. If you groom him in the crossties, use two ropes (long pieces of clothesline will do nicely). Run them through the rings and back to your hand so that he has the sensation of being tied but you are still able to release him if he pulls. The resistance to his pulling back should be gradually firmer and firmer, with a determined "Whoa," and perhaps even a tap on the rump. When you are certain that he understands, it should be safe to tie him and he will probably not resist. But be certain never to tie any young horse and then walk off and leave him. If he does panic and try to pull free, release him and calm him down.

Horses frequently dislocate their spine and damage the nerves running through the spinal cord by yanking back in halters. Once a horse breaks out of a halter, he may forever be a confirmed halter puller.

Your aim is to teach your horse to love, trust, and respect you. You must have the same feelings for him. If you have no affection for him, your praise and petting will have no meaning, for the horse can feel instinctively many emotions of which we are not even aware. If you fear him, you will smell of fear and will fill him with an uneasy dread; and if you do not respect his strength, he will one day master you in a contest of strength.

Much as you may love your horse, he will grow up to be a big animal. Now is the time for him to realize that he is not a lapdog. Do not allow him to rear, yank around, eat grass while you want to walk, and so on. Be firm, as the leader, but never lead him into a situation in which he will get hurt.

Weaning

Foals generally are weaned from four to six months of age. Much depends on the condition of the mare and the growth of the foal. Mares do not spontaneously wean their foals. You must separate them and plan on continuing to do so for at least three weeks and even up to two months or more. The mare will allow the foal to come back and nurse as long as she has milk, and she will continue to produce milk as long as he nurses.

Weaning is a period many people dread more than any other with their foals. In fact, the time to prepare him for being taken away from his mother's side—four to six months hence—is when he is newborn. The biggest problem foals have at weaning is that everything changes suddenly, and their security and happiness is shattered. If they are happy with people and at ease with the world, they do not mind the weaning process nearly as much.

OUR GRADUAL PROGRAM

We start the foal on his own feed bucket at the side of the mare. Gradually, we move the bucket farther away as the foal's interest in the grain grows. It is his mother's milk you are going to deny him, not her company or her love, so what you want to do is to replace his dependence on milk with a dependence on grain. If the mare can be tied, we tie her in her stall and give her grain. We entice the foal out of the stall door, but just outside, so that his rump is still inside. We leave the stall door open and feed the foal there. After a few days of this, we move the foal's bucket all the way out of the stall door, but leave the door open. The foal can run around or run back to his mother when she calls. We stay there all the time the foal is eating, so that he doesn't run off and leave his frantic mother straining on her rope.

When they have both accepted the separation as an everyday event, we leave the mare untied and shut the stall door, with the foal loose in the hallway. His bucket is tied near his mother's stall, and we "babyproof" the barn so that he will not eat saddles or lead ropes, or disrupt the area. Leave the colt running free until his mother calls him or until he goes to the stall door and pleads to be let in. Pet him and groom him and be his friend during the separation. By the time he is six months old, he will have gone off for hours at a time on his own and his mother will relax and let him go. At weaning time, you can put him in a stall next to hers and just never put them together again for nursing for two or three months. This way they can still enjoy each other's company, and need not be taken out of sight of one another except in pasture.

Never tie a foal up and take the mare away. Do not lock the foal up in a stall and remove the mare unless you have someone stand by to reassure the foal. He can dash himself against the stall wall repeatedly. He can jump much higher than you anticipate and get straddled over the top of the stall partition or door. Use sense with foals; they have very little of their own.

A gradual weaning program is time-consuming and not everyone wishes to spend this long sitting and watching to see that mare and foal don't get upset. It is a fine time to clean tack, write letters, catch up on your reading, or for the kids to do homework. You will have to stop and enjoy the foal's antics once in a while, but what's wrong with that? You cannot expect to take him off and teach him something all that time. Remember you are replacing food with food, and the growing independence and relaxed acceptance depends upon his going off on his own volition and enjoying himself. His mother's acceptance depends on his being able to return to the stall if she calls him.

Many people find they can leave the foal in a stall or paddock with another gentle horse as a babysitter while they ride the mare. Obviously, if the two of them will accept this separation, there should be no problem in weaning. However, don't miss the opportunity of training the foal to be a good trail horse by letting him accompany his mother on some of her rides.

We have had a mare go crazy when we weaned her first foal. I am not exaggerating when I say that she broke the gates off seven oak stalls with 5-inch hinges. She tore down fences of our strongest paddocks, dived through a hole between walls that was no wider than her head and became lodged there. She broke four "unbreakable" halters and nylon ropes and finally a large chain. I had to hold her and longe her on a rope while my husband came from work and built a solid new stall clear to the ceiling. We put her in, slid hay under a crack in the boards, and filled her water bucket with a watering can through a small hole. We kept her confined like this for three days. Then, when we let her out, all was peace and quiet and she never made any more fuss. What had happened to her was a hormone change. When there was no longer a demand for her milk, her body started to reverse the mechanisms that had produced the milk flow. It should be stressed that she did not go berserk the moment we separated her from her foal. They had been separated gradually, as all ours are for weeks; but once the demand for milk had ceased completely, she suffered this traumatic change.

SWIFTER METHODS

If you have no patience with slow weaning, then you have to figure some way of keeping both mare and foal from injury. They will be best separated if you ship the mare off to a friend's farm for a month, far enough away so that mother and child cannot hear or smell each other. Failing that, put them in separate barns, and be sure the stalls are screened or boarded up all the way to the ceiling. Give the foal something for company. The mare is not going to be as lonely. She will be upset for the safety of her foal; the foal will be lonely and upset for himself. Cut way down on the mare's grain and give her hay several times a day. This will reduce the milk supply and give her something to do. Do not cut down on her water. *Do not milk the mare,* no matter how hard her udder may get or how swollen and painful it looks. That would only stimulate her to keep producing more milk. If you are worried about pain, rub her bag gently with camphorated oil three times a day. Do not put her on a fresh green pasture, as that will make more milk. Nor should you work her hard while her udder is distended, for you may damage the tissues, which are under pressure. She can have exercise, but may have to go quite spraddle-legged and might really not want to trot at all. It shouldn't take more than a week for her udder to reduce and be comfortable again, but it will take longer—as much as two months—for the milk to dry up to the point where she can be reunited with her foal and not go right back to nursing again.

THE ADVANTAGES OF WEANING IN COMPANY

Some people put foals in pairs to wean them. If you have two foals, this is much the best system, for they play and forget their problems. Both the mare and the foal should have some time in separate pastures every day. No horse should ever go without exercise for a day unless he is sick or injured in such a way that exercise will cause harm.

Horses tend to stay together in families. The older siblings will baby-sit the younger ones. When you wean the foal, if you have an older sister around, it is often a great help to put them together.

Finally, remember that weaning is as much a psychological disturbance as a physical one. If mares or foals are locked in solitary confinement with nothing to do but cry, they will become morose. Help them through this time by being understanding, patient, and careful, so that they do not get hurt or depressed.

CHAPTER 17

Training: Weanling to Maturity

EVERY YEAR FAMILIES DECIDE to purchase a first horse, and in many cases the most practical choice is a weanling foal. The mysteries of caring for and training this young creature can be fun and amusing or baffling and frightening. This chapter is dedicated to those hapless parents, delighted children, and defenseless foals. Since the novice who is training one horse is not likely to buy all the training equipment or study all the training procedures of the professional, he must go slowly and use methods suited to his limited strength and knowledge. He must have realistic aims for his training program, and select a horse who will be both responsive and suitable.

Some General Advice

If you are impatient, do not even attempt to train a foal. Impatience mixed with inexperience and ignorance can ruin a good horse. You will hear plenty of people say there is no need to wait until a horse is two to harness-break him, or three to ride him, but it is always a mistake to rush his training and it is a hardship on the horse. There is a great deal that you can do to teach a foal to be a fine pleasure horse without any formal lessons with harness or saddle. Your lessons should offer variety, freedom, and interest. He should have time off to relax and play. Here you must also make it clear in his mind that although work need not be unpleasant or uncomfortable to him, work is one thing and play another.

You should be aware that horse development does not parallel our human lifespan in a neat ratio of one year to every five. At first the horse develops and matures at a very much faster rate. A yearling is an adolescent much like a human being at age eleven; he experiences the same hormone changes, emotional crises, and crash behavior. He needs sleep, tires easily, and often gets temperamental and sulky. He can develop self-control and skill with the help of his trainer, but he is not up to any amount of real physical work and cannot concentrate for long periods of time.

At two, the horse is about like a person at fourteen. He can do short bursts of work, but will be unable to sustain effort over a long period. At three, the development has slowed way down and the horse is only equivalent to about a seventeen-year-old level. Most of the emotional upheaval is over, and the horse can take longer periods of work but still no heavy work or very strenuous effort. Mentally, a horse never progresses much beyond a human being at about eight or ten; emotionally he matures beyond that point; and physically, he reaches the level of maturity of a twenty-year-old person by about age five. From then on, he matures at a rate of less than three to one. A twenty-year-old horse is about like a person in his seventies. And like people, some go on much longer while others have come to the end of their normal life expectancy. If you keep these approximate age equivalents in mind as you train the horse, you will refrain from overtraining and asking him for too much too soon.

I do not advise any novice to attempt to train a horse to be a top show horse. Certainly, it can be done, but the temperament that makes a horse a really top performance animal makes him too great a challenge for the average novice. The boundless energy, high-spirited nature, and competitive mind of a top contender require talent and experience to bring them to their fullest promise.

ARE YOU PREPARED?

You would not attempt to teach someone to drive one of today's high-powered cars if you had not learned to drive first yourself. Training a horse is even more complicated, although it need not be hazardous or difficult. It requires only that you learn a little before you attempt to teach. Successful trainers have a plan. Horses have an average rate of growth and mental ability to grasp ideas. They learn certain jobs best at certain stages of their development, and one lesson will logically follow another. The schedule suggested here is based on this average horse and will serve best for most novice trainers and most foals. It should turn out a nicely schooled and useful animal, who has been given ample time to fully understand each lesson. It is not intended here to suggest that one horse be taught all the things listed in a year, but rather that these are the appropriate lessons for the particular age. The breed and eventual aims of the owner will determine which lessons should be undertaken.

Training Schedule

Newborn to Weanling—He should learn to:

Know the sound of your voice
Know his name; the word "Whoa"
Halter and lead at walk
Stand tied
Pick up feet and stand for grooming
Be handled all over
Stay alone in stall
Go for walks away from dam
Load and truck
Pose
Come when called

Weanling to Yearling—He should learn to:

Lead over obstacles
Back up in straight line
Follow on trail rides
Know the words "Walk," "Trot," "Stand," and "Easy" or "Steady"
Understand the meaning of the whip
Start in bitting rig (late yearling)
Ground-drive in long lines
Accept the bit
Cavalletti work

Two-Year-Old—He should master:

Harness in two wheels
Slow and fast trot, serpentines
Back-up in harness
Developing balance and rating gaits
Bitting toward saddle work

Three Years—He should master:

    Saddle work
    Four Wheels
    Short trail rides
    Carriage drives
    Pleasure classes; limited park classes
    Basic dressage

Four Years—He should master:

    Developing more action if showing
    Figure eights and turns for stock work
    Advanced dressage

Five Years Onward—Your horse is now mature, go on to:

    Endurance and/or competitive trail rides
    Developing full action or speed
    Working stock or jumping
    Marathon driving

General Training

VERSATILITY

Our ring is full of "junk"—an old cow skin, a braided rug, an assortment of jump standards and rails, sheets of plastic and wallboard, and sometimes water troughs, kegs or oil drums, and tires. The large cardboard cartons that refrigerators come in, beach umbrellas, newspapers, laundry, and gas-station flags have all adorned our obstacle course at one time or another. We do our carpentry with electric drills and we work while the horses are in the stalls. We have had banty chickens that flap and squawk and sit on their heads while they eat. Granted, when our horses go into a show ring, they stand and gaze around with more amusement than animation, but for trail and family horses they are safer than if they had never been presented with all the excitement. Since versatility requires a certain amount of steady nerves and calmness, we feel any versatile family horse should have at least a part of this training.

One lesson on something that really frightens an animal is never enough; but if the horse does a job right, do not repeat the lesson that day. Stop, praise him, groom him, and put him away or reward him some other way so that his mind remembers the experience as pleasant. If you repeat and work over a hard job, you can sour the animal and cause a problem. Learning when to quit is probably the hardest thing in training.

Some horses are easily distracted, and when you are training you need their complete attention. Try to take the horse off at some distance from other horses or traffic. A quiet walk in the woods is a marvelous place to school a youngster. While you are leading, break off branches or pick up a fallen branch and drag it along by your side. Find a brook and sit down by it. When you walk across it, step into the water, don't avoid it. If the horse wants a drink, let him have his fill. He may back off and snort. Don't force the issue. Go there the next day and the next, bring a book or your lunch, and just spend the time there until the noise of the water holds no fear. If your horse is ever injured and you have to soak his legs, you will be glad he learned to stand quietly in the running brook. If traffic is heavy and you have to ride near roads, start to accustom the horse to the road just as you did to the stream. Sit in a field by the highway and let him graze, or bring his lunch along with yours and stand at a safe distance from the cars but where he can hear and see them. Remember to make sure he sees them out of both eyes. If he faces only one way, they'll be new to him on the other side of his head.

GROOMING TIME

Tying and grooming should become daily routine with any horse you intend to train. It does a number of important things besides making the animal look nice. Tying him up is a gentle form of discipline and grooming him is a reward that most horses like immensely. Proper grooming stimulates circulation and aids digestion. You can spot any signs of sores or injuries, and the horse will relax as you touch and handle him.

Grooming time is also the time to introduce them casually to all the pieces of equipment they will wear in their lifetime. Start with a rope. While you groom, let the rope lie across the back, over the rump, and even down along the tail. Next, bring out a towel. Just lay it on his back, head, over the eyes or ears. Drape his blanket on his back, but do not put it on and buckle it up the first time. If he is curious about anything, let him look at it and sniff it. If it smells like him or another horse, he will like it a lot better than if it smells "brand new" or of mothballs. Place saddles, bridles, bitting rigs, and harnesses in view of his stall or crossties, where he can see them but can't get hold of them with his teeth. Carry things past him and raise them up above his eye level, but do not try to put anything on him that he fears. Let it become a familiar sight while he is enjoying his daily grooming. If his halter has been allowed to get too tight or to rub a sore on him, he will view other equipment with an understandable suspicion. If he was left blanketed in his stall and got all tangled up, don't expect him to accept more new gear without question.

INTRODUCING TACK

Tacking up on the first occasion should be just that. Put the equipment on one piece at a time and adjust it so that it is somewhere near the right size. Do not make anything tight, especially the girth. Lay the equipment on his back and move it gradually and calmly into place. Do not try to be sneaky about it. He will know instinctively if you are trying to pull a fast one on him and will be apprehensive. After all, the equipment shouldn't hurt him, and there is no reason to act as if it might. He should have confidence in you and anything you do to him. Some horses, no matter how calm and gentle, hate to have a crupper put under their tail or a britching strap around their rump. Go slowly; you have months. Roll up a dishtowel and lift the tail. Place the rolled-up towel high under the tail, and let him jump or clamp his tail down and shake all he wants. Speak quietly and hold the towel so that it doesn't slip or fall down. Be patient for a few moments, then, if he doesn't stop his nonsense, scold him. Do not yank on the towel or cause any pain in connection with it. Some horses are inordinately sensitive in one area of the body or another. A horse sensitive at the tail will very likely end up getting sores from a crupper, if it isn't kept very clean, because he will tend to clamp down and pull on it. It sometimes pays to tan or toughen areas of sensitive hide on a horse. Ask your veterinarian for a nonirritating substance to help. Strong tea, vinegar, salt water, and various other things can be used, but unless it is a real problem, just patience, time, and clean equipment are usually all that is necessary. Sweat causes rubbing and irritation, even in normally tough horses. Pressure causes ruptured blood vessels, and sand and grit make holes. A young horse is tender. Consider this when you work the youngster, for he cannot do his best or concentrate on a lesson if he is uncomfortable or in pain. Sheepskin or acrylic padding helps.

One piece of training equipment well worth its moderate price is the nylon longeing cavesson, which is rather like a cross between a bridle and a halter. The average novice trainer is not really skilled enough to start a young horse in a bit. This gives good control, communication, and time for both horse and trainer to get used to training procedures.

Ground Work

From the beginning of serious training until the horse is actually hitched to a cart or ridden, all training is referred to as "ground work" or "working from the ground." Leading is the obvious first step. Ground driving and longlining are the next step, and they are done alternately, depending on your aims with the horse. Longeing will not be discussed in this book, because in my opinion it is a very poor method of training, usually carried out badly, to the detriment of the horse's bone development. Longlining does all the good things longeing can do but maintains the horse's balance and control to a much greater degree. It is not beyond the ability of anyone to learn to ground-drive and longline properly.

THE BITTING RIG

Ground work is done with a bitting rig. This can be a professionally made setup, or fashioned in a variety of ways at home. If you plan to train more than one horse, a properly made rig will pay for itself, since having one that is adjustable and comfortable will make training go faster and easier. The bitting rig consists of a surcingle or saddle, like that on a harness, with rings for the attachment of the crupper, a pair of side reins, and an overcheck or side check. Side reins should have elastic ends of some kind. These can be bought separately to be used with a homemade surcingle. Check reins can be made of sash cord and some snaps. If you cannot locate side reins with elastic ends, any rein or cord with a section attached to it cut from an inner tube will suffice. Shock cord—available at marine hardware stores—can also be attached to reins for this purpose (8 to

10 inches of elastic is about the right length). A crupper can be a simple dish towel or a soft roll of fabric tied with a clothesline; adjustment is more important than looks or materials. The surcingle should be placed well behind the withers, in the middle of the back. Most people put them on too far forward. The crupper should be adjusted to hold the surcingle in place. The bridle or longeing cavesson should be comfortable and snug so that it cannot twist about on the horse's head. If it is equipped with side check rings, run the check rein from the side rings of the cavesson or the bit up through these check rings (also known as ear drops), back to the surcingle, to the ring on the top center or check terret. The side reins attach to the two outer rings on the longe cavesson or else to the bit. These go back to the side rings on the surcingle.

None of this should be very tight, but everything just snug, so that things don't flop and hang and twist. Often people fear they will irritate the horse by making his tack too tight, but it is just as irritating for the horse if it is too loose. The bitting rig should not at first make the horse hold his head higher or more tucked in than his natural head carriage. A horse should never be set up in a bitting rig and then left in a stall without supervision; many horses die of

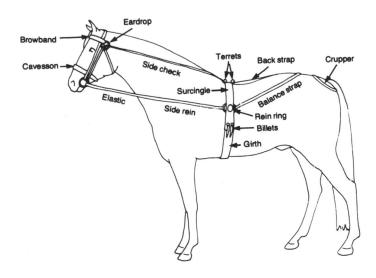

The parts of the bitting rig.

cracked skulls from this practice. Lead or chase the horse about a small enclosure or paddock if you do not want to start off ground-driving him, but don't let him stand still and hang his head on the bit or he will develop the habit of "boring" very quickly and it is a difficult habit to break.

As the horse works, the bitting rig is gradually adjusted to encourage him to hold his head in the desired position. If the horse is to go Western, his head is not lifted at all. The check rein simply prevents him from eating grass or rolling his neck down and bucking. If he is to go on a relatively loose rein as a pleasure horse, his side reins will not be taken in enough to put constant pressure on his mouth. They will serve only to prevent him from turning his head around or from poking his nose way out in front of him in an unnatural position. If your purpose in using a bitting rig is to set the head, you will take it up in stages and make the horse carry himself in an unnatural position until the muscles are accustomed to the position and strong enough for him to carry himself in the desired way without needing to be held up by the rider or driver. Such work is tiring for the horse. His head is heavy and his neck will become very stiff and sore. Caution is needed here or you will make him resentful and angry. The horse should not work in pain; he will not learn if his mind is on discomfort. As soon as a lesson is over, release the check reins and allow him to hang his neck for a few moments until the stiffness is relieved. Massaging the neck eases the stiffness and rewards the horse. Keep all lessons short while you are asking the horse to use new muscles or to take a different position.

Our practice is to use the longeing cavesson for the first month. We take the horse for walks, and get him used to his trainer either ground driving him from behind or longlining him from the side. He learns to travel at a rated speed and to stop on command. Once we are sure he understands most of the whip and rein signals, we hang a bit in his mouth, completely independent of the cavesson and reins. He is allowed to grow accustomed to this bit for as much as a week before we attach anything to it. Then we attach the check rein one day and work him as usual off the cavesson. The following day, if he seemed comfortable, the side reins are attached but the long lines are still on the cavesson. Remember that it takes time for the horse to adjust to the bit and for the mouth bars to toughen enough not to blister or get inflamed from rubbing. Since the horse can adjust the amount of pressure he receives from the bit by lifting his head or tucking his chin, he will learn to respond to it on his own.

STARTING TO GROUND-DRIVE

It will help tremendously to have a helper when you start to ground-drive your horse. Have the helper snap a lead onto the center ring of the cavesson or put a halter on the horse and lead him by that. The trainer should work behind the horse and give all voice commands, and snap the whip or gently tap the horse as he gives them. The leader should never give a command out loud, nor should he actually pull the horse to start, turn, or stop him, unless the horse does not understand or respond to the trainer. The leader should work on the direct instructions from the trainer and just stay next to the horse as an assistant. One of the first things the horse might respond to is seeing and hearing the trainer behind him. Some horses "blow up" or shy, and some wheel to face the trainer. Other horses are not upset by the sight or sound, but they are panicked by the sensation of the reins or long lines on their back, rump, or around their legs. Some horses kick, some bolt or scoot and tuck their tails. Be careful not to let the long reins get up under the horse's tail. Frequently, a horse will clamp his tail down hard on the rein, and pulling on it makes him frantic. So the trainer has several things to consider—the least of which is actual control or training in the first few minutes of the lesson.

The handler at the lead keeps the horse calm, with gentle words of reassurance and a steady hand on the lead. If your first attempt to train a horse is not a disaster, be happy to praise the horse for his good sense and quit within five minutes. Once around the ring is plenty for the first time. If it *is* a disaster, lead the horse about in the bitting rig to calm him. Do something he likes to do, such as a short walk with just the leader at his head, and finish on a calm and pleasant note. He must be made to feel that things are all right even though there was a period of fear.

STANDING

Standing still is one of the horse's most important lessons. Stop him several times during each session and count slowly to twenty-five. If the horse takes a step, stop him at once, and continue to keep him still until you reach twenty-five without a wiggle. Then give a decisive command to walk or trot. Do not let the horse start up on his own. You need not work much on backing. Horses get to like it and will tend to back when you want them to stand still.

NEW EXPERIENCES

Once you have him ground driving quietly and standing still on command for a count of ten, you are ready to solo. Have the leader unsnap his line but let him still stay walking along beside the horse. This may take a week or a month, but it is important to get the very first lessons down pat and the horse relaxed and calm about training. If the horse walks out freely and happily without being led, the leader can drop back and walk beside the trainer, then stand in the center of the ring and just be on hand for emergencies. Once the solo working is steady, the helper can start to drag sticks in the dirt at some distance in front of the horse. We use a little red wagon with great success, but anything that will make the horse see and hear strange things but not create an accident is fine. We then drive the horse past the object being pulled. Most horses will give a wide berth to such things and walk on their toes. Some will walk boldly by as if they don't care, and then suddenly bolt forward.

Ground driving should include turns and serpentines. You are trying to get the horse to be responsive to your commands and to get him as supple as you can. We use regular highway pylons here, but lines of plastic wastebaskets, piles of rocks, or any such markers will do. Put them in a row about eight paces apart and drive the horse "in and out the window." Most horses have more trouble turning to the right than to the left; now is the time to help the horse gradually over this onesidedness. Take him on trails in long lines. You will be surprised that some things he would cross with you at the halter are suddenly frightening to him if you are behind him. Work on your ability to reassure him from this remote position, for he may need your support when he is pulling a cart and you can't get to his head.

Ground driving is easiest done with two longe lines. The trainer works directly behind the horse. The lines can be attached to the longe cavesson or to the bit, depending on the trainer's skill and the horse. Some people run the lines through the side rings on the surcingle; some run them through terrets on a harness saddle; and others run them through the stirrups of their saddle. Any method that keeps them from getting down under the horse's feet is fine.

In longlining you are going to need longer lines than the usual longe line. Long web straps are the easiest on your hands, but you can use any soft, light rope if you prefer. These can be anywhere from 50 to 100 feet long. You will work from the side of the horse, maintaining a position just about directly in line with the girth, with the near rein running directly from his head to your hand, and the far rein going around his gaskins. The trick is to maintain a light, steady pressure, which is even on both sides of his head, in order to prevent him from turning either toward or away from you, and not to let him step over the reins while you walk sideways and handle the whip. It's fun to learn to do it, but the horse might not be amused if you step on the lines, trip and yank his mouth, flop the whip about, or tangle him all up. So start back with a helper at his head for the first few tries until you get organized and comfortable with all these maneuvers.

In the event that a horse turns, faces you, and backs up, *don't* pull on the reins. Speak quietly, release pressure, and walk slowly toward the horse. Turn him facing the right way and slowly start again until he understands. One of the new sensations for both of you will be the fact that when you longline, the horse changes his direction by turning away from you. This is the trickiest moment for many handlers, because you must let out line in one hand and reel it in with the other without overturning the horse, and must then release him enough to allow him to move forward. Most horses get confused and stop. Some jump when they see the trainer appear on the other side of their head. Give the horse room when you turn so that you don't run him into the fence.

Longlining is the best way to train a horse to the necessary gaits and voice commands. It takes energy on the part of the trainer, for he must do quite a bit of walking, but it is possible to exert a great deal of control on the animal. You can get the gait you want and control its speed. You can demand a stop, and back up the command with a steady pull on both reins at once. This is a far better way to train than the longe line, and you can see how your horse is learning balance and self-control. The horse is not pulled from the head into a circle, as he is in longeing. These lessons can be carried out all winter and the horse can be both longlined and ground-driven on trails and over obstacles.

Introducing Him to a Cart and Harness

Now that you have worked on ground driving to get the horse to go any place you want, have him standing quietly and relaxed on the word "Whoa," and worked at longlining to get him going steadily at a walk and a trot, you are set to start with a cart.

The cart goes before the horse, just like the dragging sticks and the little red wagon. Have your assistant play pony and pull the cart about, while you drive the horse behind, alongside, past, and then in front of the cart. Do this until there is no evidence of nervousness on the horse's part. When you are sure he is not frightened of the cart in his bitting rig, fit him to his harness and work him in the blinker bridle. This may upset him terribly. Some horses refuse to walk forward; some turn around; and some shy and wheel at every noise. Drive him in his full harness with the straps hanging where they will on his sides. Put on the breast collar and have your assistant walk behind the horse, putting gentle pressure on the traces to simulate the pull he will feel with the cart. Once he has accepted this, start again with the helper pulling the cart in front of the horse. Take turns passing and being passed by the cart. Make certain it goes by on both sides. Take the reins off to the side and stand the horse still.

Now have the handler turn the cart around and gently push it up against the horse's hind legs. Bump him lightly. Reassure him but be firm that he must stand still. Pull the cart up alongside the horse and push the shafts against his sides slowly but enough to make him feel them. If he takes this well, run the shafts on both sides of him so that he stands between them. In doing so, be careful not to poke him or bang the wood against his hocks. When the shafts are in place, the trainer can hold the horse by the head and the end of one shaft. The helper should stand on one side and push the shaft against the horse firmly enough to make him move sideways a step or two. The handler then repeats this from the other side, again actually making the horse step over. Raise and lower the shafts against the horse's sides a few times. Now back the shafts up enough to slip them into the shaft carriers and run them forward where they will be when the horse is hitched.

If the horse has been calm about all this, the trainer can now go to a driving position beside the cart, while the helper holds the shaft firmly just in front of the shaft carrier. He is going to act as a stop so that the carrier can't slide off the shaft. This is actually much safer and easier with a helper on each shaft. The horse is asked to walk and the helpers pull very slightly to get the cart going, but then they let the horse do the pulling. The horse is not in fact hitched to anything. Some very nervous horses even require a further assistant, to act as a strong, steady leader who runs a chain over the horse's nose and walks by his head. The horse should walk forward and only make gradual turns. He may be fine in a straight line and then jump when he turns a corner. Do this with the horse for days. If he jumps forward, the helpers on the side should be ready to push the cart back and off him to avoid injury. The driver should be off to one side so that the cart can stay while the horse and the driver move forward. If the horse jumps forward and out from between the shafts, stop him and put him back into the cart again, but be sure he understands that you know he is afraid and that you are not angry with him. After this session is over, take him for a quiet walk and let him settle down. Be companionable for a while and end it all on a good note. You have time. These first few tries in harness will establish how he feels about driving. You want him to feel safe, for a runaway in harness is the worst kind there is. Work him with people for helpers for a long time before actually hitching him.

Some trainers use a travois for training while others drag logs. A travois is two poles of springy live wood, with a board nailed to them to hold them apart. The poles must go through the shaft carriers on the harness. If you want to make up a travois rather than using your cart to get the horse used to shafts, that is fine, but be sure to make the poles long enough so that they are high at the horse's hocks. Most people tend to make such a device too short and the ends of the poles are at fetlock level. That's asking for trouble. The board should be well behind the horse's hind legs so he won't hit it if he kicks back. If your harness has a breeching, it is well to attach the poles to this to make certain they stay high and in line with his body if he tries to turn around. If you drag a log, you have to make certain the traces are supported by the breeching or else run a strap over the horse's rump to hold them up. Should the horse step over the traces, he may well blow up and get hurt. Tape the strap or support to the crupper strap to make certain it does not slip back off his rump.

HITCHING TO A CART

Hitching the horse to a cart should be done in the following order: Have your assistant "head the horse"—that is, stand facing the horse holding both sides of the bridle and keeping the horse facing forward. He is to prevent the horse from going forward and from rearing. Bring the cart up behind the horse and insert the shafts into the shaft carriers. If the harness has thimbles, the shaft tips must also be inserted into these as the cart is run forward. The shaft tip should be at the point of the shoulder. If it is too far forward, the horse can catch the reins over the tip, and if too far back it will poke the horse in the side while he turns. The traces are then taken back to the whiffletree or to the trace bolts on the cart and fastened. The traces should be snug, with no hanging excess. They should not be so tight as to cause a constant pull or chafing on the horse's chest. Most carts are fitted with loops of leather on the shafts to guide the trace and hold it away from the horse's side. If the traces are too long or if there are no loops, run the trace once over the shaft before attaching it to the whiffletree. If the traces are too short you must use trace extenders. Do not tie or wire the traces to the cart, because it will be difficult to free them in an emergency. If the whiffletree has a small hole in each end and a rawhide thong, the trace is pushed onto the end past the hole and the thong is inserted into the hole to prevent the trace from slipping off. Some whiffletrees have a turnfitting on the end that locks the trace on. Make certain this turns easily and oil it if it is stiff.

If you have a breeching-style harness instead of a thimble harness, the holdbacks are attached next. These should run forward between the horse and the shaft through a footman's loop which is located on the bottom of the shaft. Then it is wrapped over the shaft, around itself, and back to its buckle. There should be about 4 to 6 inches of play between the breeching and the horse's thigh. This should never be so tight that it puts pressure on the horse while he is pulling forward on the flat or standing still. It is there to prevent the cart from riding up on the horse's hind legs when he stops or goes downhill and it pushes the cart back while he is backing.

The next step is to tie the shafts down with the hold-down strap which runs under the girth. It is brought up between the horse and the shaft, through the shaft carrier, over the shaft, around itself and the shaft once, and then back down to its own buckle. It should not be excessively tight. The purpose of this strap is to prevent the shafts from lifting up over the horse's back, but it should not restrict the up-and-down motion of the shafts completely, for this will irritate the horse and make for a very rough ride for the driver when the horse trots. Most people err by cinching these straps down, thinking they are there to hold the cart from moving forward and back. It is customary to hitch the horse with his check rein loose and to check him up just when the driver has seated himself in the cart. This signals the horse that he is to move and while the check is free he is to stand still.

Once you start to drive a young horse the first time, he should be driven every single day for at least two weeks without fail. Do not hitch him at all until you are fairly certain you will have the time and the help to get him going every day. Don't allow bad weather or family activities to interrupt this schedule.

The next stage is driving with another horse in harness, for seeing another cart come by and hearing the sound of overtaking hoofbeats can startle some horses.

PERFECTING THE DRIVING HORSE

The good driving horse must go at the speed you ask. It takes quite a while for a youngster to learn to rate himself and go at a steady pace. Show gaits require a high park or animated trot, which is not excessively fast, and a fast, ground-devouring trot called a road gait. It is good to school the horse to jog quietly in harness also—that is, simply to trot at a slow, relaxed, and easy gait in a light rein. The walk, whether in harness or under saddle, should always be fast. Make the horse pay strict attention and go at the rate you wish. Make him travel in a straight line, not wander all over the lot. Walk toward home. Do not drive to the barn and unhitch. Go beyond the barn or to a regular place to store the cart, but do not let the horse think that going to the barn is the aim of the ride. He may decide to end the ride before you do.

Standing perfectly still is an absolute must in harness. Backing in a straight line is also mandatory. If the horse tries to twist in the shafts, he can upset the cart. If the horse does not back in a straight line, work him out of the cart but in full harness along a solid-board or other fence. Get him to back quietly for as long as you ask him to and then to stand perfectly still at your command. He must not move forward until you give the signal to do so.

For backing in harness, martingales tend to keep the horse from putting the head too high and from rearing. You can't back along a fence to stay straight once you are hitched to a cart—and backing a four-wheeled vehicle is of course much harder than backing a cart —so I would advise backing unhitched until there is absolutely no problem of understanding and control. The closed (blinker) bridle makes more problems, but since that is the right equipment you had best train in it. It is a good idea to have someone near the horse's head on your first attempt to back in a cart. He need not touch the horse, but just in case the animal jackknives the equipment and gets frantic, it is much quicker for a person on the ground to come to his aid than for the trainer, who is behind him.

If your horse shows some signs of speed and you want to increase it, be sure to condition him carefully. Do not try to get all his speed as a young horse but gradually ask for faster time on each drive. Keep the distance short and give him time to mature and develop sound feet and legs. Speed requires good wind and firm muscle. Fat will hamper his speed, so the diet of a roadster should be tailored to lean, hard condition.

At this stage of development, about two years old, the horse begins to show more ability and aptitude for some types of use than others. The horse that is everything—show, pleasure, endurance, and speed —is a rare creature. If yours shows signs of real aptitude for some special job, he will probably do it well all his life. He may become equally proficient at other tasks, of course. But horses, like people, have preferences and specialties. The important thing is to keep the job of learning fun for him and to encourage his curiosity and cooperation all you can.

When your horse is driving nicely in two wheels, he will understand turns that involve leaning on the shafts. He will not attempt to turn in a tight circle and upset the cart. He will back in a straight line or in an arc, as you direct, and he will work at a slow and brisk trot as well as a lively walk. Traffic should present no problems by now, but the sound of another horse approaching from the rear may excite him.

Working with Other Vehicles

When you introduce him to four wheels, the buggy will again present a new sensation to him. It will pull a bit heavier and turn in a slightly different manner, but what will feel different to him is the looseness of the front axle turning with him, and the body of the buggy trailing behind. Some horses are terrified by this change. You will find backing four wheels a unique experience the first time you try it, too. Buggies tend to make more noise than comparable carts, so it will do no harm to pull any new vehicle behind the horse before hitching it.

Hitching to a sleigh is essentially the same as to a cart. The one precaution with young horses is to be sure the runners are not iced up or frozen to the ground, as this may cause the youngster to lunge forward or to rear and come over backward. Some will scramble and fall and become frightened by this. Be sure the horse is properly shod for snow if you plan to use a sleigh. Heavy snow is exhausting, and a snappy trot dragging a bunch of bundled-up passengers through knee-deep drifts is a job for a well-conditioned, mature animal.

PULLING A LOAD

Pulling a log or a load requires a different approach to driving than does jogging along in a light cart or buggy. The horse must be taught to lean into the collar and push forward. He will learn to dig his toes in and heave against the harness—and it had better be a strong one. Heavy pulls are too much for a two-year-old, but he can learn to tow a log along a road or in a field.

Get him used to the collar and harness and chain traces about him. Pulling harness is much heavier, and often the hardware clanks in noisy fashion. You can use a spreader—or whiffletree—on the traces and a single chain from that to the log. Make sure you can unhitch quickly. Back him to the log and attach it. He should drive forward quietly on command. Allow him to walk about 15 or 20 feet. Then he should stand quietly while he is unhitched. Do this with increasingly heavy logs over a period of time. Asking him to pull too much at first will discourage him, but a very light stick won't teach him anything. He must learn to lean forward and push against the collar. The collar is new to him and it may cause irritation, just as a new pair of shoes can give you corns and blisters. Small bumps that are caused by chafing and sweat under leather should never go unattended; vinegar washes and salt-water treatments will help to toughen the hide and prevent big sores.

Time for Riding

When your horse is three years old, he is ready to start feeling weight on his back. You have probably not been able to control yourself and have sat on him a little, oh, just for a second, to see what he would do. I, for one, hope he bucked you off, but he probably didn't. Once satisfied that he wouldn't buck, you went back to his driving and obstacles and let him grow, mature, and develop as he should. Now he is old enough, understands enough of his voice commands, and is well enough used to the bit in his mouth so that the only new things will be the feel of the saddle and the sight of someone behind his head.

HIS FIRST LESSON

First, remember that your horse can face forward and see you sitting up there on his back and will be watching every move you make. If you are kind and quiet with him, he has no reason to fear you up there, and he is not resentful—but he may well be curious. Talk to him and praise him for standing quietly. Don't go anywhere the first time up. It is important for him to stand still when you mount and dismount. That is the first thing to teach him. People tend to girth young horses up tight and mount from the ground, just as they do an older horse. I urge you not to do this the first few days. His back is tender, you will be awkward in mounting him slowly, and the girth will hurt him. Tie him in crossties and get a box or mounting block. Stand on that and lay your weight over his back. Let him get used to that. Get back off, and then on and off again a few times. Be sure he understands that all you are asking is that he stand quietly. Praise him when he behaves by doing nothing at all just as much as when he does some active thing on command. When you slide your leg over his back, take care not to thump him on the hindquarters. Sit up slowly and speak to him in your normal voice. Once he accepts mounting calmly, cast off the crossties and ride him forward on the word "Walk." Do not use your legs or heels, just your voice.

BE READY FOR A BIG JUMP

It takes a few rides before the horse gets used to the weight and strange feel of a rider on his back. A more experienced horse is a source of comfort and reassurance to the young one, and a mounted assistant is a safety factor to the rider on the green mount. Horses are not likely to buck the first time they are ridden. Somewhere around the third time, they have figured out how to hold the weight, and some are then disposed to see if they can unload it. Hold the reins lightly but do not allow the horse to get his head down. Make sure your own balance is good and that you do not depend on the reins or the saddle for your safety. There will be a number of things which are new to the horse: your voice coming from above, rather than behind him, the weight on his back, the bit held at a different angle in his mouth, and the feel of your legs along his sides.

TRAINING TO LEG CUES

Training the horse to respond to your legs is next on the agenda. He knows by now that "Walk" means start moving forward, and "Whoa" means stop and stand still. When you use these commands, squeeze him with the calves of your legs, and lean forward to Walk and back a little for Whoa. Do not kick but squeeze rather firmly so that you are sure the horse is aware of your legs. Once he starts to move forward, release your leg pressure. It is to be hoped that you have taken riding lessons and know the use of the aids—you cannot expect to teach the horse something you yourself do not know. Use exaggerated aids for all your signals, but do not alter them otherwise. In other words, if you train the horse to turn on one leg while you push him with the other, do not signal with your heels; use your legs only. At the same time that you make turns and stops or changes of gait, you will use the familiar voice commands, which he fully understands. You will also lean your body in exaggerated emphasis. As he responds, you can reduce the amount of "body English" in your signals.

If the horse simply does not respond or react to your legs, dismount and stand at his side. With your knuckles push his ribs firmly and pull his head to make him step in a circle. When he responds, praise him. Repeat this lesson several times on both sides until he turns at a touch of the hand and does not need the pull on the bit. Then mount and try again. He should understand what it is you are asking. Some horses are so concerned with weight on their backs at first that they can think of nothing else.

THE BIT

When you start to ride, use the same bit you have used in driving, for it will be familiar to him. One new thing at a time is always enough for a horse. After your weight and legs are accepted, you can start him in a new bit if you feel he will go better. However, keep to a similar type for a while. Make all changes gradual. The horse will carry his head low when first learning to carry you, but after a while he will bring it up to his normal position with no urging on your part. However, if you want higher head carriage, you will want to raise your hands slightly. Shift your weight back in the saddle a little and he will lift his head.

WORK TOWARD GOOD MANNERS

For the first month, the young horse should do *nothing* but walk. He should go backward as well as forward, up and down hills, carry a sack or a slicker over the saddle, allow you to take off and put on a jacket. But most of all he should learn to stand still when you want him to. You should never pull on his mouth and he should never pull on your hands. Get him to understand and to respond in a willing and cheerful manner. It is a temptation to go as fast as he can learn, but he will not learn as well and will, in the end, know less than if you take your time. If you can find friends who are willing to go on long, quiet trail rides and whose horses are kind and willing, both you and the horse will enjoy that far more than the constant circle of the ring. This is particularly true of a horse you wish to show, for a bored horse has no presence and a ring-sour horse is always scored down. When using obstacles, try to bend the horse's body in an arc as he turns in and out of poles; let his head nod as he crosses logs. You want to make him as flexible as you can until he has gained his own natural sense of balance with the added weight of the saddle and rider.

BUILDING HIS ENERGY

The more work a horse does, the more he develops ability and stamina. I am not suggesting that you ride a three-year-old for two hours at a time, but he will enjoy an easy ride on the trails and should be worked every day—he will grow stronger as his balance improves.

TROTTING

Your horse's natural drive will let you know when it is time to start to work on the trot. Keep trotting (steady and medium pace) for a short distance, and avoid working on corners at first. Trot only on the level and uphill, never down with a youngster. Make sure he is not allowed to take the trot until you clearly ask for it, and that he is not allowed to break into a canter. If he is extended too soon, he will do one of two things: learn to break or skip behind, or overreach and cut his heels. Working downhill will bring on both these faults in short order. The horse should trot with his head up. If he is harness-broken, he will have worked this way, providing your check was properly adjusted. He may tend to stumble and grab his front shoe and trip, even though his head is up. Slow him down and sit farther back in the saddle. Post strongly and establish a regular cadence in his stride. Most horses hit themselves because of the rider's position. Firm leg contact, raised hands, and playing lightly on the bit will usually correct this problem. You want the horse to work off his hindquarters. When he was pulling, he leaned into a harness with his forehand and pushed with the rear legs. Now he must support weight and drive off his hocks. It takes experience for a horse to learn this and it is hard and tiring at first. Be absolutely certain you know *how* to post so that you are not pounding his kidneys unmercifully at every stride. If you ride correctly, there is no daylight between you and the saddle; you post forward, not up; and you never come fully down into the saddle again. If this is news to you, go practice on an older horse.

Horses are usually trained to trot on contact with the snaffle bit. That is when you hold the reins just tight enough to feel the horse's mouth and prevent him from ducking down. If he stumbles, you can help to support his head until he regains his footing. The faster the trot, the firmer the contact. In this case, the horse should actually pull on the bit in a fast roadster trot and you will push him just short of a canter with your legs, while holding him steady on the bit. Never trot a horse on the curb. It will make it far harder for him to understand the signal to canter and you will complicate your life and his. If your horse is Western, jog on a loose rein and keep the speed very slow on a young horse.

When you want the horse to trot, say, "Trot," and start to post. When you want him to walk, use the word "Walk" and *sit down* even if he continues to trot. Pull him to a standstill or a walk, and hold him there until he relaxes and walks flat-footed.

When your mount has a fast walk with a light or loose rein, a slow, collected trot with the head carried well, a breezy extended trot, and a perfectly relaxed transition to any gait or standstill from any gait, he is finally ready to begin in the canter.

THE FULL BRIDLE

Start on the ground at his side. Raise his head by lifting the snaffle rein toward his jaw. If he has been bitted properly, he will respond without trying to pull down. Now take the curb lightly and pull the rein gently toward his chest. His nose should dip just slightly; his poll should flex and bend. Do this exercise a few times, but do not overdo it. When he responds to the curb by giving with his chin, he is ready to be ridden in a full bridle. If he rebels by lifting his chin or tossing his head, you are being too severe and trying to get results too fast. You are asking him to relax and give you his jaw; he cannot be expected to do this if he is hurt or frightened.

CANTERING

Ride him at a walk and trot through a usual routine in a familiar place. When you have him warmed up and relaxed, plan to canter on a level stretch of road for a specific distance. Never mind the lead he is on. If the road is straight, either lead is correct. Now lift his head with the snaffle and push him into the curb bit with your legs. He should be well up in your hands and eager to go on. Say the word "Canter," and let him burst forward. Don't attempt to hold him at a slow canter for the first few strides. Keep his head up so that he will not fall or buck, and sit down and quiet in the saddle. Before you reach the end of your chosen distance, lean back and say, "Whoa," while you pull on the curb rein. Do so gently and hold him steadily. As soon as he stops, pet him and be sure he stands perfectly still and relaxes completely. It is sometimes good to dismount and pet him until he is completely at ease. Then remount and continue your ride at a walk and trot. Pick a new spot each time you ride for a canter, otherwise he will anticipate and start to lift and toss his head or jog. Let it be a pleasant experience that never gets out of control.

Polishing the canter comes weeks and weeks after he has learned to canter on a light rein. It is most important that he comes to a full stop and relaxes. To take a lead, pick a spot where you will turn a corner naturally. Bring him in slowly and keep your weight off his lead shoulder. It must be free for him to lift into the lead. Never forget, however, that the horse actually takes his lead off the rear leg. You can feel him push forward if you sit tight to the saddle. Your ability as a rider counts more at a canter than at any other time.

Normally, the horse will automatically take the proper lead when he turns in his pasture. And he will do the same with you in the saddle if you ride well and never interfere with his balance. If he takes the wrong lead, it is because he is trying to compensate for your weight. Cantering in a small circle does three things: (1) it slows down the gait; (2) it forces him to take the proper lead in the front, and hopefully to follow with the rear; and (3) it puts a severe strain on the forelegs and shoulders. I recommend cantering in small circles to establish the proper speed and gait *only* if you keep the limitation of strain and the horse's welfare in mind. It is a better practice to be sure he is bitted properly and will slow down on rein pressure. Keep your seat without squeezing his sides for your balance. Don't get excited and transmit your excitement to him.

There must be nine million "proper ways" to signal a horse for the canter—from the hunter kick to the equitation toe-in. I don't advocate any of them specifically. The only thing to keep in mind is that you want the horse to start his canter off a hind foot on the inside of the turn and make his front legs follow suit. If he learns to canter off the front shoulder, he might well learn to go disunited and switch leads on you at will.

Some people always allow a young horse to take a canter from a trot; some never do. If you plan to show the horse, he must never be allowed to "break" from a trot to a canter, whether he is an equitation horse or a road hack. Dressage horses are schooled to make a smooth transition from a trot to a canter, but they don't break into it on their own.

If the horse trots, then canters, then breaks back to a trot or quits on you, it is your fault; you are not supporting him with your riding. You can feel a horse start to change gaits—then, and not a second later, is the moment to signal him. Remember that if you are not a good rider, you cannot expect the horse to figure these things out for himself. He is young and ignorant and his education depends upon your ability. If you realize you are not so hot as a rider, you will have patience with his goofs and can adjust your training to a level you can both reach.

BACKING

One of the things I have not touched upon much is backing. No horse is truly well trained until he can back straight and smoothly and willingly. The horse must back without resistance and continue to do so until told to stop. I have not stressed this until last for a very good reason. Young horses sometimes learn to back in order to avoid work, or from fear and ignorance. An experienced trainer can teach a horse to back properly at the outset of his work, but the novice would do best to leave it until after he has established the forward gears and the brake. Reverse can get out of hand. Some horses back easily and naturally, and some find it nearly impossible. They would rather rear and throw themselves than go backward. Horses rarely back up in a free state. So again, as when we first started to halter-break the foal, we are training the horse to something which is naturally not his normal behavior.

If you have trained him to back up while you were leading him, and he can back out of a trailer and take the few steps back required in harness and pleasure classes, that will very likely satisfy you. However, a horse that works cattle (or performs in stock horse classes) and a really useful harness horse must be able to back straight and smooth, and under the handler's full control. Rein the horse back very gently. His head should be low, with chin tucked and neck flexed. He should be as relaxed as possible. If he stiffens his jaw and tries to stick his nose in the air, you have not schooled him properly. With patience and tact, you should be able to correct the problem, but if not, there are a number of things that may help. Don't try them all at once, or one after the other without giving each a proper chance at success, or you will only cause more confusion and problems.

If you are backing under saddle first, try putting your left hand forward over the crest of his neck and *gently* tapping or pushing down when he lifts his head as you pull back. If he pulls forward and down, make your pull intermittent, not a steady straight pull. Light jabs will not give him anything to pull back on. With some horses, a vibrato or tremor on the reins will work as a signal to back. Remember always that you must do more than just use your hands. Your legs can pull the horse back with calf pressure. Some horses respond to the rider pushing the stirrups far forward. Some shift in weight must always come with a new signal on the reins. And never forget that if you have taught your horse a vocabulary, you should continue to use it. Try attaching a rein to the cavesson and pulling that down and back in conjunction with the reins. He may still plant his feet and grow roots. Try tapping his chest with a crop. That will mean you will be leaning far forward and can push back on the stirrups as you do. Don't unhook them out of their safety bars, however, which is quite easy to do in that position.

If all else fails, rig a draw rein. Professionals have varying methods of doing this, but the novice tends to get himself into things that are hard to get out of, so I recommend the following system. Get two simple round rings, like the lead ring on a halter. Buy some new rawhide lace. Tie one ring to the girth buckle on each side of the saddle. Take two long reins which are separate (Western reins are good for this). Attach them to the rings, one on each side, and then run them through the snaffle ring of the horse's bit and up to your hands with the regular reins. Try using just these reins to make the horse back. If he still is uncooperative, take your feet out of the stirrups and with your heels kick him on the points of both shoulders as you pull. If you are adept at using spurs, you can apply them here; if not, this is not the time or place to practice. Just one step backward is cause for lavish praise and an end to the lesson for the day. Even if you are convinced that the horse stepped back by mistake, quit while you are ahead.

Don't make an issue of backing unless you are sure you know what is causing the resistance and then be prepared for the horse to rear violently if you get tough about it. If the draw rein works, always lean forward and pull down and back on the snaffle bit as a signal to back.

The horse does not walk backward—he trots backward—that is, he moves his legs in diagonal pairs as he does when he trots. This accounts for some of the problem. If he is foundered, then backing is exceedingly painful for him. If he is a wobbler, he may be physically unable to back. Backing for the normal horse should not be a problem and probably will not be one if he has been good about everything else in which you have trained him.

BACKING IN LINE

The next project is to back in a straight line. Use a fence or the side of a building at first. Do not turn in the saddle to look back. Don't even turn your head or eyes, for it will twist your position and make the horse turn sideways. Make sure there is nothing behind you. Line your eye up on some object in front of you and judge your position from that. Then sit perfectly straight in the saddle and back the horse.

Backing an "L" causes no end of problems for some riders, but I am sure it is because the rider twists and turns in the saddle and guides the horse off course. When you practice at home, ride into the L and at the corner of the first leg, spot an object to line up on. Then proceed to the start of the L, line up, and back until you are near the bend. Turn your head slightly to locate the new sightline, but keep the horse backing straight until you want to swing his hind legs one way or the other. Then turn your body to face the new sightline and he will probably make a smooth turn down the second leg of the L. Often when you show in pleasure or trail classes, you are not permitted to ride into the L, nor may you start with the horse's hind legs in the L. Practice at home. Scold the horse if he steps on or knocks over a barrier, but do not punish him, particularly not with the reins. Move the L from place to place and bend it to both the right and the left. I have seen one class in which the contestants had to back over a pile of scattered jump rails. Try it out for size sometime—even a good trail horse may prove reluctant on that one.

For some reason, horses sometimes get to like going backward so much you can't stop them. Under saddle this is irritating; in harness it is downright dangerous. The logical end to backing is the word "Whoa," enforced with a touch on the rump and a step or two forward. If you have to back into a fence or a building, do so (under saddle). In harness, have someone grab the horse's head and pull forward if he refuses to quit. Do not panic and pull on the reins. Do I need to tell you not to pull? Certainly. I have seen people pull horses over on top of them, both in harness and under saddle. Fear is, and has been from the beginning, the major problem in training horses. Ignorance is in second place. Study, practice, and experience can do a great deal to minimize ignorance, but fear is something only you can master. Don't expect the horse to be calmer than you are. If he is, you are at a disadvantage. If you are genuinely afraid to teach a horse anything, leave it up to someone braver and more experienced. Not everyone is temperamentally suited to raising and training horses. But if you can master your own timidity and educate first yourself and then your horse, you will have the finest companion anyone could wish.

Toward Maturity

DO YOU WANT TO SHOW HIM?

When your horse has reached his full height and weight, he is still not mature and his bones are still hardening. Since he will have a certain amount of energy and enthusiasm for work and a good basic knowledge of what he is expected to do, you can start to polish his gaits, encourage greater action, and help him to develop his own style and personality. If you have worked him toward being a pleasure horse but find he is always bold, inclined to "ham it up" and show off, perhaps you should reconsider only hacking him on the trails and give him a whirl at a few small shows. If you plan to show in English park or pleasure classes, you will want to develop his action and animation further. Study his way of going and his head carriage. In order to increase knee action and hock action, you must get him to work with his legs well under his body and his head high. If he lifts his head and arches his neck, it frees his shoulders and makes it possible to lift his knees and snap his fetlock up.

You have tried to develop a light and responsive mouth; to pull the head up and hold it there with the reins will undo all your work, so you must work on your legs, your position in the saddle, and the position of your hands. Sit still on the saddle and let the horse relax completely. Let him move off at a walk with your hands down and quiet on the reins. Now, without changing anything else in your position, raise the reins slowly but do not pull up on them. Does he respond? He should at least be aware of the change and flick his ears or pay more attention to you. If he does so, you should have an easy time collecting him. If he responds with fear, you have done something wrong in the previous training. If he ignores you, speak to him; jiggle the reins slightly or actually vibrate the bit in his mouth lightly. Some horses respond to this by yanking down and extending their neck to pull the reins free. If you set up and pull, he will pull harder, and you have the start of a fight and a spoiled mouth on your hands. He has the strength, so use your intelligence.

Assuming that you get any of the proper responses, put your hands back down to their normal position and without making any other changes, squeeze him with your lower legs. He should raise his head or walk faster. If he does not, then squeeze harder. If there is still no response, you must go into a schooling on legs, for you cannot have a properly trained horse if his sides are not responsive to leg pressures. After all, you don't want to have to hit or kick him all his life to get him to go. So return to that same relaxed walk, and wait. In a moment or two, lower your stirrups a little and slide back in your saddle. Does he raise his head? Now squeeze with your legs and raise your hands and see if he doesn't take a deep breath and lift his front end a little. Praise him if he does and ask for a trot. Keep it a slow trot but *not* a jog. Make sure it is a regular and cadenced trot. Post very low and close to the saddle. The horse who has not responded at a walk may suddenly do so at a trot. Be satisfied with that and a short workout at a time until he gets the hang of it. He is supporting your weight in a different way on his spine and it will make his back a little tender if you overdo it at first. Even if he does not respond the first day you try this, he may well think this lesson over in his spare time and realize what you were after.

The next lesson may show a vast improvement. If he is dull and remains dull, forget the whole thing and just hack him. You can't make a good, responsive light-going horse out of one that hasn't the mental or emotional capacity for the work. All you can achieve is to bully him into doing what you want in a very grudging or frightened manner.

THE IMPORTANCE OF SPECIFIC EQUIPMENT

When you teach something you know how to do, it is not so difficult to communicate as it is when you are both learning together. Your signals may get crossed and your vocabulary may be less clear until you work out the system that suits you both. I would suggest that you make things clearer by using specific pieces of equipment for each phase of training in versatility. In other words, you use a fine harness with a snaffle bit and an overcheck for park harness. If you wish to work the horse as a roadster, use a thicker bit or some different type of a snaffle, and add quarter boots on his feet, as well as switching to a light sulky. In this way, he realizes that with the different equipment, you expect a different kind of performance. When you ride him as a show saddle horse, you should use a very lightweight set of show bits, Weymouth, and bridoon. When you ride him as a road hack or trail horse, switch to a pelham or a heavier bit set. If you go into dressage, use the proper bit set as specified by the American Horse Shows Association. Western bits are also specified in that rulebook and, of course, with Western work you will switch to the whole outfit—saddle, bridle, and all.

Saddles are changed as well, from the very flat show saddle to the balanced seat for dressage and a fully forward seat for jumping. It is a good idea to use the dressage or balanced seat in pleasure or trail (if you don't go Western), because in both of these endeavors the horse is at his best when relaxed, flexed, and in the rider's full control. He will respond to the change in placement of the rider's center of gravity, to his balance and new leg positions, and he will learn to know what the rider is going to do the minute he is tacked up.

One of the prime things to keep in mind during all facets of training is that you must not confuse the horse. Always be certain he fully understands one lesson before trying the next. This is done by repetition for a realistic period of time after he has carried out your bidding without mistake. I don't mean that you should drill him repeatedly on the same lesson on one day. That would sour him and bore you both to death. But each lesson should repeat those things he knows well and one of the new things he is still learning. When he has succeeded in performing the new task, reward him by a word, a caress, and by doing something he likes to do.

Every time you have taught him a new thing, you have probably also taught him a new word, such as "Walk," "Trot," "Stand," "Back," "Easy," or "Whoa." These cue words are a big help to him, for it is clear in his mind that you expect a given response for a particular word. In most cases you are probably consistent in giving clear signals and cues because you are aware that you are training a young mind to respond. As your horse gets older, it becomes harder to remember that mentally he remains a child and every new thing you teach must be taught with the same method.

You can make a good pleasure horse with easy lessons that are a delight to both you and the horse. You can teach a horse anything you really know—and you will be surprised at how much you know if you take your time and learn together. It takes only a few months for a good professional trainer to make a top show horse from one with good basic ground work and some maturity. It takes fully five years to make a good trail and pleasure horse that is reliable and has endurance and versatility, but the making of that horse is totally rewarding and exciting.

CHAPTER 18

Where to Get Help and Find Company

You won't always want to be alone with your horse. Horses are gregarious and so are people. Many hours of your life with your horse will be just the two of you; but there are times when you will want to share your horse with other horsemen, and also times when you will need help or further education.

There are horse clubs of many kinds, including the national breeding associations and their statewide affiliate clubs. It is safe to say that nearly everything you would want to do with a horse has become a sport, with devotees and fans, and probably an organized club making rules and having meets or sending out newsletters.

If you want to learn more, or if you and your horse are having problems with some specific point of learning, there are professional trainers and riding masters specializing in every form of the "equine art." Helpful people at local state universities or agricultural departments can also either offer assistance or refer you to someone who can help. Your grain store and local tack shop can usually give you the names of people to contact in your area, or can refer you to a horseman in the agricultural department who is familiar with professionals in the area. Many states now have equine councils, which help with everything from zoning regulations in individual towns to tax questions, laws governing shipping and health regulations, and trail usage. Most horse people are pretty sympathetic to problems that come up and are ready and willing to help if they can. Horse clubs are usually willing to take new members. Some clubs are very active, with camping trips, shows, rallies, hunts every weekend, the sponsoring of children's trips and camp stays and the like; while others are mutual admiration societies, which specialize in coffee klatsches, drinking bouts, and gossip. You will have to choose the people and clubs that best suit your tastes. I will not attempt to give addresses for all the major organizations because these change quite frequently, but I will outline some of the major areas of horse activity and the clubs connected with them. Magazines often carry news columns from these clubs, or you can get current addresses from some of the breed organizations.

Shows

The American Horse Shows Association is the one ruling body for all major shows. In this association the rules are set up and constantly revised for the exhibition of nearly all breeds and types of horses in the United States. The judges who officiate at these shows are certified by this association, as are the stewards. You can become a member of this club and receive a copy of the current rulebook by paying annual dues. You can get an application blank from the program of any recognized horse show. If you plan to show, even on a local level in nonaffiliated shows, it is advisable to become a member for at least one year, study the rules as they apply to your horse, and go to shows with rulebook in hand to see what the rules mean in action. There are specific qualifications for classes. The proper attire, tack, and appointments are spelled out with great care. The AHSA is by no means the only association which governs horse shows, but it is a valuable source of information on all phases of the horse show world.

The rodeo associations, such as the National Rodeo Association, function much the same way as the horse show associations. They coordinate rules and rodeo dates to avoid conflicts. Most such organizations arrange their events in a kind of circuit, so that competitors can go from one event to another gathering points for a total high score award from the association at the end of the season. The National Cutting Horse Association sponsors events for horses cutting cattle. The Masters of Foxhounds Association of America organizes hunter trials. The Eastern Competitive Trail Ride Association sponsors events judged on both the conditioning of horses and time. The American Carriage Association devotes itself to carriage rallies and restorations. The American Driving Society is a similar organization, but with more emphasis on conducting driving meets and competitions. The National Steeplechase and Hunt Association is Eastern-based; the West Coast has the Pacific Coast Hunter, Jumper and Stock Association. The United States Combined Training Association is the club for three-day events. Many of these associations, plus all the breed associations, have a newsletter or magazine.

In addition to the information on a given field available from the parent or sponsoring organizations, there are specific books on most phases of horse sports, such as show jumping, dressage, and hunting. There are some specialized books on showing three- and five-gaited American Saddle Horses, many on Western horses, and a very few on driving horses, in either harness racing or carriage driving. A few are also available on conditioning and competing in trail rides. Most tack shops carry books and there are specialty horse bookshops, too.

If you feel you would like to try your hand at some of these sports, the best place to start is at a meet rally or gathering, race or show, as an observer. I can't tell you how many people I know who have loaded up their horse and trucked happily to a Class A show without previously having watched a single horse show class. They come away a little taken aback, embarrassed, and often discouraged. Get your feet wet before you take the plunge—that water can be awfully cold!

Shows vary in size from a one-day affair in a vacant lot, fenced in with sheep wire and a half-dozen horses, to a mammoth annual national competition which lasts a week or more, complete with movie stars, cocktail parties, and dances. Some shows are open to the public and to any and all manner of horses; some are closed affairs for the members of a particular club, a summer camp, or are limited to members of the 4-H or Pony clubs. There are single-breed shows, such as the Arabian International, the Morgan Grand National, the Quarter Horse Congress, and end-of-the-year shows for a variety of horses, such as the National at Madison Square Garden.

At the one-day shows, most people trailer their horses there in the morning and show from the trailer, tying their horse to it and using it as a dressing room and tack room. Some ride to the show if it is close to home. At the longer shows, each horse has a box stall, and each stable often has one or more extra stalls for tack, feed, and sleeping quarters for the grooms who watch over the horses at night.

Races

Races are a much more formal affair and are more closed. There are specific races for specific breeds. There are open races over fences, "farmers' steeplechases," and the like in hunt country; but races on the track are a very carefully regulated business. The old tale of the girl who captures the black stallion and wins the Derby is pure fantasy. Racehorses are registered, carefully scrutinized, and handled by licensed trainers and jockeys. Races are rarely of mixed breeds—that is, Quarter Horses rarely race against any horses but Quarter Horses. The same is true for Arabs, Appaloosas, Thoroughbreds, and Standardbreds. There are mixed-breed races in harness for ponies; pony racing is a much freer and more open form of sport, rapidly gaining popularity. Horses are usually trained at a professional training stable and taken to the track, where they work out for a period of time or stay in training for an entire season, entering in a race or two a month. Some horses go from track to track and race in special races.

Rodeos

Rodeos, like horse shows, are sometimes closed affairs, but more often open competition. Here the events range from wild cow milking and chuck wagon races to cattle roping and bronc riding. These rodeos were at first local get-togethers of cowboys who spent an afternoon on a sort of busman's holiday, doing for fun what they did for a living the rest of the week. The competition somehow made their work more fun. Today, rodeos have become highly complex, with animals owned by rodeo promoters that are used for no other purpose. These are hauled from one rodeo site to another, but the cowboys still bring their own working ponies to compete on.

Polo

Polo matches are held between clubs or collegiate teams. There are no open polo matches that I know of, where anyone can bring his horse and enter a game. If the sport interests you, contact the nearest polo club. If there is none in your area and you want to start one, it is not very difficult. Put up a few ad cards at the tack shops and spread the word, and you will probably find enough takers to start a group. You will have to find a field and gather the equipment, but this sport is experiencing a real comeback and women are now eligible to play.

Rallies

Sleigh rallies in the winter and carriage rallies in the summer keep the harness and antique buffs busy. In New England, the competition is much like the open horse show: you bring your animal, harness, and vehicle, and compete in a variety of classes for which you are qualified. The rules for sleigh rallies are not as rigid as for the formal horse shows, the sportsmanship is on a high level, and the turnouts are often magnificent. Sleighs vary from bobsleds to ornate vehicles —many from Russia and Canada, where a sleigh probably sees as much use as a buggy. The harnesses are fitted with gleaming brass or polished nickel fittings. Sleigh bells, some of which are as old as America itself, jingle and tinkle around the ring. Currier and Ives scenes can be found in glorious animation as soon as there is enough snow to pull a set of runners. Some sleigh rallies end up being run on grass, but the competitors and the horses don't seem to mind.

Carriage rallies are more formal affairs, open to both horses and ponies, adults and children, and vehicles of all descriptions. There are classes for dressage, and obstacle races, marathons (which troupe the whole class through the town roads and waterholes, woods, trails, and hillsides), and events judged on appropriateness of the team of harness horses, the carriage, and the costume of the driver and his passengers. Some of the competitors are children dressed in costumes of the eighteenth and nineteenth centuries driving tiny ponies; some are teams of six, eight, or twelve huge draft horses—all marvelous scenes for the keen photographer.

Anyone with any interest in driving owes it to himself to join the American Driving Society. There are beautiful collections of carriages in many parts of the United States, and their owners are no less fanatic than those who own old cars. These people are excited by their treasures and happy to share their knowledge and enthusiasm with anyone who expresses an interest. The restoration of antique vehicles is an activity that is growing in popularity, and there is now such a renewed interest in driving for pleasure and show that fewer beautiful carts, sleighs, and buggies are degraded into pots filled with geraniums sitting out on front lawns in the suburbs.

Besides racing, carriage, and show driving, harness horses are used in pulling contests. I have said little about draft horses, but they, too, are making a comeback, especially as a sporting animal for pulls and carriage rallies.

Pulling horses are classified by weight—from the lightest teams, those under 2,800 lbs., to the heaviest, who weigh 3,200 lbs. and over. The horses vie to see which can pull the stone boat, loaded with weights, the farthest distance in a single pull. These beautiful big horses compete at fairs and agricultural expositions all over the country, and in national competitions the prizes may run as high as $4,500. Most of the teams are the regular draft breeds: Shire, Percheron, Belgians, and Clydesdales. To stay in shape between events, the draft teams are usually exercised hitched to a bobsled. Many draft horses are still used regularly in lumbering to replace motorized skidders because horses cause less damage to the woodlots, and don't burn gasoline.

Some teams are regularly employed for hay rides, and many horses still rake hay and cultivate gardens in addition to their competitive activities.

Competitive Trail Riding

Competitive trail riding is another rapidly rising sport and one anyone can join. To be sure, many rides are dominated by Arabians and Morgans, but the majority of horses are unregistered animals. Rides vary in length from 15 to 300 miles, and are judged more or less by a standard set of criteria, although this is such a new sport in some ways that there is still a great deal of change going on. A typical 25-mile ride is run in a state forest, starting at a camp where the riders gather with their trailers. There is a coffee and donut breakfast while everyone has a chance to prepare for the ride. Then a "weigher-in" weighs every rider with all the tack and clothing that the horse will carry. The veterinarian and another judge, called the lay judge or horseman judge, give each horse an individual examination. Finally, the horses are sent out at timed intervals.

The judges race in cars to checkpoints along the way, hoping to arrive there before the first horse has had a chance to get through.

After each horse has gone by, they jump into their cars and head for another checkpoint. Horses are stopped on the trail at each checkpoint and examined for pulse, respiration, and general condition, then allowed to continue if they are still in good shape. If a horse shows signs of trouble, he is either held for additional time and checked again before being allowed to continue, or he is "pulled"— picked up by a trailer and taken back to the starting line, to the veterinarian's clinic, or if he can go home on his own, ridden quietly back to the starting line. There is a lunch stop along the trail. At the end of the ride, the horses are scored on their condition throughout the ride, and checked again an hour after the ride for recovery rate. This is not a race. There is a minimum as well as a maximum time limit, and horses brought in too early or too late are penalized or eliminated altogether.

Hunting

Hunting is one of the earliest group sports of man. Today, of course, the whole thing has become a very stylized art—from the formality of dress to the stirrup cup drinks after the kill. Not all hunts end up with a kill. As a matter of fact, many hunts no longer chase a live fox; instead, a scent is laid and the foxhounds follow it over a predetermined course. The riders in these "drag hunts" have just as much fun, and a much clearer idea of where they are going, how safe the terrain is, and when they will be back at the clubhouse. Hunting is virtually limited to private clubs—in order to go on a hunt, you must do so as a guest of one of the members. You are expected to know all the rules and dress appropriately. If you are ever invited to go on a hunt, get some books on the subject and familiarize yourself with the sport, or you will prove an embarrassment to your host. Somehow, people connected with the hunt are particularly sensitive about their traditions and formalities. And please, don't tell anyone you know how to ride a hunter until you have a little experience cross-country. It is not the same thing as taking schooling jumps in the ring, or even over a hunt course at a show.

Dressage

Dressage is a sport that used to be forbiddingly formal, but is beginning to be better understood, so that the average horse person feels he can take a crack at it and not get laughed out of the ring. Dressage is actually a system of training, the purpose of which is to establish confidence, obedience, and action in the horse that makes him simultaneously responsive and relaxed and flexible. It is based on understanding how and why a horse moves as he does, and then on how he responds to signals and puts those responses to work. There are levels from that of training to expert, and level tests have been designed to tell the rider how he has progressed. The show aspect of dressage is the performance of these tests. You are not simply placed first, second, or third as at a show, but are scored for each maneuver, each change or transition, for control, posture, and flexion of the horse. Dressage is something you can start to do on your own, with a few good books, or in a class with a teacher, and in competition with other enthusiasts. If I were going to start riding lessons now, or if I had known of dressage when I first learned to ride, I would certainly have started out this way. Once you have learned the fundamentals of dressage riding, you can then apply your skill to all other "seats" and do a better job of communicating with the horse.

Group Riding

There are noncompetitive clubs like the trail-ride groups, which have long pack trips, overnight rides, campouts, and one-day rides, complete with barbecue lunches. There are drill teams, in which groups of riders get together and practice in formation and then perform at shows during the intermissions or for any occasion where they will have an audience. Colleges and police units have beautiful uniformed teams which are a thrill to watch, the best known being the Royal Canadian Mounties.

We have had an informal drill team here on the farm and my husband learned more about riding the summer he took part in one than he had in years of riding out on trails. The discipline and control of the horses has to be very quiet and unobtrusive, yet you are asking them to do things that are not natural to them. Every horse has to walk or trot at exactly the same speed; they have to turn 90 degrees, crowd tight, and even bump into each other. It takes a long time to get a group of horses to work together without resentment and fights. Years ago we started a drill team of my broodmares, complete with foals running behind during practice. They performed flawlessly after six weeks of drill, although several riders had never ridden a drill team before and several of the horses had hardly been ridden.

There are other kinds of group rides. The Governor's Horse Guard is a state group. Many sheriffs' posses and Shriners have mounted patrols. There are groups that ride in parades, such as the Rose Bowl parade, with matching uniforms and silver saddles. Recently, there has been a growing number of rides-for-a-reason, in which horse people have taken to the roadways and trails to solicit money for veterinary research, or for the handicapped, or to emphasize the need for better trail systems or prevent destruction of existing trails.

These are but a few of the many things people find to do with horses. Every section of the country has its particular emphasis and areas of horse sports. Each sport varies in its degree of competitiveness, community activity, and formality. Some breeds dominate certain sports, but there is no sport except racing that is specifically limited to special breeds or only registered animals. Some of the sports are more demanding than others in terms of athletic ability or riders' capabilities, and some of them require a large outlay of money, while others are really everyman's game. Some, like competitive trail riding and sleigh rallies, are great for beginners, for the attitude among the competitors is to encourage newcomers, even during the competition itself. Experienced horsemen are eager to share their knowledge and spread the sport, and by the very nature of the sport there is a great awareness of the horse, his well-being and ability as an individual. Other sports—those that are the most lucrative, such as racing and horse shows—are far more competitive. However, I have always found people willing to help their own competition, if need be.

There is good sportsmanship along with the bad in every sport. Money, vanity, status, and prestige do nasty things to people; drugging, "soreing," beating, and bribing certainly go on, but you do not have to get involved if you never allow yourself to take winning too seriously. You do, of course, have to take the sport seriously enough to do your best, presenting your horse properly and competing according to the rules.

Finally, I should mention an unusual group you may someday want to join. These are the people concerned with the riding programs of therapy for the handicapped. Acceptance on the part of the medical profession is growing, and there is a swelling and very heartwarming stack of evidence to show that horses have proved exceptionally effective in the rehabilitation of both mentally and physically handicapped people. Whether your interest in this field is to help a fellow human being or to get assistance for yourself or a handicapped friend, the address to write to is: The North American Riding for the Handicapped Association; Ms. Diana Seacord, Treasurer; Thistlecroft; Mendon, Massachusetts. Schools and programs are being established throughout the country with volunteer workers, donated horses and equipment, and trained instructors under NARHA's guidance. Perhaps the inspiration for the title of this book stems from a lingering memory I have of a conversation with a girl in a wheelchair who told me of the day she was allowed to solo in the woods on a horse. This was the first time this girl had ever been able to see trees, birds, and the quiet of a forest without an assistant. To her there was no greater feeling than being alone with her horse.

GLOSSARY

BAR SHOE—a horse shoe that is made with a bar across the open end to afford added support to the frog and heel.

BREAK DOWN—to go unsound or come down with disease.

BRIDOON—a second bit, the smaller of a pair; usually snaffle style.

BUCK KNEES—knees that are sprung forward or flexed.

CANNON BONE—the bone from the hock or knee to the fetlock joint.

CAVALLETTIS—a series of poles or rails, usually slightly elevated and spaced evenly, over which a horse is walked, trotted, or cantered.

CAVESSON—a noseband; there are a variety of styles with varying uses.

COGGINS TEST—a blood test to determine the presence of antibodies in a horse for the disease equine infectious anemia (EIA).

CONFORMATION—the term used to denote how a horse is built, or put together; a total of all its parts.

COPPERING/COOPERING—filing down the teeth in an effort to make a horse appear younger than he is.

CORONET—the cuticle, quick, or upper edge of the hoof wall.

CROSS-CANTER—to canter on one lead with the rear legs and the opposing lead with the front legs.

CROSSTIES—a set of ropes or chains used to secure a horse for grooming, etc.

CROUP—the top of the rump from the back of the loins to the root of the tail.

CULL—to weed out and select.

CUTTING HORSE—one that is used to separate cattle out of a herd.

DEES—metal rings in the shape of a D.

DISHED FACE—one that is concave in profile.

DISHING—a way of going characterized by circular motion of the hoof.

DWELL—the period of time the horse's foot remains suspended during its stride.

ECLAMPSIA—milk fever.

FISTULA—an abcess.

FLEXION—bending of the neck.

FLOATING TEETH—filing sharp points off teeth.

FOUNDER—breakdown of the laminae of the hoof and rotation of the P_3 bone.

GAIT—walk, trot, canter, rack, pace, singlefoot, running walk, jog lope, and other rhythms or sequences of step. (See WAY OF GOING.)

GASKIN—the portion of the rear leg between the thigh and the hock.

GROUND DRIVING—walking behind the horse while training in bitting rig or harness and schooling with reins and whip.

GROUND WORK—all training and handling of a horse while he is neither mounted nor hitched.

HAMES—metal bars with rings which clamp around the collar of a harness.

HAND GALLOP—a controlled gallop, not a race.

HEAVES—asthma.

HOTNESS—a term for a temperament that is mettlesome, excitable, and alert.

LATIGO—leather tanned so that it remains very flexible and tough.

LINE-BRED—horses bred to descend from the same relative a number of times.

LONGEING—working a horse in a circle on a single longe line.

LONGE LINE—a web line about 20 to 25 feet long.

LONG LINES—a pair of web lines 50 to 100 feet long.

LONGLINING—ground working a horse in a bitting rig with long lines.

NAVEL ILL/JOINT ILL—a disease of the joint affecting a foal at birth, believed to gain entry through the umbilical cord.

OCELETS—enlargements of the pastern bone and occasionally the cannon bone as well.

OVERREACHING—striking the front foot with the rear foot.

PASTERN—the area between fetlock and hoof; also the two bones that form the top part of the foot.

PERIOPLE—a thin layer of material that covers the hoof and controls evaporation.

POINTING—resting the foot on the toe with the pastern flexed.

POLE-BENDING—the sport of slalom on horseback, zigzagging between a series of obstacles against the clock.

POLL EVIL—an abscess at the poll.

POSTING—raising the body and then lowering it gently in the saddle while trotting.

PROUD FLESH—excess tissue which grows during the healing of a wound.

PUREBRED—of two parents both blood-related and registered.

RACK—one of the man-made gaits of American Saddle Horses: a syncopated four-beat gait.

RING-SOUR—said of a horse that is bored and sullen from too much ring work.

SOREING—deliberately irritating the coronets and pasterns of horses with chains, boots, caustic oils, mustard, or driving nails upward through the soles of the horse's feet, to make them move with exaggerated action (a federal offense).

SPAVINS—any one of several ailments of the hock joint.

SPLINTS—enlargement of the splint bone on the side of the cannon bone.

STOCKING UP—swelling.

STOCK WORK—herding and cutting cattle, sheep, or horses.

SULKY—a small, light racing cart.

TANBARK—shredded bark which is a waste product of tanning leather.

TERRET—a ring or hook on a harness, to which or through which other parts of the harness go.

THUMPS—a painful condition in which the horse's heart and breathing are affected from overwork.

TIEDOWN—any strap or rope used to tie something down; often the Western term for a standing martingale.

TOE IN/TOE OUT—standing with toes turned in or out.

WAY OF GOING—combination of motion, action, straightness, and regularity at any gait.

WIFFLETREE—a bar which attaches to an object to be pulled, and receives the traces on each end to keep them separated. Also called an evener or spreader.

WOBBLER SYNDROME—an affliction of the spinal nerves.

WOLF TEETH—teeth that grow in various places in the mouth, not used for chewing, which often cause extreme discomfort.

Index

Encyclopedic in scope, *Alone With Your Horse* is an indispensable guidebook for the new as well as the experienced horse owner. It is a personal book based upon the author's lifetime association of living with, caring for and learning about horses. Mary Jean Vasiloff covers such topics as prerequisites for owning a horse, necessary facilities, how to select the horse that will be best suited to one's personality, and most importantly, how then to care for the horse. She also provides detailed instructions for the experienced horseman who wants to breed a mare or train a foal.

Mrs. Vasiloff further enriches this comprehensive book by sharing her love of horses with the reader and offering anecdotes about the horses she has known and loved. Richly illustrated with photographs and line drawings, *Alone With Your Horse* is designed to increase one's pleasure in owning a horse, and, at the same time, to maximize the health and well-being of the animal itself.

0178

Mary Jean Vasiloff with Whippoorwill Duke

Mary Jean Vasiloff has been a well-known breeder of purebred Morgans since 1945. She established a distinctive family of Morgans known as Whippoorwill, and then organized the Whippoorwill Horsemen's Club for children. Mrs. Vasiloff is a contributing editor to *The Horseman's Yankee Pedlar* and *Northeast Horseman*. Her articles have also appeared frequently in *Horse, Of Course!* and *Chronicle of the Horse*. Mrs. Vasiloff and her husband, Alex, preside over The McCulloch Farm in Old Lyme, Connecticut.

Jacket photograph of Ellen Kilmer astride Whippoorwill Tempter by R. Black